Moanin' at Midnight

Moanin' at Midnight

The Life and Times of Howlin' Wolf

James Segrest and Mark Hoffman

Pantheon Books  New York

All rights reserved under International and Pan-American Copyright Conventions. Published
in the United States by Pantheon Books, a division of Random House, Inc., New York, and
simultaneously in Canada by Random House of Canada Limited, Toronto.

Pantheon Books and colophon are registered trademarks of Random House, Inc.

A portion previously appeared in *Living Blues*.

Grateful acknowledgment is made to *Bug Music, Inc.* for permission to reprint excerpts of the
song lyrics from "Back Door Man," "Down in the Bottom," and "Red Rooster" written by Willie
Dixon. Copyright © 1961, 1989 by Hoochie Coochie Music (BMI)/administered by BUG.
Excerpts from the song lyrics "Evil" and "Spoonful" written by Willie Dixon. Copyright © 1960,
1988 by Hoochie Coochie Music (BMI)/administered by BUG. Excerpts from the song lyric "I
Ain't Superstitious" written by Willie Dixon. Copyright © 1963, 1991 by Hoochie Coochie Music
(BMI)/administered by BUG. Excerpts from the song lyric "Tail Dragger" written by Willie
Dixon. Copyright © 1964, 1992 by Hoochie Coochie Music (BMI)/administered by BUG.
All rights reserved. Reprinted by permission of Bug Music, Inc.

Library of Congress Cataloging-in-Publication Data
Segrest, James, [date]
Moanin' at midnight : the life and times of Howlin' Wolf / James Segrest and Mark Hoffman.
p.   cm.
Includes bibliographical references (p. 375–84) and index.
ISBN 0-375-42246-3
1. Howlin' Wolf, 1910–1976 2. Blues musicians—United States—Biography. 3. Rock
musicians—United States—Biography. I. Hoffman, Mark, [date] II. Title.

ML420.H72S44 2004
781.643′092—dc22
[B]   2003066365

www.pantheonbooks.com

Book design by Iris Weinstein

Printed in the United States of America

First Edition

2 4 6 8 9 7 5 3 1

You Can't Be Beat

For my mother and father, Hilda and Murdock, without whose love and support this book would not have been possible

—JAMES SEGREST

For my parents, Eugene and Dolores, who have given me so many priceless, lifelong gifts—especially books, music, and the love of reading and listening

—MARK HOFFMAN

Tell Me

See, like me, probably—later, I be done forgot about: dead and gone. Well, they got some kids gonna come up in charge of the future. . . . After I'm dead and gone, you see, well, these undergrowth'll be sayin', "I heard of this cat, but I never seen him. Here his name and here his picture in the book!"

—HOWLIN' WOLF, BOSTON, MASSACHUSETTS,
DECEMBER 30, 1973

Won't somebody tell me? Answer if you can!
I want somebody to tell me: Just what is the soul of a man?

—BLIND WILLIE JOHNSON, "SOUL OF A MAN"

Contents

Acknowledgments

Who's Been Talking?

Reconstructing the life of an artist as complex and mercurial as Howlin' Wolf reminded us of the story of the blind men tapping their way around the elephant to try to fathom its mysterious nature. Fortunately, as we stumbled along, often in danger, we had hundreds of guides to help us sound out and make sense of those massive flapping ears, trunk, legs, tail, and, well, the other parts. You'll never know until you attempt a biography like this how very much it is a collaborative effort, and how much you must depend upon the kindness of friends and the witness of strangers to see it through. We could not possibly have written this book without the help of hundreds of generous people, and we'd like to thank them all here.

First, we'd like to thank the tireless music producer, blues scholar, raconteur, and world-class punster Dick Shurman, without whom this book might never have appeared. Dick could have written this book or maybe even a better one about the Wolf if he wasn't constantly busy producing so many fine blues albums and helping other writers finish their books. Thanks to our agent, Sandra Choron, an unsung hero of rock 'n' roll, who always lifted our spirits with her sage advice. Thanks to Erroll McDonald of Pantheon Books, who had faith enough in this book to see it to print. Thanks to the rest of the team at Pantheon who made the process painless: managing editor Altie Karper, production editor Rita Madrigal, editorial assistant Robin Reardon, and art director Archie Ferguson. Thanks to Peter Guralnick and the late Robert Palmer, whose books about the great blues musicians inspired us to begin writing this one. Thanks to Don McGlynn, Joe Lauro, and Christian Moltke-Leth, who shared stories, contacts, and photos with us during the making of the definitive film about the Wolf, *The Howlin' Wolf Story*. Thanks to Tony Glover, Scott Dirks, and Ward Gaines, authors of *Blues with a Feeling: The Little Walter Story*; to Robert Gordon, author of *Can't Be Satisfied: The Life and Times of Muddy Waters*; to Nadine Cohodas, author of *Spinning Blues into Gold: The Chess Brothers and the Legendary Chess Records*; and to Bill Keenom, coauthor of *Michael Bloomfield: If You Love These Blues*, all of whom shared information with us and set a standard of excellence that we tried to match. Extra special thanks from James to Marvin Flemmons for his warm friendship and generous hospitality, which made much of the research for this book possible. Special thanks from Mark to Cheryl Lockwood, who accompanied him on his fateful first foray into the Delta so many years ago. Thanks from James to Elvira Adams, Worth Proffitt, Felicia Woodson, Robert Gee, Bill Steber, James Fraher, Larry Hoffman, Mae Smith, Nancy Kossman, Jim Ellis, and Bill Balcerzack for their friendship and encouragement through the many years and ups and downs of this project. Thanks from Mark to Marlee Walker for giving him a forum for ten years and for getting him into so many great blues shows. Thanks from Mark to Judy Guill for putting him up during his research trips to Chicago. Thanks to Dr. Joe Stephens, Jon McDonald, Steve Arvey, and Steve Cohen, who introduced us to people we wanted to meet. Thanks to Adam Gussow, Art Hanlon, Chris Dortch, Emily White, Matt Harris, Pete and Artis Palmer, and Richard Haslop, who read our manuscript and made sound suggestions, and to Vince Cheney, who did vital last-minute fact-checking and research.

Thanks to all the musicians who gave so generously of their time and insights: A. C. Reed, Aaron Moore, Abb Locke, Abu Talib, Albert Vescovo, Andy McKecknie, the late Archie Edwards, Aron Burton, Arthur Williams, B. B. King, Barry Goldberg, the late Big Amos Patton, Big Joe Duskin, Bill Thorndycraft, Billy Boy Arnold, Billy Branch, Billy

Davenport, Bo Diddley, Bob Corritore, Bobby Bland, Bobby Rush, Buddy Miles, Byther Smith, Calvin Jones, Candy Shines, Casey Jones, Cash McCall, Charlie Musselwhite, Chico Chism, Chris Barber, Clifton James, Clyde Leoppard, Clyde Stats, Colin Linden, Corky Siegel, Dale Hawkins, Danny Russo, Darlene Love, Dave Kelly, the late Dave Myers, Dave Sproat, Detroit Junior, Dusty Brown, Easy Baby, Eddie C. Campbell, Eddie Clearwater, Eddie Shaw, Ernest Gatewood, Floyd Murphy, Francis Clay, the late Frank Frost, Frank Vick, Fritz Richmond, Gene Barge, Harvey Mandel, Henry Gray, Honeyboy Edwards, Hubert Sumlin, Ian McLagen, Ike Turner, Jerry Portnoy, Jessie "Little Wolf" Sanders, Jim Dickinson, Jim Rooney, the late Jimmie Lee Robinson, the late Jimmy Rogers, Jody Williams, John Anderson, the late John Brim, John Dummer, John Hammond, Jr., the late John Lee Hooker, John Stephan, the late Johnny Littlejohn, the late Johnny Shines, Johnny Williams, Kim Field, Koko Taylor, Lacy Gibson, Larry Johnson, Lee Eggleston, Lee Shot Williams, Lester Davenport, Little Arthur Duncan, Little Hudson Showers, the late Little Mack Simmons, Little Smokey Smothers, Long John Baldry, Lucky Lopez, Malcolm Yelvington, Mark Kazanoff, Mark Naftalin, Mary Lane, the late Maxwell Street Jimmy Davis, Melvin Peterson, Mick Clarke, the late Mighty Joe Young, Monroe Jones, Necktie Nate Haggins, Nick Charles, Nick Gravenites, the late Oliver Sain, Pat Ford, Paul Asbell, the late Paul Burlison, Paul Pena, Paul Rishell, Phil Upchurch, Pinetop Perkins, R. L. Burnside, Robert "Bilbo" Walker, the late Robert "Huckleberry Hound" Wright, Robert Lockwood, Robert Plunkett, the late Ronnie Hawkins, Ronnie Smith, the late Rosco Gordon, the late S. P. Leary, Sam Andrew, Sam Lay, Sam Mitchell, Sam Myers, Shorty Gilbert, Sonny Blake, Sonny Payne, Stuart Parkes, Sugar Pie DeSanto, T. J. Wheeler, Tail Dragger, Taj Mahal, the late Tommy Bankhead, Tony McPhee, Tot Randolph, Tracy Nelson, Twist Turner, Vaan Shaw, the late Vera Taylor, the late Wade Walton, Wild Child Butler, Willie Kent, Willie King, Willie Mitchell, Willie Young, Wilson Lindsey, and Zora Young.

Thanks also to Wolf's family, friends, fans, neighbors, and associates, who shared with us their precious memories: A. J. Burnett, Ada Swift Cook, Amy Van Singel, Annie Eggerson, Annie and the late Margaret Malkentine, Bill Morris, Bob Koester, Chester Burnett, Chris

Strachwitz, Dan Curry, David Hervey, David Little, Dick Waterman, the late Dorothy Mae Scott, the late E. Rodney Jones, the late Early Wright, Elizabeth Clay, Emma Williams, Ernestine Mitchell, Evelyn Sumlin, the late Floyd Frazier, Gertrude Burns, the late Ida McMahon, the late Israel "Wink" Clark, James Ausborn, James Hart Morrow, the late Jannie Taylor, Jim O'Neal, Joe Bihari, John Fishel, John Sinclair, Laura Towner, the late Leroy Swift, the late Lillie Burnett, Lucy Marshall, Lucy Wiseman Swift, Magnolia Frazier, Malcolm Chisholm, Marshall Chess, Mary Strong, Michael Frank, Minnie McKenzie, Monroe Burnett, Myrtle Gordon, Nat Richardson, Norman Dayron, Osborn Holloway, Pat Quinn, the late Perry Payton, Pervis Spann, Peter Riley, Phil Chess, Priscilla Swift Henderson, R. L. Larry, the late Ralph Bass, Ruben Hughes, the late Rosie Griffin, Rosie Whitehead, Ruffin Scott, Sadie Jones, the late Sam Phillips, Sonny Payne, Stan Lewis, Steve Cushing, Susan Stroud, the late Tom Cannon, Tommy Williams, Walter J. Brown, Wes Race, William Hardy, Jr., Willie Richard, Sr., and Willie Walker.

Thanks to the many correspondents who shared tapes, CDs, videos, and other information with us and helped us track the Wolf across decades and continents: Anton Mikofsky, Art Simas, Barry Lee Pearson, Bill Donoghue, Bob Pruter, Cheryl Line, Cilla Huggins, Dan McClosky, Dave Clark, Dave Richardson, Dave Voorhees, Dave Whiteis, Denise Tapp, Ed Komara, Felix Worhstein, Gayle Wardlow, Graeme Moss, Greg Freerksen, Guido van Rijn, Jacques Demêtre, Jacques Lacava, Jacques Périn, Jeff Gold, John Byrne Cooke, Kurt Hriczucsah, Margo Bruynoghe, Mark Jickling, Norm Rosen, Phil Chesnut, Robert Sacré, Sanford Horton, Thomas Partlow, Tom Ellis, Tony Russell, and Trevor Duplock.

Thanks finally to the fabulous photographers who captured the Wolf in mid-prowl: Charles Sawyer, the late Doug Fulton, Dave Hatfield, Ernest Withers, John Phillips, Mick Huggins, Peter Amft, Rae Flerlage, Sam Lay, Sandy Guy Schoenfeld, Sylvia Pitcher, Willy Leiser, and the late Yannick Bruynoghe.

Our guides never deserted us. If we lost our way or our nerve, the fault is entirely our own. Please send us your thoughts at our Web site, **www.howlinwolf.com.** You'll find many of the documents that we uncovered in our research at **www.howlinwolf.com/docs.**

Introduction

Just My Kind

I've been listening to Howlin' Wolf's music for more than half a century. I first met him in 1949 at a place out from Memphis called Black Fish Lake. A guy called Willie Ford had a club there called the Top Hat and Wolf had been playing for him. I think Wolf had a death in his family, so he had to go back to where he lived at the time. While he was gone, Willie Ford hired me to play in his place. I was there for two weekends before Wolf came back. Willie Ford liked us both, so he didn't want to fire either of us, but he couldn't afford both of us, so he let us both play that night. Wolf played and I played after him. He played harmonica in a rack and guitar, but what I remember most was his voice. I'm telling you, I've never heard anybody sing like Wolf did that night. He sang so well till I almost cried. And Willie Ford would ask the people to choose. He'd put his hand over my head and they'd say, "Yeah!" Put his hand over Wolf's head and they'd say, "Yeah!" Finally, after a long time, he decided that they selected me over Wolf. But I told Wolf I didn't want the gig—he could have it. That's how good I thought he was when I first met him.

A couple of years later, Wolf had a record out called "How Many More Years?" It became a great big hit for him. We used to see each other pretty often then. We'd meet up after shows at places like Miss Annie's on 16th Street in West Memphis or Sunbeam Mitchell's in Memphis. Usually when we got together, it was the regular old musicians' talk: Where we played and what was going on in places and "Man, those are some pretty girls over there!" He was a nice guy. I was a big fan of his. I just loved his singing. His voice was so distinct, but so natural and believable. He wasn't a fancy singer, but it seemed like his voice was hooked up directly to his feelings. To me, singing is like talking. If it ain't natural, it ain't right. Howlin' Wolf was a natural.

He was fifteen years older than I was, but I found out he and I listened to a lot of the same blues singers when we were coming up. Like me, he loved Blind Lemon Jefferson, a bluesman who came from Texas, not the Mississippi Delta. Like me, he sang along to the records of Jimmie Rodgers, the Father of Country Music, who was really a blues singer who happened to be white. Wolf listened to many other people I admired, like Lonnie Johnson and Tampa Red and the great women blues singers like Ma Rainey. Wolf also knew Rice Miller—Sonny Boy Williamson II—who helped me get started in radio. Wolf even knew my cousin, Bukka White, who was born in Aberdeen, Mississippi, not far from where Wolf was born. But no matter who Wolf learned from, he made the music his own. He may have done some songs by Charlie Patton, but when he got through with them, they sounded like Howlin' Wolf—nobody else.

A lot of blues songs are about survival. Reading this book, you'll find out just how hard Wolf had to work to survive and to make his music. One of the things I admire about Wolf, though, is he didn't just sing about tragedy. Like all great bluesmen, he sang for the sinners, which meant he sang for everyone. He had a God-given talent to express beauty and human emotion of all kinds in his songs. He'd sing the kind of blues that would make you cry, but he'd also sing blues that would make you forget your problems and laugh at all the contradictions in the world. And he didn't show up to sing in rags with a whiskey bottle hanging out of his pocket. He dressed and acted like a gentleman onstage, and he expected the same from his band. His music demanded respect, just like he did.

When I was working for radio station WDIA in Memphis, Wolf had his own radio show at a station across the river in West Memphis. Later, after he moved to Chicago, he came back to play for a WDIA "Good-will Review" benefit with me and Muddy Waters and Ivory Joe Hunter for kids who wanted to play little league baseball. I saw Wolf many times up north. One time, I ran into him in a studio in Chicago when he was working on a record. He introduced me to one of his guitarists, who could play just like me when he wanted to, and we cut a record together that day—the guitarist and I. I'd also go see Wolf in the clubs sometimes on the few nights when I wasn't working.

The last time I talked to him, we were playing at the University of Michigan. He talked about his health and told me his kidneys were in bad shape. But he gave it everything he had that night. I don't remember a single show where he didn't.

I always was a fan of his. That's why I was touched to find out from this book that at his last big show, not too long before he died, he didn't want to go home until he heard me play. That means a lot to me, because his music always moved me, whether he knew it or not.

The country has changed so much for black people since Wolf and I were young. The whole world has changed for our kind of music since he and I were starting out. Back then we were local musicians who were just happy to have a record out, and now blues music is known around the world. That's happened in just one lifetime, and I'm of course glad it has.

But some things never change. The greatness that bluesmen like Howlin' Wolf had will never change. He was one of a kind. Nobody I heard before him or after him has had that fantastic delivery—that certain something in his voice that seemed like a sword that'd pierce your soul when he'd sing. Wolf was already a great singer and musician when I first met him. To my mind, he's one of the greatest ever. We'll never see another like him.

B. B. KING,
January 2, 2004

Moanin' at Midnight

1. Poor Boy

Halley's Comet burned across the Mississippi night like a brakeman's lantern during June 1910, leading to suicides and whispers of Armageddon. Up north in Hartford, the Connecticut Yankees were lamenting the recent passing of the brightest star in the American literary firmament, Mark Twain. In New York City, W. E. B. Du Bois, anguished about race riots and lynchings around the nation, was preparing the first issue of *The Crisis*, the magazine of the new National Association for the Advancement of Colored People. In Reno, Jack Johnson, the first black heavyweight boxing champion, was training for his July 4th title defense against former champ Jim Jeffries, "The Great White Hope," a spectacle that would lead to more race riots. In Washington, D.C., Congress was debating the Mann White Slave Traffic Act, which would ban "the interstate transportation of women for immoral purposes"—a law specifically targeted at Johnson that would soon send him to jail for traveling with his white girlfriend.[1]

Across the South, Jim Crow and Judge Lynch were triumphant. Black people were subject to vicious but legal discrimination, voting restraints, violent customs, and state-sanctioned terror that negated their rights and blighted their hopes. A half century after the horrific war to end slavery, black people in the South were again living in near slavery.

In West Point, Mississippi, the news in the *West Point Leader* ("Conservative in All Things; Radical in Nothing") was all about a new brick schoolhouse for "colored" children that cost $7,000, the Elk Club's drive to raise $25,000 for an opera house, and the rising price of live meat hogs: $11 per 100 pounds. West Point, situated in the state's eastern hills near the Alabama border but formerly the westernmost point in Lowndes County until it was incorporated into Clay County, covered three square miles, and had a population of 5,500.[2] A small town, it was big enough to rate a train visit by President William Taft the October before.[3]

Into this violent, radically divided world, Chester Arthur Burnett came howling on Friday, June 10, 1910, at White Station, Mississippi, four miles northeast of West Point.[4] The baby who would grow up to sing so hauntingly about trains could hear the Illinois Central chuff to a stop three times a day to pick up passengers at the tiny White Station train depot.[5] Because of a nineteenth-century border dispute, people in White Station in 1910 weren't sure whether they lived in Clay County or Monroe County to the north.[6] The hamlet is near the county line and most of White Station Road lies north of the line in Monroe County.

Named for the twenty-first president of the United States, Chester, like most black children in Mississippi, spent his early years in crushing poverty. His neighbors were poor families like his own who struggled to survive a repressive racial caste system while farming the unusually fertile, fifteen-mile-wide belt of "black prairie" soil that ran through the region and across to Alabama. Twenty years before he was born, black people in White Station were so desperate that they formed a committee and wrote to the president of the United States to beg for help:

> We want such things as meat, flour, sugar and coffee and clothes and shoes and also our little children is starving and is naked and crying for bread and we is not able to give it to them. . . . If you all don't help us we will all be dead by July sure, without a doubt, and please for God's sace help us for we can not live this way. . . .[7]

In 1904, Reverend C. S. Buchanan, a black West Point merchant who owned a thriving printing business, was condemned at a meeting of a hundred white men who objected to his "prospering." Ordered under threat of death to sell his business, Buchanan and his family fled with little more than the clothes on their backs. A few years before, a successful black grocer in West Point was forced to leave town, another black retailer was ordered to "sell his buggy and walk," and a third, who owned two horse-drawn cabs, had to sell one lest he, too, risk prospering.[8] Just thirty-five miles northeast is the town of Vardaman, named for Mississippi governor and U.S. senator James Vardaman, who vowed to repeal the Fifteenth Amendment, which gave black people the right to vote, and claimed that the only effect of educating a black man is to "spoil a good field hand and make an insolent cook."[9]

In this bleak, unforgiving land, Chester's father, Leon "Dock" Burnett, toiled as a sharecropper, while Chester's mother, Gertrude Jones, worked as a cook and maid. Dock, born in nearby Aberdeen in December 1891 to Albert and Amelia Burnett, was eighteen when Chester was born. Gertrude, born fifty miles south in Shuqualak, Mississippi, in June 1894 to John Wesley Jones and Catherine Tripplett, was nearing sixteen.[10] Chester's paternal grandparents were African-American; Chester said his father was "Ethiopian."[11] Gertrude, like so many "African Americans," also had American Indian ancestors. Her father was a full-blooded Indian, probably of the Choctaw tribe, who had a reservation twenty-five miles from Shuqualak.[12] Dock and Gertrude married in Aberdeen on November 20, 1909.[13] Chester was her only child.

Chester was nicknamed "Wolf" by his maternal grandfather, whom the boy described as "one of them away-back guys, an old guy, whiskers way down to there."[14] Grandpa Jones used to scare young Chester with stories about the wolves that roamed the nearby woods. "I was bad about getting my grandmother's little chicks," Chester said. "Every time I'd get one I didn't have enough sense to just hold him—I'd squeeze him and kill him. So I got so bad about it they told me they was going to have to put the wolf on me. Scared me up like that. So everybody else went to calling me the Wolf. I was real young."[15] One day, his grandfather brought home an animal that he'd shot. Chester thought it was a dog, but his grandfather assured him it was a wolf, and then told him "the story 'bout how the wolf done the Little Red Ridin' Hood."[16] "And me being just a kid I'd believe what he say," Chester said. "And it got to where everybody called me Wolf if I'd do some misdemeanor, you see, and I'd run and hide under the bed and they'd howl after me. That was where my name started. I've always been the Wolf."[17]

Dock traveled down to the Mississippi Delta every spring to work as a farm laborer. He and Gertrude separated when their son was a year old, and Dock moved to the Delta permanently. Gertrude and Chester moved north into Monroe County. She was showing signs of mental instability—becoming an eccentric religious singer who performed and sold self-penned spirituals to passersby on the streets of Aberdeen and West Point.[18] She and her son sang in the choir at Life Board Baptist Church, thirteen miles north of White Station, near Gibson, Mississippi.[19] Chester later said he got his musical talent from his mother.[20] It was one of the only things he ever got from her.

When Chester was still a child, Gertrude sent him away. We'll probably never know why precisely. Maybe, as Chester told a friend, his mother became enraged because he wouldn't work in the fields for 15 cents a day.[21] Maybe, as he told his last wife, his mother rejected him when he refused to sing spirituals with her because he already had his sights set on another calling—singing the blues.[22] Maybe, as a friend of his wife heard, his mother got involved with a man who didn't want Chester around.[23] (By 1920 Gertrude was living with a man almost twice her age.)[24] Maybe, as Chester told another friend, his mother, half-Indian, didn't want him simply because he was "too dark."[25] Maybe all of these stories were true to different extents or at different times in his grim childhood. Who can know why a mother would reject her only child?

Whatever the reason, one cold winter day, Gertrude cast her young boy out to fend for himself, saying, "Don't come back."[26] Chester walked many miles across frozen ground with burlap "croker" sacks tied around his bare feet before he reached the home of his great-uncle Will Young, his father's mother's brother.

Born the year the Civil War ended, Young was fifty-five years old in 1920. He and his forty-year-old wife, Eliza, were working to pay off the loan on their small farm and two-room house in White Station. Also in their household were Chester's retarded aunt, Lyda "Laddie" Burnett, sixteen, her brother Gaddis Burnett, ten, and an unrelated girl, Lucy

Mae Wiseman, seven, whom the Youngs took in as a toddler not long before the Spanish flu epidemic of 1918 killed her mother, sister, and two brothers.[27] It may seem odd that the Youngs were raising so many children who were not their own, but in White Station almost everyone was related by blood or marriage, and poor Americans at the time often relied on relatives and friends to raise children.

Standing six feet tall, dark-complexioned, and weighing more than two hundred pounds, Young was half-deaf and had an odd habit of clearing his throat noisily before he spoke. He had very little patience with children, or anybody else, for that matter, and often displayed a violent temper. Annie Stevenson, who married Chester's cousin Levy Eggerson, said, "Will Young was mean to all them children."[28] Chester's childhood friend Leroy Swift said, "I ain't never seen a man like that in my whole life."[29] Leroy's sister, Priscilla "Silla" Swift, Chester's first girl-friend, said Will Young "was the meanest man between here and hell."[30] But Will and Eliza were the only parents Chester had then, so he called them "Daddy" and "Mother."

Young had three "outside" children with an unmarried woman who lived nearby—ironic, in that he later drove out his own daughter for conceiving a child out of wedlock.[31] But Young and his wife needed the helping hands of the strapping young Chester and the other children. Life was hard in rural Mississippi in 1910, especially for black people, and the children of farmers had to work long hours in the fields every day. One sharecropper said, "Life was a struggle and there was so much work—work all the time for children as well as for adults."[32] Another said, "Every day I lived in the field chopping cotton, hoeing corn, plow-ing. . . . Rise 'fore daylight, eat your breakfast in the field setting on the plow. That's the truth."[33]

Young was especially hard on Chester, beyond the already brutal conditions for farmers in the area. He humiliated the boy by making him sit apart from the other children during meals.[34] He worked him constantly like a beast of burden. "Did he make him work?" Silla asked sarcastically. "Tear his ass if he didn't work all day long! He got to work all day long, come back and get a little meal and get his ass to bed."[35] Annie said, "He was raised in the field, workin' cotton and pullin' corn. That old man would work you till you about fall out—till you just fall down."[36]

When Chester's uncle got angry, the punishment was severe—often delivered with switches cut from trees or even a leather plow line: a "bullwhip," as the neighbors called it.[37] The neighbors never intervened. "Nobody would report [Young] for whippin' with no bullwhip," Annie said. "There were grown peoples afraid of him, he was so low-down. It wasn't just the children. He'd even whup the grown folks if they messed with him. His wife was scared of him, too."[38]

Deacon R. L. Larry, a lifelong White Station resident, said, "That old guy would yell, 'Chester! Chester!' . . . When Chester hear him callin', he'd come runnin', he was so scared of him. 'Yassir?' 'Bring that water!' 'Yassir!' Old Chester used to be plowin' and singin' so well, but he had to go get that water for Will Young. 'Heeeeeeeeey boy—bring me that water!' "[39]

Lucy said, "He'd whup you if you didn't do right. He used to whup Chester a lot. In fact, he whupped all of us if we didn't obey. . . . I don't think he knew any better. He thought that's the way you're supposed to do it." Young beat Lucy once for a minor mistake. "He told me to shuck twelve ears of corn and put 'em in the trough for the mules: twelve ears of corn apiece. I shucked the corn and then I made a mistake, and instead of putting twelve, I put eleven. I got the worst whipping I ever got about that."[40]

Though Will and Eliza Young could read and write, they didn't bother to send Chester to the local schoolhouse, which was built and paid for by contributions from the community, and doubled as a society hall. "He didn't hardly go to school—just worked all the time," said Deacon Larry.[41]

Chester might not have learned much even if he had gone to the school. "You did good to get any kind of education," Lucy said. "If you lived in town, you had nine months of school. But they just had three months of school out in the country. If there was work to be done and the weather was nice, you couldn't go to school at the time there. . . . One thing I regret so bad is that I didn't get no education."[42]

Young often let Chester go hungry. "Will Young had food, but he wouldn't give him none. He was just a low-down man," Annie said.[43] "All Will Young would give him was milk and bread, dry, and when he get done there, he had to go to the field," Silla said.[44]

Famished, Chester would walk the train tracks to scavenge scraps of food thrown out by railroad workers. He went about shoeless and in rags—"a barefooted, raggedy-haired nigger havin' a hard time," as Silla described him.[45] Chester was overjoyed when his uncle bought him his first pair of shoes. "They took him to town in the wagon," said Leroy. "When he come back, he put his feet up so everybody could see those shoes."[46]

The Young house rested on trusses a few feet off the ground, with steps on one side leading to the front porch and door. Overworked and afraid, Chester sought sanctuary in the dark, cool space under the house. "He liked it under the house," Silla said. "He didn't go in the house much. He'd go in the house and eat, come back outdoors and sit up under the house. We'd go out there and sit up under there, too, with him. We all would sit up under there and play."[47] When Chester's uncle returned, all play came to an abrupt end. Silla said, "We see him coming, we better get our ass out of there and run away from that house because we been there with him. 'Here come Will Young!' "[48]

Chester also found refuge in the home of his friends the Swifts, whose mother, Emma, was kind to him—seemingly the only parental love he got as a child. Chester often spent the night there because he didn't want to go home.[49] Silla's sister Ada said, "I used to hear my mother talking to my daddy, 'They ought to not do him like that. . . . Mr. Will Young, he's mean to kids.' They always would say that. Like on Saturday and Sunday—that was the days of rest, but he never did get none. . . . They wanted him to work all the time. He had a tough time. He used to come over and talk to my mother all the time. He used to come over and eat all the time. My mother would talk to him and feed him cornbread and hotcake biscuits."[50] Ada's and Silla's brothers, Jimmie and Sharpie, were Chester's best friends, and they would join him in childish "devilment," as he called it, such as sliding in the mud when it rained, and playing marbles.[51]

Chester often complained about his mistreatment. "He said he was going to leave, and when he comes back, he was coming after my sister," Ada said. "He promised her. He said, 'I'll be back and I'm coming after you.' He was always crazy about my sister."[52]

Her sister was crazy about Chester, too. "He was good—I swear he was," Silla said. "No mother, no father, nobody but them people that took him and raised him. That boy sure had a hard time. . . . He was sad, but he could sing. He'd sing so pitiful and so sweet, and we just loved him. He sure was a nice person. He was a good-hearted person, and he'd teach us how to sing. . . . He couldn't read or write, but damn, could he sing!"[53]

Wearing blue bib overalls and a large straw hat, Chester would sing while plowing behind a mule. "He'd whistle and then he'd sing something like 'Baby, I'm leaving you,'" Ada said. Chester also used to beat on a tin bucket while singing. "He really knowed how to sing the blues," Annie said. "He'd just lick 'em up and sing 'em with his tin bucket."[54] Chester fashioned a one-stringed diddley-bow out of boards and baling wire and also started to learn how to play harmonica. "He got a harmonica every Christmas and he was tryin' to blow then," Leroy said.[55] Harmonicas, which cost just 15 cents at the time, were common presents for poor children, and dozens of White Station children learned to play them over the years.[56]

Will Young was more obsessed with preparing his place in the next life than with parenting in this one. He always made Chester and the other children recite a verse from the Bible before they ate.[57] At nearby Mt. Zion Baptist Church, Young sang in a strong, clear voice in the choir and took his duties as a volunteer deacon so seriously that neighbors called him "Brother Young."[58] Chester also attended Mt. Zion Baptist on Sundays, but he often had to go right back to work in the fields when he got home.

Chester felt his "daddy's" whip for the last time when he was thirteen. He'd been working in the woods nearby, cutting railroad ties to make enough money to buy himself his first pair of long pants. "I wanted to prove to the girls that I was a man," he said, "and I figured if I had the long pants, the womens would pay more attention to me. I worked in the woods about seven or eight weeks for fifty cents a day. And when I got my money, I went and bought me a pair of them good pants. Pants at that time ran about nine, ten, eleven dollars, you know, because things wasn't as high as they is now. . . . First, I taken care of my father's stocks and cows and everything. I was in a hurry to take this gal to Sunday school. Also didn't want the other boys to beat me to her. She was very pretty, you know?

"So I went in and changed clothes and put my brand-new pants on, white shirt and collar, shined shoes. I thought I was dressed up. Well, I was a rough sport, you know? When you're not plumb dressed, you's nothing but a rough sport. With a white shirt on, and nice collar, tie, shined shoes, and trousers, that's what you call a 'rough sport,' but a 'sport' is dressed fully.

"I got ready to go. My daddy, every time he say something, he cleared his throat. 'Uhmmm, did you slop the hogs?' Said, 'No, sir.' He was kind of mean, you know? He say, 'Well, go slop the hogs.'

"I goes and gets this grease bucket that my mother throws the dish-water in after she gets through washing the dishes—had a lot of grease in the bucket. Well, I was trying to tote it way away from my body to keep the grease and stuff from splashing on my trousers because I loved 'em so well, you know—the first pair I ever owned in my life—'cause I was going to show off. You know how boys do when you get something? You want to show off.

"So I carries the slops to the locked gate and I runs the hog back. See, my daddy paid about $150 for this registered hog. I think they called it a big-boned Poland-China or Duroc-Jersey. I don't know the brand, but I know it was a brand. And so I ran the hog back—whiles I was toting the slops to the hog trough, I run him back. He stood there just as quiet like he wasn't going to do nothing. I thought everything was all right.

"I went to tearing to the trough with the bucket. And all at once he made up a mind to break out, man. And he caught up with me and run 'tween my legs and knocked me down and ruined my britches and slopped this goo all over me. So I taken the pail and hit him around his ears and killed him, you know?

"My dad is sittin' at the breakfast table. It's Sunday morning. He cleared up his throat and said, 'Hurry up and come in here. I'm going to whip you.' "[59]

Chester knew he'd get a severe beating. The $150 Young had paid for the hog was a fortune for a small farmer, and pork was one of the staples of their "3M" diet: meat, meal, and molasses. "You got to root hog or die poor then," said a neighbor.[60]

Chester took off running toward the railroad tracks a few hundred feet away.[61] Young, seeing him flee, mounted a mule and chased after him. "Yeah, Lordy!" Leroy said. "Will Young, Lord, that man whupped that boy, runnin' behind him with a mule, whuppin' his ass with a bullwhip!"[62] Chester outran Young and hid out in the woods overnight. The next day, he sneaked back into the hamlet, borrowed some old pants and shoes from his friend Jimmie, and then "hoboed" away—hopped aboard a train as it rolled down the tracks. Silla watched her young swain go.[63] "I saw him leavin'! That boy caught the train right back of my mother's house. I was standin' there and looked at him."[64] Despite Chester's promises, he never returned for Silla. They didn't see each other again for decades. He was alone again.

Chester's grim childhood scarred him emotionally. Decades later, his wife said, "He went along and the things he really told me, how he really came up, would just really make you cry. 'Cause a lot of times he'd say he would walk from house to house—sometimes they were strangers, sometimes it was relatives—and they would turn their back on him. But he made it. And to hear the stories about just how he was brought up, it's heartbreaking. And he would cry about it.[65]

"So many of them mistreated him. Disowned him because he was a little black, barefooted, raggedy boy from here and there trying to make it. He remembered it, too."[66] He had nothing good to say about most of his White Station relatives. "Baby, you welcome to treat 'em nice," he told his wife. "You do just that if you want to, but I know what happened to me."[67] He told a friend's son that his own childhood was "dark . . . that he got beat, but he knew how to run. He even knew that he was going to be a big man, and nobody was going to hurt him again."[68]

Chester rarely talked to anyone about his earliest years. His pain came out in his dark, disquieting, autobiographical music. In "Smoke-stack Lightnin'," one of the most powerful American songs ever recorded, he sang, "Stop your train; let a poor boy ride. Why don't you hear me crying? Awooo-hooo. Well, fare you well; I'll never see you no more. Oh, don't you hear me crying?" Chester's flight down the train tracks in 1923 took him deep into the heart of the Mississippi Delta, where he went looking for the father and family he had never known.

2. Down in the Bottom

Rolling down slowly by train from the state's eastern hills into the low-lands of the Delta, his grim childhood behind him and an uncertain life ahead, Chester Burnett, age thirteen, entered a new world. The Delta was a green, fecund Eden dripping richness and promise. Formed over eons by the flooding of the Mississippi River to its west and the Yazoo River to its east, two hundred miles long and seventy across at the widest, with Memphis at its northern end and Vicksburg at its south, the flat pan of bottomland in the state's northwest corner offered vast possibilities to a young man.

Until the late nineteenth century, the Delta was a swampy wilderness notorious for mosquitoes, malaria, and yellow fever. Folks in the Mississippi hills considered it so hellishly unhealthy that they called it simply "the Death House."[1] (Ironically, Yazoo means "river of death" in the local Choctaw Indian tongue, and Memphis was "the city of the dead" in Egyptian mythology.) William Faulkner described the Delta of 1908 as a "vast alluvial swamp of cypress and gum and brake and thickets lurked with bear and deer and panthers and snakes."[2]

By the time Chester arrived in 1923, though, the plantation owners and their many hardworking hired hands had drained and cleared most of the swamps, hunted down the last wolves, bears, and panthers, and

plowed the land for King Cotton. The landowners stood to make for-
tunes. With topsoil fifty feet deep in places, the Delta includes some of
the richest farmland on earth.[3]

But as in every Eden, there was a snake in the tree, a worm in the
apple: the racial caste system that kept black people from getting ahead.
The Delta was overwhelmingly black—its soil black and rich, its people
black and poor. Black people outnumbered white in the Delta two to
one in 1923 and three to one by 1930.[4] Because Delta plantations relied
so heavily on the work of sharecroppers, 95 percent of whom were
black, local plantation owners struggled constantly to keep their hired
hands tied to the land—a struggle as obsessive as keeping the great
river's waters penned up behind the levees. Many planters were willing
to use any means necessary, legal or extralegal, to keep 'croppers in the
Delta, and white-cappers, lynchers, and labor agents out. A common
technique was to keep sharecroppers in perpetual debt by underpaying
them for the cotton they produced and overcharging them for everything else.

Given the savage racism in Mississippi in the 1920s, the Delta
looked relatively progressive to black folks from elsewhere in the state.
"The Klan never functioned in the Delta," observed blues scholar
Gayle Wardlow. "The planters would not let it start. . . . They were not
going to give their control over the black man, the sharecropper, to
these guys who wore these white sheets."[5] But even in the Delta, violence against black people was common. B. B. King, Honeyboy
Edwards, and many other bluesmen witnessed racially motivated murders there.

Compared to the rest of Mississippi, the Delta was also affluent. In
the state's hill counties, a sharecropper might make a quarter a day,
while down in the Delta they made a dollar or more.[6] But that was only
on a plantation run by an honest man. The trick, of course, was to find
that man. Black people drifted from door to door, often in the dead
of night, searching for a home where they wouldn't be cheated and
mistreated.

Chester was also searching for a home. He lived for a time with a
Jewish family and an Italian family that he met in his travels. "Those
Italians . . . they treated me *very* nice. But those first white peoples I
lived with, they treated me a little cold, the Jews, you know, because

they was in the South and they was taught to hate Negroes like a lot of more peoples, you know. But the other people, they treated me swell. Treated me as one of the family."[7] Chester eventually found Dock Burnett and his new family living on the Young and Morrow Plantation on the Quiver River, between Ruleville and Doddsville. Chester at last had a real father who truly cared about him. Everyone liked honest, hardworking "Mr. Dock." Jannie Taylor, who knew the family in the late 1920s, said Dock was a "fine man—Christian man."[8] Chester said, "Nobody ever gave him any trouble. He was just so nice to everybody."[9] People said thirty-two-year-old Dock and thirteen-year-old Chester looked more like brothers than father and son.[10] In his spare time, Dock loved to go hunting with friends both black and white, which is where Chester got his lifelong love of hunting and fishing.[11]

Chester's father had a beautiful new wife: Ivory Crowley. "She was kinda built like a Coca-Cola bottle," said her niece. "She was real neat in the waist. She had kind of a heavy bust and she had beautiful hips and legs and feet. And she was a very friendly person."[12] Chester had other relatives nearby. An infant half-sister, Dorothy Mae Burnett, was born in 1923.[13] Dock's sister and brother, Daisy Clay and Will Burnett, lived on the plantation, and on nearby Dockery Plantation lived Chester's mother's sister, Mrs. McNeese, called "Aunt Sis."[14]

Chester also took a new name in the 1920s: "John D."[15] His given name must have reminded him of the painful childhood he'd left behind in White Station, where his mother rejected him and his tormenting great uncle constantly called him away from his work on a whim. Everyone who knew Chester well in the 1920s called him John D, and many of his relatives called him that for the rest of his life. Like so many other bluesmen, Chester Burnett began his self-invention with a name change.

Chester's extended family grew larger in the late 1920s when Crowley's niece, Dorothy Mae Spencer (later Scott), age seven, came to stay with them. Her parents, Henry "Buster" and Elizabeth "Bessie" Spencer, sent her to the Burnetts from a nearby plantation because Young and Morrow had a better school, and their plantation's overseer, Mr. Dockett, was so violent that he shot a man who wouldn't work because he was bedridden with illness.

Dorothy Spencer loved her new family and became close to her new cousin Chester. "He was a nice-lookin' black man," she said. "He was! He was kind of like his daddy, but he talked slow." She described Dock as "real dark—not too dark. He had a smooth dark. He had big beautiful eyes. . . . He was a very intelligent man."[16]

Chester was strict with the dueling Dorothys. "John D would check us," said Dorothy Spencer. "He talked slow, but he was sure. John D was just the boss." When Dorothy Burnett spat on her cousin Dorothy Spencer's food once and began to cry, John D disciplined her with a leather strop.

Chester tried to teach both girls to write, pressuring them to study a board with letters and numbers on it that he got from his stepmother, but his illiteracy made him a poor tutor. His belief in the value of self-education was a lifelong habit.[17]

Sam Young and Will Morrow's plantation spread over 1,100 acres and had a commissary, a cotton gin, and a barn full of mules. About forty sharecropper families lived and worked there. Its "rider," or manager, was Tom Booth—"Mr. Boosey" to the sharecroppers.[18] Chester's Aunt Daisy cooked for Booth, who lived in a big house on the property but moved to the commissary whenever Morrow visited from his home fifty miles away in Winona, Mississippi.[19] Booth made the rules and ran the place on a strict schedule. A bell at 4:00 a.m. woke the 'croppers; at 5:00 a.m., it reminded them to hitch up mules for the day's work. Booth rode over the plantation on horseback every morning and afternoon to make sure the 'croppers were hard at work. The plantation made money for its owners and "gave the people something to do," said Morrow's son.[20]

All rules disappeared when the workday was done; like many Delta plantations, this one was lawless at night. "They killed somebody every Saturday night," said Dorothy Spencer. "It was some rough people there." Murderers went unpunished if they were good workers. "They didn't do nothin'. Mr. Boosey didn't care if you killed. If you stayed out of the graveyard, he kept you out of the jail. They just killed one another, went on to the field Monday morning."[21]

Chester stayed out of trouble and went to work every Monday. "At that time I was working on the farm with my father, baling hay and . . . fixing fences, picking cotton, and pulling corn," he said. He also worked a plow behind a team of mules, accompanied by his own voice. "There was a lot of music around there—work songs. Some of the fellows was making songs like 'I worked old Maude, and I worked old Belle'—things like that. They'd just get out there and sing as they worked—plowing songs, songs to call mules by. They'd get out there mornings and get to plowing and get to hollering and singing. They'd make these songs up as they go along. . . . See, people make their music just like you think about what you want to do. They make their sound and their music just like they feel, and they sing like they feel. They made up the work songs as they felt. If they felt . . . somebody had taken something from them, that's what they sang about—however they felt."[22]

Delta sharecroppers all too often felt the blues, born of hard times and injustice. Blues songs sprang from work songs, field hollers, and spirituals, with roots that stretched back to the rhythms and melodic scales of Africa and the harmonic and lyric structures of Europe. Born in the early twentieth century, the standard blues song evolved into a series of twelve-bar musical phrases based on three chords and an A-A-B rhyme pattern. Simple and evocative, the blues was infinitely adaptable for expressing deep emotion. The blues dealt with the day-to-day travails of poor folks just barely getting by. The best blues, like country and western, its light-skinned twin, are concise, powerful, and aphoristic: three chords and the truth. The blues often addressed the strained relations between black men and women in trying circumstances.

The blues gained widespread popularity in the 1910s through the sheet music of composer W. C. Handy, who heard one of the first blues singers in 1903 while waiting for a train in Tutwiler, Mississippi.[23] Blues reached a wider audience in the 1920s with the popular "race records" of classic blues singers such as Ma Rainey and Bessie Smith, who had musical roots closer to vaudeville than to cotton fields. Toward the end of the 1920s, male blues singers began recording, often accompanied by the portable and affordable guitar, and country blues became popular.

One of the most popular early country blues artists was Charlie Patton, who cut his first records in 1929.[24] Born in April 1891 near Bolton, Mississippi, Patton was by the 1920s living on Dockery's plantation near Ruleville. An immensely creative guitarist, singer, songwriter, and performer, Patton was by far the most popular musician in the Delta. Some Saturdays when Patton came to play, Dockery's plantation looked like a sizable town, as people traveled from far and wide to hear him make his guitar talk.[25] Osborn Holloway, whose father was mentioned in Patton's "Tom Rushen Blues," said, "He'd sing them old songs and then they'd be dancin' and drinkin' their corn whiskey and goin' on. He'd lay that guitar across his lap and man, he'd have 'em jumpin'! And they'd be hollerin', 'C'mon, Charlie, play that again!' "[26]

Patton was the best guitarist in the Delta, with a percussive drive and aggressive edge that no one could match. Snapping and bending strings with his fingers or making them sob and moan with a slide, he attacked the neck of his instrument like a hound dog shaking a stick. An astounding showman, he beat his guitar like a drum, played it between his legs or behind his head, rode it like a pony, and threw it up in the air and spun it, all while maintaining a driving dance beat in 4/4 time with the accent on the 2 and 4—a metric novelty that he popularized and may have invented. His singing was ferocious. He roared out lyrics in a hoarse, nearly unintelligible voice, and carried on running conversations with himself through spoken asides in different voices, often switching between his rough, affected singing voice and his natural speaking voice. Raw talent and constant practice made Patton the most popular bluesman of his time and place.[27]

Patton's dynamic performances inspired other early Delta bluesmen such as Son House, Willie Brown, Robert Johnson, and Bukka White. Patton perfected many of the acrobatic guitar tricks used by later bluesmen and rock 'n' rollers such as Jimi Hendrix and Stevie Ray Vaughan. His hoarse, throaty, histrionic vocal style became one of the common sonic threads of popular music, echoing all the way down through the rock 'n' roll singers of the 1950s and 1960s to the grunge and punk/blues singers of the 1990s and beyond. Chester once told a table full of friends, "He had a voice like a lion. You'd hear him in a house, you'd think it's a man in there big as all us put together. Wasn't nothin' but a little rascal."[28]

Patton enchanted young Chester, who said, "I was plowin'— plowin' four mules on the plantation. And a man come through there pickin' a guitar called Charlie Patton, and I liked his sound. So I always did want to play a guitar, so I got him to show me a few chords, you know."[29] Chester remembered with great accuracy when he got his first guitar. "My daddy bought me a guitar on the fifteenth day of January in

1928," he said. "He cleared a good crop that year. . . . I done well with it and I been goin' ever since."[30]

Fascinated by Patton, Chester listened to him nightly at a nearby juke joint and tried to play along as Patton roared out his music. One night Patton heard the young man plinking away outside. He marched out, grabbed Chester, and said, "Come on up here and play with me, son!"[31]

It was a life-changing event for the young man. Playing guitar did not come easily to Chester, whose huge and powerful hands and fingers — ideal for farming — made it hard for him to play a string instrument with subtlety. But Patton's rhythmic style was perfect for the aspiring young bluesman, who relied on guitar mostly to accompany his startling voice. "He showed me things on the guitar," said Chester, "because after we got through picking cotton at night, we'd go and hang around him, listen at him play. He took a liking to me, and I asked him would he learn me, and at night, after I'd get off work, I'd go and hang around. . . . I remember he was playing the tune "Hook Up My Pony and Saddle Up My Old Black Mare" and also "High Water Everywhere," "Spoonful," and "Banty Rooster" — oh, lots of tunes. I done forgot most of them, but at one time I could play his music. After all, he done taught me. I don't play it now much, but I *can* play it."[32] Chester mastered Patton's "Pony Blues" straightaway. "The first piece I ever played in my life was . . . a tune about hook up my pony and saddle up my black mare."[33]

Chester learned to play guitar in two of Patton's tunings: standard (E-A-D-G-B-E from the lowest string to the highest) and open G (D-G-D-G-B-D), called "Spanish" tuning in the Delta.[34] He did not learn to play in open D (D-A-D-F#-A-D) or its variant a whole tone higher, open E (E-B-E-G#-B-E). "I never did hear him play anything in Open E," Chester said.[35] Chester also learned from Patton how to grab and hold a crowd. "He was a real showman," said Chester. "When he played his guitar, he would turn it over backwards and forwards, and throw it around over his shoulders, between his legs, throw it up in the sky. He was more a clown than he was a musician, it seems. But I never did hear nobody else playing like him — playing that bass, patting on the guitar — nobody mocking and using his patterns much."[36] Chester could perform the guitar tricks he learned from Patton for the rest of his life.[37]

Patton's niece said, "Different ones from different places would come and try and learn like Uncle Charlie, and they would hang on to him, trying to learn to play like he could play. . . . When they couldn't learn, Uncle Charlie dropped them and catch on to the best ones."[38]

Chester learned his lessons well and played with Patton often around Ruleville.[39] They were an odd-looking pair. The younger man, at that point lanky and muscular, stood six foot three and weighed more than two hundred pounds.[40] He had a huge head and large hands and feet.[41] His smooth skin was a deep, rich, dark brown color and he had a thin mustache.[42] Patton was short, slight, and light-complexioned, and had wavy hair and large ears; he was often thought to be Mexican, Puerto Rican, or Indian.[43] "Charley Patton was more Indian than he was Negro," Chester said.[44] "He was a half-breed, you know, but he was a nice person."[45]

Chester took his last lesson from Patton in Cleveland, Mississippi, in the early 1930s. Patton's girlfriend, Bertha Lee Jones, said, "Charley worried with him all day before that man would leave him alone."[46] The all-day lesson, during which Patton puffed through five packs of cigarettes, left the older man exhausted.[47] It was the last time Chester saw his idol.[48] Bad health and fast living soon caught up with Patton. He died in 1934, at the age of forty-three, from a chronic heart condition, not long after someone cut his throat from ear to ear in a juke joint fracas. Chester always idolized him. "You askin' me for my all-time favorite singer? That was Charlie Patton."[49]

Chester also learned a bit of blues from Dick Bankston and Jim Holloway, who lived near Drew, Mississippi. "Bankston was a brown-skinned fellow; he worked at the compress, while Jim farmed," Chester said. "They were older than me, but they were right along there behind Patton in age, a little younger than him. But they couldn't play that sound like Charlie could, because Charlie would strum his guitar and would kinda drum on it with the back of his hand. Dick Bankston and them played nice but they just couldn't put the strum in it."[50] Mott Willis, who knew Bankston, said, "He could sing good, but he just would holler so loud. You know, he'd deafen you, near 'bout, if you setting there helping him."[51] Chester didn't learn much from Bankston and Holloway. "I didn't fool around with them like I did Charlie."[52]

Chester learned chords from Long Nathan Scott, who was not

much older than he was.[53] He also learned a few techniques from Nathan "Bear" Taylor, who lived on the Young and Morrow Plantation.[54] "See, my husband used to play for big parties—jukes," said Taylor's wife, Jannie. "They danced, they cursed, they drank and they fell out, and they fought, and they done everything. . . . John D, he just liked the music and he wanted to learn how to pick—and he did. My husband learned him sittin' on the front porch. When Bear turned him a-loose, he could play."[55]

Chester also liked the Mississippi Sheiks, a sophisticated string band made up of members of the Chatmon family and family friend Walter Vincson. The Sheiks played blues and jazz, and at parties for white folks could switch to waltzes, hillbilly tunes, and pop hits. Chester said, "They had a beat to their music. I think they were about No. 1 around that part of the country. In those days I preferred the Sheiks' music to Charlie's music because the Sheiks had an up-tempo beat. They were a little more modern."[56] He later recorded the Sheiks' "Sitting on Top of the World."

Little by little, Chester learned from many other local players. "I was inspired by all the singers and guitar players who sprung up everywhere in the black quarters. Some of them I would only see once; they would appear one day to sing the blues on the street corner, and then go back wherever they came from as soon as they made a little money."[57]

Two of the first songs that Chester mastered were among the biggest race record hits of the day: Blind Lemon Jefferson's "Match Box Blues" and Leroy Carr's "How Long How Long Blues."[58] "What I liked about Lemon's music most was that he made a clear chord," said Chester. "He didn't stumble in his music like a lot do—plink. No, he made clear chords on his guitar; his strings sounded clearly. The positions he was playing in—that made his strings sound clear."

Wolf heard Blind Lemon in person one Saturday night at a picture show in Greenville, Mississippi, but didn't get a chance to meet him. "So many peoples I couldn't get up there. And I was young then; they pushed me out of the way."[59] Honeyboy Edwards saw the young Wolf perform and said, "He had some little old, small eyeglasses on his eyes, tryin' to play like he was like Blind Lemon. Little bitty glasses—just could see out of them, just big enough to cover his eyes."[60]

Chester also listened to records by Gertrude "Ma" Rainey, Lonnie

Johnson, Tampa Red, Blind Blake, and especially Tommy Johnson.[61] Born in Terry, Mississippi, Johnson had lived in Drew near the Young and Morrow Plantation but moved away before Chester arrived. The young bluesman adapted some of Johnson's vocal tricks—especially his distinctive falsetto—and learned Johnson's tunes, such as "I Asked for Water, But She Gave Me Gasoline," from his records and from local musicians who'd known him when he lived in Drew.

Chester developed the howl that made him famous by listening to the first great country music star. "As far as singing goes, I wanted to do something new and have a style that wasn't too common," he said. "I was inspired by the records of Jimmie Rodgers, a white singer of that time. He was called the 'yodeling singer,' because he would sing some parts in a head voice, like the Swiss yodelers. I took that idea and adapted it to my own abilities."[62] "I couldn't do no yodelin' so I turned to howlin'. And it's done me just fine."[63]

Searching for an identity, Wolf played under many names in the Delta. Honeyboy Edwards, who first met him in Greenwood, Mississippi, in 1932, knew him at various times as John Dee, John D. Burnett, Chester Burnett, Foots, Buford, and Howlin' Wolf.[64] Only seventeen at the time, Honeyboy said, "He come walking into town with his high-top shoes on and we called him Foots. He had the biggest feet—he wore about size 14!"[65] Wolf said, "I don't know how that name started—just because they say I had big feet. And some of them called me the Bull Cow. They just give me different names. But I just stuck to the Wolf."[66]

Chester used his famous stage name, "Howling Wolf" or "Howlin' Wolf," right from the start of his career, though some scholars have speculated that he took it from Funny Papa Smith's record "Howling Wolf Blues," released in 1930. Jannie Taylor insists that John D. Burnett, as she knew him, called himself "the Howlin' Wolf" in 1928.[67] Dorothy Spencer and her husband, Ruffin Scott, in separate interviews years apart, also said he called himself Howlin' Wolf in 1928. The popularity of Smith's song, which Chester knew well, encouraged him to keep using the name. "Howlin' Wolf" fit his persona, performance style, and voice perfectly. Wary by nature to the point of paranoia—the result of his childhood physical and emotional abuse—he was, in his early years, a musician who roamed by himself: a lone wolf. His unusual blue-gray eyes, so like a wolf's, seemed to glare right through people rather than at them.[68] A tall, strikingly handsome man, he was a proverbial wolf with women, and had many female fans. His stage antics were positively feral. He'd crawl around on all fours and shake his hips like a wild beast. His lupine howl gave him the aura of some unsettled creature of the night. His rough, raw, hypermasculine voice was also capable of great delicacy and subtlety. It could convey a huge range of emotions, from homicidal rage to deep affection, sublime joy to utter despair, burning hurt to prideful boast. Blues scholar Dick Shurman wrote, "The moans, howls, whoops, spoken questions to himself and asides to the world in general, leaps and drops in pitch, sense of menace and intensity could never be chalked up to emulation; they came from Wolf's own being."[69] Ruffin Scott said simply that he had "a voice like a lion."[70]

The gravel in Wolf's voice came naturally. He suffered from many childhood bouts of tonsillitis, which damaged his vocal cords.[71] Unlike Charlie Patton, who affected a growl, Wolf's natural voice sounded like he subsisted on a diet of broken glass and caustic lye, washed down perhaps with kerosene. Like the bellowing "goat roar" of the South African singer Mahlathini, who inspired a generation of African vocalists, Wolf's vast rasp seemed to come from a mythic beast rather than a man.[72]

Wolf had rich, resonant overtones in his booming baritone, and he could manipulate it into separate tone streams like the multi-harmonic "throat singers" of Tuva, Tibet, Uzbekistan, South Africa, Finland, Canada, and Japan. San Francisco bluesman Paul Pena played with T-Bone Walker, B. B. King, and Bonnie Raitt before becoming the first American to win Tuva's annual contest in the deep, difficult "kargyraa" style of throat singing. Pena grew up listening to Howlin' Wolf, and he teaches throat singing by making his students mimic a famous Howlin' Wolf impersonator. "Something that Howlin' Wolf does with his voice is very similar to what's done in certain types of Tuvan music. To be able to do throat singing, you have to constrict your voice, and we were trying to find some way to explain this that everybody would understand, so we picked on Wolfman Jack because that's what he does." (Deejay Wolfman Jack, born Robert Weston Smith, got his radio voice largely from Howlin' Wolf.) "Charlie Patton and Wolf stumbled onto one of the basic techniques of throat singing. They don't take it as far, but it is the same thing that you do with your throat. It's the constriction of certain muscles in the throat to create resonance chambers for the sound to go through, and then you shape that sound with parts of your vocal cords and different cavities that you have in your mouth, like your oral cavity and your nasal cavity and sinuses."[73]

Wolf's unusual voice was a gift of nature that he worked hard to develop. Dorothy Spencer said Wolf "started with his voice—trying to grow it."[74] He sang at work and play, often singing all day long while plowing, then singing on weekends wherever people would listen. "It was in the late 1920s when I decided to go out on my own, to go for myself," he said. "I just went running 'round through the country playing, like Charlie and them did."[75] "When I learned to play I'd play on the plantations at Saturday night 'breakdowns,' sometimes we'd call 'em Saturday night balls. . . . I'd just play on the weekends at the Saturday night fish fries and things . . . until I got good, then I decided to stretch it out and play for dances."[76]

Wolf rambled around to play in Drew, Ruleville, Boyle, Doddsville, Cleveland, Moorhead, and Dockery's plantation. He played on the street in Drew and Ruleville, at local jukes, and for house parties.[77] Spencer said, "He'd always hit that guitar. 'Tunk-a-tunk-a-tunk-a-tunk,' he'd play. Then he'd go to hittin' it with his hand at the top. Then he'd pat them big feet. Then he'd holler, 'Ooh baby, oooooooohhhhhh.' And that's all the people liked to hear him sing. People liked him."[78] Though he usually performed solo, he sometimes teamed up with accordion player Homer Lewis, who also played with Charlie Patton.[79]

Roebuck "Pops" Staples, who lived on Dockery's plantation and later fathered and founded the famous Staple Singers, often heard Wolf. "Howlin' Wolf would be playin' on the streets, standin' by the railroad tracks, people pitchin' . . . nickels and dimes, white and black people both."[80] "Charlie and me was on the same plantation, he'd always be playing there, and Wolf came along later. Wolf was my main man. Charlie Patton was a good man, far as I know; I was young and didn't know about his life or anything. But Wolf, I thought he was the greatest thing. A big guy, a real tall handsome man, he was really something else. He was just a few years older than me, but he was so powerful I wouldn't even dare speak to him. They were already calling him 'Wolf' then. He was playing with Charlie. I think he was maybe playing Charlie's songs, but he was something different altogether. As far as I was concerned, he *was* the blues."[81]

Soon after Wolf began performing, tragedy struck his family: His stepmother died unexpectedly. Wearing a beautiful white, beaded dress, Ivory had gone to a plantation party, where she ate and drank and soon felt sick to her stomach. By the time she got home, she was deathly ill. Her tongue swelled up and she suffered, unable to talk, for almost two weeks before dying. She'd been poisoned; deliberately or not, no one knew.

Ivory's death hit the family hard. Wolf, who was very fond of her, was grief-stricken, and her daughter Dorothy Burnett, only five years old, was inconsolable. Dock took it hardest of all. Dorothy Spencer said, "Cousin Dock thought the sun rose and shined in her."[82]

Misfortune struck again with the start of the Great Depression in 1929. In the South—already the poorest region of the country—the Depression sank people even further into despair. Money and work grew scarce as cotton prices plummeted. For black sharecroppers on the bottom rung of Southern society, hard times grew harder and hopes for improvement largely vanished.

Wolf hit the road, playing wherever he could for whatever he could get. It was a hard life, but he was doing what he loved and was free to come and go as he pleased—provided the local law didn't arrest him for vagrancy and force him to work on the county farm or local levee. The blues life offered escape from the backbreaking cotton fields and the insufferable labor of sharecropping. "I never knowed him to do a thing but pat his foots and sing those songs," said Spencer. "Now he was sure lazy—I'll tell you the truth!"[83] Wolf would have called it wisdom— choosing a better life.

Wolf's choice let him travel widely at a time when sharecroppers were tied to someone else's land. "The places I'd hit: I'd go to Greenwood, Winona, and back to my home, West Point, Mississippi, and go to Columbus, and then I'd go to Indianola and Greenville, Mississippi. Then I'd come over to the Arkansas side of the river around West Memphis and Parkin and Pine Bluff and Brinkley, Arkansas. Just all through the cotton-belt country, and mostly by myself."[84]

Like other migrant workers, musicians went where the money was flowing and circled back with the seasons. In the fall, during cotton-picking time, money rolled into the Delta as fast as the cotton bales rolled out. Wolf's contemporary Booker "Bukka" White, born just north of West Point in Aberdeen, said, "I always did like the Delta, 'cause of the money. There was so much money down there: Money wasn't no problem."[85] Honeyboy Edwards said, "There used to be a lotta money down through that Delta, man, you know when them guys in the fall of the year started picking that cotton."[86] A bluesman could make as much money in a few hours playing at a juke or in front of a store as a share-cropper made in a week manhandling a plow behind four farting mules. Saturday night jukes and house parties paid especially well. Blues historian Gayle Wardlow said, "In those days, there were a mil-lion people in the Delta with nothing to do and no place to go except the jukes on a Saturday night."[87]

In the winter, musicians moved up into the Mississippi hills or down around Jackson, where sawmills paid out every two weeks. Levee camps also provided a paying crowd, but musicians had to take care not to be pressed into service actually working on the levees—absurdly dan-gerous places where workers were murdered daily.

Wolf met blues pianist Albert Luandrew, better known as Sunny-land Slim, in the early 1930s. Born in 1907 in Vance, Mississippi, Sun-nyland had played the blues for a decade by then and was already an established performer in Mississippi, Arkansas, and Memphis. "I really knowed Wolf good in 1930, '31," he said. "Wolf never did come to Mem-phis. He played out in them little country places. In those days, you'd have a farm with two or three hundred acres and there's a roadhouse on your farm, one on his farm, roadhouse over there. Peoples was hard up for musicians. He played where they couldn't get . . . nobody else. I don't remember him being popular. . . . That's the kind of place Wolf played at."[88]

Wolf said, "Back in the country the people weren't able to pay you too much. Sometimes you'd work all night for a fish sandwich—glad to get it too."[89] "When I'd go out on them plantations to play, the people played me *so* hard; they look for you to play from 7 o'clock in the evening until 7 o'clock of the next morning. That's too rough! I was get-ting about a dollar-and-a-half, and that was too much playing by myself. People would yell, 'Come on, play a little, baby!' A bunch would come in, and they was ready to play and dance."[90]

Honeyboy Edwards was impressed by Wolf's passion, if not his play-ing. "Howlin' Wolf was trying to play guitar back then. He always was a good singer but he never was much of a guitar player. In the country at that time you could play any kind of music if you had a good voice and your guitar was tuned up. The country people went for it because they didn't have no other kind of music but that. Wolf could phrase it and make a few chords and he had that good, heavy voice. He played for some country dances around there. He'd set himself down on a cane-bottom chair and play and be scooting all around the room in that chair. When he'd get through scooting, he'd be all around the other side of the room! He'd tap that big foot and you could hear it all over, like a drum."[91] At the time, Wolf was playing a small, beat-up guitar held together with tape.[92] Wolf sang Funny Papa Smith's "Howling Wolf Blues," Tommy Johnson's "Cool Water Blues," and songs by Charlie Patton and Blind Lemon.[93]

When bluesman Johnny Shines was seventeen, in 1932, he saw Wolf playing for a crowd on a street in Hughes, Arkansas. "They was pitching him nickels and dimes," Shines said.[94] "He looked different than anyone I'd seen. He was a long, linky man with black velvety skin. It looked like it would ripple if you would blow on it, like a vial of black oil. The hair stood up on his head like hog bristles. He had this deep, raspy voice. That day he was doing a song called 'Howling Wolf,' and then he whooped on a song, 'Smokestack Lightning,' like I'd never heard anybody ever do."[95] In a famous description captured by writer Peter Guralnick, Shines said, "I first met Wolf, I was afraid of Wolf. Just like you would be of some kind of beast or something. Because it was an old saying, you know, people thought about magic and all such things as that, and I come along and say, a guy that played like Wolf, he'd sold his soul to the devil. And at that time Wolf had the most beautiful skin anybody ever seen in your life, look like you can just blow on it and it'd riffle. And I was kind of afraid of Wolf, I mean just to walk up and put your hand on him. Well it wasn't his size. I mean, what he was doing, the way he was doing. I mean the sound that he was giving off. That's how great I thought Wolf was."[96]

Shines often spoke of Wolf in mystical terms. "As far as I knew he could have crawled out of a cave, a place of solitude, after a full week's rest, to serenade us. I thought he was a magic man. They had an old saying about people who sold their soul to the devil to be able to play better than anyone else. I thought Wolf was one of these."[97]

The young Shines followed Wolf like a convert. "I would go over to where Howlin' Wolf was playing at because I thought Howlin' Wolf was the greatest guy I'd ever heard in my life . . . the greatest throughout the area of Hughes, West Memphis, Roundtree, Parkin, and Twin Bridges and around there."[98] Shines, who had heard local bluesmen Willie B. Borum, Jim Christian, Tad Owens, and Ollie Burks, Jr., said, "Couldn't any of them beat him singing!"[99]

Shines described a juke run by a whiskey-making entrepreneur named Will Weillers. "He'd take his beds and things down and they'd dance in one room and shoot dice in the other one. He didn't charge admission to them; this was free. The thing was to get the womens there to get the mens there so they'd gamble. And he'd cut the game, get his money that way. Sell whiskey too. Because he had to pay the men for playing, he charged a nickel more on a half-pint of whiskey; he charged 35 cents for a half-pint of whiskey. This was 'fist-made' whiskey, that's what I call it: tom-cat whiskey. It wasn't bonded liquor."[100]

Shines borrowed Wolf's guitar one night at Weillers's juke. "Wolf got up and stayed out a pretty good while. I don't know whether it was a woman or not. He'd set his guitar down there. While I had the idea of what he was doing in my head, I just couldn't wait to get to his guitar. I guess I was still caught up in the trance, spellbound, when I started playing it in Wolf's style. Before I knew it, I had an audience working like I was paying them, just dancing away. Then Wolf came in. I'll never forget the look he gave me. He silently took away the guitar. He said that'd be the last time he'd ever leave his guitar for anybody to learn how to play."[101]

Shines described this pivotal event in another interview. "One Saturday night I was over to where he was playing at and Wolf set his guitar down. I'd been setting there watching him and I figured, I said 'Heck, I can do that.' He was playing it in Spanish then. . . . So I watched Wolf. He's playing 'Roll and Tumble' and many different pieces, and I'd been trying to play these things but I hadn't had no luck. Watching Wolf, I really seen what he was doing. So when Wolf taken his break I got his guitar and I'd taken a knife or a bottleneck, I don't remember what it was I had, but anyway when Wolf came back I had the joint rocking. Playing 'Roll and Tumble,' 'Smokestack Lightning,' 'My Black Mare' and everything else he played, all his songs. Wolf got mad about that; he didn't like that very well, 'cause I had the place rocking."[102] Wolf, who was much larger than Shines, did not react physically. "Wolf was very easygoin'," Shines noted. "He wasn't no problem."[103] Wolf alluded to events like this when he said, "Myself, I was singing and playing solo, all over the place. It was a real blues atmosphere; an unknown customer might pick up a guitar and do just as well as a professional."[104]

Shines imitated Wolf so well that people started calling him "Little Wolf." "Howlin' Wolf was an idol of mine when I was starting out," he explained. "I used to flip the guitar, slap it around, play it behind my back and my ear. Then one day I asked myself why am I doing this and I couldn't find an answer. All the answers I could find was 'cause Wolf did it. Well, why did Wolf do it—'cause Charlie Patton did. Well, why did Charlie Patton do it? I couldn't answer that so I quit it. Am I a musician or clown? So I chose to be a musician and let the other fellows do the clowning. If I wants a clown I hire one."[105]

But Wolf was no clown. A serious bluesman with a knack for capturing a crowd, he never forgot that his audience of poor people desperately wanted to forget their misery for a night. Even Shines knew who was more popular. "If they couldn't get Wolf, they'd have to settle for me because we were the two best."[106]

While Wolf rambled part of every year, his family back home continued to grow. His father remarried in the early 1930s. Dock's new wife, Abbie Davis, was a widow with four children—Rosie, born in 1919, Lucy, born in 1921, Sadie, born in 1923, and J.D. (for Jefferson Davis), born in 1925. Her first husband, William Davis, worked as a coal miner but died from tuberculosis and exposure.[107] When he died, Abbie and her children moved to the Young and Morrow Plantation to live with her brother, Early Lane. Rosie said, "I guess she went out one night and got acquainted with some guys, you know. And so they started corresponding together; and finally later on she came home and told us that, 'I done found you all another daddy.' I said, 'What we goin' to call him?' She said, 'Call him Daddy.' I said, 'I'm not goin' to call him Daddy unless you do.' And so she started callin' him Dad, too."[108]

Rosie said Dock was "a tall, heavy, real dark person who had pretty white teeth and whites of his eyes. All them Burnetts were real dark people."[109] Dock was "a real nice stepfather" and Wolf was "more like a real brother than our own brother was. He was really free-hearted." She also recalled Boosey, the plantation overseer. "We had to carry water from up there to Boosey and lots of time we go up there and get water and he would have us dancin'. And we'd stay so long, Mama have to come around the corner and see us dancin' and she had to run us home."[110] The image of black children dancing in the Mississippi dust for the overseer's amusement conjures up troubling images of the Old South, but Rosie didn't remember it as unpleasant.

Rosie said her mother "was a lovely woman. There wasn't nothin' she wouldn't do for peoples."[111] Sadie said, "It wasn't a Sunday passed we wasn't in Sunday school, and she would make it for church."[112] Both daughters said Wolf became close to his new stepmom and called her "my mother."[113]

But Dorothy Burnett felt Abbie was unkind to her and her half brother. "My life was not pleasant," she said. "I could be sick and cramping with stomach pains and my stepmother, Miss Abbie, would say to me, 'I hurt, I be sick, and I still work.' . . . Nobody ever told me I could lie down. I had to work sick in the hot sun all day long in agony. . . .

"My brother always came home in the spring of the year to break up the land for my father so he could plant cotton and corn. . . . One day my father went to the store and bought him a pair of pants. My stepmother asked, 'Who are those pants for?' My father said, 'They are for my son, because he plows for me.' My stepmother did not want my father to buy my brother a pair of pants after he had broken up all that land."[114]

Despite the family drama, Wolf kept returning like the prodigal son every year to his father's home. Sadie said, "He would go play for different people. Maybe go through Mississippi and stay down there a long time. Go in Tennessee; he'd stay in Tennessee a long time. And then, about the time to break up the land, he would come home. Break up the land, take them mules—he would plow a mule to death, boy! He'd break up that land every year for Daddy. . . . When he finished, he'd be gone again."

While home, Wolf practiced guitar constantly. "He would come home and sit up at night and play, thumpin' on that guitar," Rosie said. Sadie said Wolf would "sit up all night long to learn. He had him a little music book and he would take that book and learn how to play that music. And I couldn't understand nobody didn't know how to read and write and could learn how to play music, but he could."[115]

Sadie had a lot to learn about Wolf. He courted a sanctified woman who wouldn't go out with him unless he joined her church.[116] One Sunday, he announced that he was saved and had to be baptized. "Women lost their panties and everything that day," said Sadie. "They was shoutin' and goin' on because he joined the church. All them people got up there and went to shoutin'. And when it come time to baptize him, he was two hundred miles away, playing the blues!"[117]

Another time, Wolf and a young woman dodged church services by sneaking to the back of the building and clambering down into a recess in the church chimney. The couple were just getting friendly when an old woman opened the trapdoor to the space, dropped her drawers, and peed all over Wolf's face. With services going on close by, Wolf couldn't howl at the indignity.[118]

Wolf's father took religion more seriously. After he married Abbie, Dock started going to the Old Bethlehem Baptist Church.[119] "He was searchin' to get religion," said Rosie, "and one morning before day I heard him in there hollerin' he had it. 'I got it! I got it!' He gets up and so he was talkin' to Mama. He said he thought he was comin' like a natural man. He went on up to the barn and caught the horse and he was goin' all around the neighborhood and tellin' 'em about his religion, that he'd got it. He had found God." Dock's conversion didn't change how he felt about his son playing the blues. "He never did say nothin' about it," said Rosie. "Just said, 'Well he's out there.' "[120]

Dock hated injustice but knew that a black man could be killed for defending his rights in Mississippi. Sadie said, "He was nice but he just didn't take no stuff. He don't allow nobody to curse him! If it was a white man, ooh, he ready, he better hear it. He'd tell him, 'Man, don't curse me. . . . Please don't do that no more.' He said, 'Don't curse me 'cause I'm not goin' to curse.' "[121]

The big book at Old Bethlehem Baptist said the meek shall inherit the earth, but Wolf thought his father took the saying too literally. "My father was a ass-kiss . . . so they give him what he want. But I was a little boy and there wasn't nothing I could do about it. The best thing was for

me to move away when I growed up. . . . A man got to stand up for himself regardless. If you don't stand up for the right, what is you going to
stand up for?"[122]

In the darkest incident of his life, Wolf fell into catastrophic trouble
while "standing up for the right." Wolf had a fling with a woman in
Hughes, Arkansas, and her regular boyfriend found out about it and
beat her severely. Wolf learned of the beating, sneaked up on the man
while he was sitting on his porch and, according to Johnny Shines,
"chopped him in the head with a cotton hoe—killed him."[123] Shines
said Wolf avoided prison for the killing, pointing out that he got a pass-
port in the 1960s, which would have been impossible with a murder
conviction on his record.[124] But Sunnyland claimed Wolf spent two
years in prison for it.[125] Sunnyland told several people in Chicago about
the killing, including Eddie Shaw, who played in Wolf's band,[126] and
Zora Young, a blues singer who is Wolf's distant relative.[127] Another of
Wolf's band members, Detroit Junior, said, "Wolf told me he was on
Parchman Farm [Mississippi State Penitentiary] for a few years. He got
in a fight and, I guess, somebody died."[128] Honeyboy Edwards also heard
about the killing.[129]

Wolf and Sunnyland were arguing on the way to a gig one night.
Sunnyland ended the argument by yelling, "Hey, I didn't tell you that
when you chopped that man's head off with a hoe!" Wolf's guitarist,
Hubert Sumlin, asked what he was talking about. Sunnyland said, "I'm
just telling it like it is. The motherfucker did chop a man's head off!"
Shaken, Wolf stopped the car and walked away. Hubert approached and
found him upset. Taking Hubert home that night, Wolf told him it was
true; he'd killed someone. He'd gotten into a fight with a man and hit
him with a hoe, slicing the top of his head off and killing him instantly.
Terrified, he ran and hid in a drainage ditch while a posse hunted for
him with hounds. The next day, his fellow Masons helped him aboard a
passing train and he fled the scene.[130]

Wolf had a violent and fearful side, no doubt due to the mental and
physical abuse he suffered at the hands of his mother and Will Young,
and to the shocking daily violence of life for black people in Jim Crow
Mississippi. Wolf's dark side—his "shadow," in Jung's term—stalked
him through life precisely like a wolf. He exhibited the classic symptoms of the abuse survivor. People who knew him well noted his dual

nature. A wild man onstage, he was the soul of conventional propriety offstage. Tough on the outside, he was tender on the inside; suspicious to the point of paranoia with strangers, yet comfortable revealing his darkest thoughts to them in song; fond of animals and children, but ferocious with adults in the rough-and-tumble world of the blues; threatening one minute, deeply sentimental the next—a sheep in wolf's clothing.

Wolf was aware of his shadow and struggled to tame it. He understood very well the ways of the weak and wounded. The repressed rage, fear, and sadness in his Delta-drenched voice infused his music with astonishing power. Wolf summed up his early Delta years decades later, in one of his last recordings, which harkened back to his idol Patton. "Every day seems like murder here. No, I can't make a dollar and I can't stay here."[131]

3. Saddle My Pony

In 1933, the Burnett family left Mississippi and moved across the river to Arkansas. Wolf said, "You know what the conditions of life are like for blacks in the Deep South, and especially in the state of Mississippi. Many people have only one dream: to get out of that place. Me, too: I left Mississippi in 1933."[1]

The Burnetts moved to a large plantation in Wilson in the fall of 1933 and stayed there until after Christmas. Early in 1934, the family moved to Nat Phillips's plantation, about fifteen miles north of Parkin, on the St. Francis River. Dock's younger sister Gillie and her husband, John Davis, lived on Phillips's plantation and got the family a place to stay.[2] At about nine hundred acres, the Phillips Plantation was slightly smaller than the Young and Morrow Plantation and supported fewer families—twenty to thirty.[3] By all accounts, Phillips treated his sharecroppers fairly and as equals. Rosie said he borrowed snuff from her mother. "Mr. Phillips, he would dip snuff in his pipe, and Mama dipped snuff. And so we be out in the field, here he'd come. He'd ask Mama, 'Hey, give me a little of that snuff you got.' He'd put that snuff in his pipe. And we'd say, 'Ooh!' We didn't like for Mama to dip the snuff. It was too strong."[4]

The Burnetts lived in a two-story house and rented out the two rooms upstairs. Besides sharecropping, Dock fed the plantation's horses and mules, riding on horseback to and from the barn every morning. Dock also loved hunting, often taking other sharecroppers with him to help carry back the game. Rosie said, "Sometime he come home with twenty-five and thirty rabbits. We had to clean them rabbits before we go to bed that night. He would kill coons and possums, too." Dock feared only two creatures: cats and babies. "They just don't feel right," he said.

Wolf came back to visit from time to time, causing great excitement in the family. Dock often had a premonition just before he returned. Rosie said, "Sometime he have a funny feeling. 'I think John D—I think John D will be in here pretty soon.' And sure enough he would come."[5] The neighbors would come over for a party whenever Wolf returned. His stepsister Lucy said they'd yell, "Howlin' Wolf comin'! Take the bed and everything and move it out. We're goin' to howl some tonight!' "[6] Just as in Mississippi, Wolf always came home in the spring to plow his father's land for planting. He spent the rest of his time at home visiting and playing guitar. Abbie would cook up plenty of food for him and Rosie would do his laundry. "He was tickled about his white shirts," she said. "He didn't want the collar rubbed too much and wear 'em out. So I would keep his white shirts clean for him."[7] A successful bluesman had to look good and sound good. Wolf must have been successful. He always brought his father money when he returned.[8]

While home, Wolf would amble about nearby and play his guitar. A woman at Birdeye, twelve miles from the Phillips Plantation, saw the giant bluesman surrounded by giggling children as he strummed his guitar and sauntered down the road like the Pied Piper of Parkin, Arkansas.[9] Myrtle Gordon, whose father, James Harris, owned the farm next to the Phillips Plantation, said Wolf "walked a lot, and he would go across my daddy's field, and Daddy said, 'Foots! Will you stay in the road and stop walkin' my cotton down?' "[10]

Wolf practiced guitar constantly. Sadie said, "He'd wake me up every night playin' that old guitar. Oh boy, he would be practicin', practicin'! He sat up there sometimes most of half of the night—over half of the night practicin' there, till three or four o'clock in the mornin'. . . . He'd lay down and go to sleep and then he'd get up and start to playin'. I guess a tune or somethin' must have come to him." Sadie said her brother played "Smokestack Lightnin'," "Moanin' at Midnight," and "The Red Rooster" at home—all of which he later recorded, the latter credited to Willie Dixon as composer. Sadie said Wolf "could make that guitar talk. . . . He was a good guitar player."[11]

Wolf also played at local parties, dances, chitlin suppers, and picnics. He played a juke in Parkin called the Bottom, and several just south of Parkin.[12] Myrtle Gordon said, "His life was barrelhousin', and that's how he made a livin'. . . . He didn't do farm work and he had no other job."[13] He even played at the Shady Grove Baptist Church, where his family prayed. Lucy told him, "Don't put yourself off for the devil all the time. Think about the Lord."[14]

Throughout his life, Wolf viewed organized religion with deep skepticism. "No. I ain't a religion man," he said. "I just believe in right."[15] He did say prayers, though, when he got older.

Wolf sometimes played nearby with Lossie Chatmon. Unrelated to the Chatmons of Mississippi Sheiks fame, Chatmon was popular locally but never recorded. He burnt his left hand when he was a baby, destroying two fingers, but like French Gypsy guitarist Django Reinhardt, he overcame the handicap to play. An accomplished lead guitarist and slide player, Chatmon played with Wolf a long time, but never ventured far from home because of his devotion to his sickly mother, who outlived him.[16]

Better known to blues fans than Chatmon was Floyd Jones. Born in 1917 in Marianna, Arkansas, Jones was a teenager when he met Wolf, who had a profound influence on him. "Well, I just see'd him around and after he moved on the same farm we were on, then I go up to his house and so I'd ask him let me see his guitar. He say, 'Be careful—don't break no strings.' Then, so he had an old guitar, he left along in the spring and he let me have this guitar."[17] When Wolf returned a few months later, they played together on Thanksgiving night.[18] Jones said, "Wolf had a real good voice. He was strong all the way, but he never would put together a song. If I hear a number, I would play it and people would ask me to play it and I would play it. Like if I heard 'Rollin' and Tumblin',' I'd sing it like it was on that record. . . . Well, see Wolf, he didn't care about that. He'd just say anything anywhere. But he had a good voice. I seen him break the floor down, man, be so many people in there and he really carried a crowd."[19]

Wolf and Jones traveled far and wide together. "I left out with Wolf and I stayed with him for two years," Jones said. "We was all through Oklahoma and back around through Mississippi and Louisiana and Georgia and all around."[20] They met bluesman Homesick James Williamson on the road. "All of us, we knew each other well," Home-sick said. "I mean all of us, we was down in them Deltas together. We'd go on up into Arkansas, Missouri, we'd play picnics on a weekend and go over to some store, and sit up on the store porch on a Saturday, and play for ballgames, and things like that."[21]

Wolf and Jones traveled on foot and hitched rides when they could. "We'd leave walkin' and we'd catch a wagon, anything, and a lot of times cotton pickin' trucks would stop and let us get on," Jones said. "All of the joints was rough then. . . . Yeah, all of 'em was rough. You didn't find no soft ones." Wolf and Jones played music to attract women, which attracted male gamblers, who tipped them well. "It wasn't nothin' but gamblin' joints," Jones said. "They play coon can, poker, and tonk. That's a card game, tonk. Yeah, man, and kotch. There's a lot of guys play kotch, and big kotch balls." Wolf, a good coon can player, watched his money carefully while gambling and advised Jones to do the same. "He'd say, 'Man, keep your money in your pocket. You don't know what's goin' on.' "[22]

Wolf's road sense also helped Johnny Shines when they traveled together. "He wasn't dumb worth a dime!" Shines said. "He was just illiterate."[23] Wolf said, "You can take my sense and put it in a paper bag and it'll rattle like two nickels. But understanding—that's all I need. You don't need no book learnin'. . . . Common sense, that's all a man needs."[24]

Shines learned the juke joints well with Wolf. "Now, a juke joint is a place where people go to play cards, gamble, drink and so on. So far as serving drinks like you would in a bar or tavern, no, it wasn't like that. Beer was served in cups; whiskey you had to drink out of the bottle. You didn't have no glasses to drink the whiskey out of, so you drank it from the bottle or you used your beer cup, and they were tin cans usually. See, they couldn't use mugs in there because the people would commit mayhem, tear people's heads up with those mugs. Rough places they were. When you were playing in a place like that, you just sit there on the floor in a cane-bottomed chair, just rear back and cut loose. There were no microphones or P.A. setups there: you just sing as loud as you can." Shines and Wolf were both blessed with powerful voices, so the lack of a microphone was no handicap, and perhaps even an asset. Where others had to struggle to be heard, their voices cut right through the din.

Shines recalled problems in the jukes. "Some places was paying a dollar and a half a night, but then you got many tips by playing requests, and like that. Sometimes people just throw you money anyway, just come and chuck it in your guitar. People attempt to pour whiskey in your guitar, beer in your guitar, anything! They'd get to drinking, see, and you'd have to watch out for people like that. Most of these places were pretty rough but I didn't have too much trouble, being a good-sized fellow."[25] Wolf, who was bigger than Shines, had even less trouble. "Wolf used to be a mean guy," said Detroit Junior. "He gambled. If he didn't win the money, he'd take the money anyway 'cause he was big. He'd take the money and carry a pistol all the time. Wolf told me this hisself." Bluesman Albert King told Detroit, "I used to go hear Wolf when he was down South. He played some hell-of-a-tough places. One night I walked in there. Wolf was howlin'. Guys were gamblin'. Some guy was on the floor and they had their feet on top of him. I said, 'What you got your feet on top of that man for?' They said, 'Oh, he dead.' They had done killed him and kept on gamblin' and Wolf was howlin'!"[26]

While Arkansas was Wolf's main stomping ground, he sometimes crossed the river into Mississippi. Lee Eggleston, who later played piano in Wolf's band, recalled first hearing Wolf in Webb, Mississippi, in 1935. "He was one of the best that I heard. He used to play that song about 'Sweet Melvina.' He used to play that all the time. Be so many people you couldn't stand."[27] Bluesman Uncle Johnny Williams heard Wolf, whom he called Foots, in Indianola, Mississippi, in the mid-1930s.[28] Minnie McKenzie saw Wolf practice at her café in Shelby, Mississippi, on Sundays, playing with a local bluesman named Tommy Jackson.[29] Honeyboy Edwards played with Wolf on the streets of Ruleville in the mid-1930s.[30] Bluesman Luther Huff saw Wolf on the streets of Rosedale, Mississippi, playing harp, acoustic guitar, and even a kazoo—an instrument Wolf may have picked up by watching Patton, who sometimes played one.[31]

Wolf also went back to his birthplace in White Station, where he played at nearby Payne Field, which was converted in the 1930s from a military airfield into a Civilian Conservation Corps camp. This gig almost turned deadly. White Station resident Gertrude Burns said, "Some of them boys went to shootin' and folks was runnin' and, ooh boy, they was runnin' over one another." Luckily, no one was hurt.[32] Wolf also played in the front yard of his White Station relative Annie Eggerson. "He used to sit right out there in that yard and play that music," she said. "And when they'd leave here, I would have to cook him some chicken and biscuits. He loved that fried chicken and biscuits." Wolf was fond of Eggerson's husband, Levy "Pee Wee" Eggerson. "He always loved my husband," she said. "That was his favorite cousin."[33]

Wolf often played in Eggerson's yard. Deacon Larry said, "He loved to play 'Deep down in the bottom, bring me my boots and shoes.' Another one he played was 'The church bell toning, the hearse come rolling slow.' You should've seen him play guitar. He could pick that thing, make it spin around in his arms. He was good. He'd take them strings and pluck 'em, and he had a strong voice. One night he was playin' two harps—one with his mouth and the other with his nose! He played in Annie's yard in 1938, playing harp with his nose and mouth. He was singin', 'My baby not at home, don't bother knocking on the door.' "[34] Larry recalled that two hot local musicians were so intimidated by Wolf that they refused to play with him. "They thought they could play! But they wouldn't play around him, 'cause when Wolf come through here, they couldn't get them to play. They were ashamed."[35]

Wolf had a powerful effect on women. Eggerson said, "Yeah, in my time, he used to tear these womens up around here! And they loved him, too! He didn't whup 'em—he loved 'em to death! Yes, they loved that man. They all loved him. They just loved him because he could sing so. And you shoulda seen him. He could get down! I just looked at him and I said, 'Boy, you can really get down with the young womens!' He said, 'Don't I tear 'em up, baby?' I said, 'Yes, you do!' And he loved it, too! He tell me, 'You better stay where Levy can see you.' I said, 'I'm goin' to be where he can see me because I don't want you to get me in no trouble!' We had to do some laughin' about it. He loved the ladies and the ladies loved him. I don't fault him for lovin' 'em. It fun to me."[36]

Deacon Larry heard Wolf play harmonica in White Station—the newest musical weapon in Wolf's arsenal. Wolf learned to play harp from a master of the instrument: Alex "Rice" Miller, better known as Sonny Boy Williamson II. Born in Glendora, Mississippi, in 1909, Williamson was an amazing harp player, singer, songwriter, and raconteur. He was the trickster figure of folklore made flesh—Bre'r Rabbit in human form. Always on the move, Sonny Boy slowed down long enough to teach Wolf the harp for one simple reason: Wolf's half-sister Mary, whom Sonny Boy supposedly married.

Therein lies a mystery, for neither Wolf's stepsisters nor his last wife knew anything about a sister named Mary, nor that Sonny Boy II ever married into their family. But the story about Mary came from Wolf himself. There seems no reason to doubt his word, as he felt no need to claim a phony connection to Sonny Boy. Wolf never lacked self-confidence as a bluesman.

"It was Sonny Boy Williamson—the second one, Rice Miller—who learnt me harmonica," Wolf said. "He married my sister Mary in the '30s. That's when I met him; he was just loafing around, blowing his harp. He could blow, though. . . . Sonny Boy showed me how to play. I used to strum guitar for him. See, he used to come there and sit up half the night and blow the harp to Mary. I liked the harp, so I'd fool around, and while he's kissing Mary, I'd try to get him to show me something, you know. He'd grab the harp and then he'd show me a couple of chords. I'd go 'round the house then, and I'd work on it."[37] In another interview, Wolf said, "When I heard him I wanted to play as well as he did, and I put all my musical energy into getting a harmonica sound as good as his."[38]

Mary's relationship to Wolf is unclear; he referred to her both as his half-sister and his stepsister.[39] Decades later, no one in Wolf's family knew if Mary was related to Wolf on his father's or his mother's side. A plausible explanation comes from "Sunshine" Sonny Payne, who after five decades still hosts Sonny Boy's old radio show, *King Biscuit Time*. He believes the two bluesmen got involved with two sisters who had very shady reputations, but soon disowned the women and destroyed all evidence of the embarrassing relationships. Who these sisters were remains a mystery.[40]

Her marriage to Sonny Boy was short-lived. "Maybe by my being around so much they didn't stay together long," Wolf said, "but anyhow

I was over all the time pestering at him to show me how to play that mouth organ. Sometimes I think he'd show me something just to get me out of the way. 'Cause he would give me something, and then I would go off by myself and practice it. Oh, Sonny Boy at that time was a wild guy. We'd play together sometimes out on the plantations, but then he would take the money and drink it right up. I just had to cut out, I wasn't making no money with him, so I had to put him down."[41]

Wolf and Sonny Boy sometimes did benefit gigs and played for children. Myrtle Gordon remembered them playing together at the Burr Plantation's Rosenwald school—the school Wolf's sisters and brother attended—to raise money for books and supplies.[42] Rosie Lee Whitehead's father took her as a child to hear Wolf and Sonny Boy at Porter's Inn in Parkin, Arkansas.[43]

The last time the two played together in Mississippi turned into a typical Sonny Boy trick. He and Wolf busked on the street for hours as money piled up in a bucket at their feet. Sonny Boy suddenly looked at all the money and said he had to use the bathroom. "Look here, there's too much money in here," he told Wolf. "You can't watch the money and play the guitar both." Sonny Boy took the money and went into the bathroom. Wolf kept playing and gathered a few more coins. But Sonny Boy didn't return. Wolf finally got up, went into the bathroom, and saw an open window in back. Sonny Boy had absconded with their earnings! Wolf said he looked for Sonny Boy for a year to kill him.[44] Years later, the two met again. Luckily for Sonny Boy, Wolf had cooled off by then.

Wolf and Sonny Boy sometimes teamed up with the legendary Robert Johnson. Obscured now by myth, Johnson was just one of many traveling bluesmen in the 1930s. An incredibly facile guitar player and an excellent singer, he was also a world-class songwriter; many of his songs are blues classics. He recorded just twenty-nine songs—a mere compact-disc-ful of tunes today—but no one has a loftier reputation in American popular music.

Wolf met Johnson, a year younger than himself, in Johnson's hometown, Robinsonville, Mississippi. "Robert was a little brown-skin, slender fellow, weighed about 160 or 170 pounds," Wolf said. "He was about 6 feet tall. . . . Robert had a nice personality. He was a nice-looking guy, and the women went for him. . . . I don't know how long Robert had been playing when I met him, but at that time he was playing pretty nice. I never did ask Robert where he learned, 'cause we was just young and would just run in and meet one another at those parties and suppers, play and jam awhile, and take off. I never did ask him too much about his life.

"Me and him played together, and me and him and Sonny Boy—Rice Miller—played together awhile. At that time I couldn't play near as well as he could; I'd just be hanging around trying to catch onto something. Rice, though, he could play with him. We took turns performing our own tunes. If I played lead and sang, they'd back me up, see, 'cause at that time I wasn't good enough to back them up. But such as I did know, they'd back me up in them."

In Mississippi, Wolf and Johnson played Greenwood, Itta Bena, and Moorhead together. "We didn't stay together too long because I would go back and forth to my father and help him in the farming," Wolf said. "I hung around with Robert about two years, off and on. He traveled a lot. Last time me and him was together we was coming out of Memphis. I was going my way to Robinsonville, and he was on his way to Greenwood." This may have been the trip when Johnson met his tragic end. Wolf said, "He got poisoned by a woman down there. I think he was getting too many girls and didn't pay her too much attention. This took place somewhere around Greenwood, Mississippi, out there somewhere. I don't know exactly when—it's been so long I've forgotten what year it was. It was in the '30s, though."[45] Johnson died on August 16, 1938, in Greenwood.[46] Most accounts say a jealous husband poisoned him. His burial place was unknown until a woman revealed in 2001 that her husband had buried him in an unmarked grave ten miles north of Greenwood, near Money, Mississippi.

Detroit bluesman Robert "Baby Boy" Warren was nineteen when he met Wolf in 1938. "I'll never forget how we'd go through Arkansas," he said, "around those little country towns in the fall of the year when they'd be gathering in the cotton. We'd hit those little towns on Saturdays—we'd clean up! Make a little money, those guys get to drinking and those women start to braggin' on Howlin' Wolf; throw him a dollar or two and he'd get down to start slidin' or crawlin'! . . . One of his favorite songs the people used to love to hear him sing was this 'Terraplane Blues' that Robert Johnson put out. He could clown and sing with it—get on his knees and all that. He had another song of his own about 'I'm that old wolf that everybody try to find out why in the world I prowl; say they never get to see me, but they always hear me when I howl.' "[47] Baby Boy traveled with Wolf and Johnny Shines in Arkansas, and played with Wolf and Robert Lockwood, Jr., in what is now Handy Park in Memphis.[48] Blues drummer Peck Curtis, born in 1912, also played with Wolf in Marianna, Hughes, Brickeys, and West Memphis, Arkansas, in the late 1930s.[49]

Lockwood heard Wolf play in the Delta in 1935. "I learned about Howlin' Wolf and Sonny Boy—Rice Miller—from Robert. All these guys was already playing, you know? I first really seen Howlin' Wolf in Brickeys, Arkansas. . . . Howlin' Wolf was playing on the streets, and I went around to the whiskey store, Charley Eula's . . . to get a little whiskey, and [Charley] asked me, 'Why don't you play a few songs?' I started playing Robert Johnson's shit and drew all the people away from Howlin' Wolf! It was funny. I looked out there in the crowd and Howlin' Wolf had his guitar on his back. . . . Back at that time, he didn't have no band, when I first knew him. He was playing by himself. At house parties, he started playing over here and he'd walk that chair all the way across the room! Before the night was gone, he'd be across the room!"[50]

Lockwood didn't think much of Wolf's musicianship, but Lockwood has extraordinarily high standards, having learned guitar directly from his fabled stepfather, Robert Johnson. "Wolf ain't never been no good guitar player—and harmonica player, either. He had a style that people liked. He was a stylist, let me put it that way. . . . He had a style, and it sold. Muddy Waters had a style, and it sold. Neither one of 'em wasn't no good guitar player. They was good entertainers."[51]

Future bluesman James "Shakey Jake" Harris also saw Wolf in these years. Born in 1921 in Earle, Arkansas, Shakey Jake said, "I was a fan of Wolf's at one time, Howling Wolf. I saw him when I was a little kid. He could blow harmonica but at the time he was playing guitar and he had a little thing that he called a flute—something, you know, that he used to blow and play guitar. I was a kid then but I traveled backwards and forwards from Chicago to Earle and West Memphis and all that. My mother used to take me around. Wolf was like Sonny Boy: he was traveling around by himself at the time, just him and his guitar. . . . I can remember him doing 'Smokestack Lightnin'' 'round about '38 or

'39."[52] Wolf got to know Jake and his mother quite well. "Wolf was sort of like my stepdaddy—he was interested in my mother. Back in those days, he used to play a thing [like a kazoo]. I remember I went to a little place he was playing for $4 a night and he was playing one of these things."[53]

Wolf often played with two Delta blues legends—Son House and Willie Brown—in Robinsonville, Mississippi. One of the greatest early bluesmen, House poured all of his being into his guitar playing and singing. Sometimes a preacher, he was torn between singing the devil's music and serving the Lord, and his personal turmoil gave his blues a power that few bluesmen equaled. An associate of Charlie Patton's, House was a major influence on both Robert Johnson and Muddy Waters. He made his first recordings for Paramount in 1930, and made many recordings after being rediscovered in the early 1960s. Brown, less well known, was a better guitarist but not nearly as good a singer as House. He made commercial recordings for Paramount in 1930, and recorded with House for the Library of Congress in Mississippi in 1941.

Wolf said, "Willie was the better musician 'cause Son House always played his guitar with that [bottleneck] thing on his hand. But Willie Brown, he fingered his, and could play all the way out. He knew more about the instrument; he didn't have to play it in open chords all the time. Now, Willie he was a good singer too. . . . Son and Willie worked well together; they teamed up pretty good. See, Willie Brown would play and follow Son House with his guitar. Mostly Son House would lead out, no matter which of them was singing, 'cause Willie kept in the background with the bass.

"I worked with the two of them at some of those Saturday night hops. I'd happen up on them at different places, and I'd jump in and play a tune or two with them. They was playing music for dancing mostly, fast numbers to dance to. . . . They had the dances every weekend. That's the only time those people would have a chance to enjoy themselves—on a Saturday night or a Sunday—'cause those landlords want them to work any other time."[54]

The jukes were so dangerous it's a wonder that Wolf, House, and Brown survived. "Them country balls were rough!" House said. "They were critical, man! They'd start off good, you know. Everybody happy, dancing and then they'd start to getting louder and louder. The women would be dipping that snuff and swallowing that snuff spit along with that corn whiskey, and they'd start to mixing fast, and oh, brother! They'd start something then!"[55]

Wolf formed more personal connections with House. They dated sisters for a while.[56] In 1938, House saw Wolf playing an electric guitar and a rack harmonica on the streets of Robinsonville.[57] Wolf also told blues scholar Pete Welding that he had an electric guitar before World War II.[58]

St. Louis bluesman Tommy Bankhead, born in the nearby town of Lake Cormorant, Mississippi, in 1931, first saw Wolf playing at a store there around 1939.[59] "He used to wear a great big hat and he had a belt made, had harmonicas all way 'round his waist," Bankhead said. "Had an old guitar, had it hung across his shoulder. He used to get out in a little town up under a tree or in front of a little store or something and people put money in the hat for him, he was playing on his own."[60]

At Robinsonville, Wolf made one of the most important musical connections of his career when he met local teenager Willie Lee Johnson in the late 1930s. Born at Lake Cormorant in 1923, Johnson was learning to play the guitar when he met Wolf. "I met Wolf in the '30s at Dooley's Spur, Mississippi, near Lake Cormorant," Johnson said. "That's right out from Robinsonville. Him and Son House and Willie Brown was playin' together. I was young, 13 or 14 years old, drivin' my dad's car. I slipped off to go down there. My dad had let me have the car to go to the show. Instead of me goin' to the show, I slipped off where Wolf and them was. Wolf told 'em, say, 'I got this boy in here. I wants him to come up and do a few numbers. He can play it pretty good.' I tuned the guitar my way and I struck out on a tune. Son House and Willie Brown, you know, backed me up and all like that. They said, 'This kid is good! He gonna be all right one day.' "[61]

Impressed by Johnson, Wolf often let the teenager play with him. "Wolf would let me play with him every Saturday night down there, you know," Johnson said. "Son House and Willie Brown was playin' together, and me and the Howlin' Wolf was playin' together. Son House's style on guitar was kinda some style like Elmore James put out. Son House is the first guy I heard that started that slide stuff. Wolf taught me how to tune my guitar and everything. He set me on his lap. You know, he was a big man. I would set on his knee and he would reach over me like this and put my hand on the guitar, show me different chords. Oh man, he had fingers that long. I used to play in Spanish [tuning] all the time. But I would play everything they play 'cause I'd know where to go on it, you know. But he taught me how to tune it from E natural on up [in standard tuning]. And then I could play in every key. I learned the chords and everything. And I got terrific with him. I got to where I could go into every joint without anybody, you know, protectin' me. I got grown then so, yeah, he regard me as a guitar player then. Then he went to harmonica."[62]

Johnson adored Wolf's music and showmanship. "I'd slip off and go to them juke joints on Saturday nights," he said. "Wolf would come down there too. He had been active a good while when I met him, playin' and doin' about, singin' and goin' on. Foots, that's what they called him. Yeah, he'd come in there with his old guitar swung over his back, stuff like that. And he'd get up and clown and do about with his guitar. Oh, he just get up and be dancin' while he playin' the guitar. He sang the same way he was singin' later on in Chicago. He got that tail dragger name from . . . he used to sweat a lot. He would get one of these big towels and put it in his belt back here. And when he would swing his hips, that was a little show-thing like. And everybody would go to hollerin' and clappin' their hands, you know. And he'd just be waggin' and goin' on tellin' 'em he the tail dragger and he drag his tracks out as he go. In those days, he would just make up songs—but he would make 'em rhyme. . . . So that's the way Wolf was. He was the kind of guy that he could make up a pretty good song. It wouldn't take him long, either."

Wolf and Johnson played together off and on into the early 1940s. "We'd pack 'em in, just the two of us," Johnson said. "I carried bass and lead. This was '39, '40, '41, somethin' like that. Sometimes we make $5 a night, sometime we make $10."[63] As Wolf put together his first electric band after World War II, the two became an unforgettable team.

Jimmy Rogers, best known as a key member of the Muddy Waters band, played with Wolf first. Born in Ruleville in 1924, Rogers said, "I was in Memphis in the late '30s. Yeah, we'd take the bus—or ride in a car with somebody that we knew—from Memphis that had a curfew to West Memphis that was wide open. Me and Joe Willie Wilkins and Howlin' Wolf would play at this roller rink in Memphis and the Baby Grand in West Memphis. We used to jam. Not too many places, but I remember those two. Sometimes we'd get $3 a night, $5 at most, a drink of whiskey and $2. [Laughs] But this was somethin' I wanted to do. . . . [Willie] Nix sometime would be with us, with Wolf, playin' on drums. . . . Willie Johnson was a guitar player in that group too. I liked what he was doin' real good. He'd listen. He'd catch on real fast. He was what you call a creative musician. Wolf, he was all right. A lot of people didn't understand Wolf. He was a man that let you know that he knew what he knew and you gotta deal with that or you weren't gonna deal with him at all. I liked Wolf. Even then he'd have blow-ups with Willie Johnson 'cause Willie was kind of wild. I've played with wild musicians: you've got to run your race, man. Wolf didn't accept that. He wanted you to be like he wanted you to be."[64]

Wolf began one of the most important relationships of his life in Pace, Mississippi—and almost died there. Situated between Cleveland and Rosedale, Pace was small even by Delta standards. He share-cropped there on the plantation of Robert Malone, who from all accounts was a fair and honest man. Also living at Malone's was Willie "Bill" and Lee Anna Frazier, whose daughter, Elven, was born the same year as Wolf. Elven's younger sister, Magnolia, said, "She weighed about 165 pounds. She had a medium waist, broad hips, and big legs and short black hair. She was friendly to everybody. To me, she was too friendly. . . . She liked parties."[65] Osborn Holloway said, "She'd drink and dance and have her fun."[66]

Wolf was irresistible to a woman who loved to dance and party. Elven met him at a local juke and began spending time with him. Magnolia said, "He'd get all down on the floor and be crawlin' like a snake! He would howl like the Wolf! I guess that's what tempted my sister. Maybe if I had been grown at that time, maybe I'd have been the one tempted." Elven, an excellent cook, worked as a cook for a man named Cal Busby in Pace when she met Wolf.[67] Wolf loved to eat, so it was a match made in heaven.

Wolf spent many evenings with the Fraziers, savoring his favorite foods: turnip greens, home-cured meat, fried fish, fried chicken, and biscuits. "My parents just loved Wolf," said Magnolia. He often wolfed down at least ten biscuits at a time. Mrs. Frazier demanded payment for her home cooking: Wolf had to bring his guitar and harp and play "Poor Boy." "I believe my Mama would stop eatin' to hear Wolf play that!" Magnolia said. "She loved to hear that song."

Elven, who hated eating in front of Wolf, once insisted that they let Wolf eat and leave before they ate. After he left, Magnolia went into the kitchen and found all their fresh-cooked food gone. She cried until her mother cooked more. Her father often cracked a joke about Wolf: "His food went in his feet." Wolf and Bill were good friends and often went out to the jukes together, accompanied by Wolf's mock protests. "My daddy was one of the ballin' types," said Magnolia. "He loved to go out and drink. Wolf'd come down there and tell him, 'Look old man, I'm gonna take you out with me, but you better not get drunk!' " Magnolia was fond of Wolf personally and musically. "I loved to hear him sing because, to me, he had such a deep, pretty voice," she said. "I just thought he was the best!"[68]

Wolf packed in full houses at Willie Towner's juke joint in Pace, which held two hundred to three hundred people. On Wednesdays, Fridays, Saturdays, and Sundays, couples danced in the front while men shot craps or played keno in back.[69] "He had a large parking space in front and on one side and there'd be cars all up and down the roadway," said Laura Towner, Willie's daughter.[70] Willie Richard, Sr., who heard Wolf at Towner's juke, said, "Couldn't hardly no more get in there." Wolf did his usual stunts: howling, crawling on the floor, and dancing with women from the audience—all while playing guitar, sometimes behind his head. "He never would dance with one long because they would all be tryin' to dance with him," Richard said. After most of the crowd had gone home, Wolf would get down on all fours and simulate sex while singing, "Let me hump you, baby."[71]

Wolf played several other local jukes: Red Boyd's in Boyle on Tuesdays, Jap's in Rosedale on Thursdays, and various nights at the Coconut Grove in Cleveland.[72] The latter, a large building surrounded by a grove of trees, attracted customers from all over. "Oh man! People was comin' from Shaw, Leland, Greenville, Clarksdale, and everywhere," said Osborn Holloway. "Everybody knowed old Wolf, 'cause they liked to hear him sing and they liked his music." Wolf's guitar tricks impressed Holloway. "He'd have it, throw it up and catch it and hit it when it hit his hands! He'd steady be playin'. I don't know how in the world he could do that! That's the reason they followed him. Just followed around with him to see him act a fool with that guitar." Well-to-do white patrons who came to hear Wolf at the Coconut Grove often dropped two or three dollars into his hat to request a song. Holloway said, "Some of them would tell him now, 'That's the colored music. Now play some white music.' He'd sing some songs they liked. That's when they'd give him some money." Holloway recalled the excitement Wolf stirred among the local women. "Man, you couldn't hear you yell, because they'd be whoopin' and hollerin'! Womens would be dancin' and huggin' anybody, and all that kind of stuff. They'd be huggin' him and kissin' him. They had to pull 'em away so he could play his guitar. . . . Them women would be around him so you couldn't hardly see him unless he stand up. For they'd be all around him whoopin' and hollerin' and huggin' him!"[73]

Tall, dark, handsome, and charismatic, Wolf attracted women like honey drew bees, though he kept coming back to Elven. For a while, he dated Josephine Anderson, but they broke up when he found out she was dating other men.[74] "Most of the ladies that he attacked wanted him, too. They chased him!" said Willie Towner's daughter, Emma.[75] Her sister Laura said, "Anybody who was half-famous the women would flock to."[76] Wolf also spent time in Pace with Coonie Ballard, and then with Rosie Smith, who was raising three of her sister's children while Wolf acted as a surrogate stepfather.[77] A short, dark woman, Smith mistreated her stepchildren, but never when Wolf was around. Wolf would spank the kids himself if they didn't pick enough cotton. One boy, age seven, had to stuff two hundred pounds a day into a cut-off cotton sack or get spanked.[78]

Magnolia Frazier in her early teens couldn't get into the jukes to hear Wolf. She and her friends got to dance to Wolf's music when he played in back of a store in Pace with Willie Gary, a young local guitarist.[79] Wolf also played in Pace with Babe Taylor, a female blues singer and guitarist.[80] Wolf often performed with local harp player Gus Lake.[81] St. Louis bluesman James DeShay said, "There weren't too many musicians down there—Howling Wolf was about the only guy down there that you'd see when you go to town. And he'd play by himself, just had a guitar and then later he got in contact with a boy by the name of Gus Lake, started blowing harp and Gus Lake played with him for a long time." Wolf used to get a nickel tip for playing DeShay's favorite song, "Highway 49."[82]

Wolf, Lake, and Gary formed a band, and along with two teenaged

musicians once played at Parchman prison for the inmates, driving
there in Wolf's car. Magnolia Frazier and her niece were interested in
the boys and went along for the ride. "He asked my mother if he could
take us to hear him play; and we wanted to go, because he had those
teenagers in the band. . . . We started up there and he pulled to the side
of the road. He said, 'Let me tell y'all somethin'—you are not goin' to be
flirtin' with these boys! And if you get up there and start to flirtin', I
done already told your mama I am gonna beat the hell outcha!' So we
went a little piece further and I told my niece, 'I'm goin' back home.'
She said, 'Wolf not goin' to take us back home.' I said, 'You wanna bet!'
She said, 'He ain't goin' to take us back.' I laid down in the van and
rubbed my eyes, went to crying. He looked around and said, "What's
wrong with you, baby sister?' I said, 'I'm sick. My head is hurtin'!' So he
taken us back to the house, but I never did tell Wolf that I wasn't sick
'cause I was afraid he would whup me for real!"[83]

Simply put, Wolf adored women, and they returned the favor. But
death stalked him and almost grabbed him in Pace because of a
woman. Bill and Deborah, a white couple, sharecropped on the Malone Plantation, and Deborah often talked to Wolf when he passed by
their house. One day she invited Wolf and Gary to come up on her
porch to play a song. They were playing for her when her husband
came home and pulled out a gun. Wolf and Gary took off running. "Bill
said that he was goin' to have him killed," Magnolia said. "He was goin'
to string him up in a tree and shoot holes in him like a sifter."[84] In those
days, most white folks in Mississippi believed that if a black man sere-
naded a woman, he had more than music on his mind. Wolf said,
"Down there the whites was mean to the colored folks. Everybody know
that. But if you could do something and they liked you, you had a break.
I had a break in the South all my life because I could play guitar. I'd
play for their parties and things. But they would beat up the colored and
drag 'em on account of white women and things."[85]

One Saturday night not long after the incident, Bill claimed he
came home and saw someone running from his house. When his wife
suggested the man looked a bit like Wolf, Bill swore Wolf was stalking
his wife. Wolf and Lake were arrested and thrown in jail the next afternoon. Wolf told the authorities that the night before, he had played at a
store in Sunflower, stayed there until it closed at eight o'clock, and then

went with a white man to a country juke, where he played until dawn. The storeowner confirmed Wolf's story, and the other white man said Wolf was out of his sight the night before only when he went outside to relieve himself, and even then he could hear him singing.

Plantation owner Malone interceded on Wolf's behalf. The authorities held him for a week, partly to protect him from Bill and his friends, and released him and Lake for lack of evidence.[86] Wolf fled Pace the same day.

Elven gave birth to a boy on June 19, 1939, and named him Floyd. She eventually told Floyd about his blues-playing father.[87] Afraid to return to Pace, Wolf didn't see his son for years.

Dozens of black men were lynched in Mississippi in the 1920s and 1930s, often in gruesome public-spectacle burnings, simply for talking to white women. Wolf was lucky to escape with his life. Soon, he'd travel to places he'd never dreamed of, far away from the Delta. For Wolf, the hard times in Mississippi were gone for good.

4. How Many More Years

On April 9, 1941, Howlin' Wolf entered the United States Army at Camp J. T. Robinson near Little Rock, Arkansas.[1] He later told a friend that some white plantation owners forced him to enter the army because he wouldn't work for them.[2] Plantation owners wielded vast power in the Delta, and they probably considered the Wolf—a blues-playing bad example who somehow avoided working in their cotton fields—an ideal candidate for the draft. Bluesmen like Wolf threatened the status quo by showing that a black man could survive and thrive without working for Mr. Charlie.[3] Now Wolf worked for the biggest Mr. Charlie of all: Uncle Sam.

Wolf's military service was very unpleasant. Thirty years old when inducted, he was ill prepared by temperament and experience for the discipline of the U.S. Army. He was assigned at first to kitchen patrol. Blues singer-guitarist Archie Edwards met him at Camp Blanding, near Jacksonville, Florida. "I was a regular soldier, but Howlin' Wolf was in the mess hall," Edwards said. "He put food on my pan when I went through the food line." Wolf often played blues for his fellow soldiers. "He played at the orderly room in the evenings, and guys would come in and take seats around in the orderly room area for mail call. And then after mail call, he and another guy would stick up their guitars and

strike up a few tunes. . . . I used to play with him in the afternoons
around the orderly rooms. He had a guy who used to play slide guitar
for him who called himself 'Black Ace.'[4] So I think he and this guy
played together more because I wasn't as forward with my music as they
were, but I did play. I played enough to let him know what I was doin',
you know?" Edwards recalled Wolf playing "How Long Blues" and
"Pickin' a Little Cotton." He admired Wolf's guitar playing, rating him
a top guitarist with "a style of his own." He also noted that Wolf did not
play a pure Delta style of blues, but "more like Blind Lemon Jefferson."

Edwards remembered fondly what Wolf said after the attack on
Pearl Harbor. "Mr. Roosevelt was going to make a speech that morning.
They didn't have but one little radio up in the orderly room window and
all the soldiers had to gather around and sit on the ground and listen to
that radio. Mr. Roosevelt declared war against the imperial majesty of
Japan. Howlin' Wolf said, 'Okay fellas, we know we at war now, and we
are goin' somewhere. We don't know where we're goin' and we don't
know who's comin' back. But one thing I want you to know. If you do
come back, keep your eyes and ears open for that young kid soldier sittin' there.' And he pointed at me. 'I like what that kid is doin', and you
are goin' to hear from him!' That's why I came to play and sing, because
this is what Howlin' Wolf said about me. He was a nice guy."[5]

Buddy Folks, born in 1916 in Alabama, met Wolf in the army at Fort
Benning, Georgia. "We'd sit on the steps and play together quite a bit,"
Folks said. "The thing was, he was so much better than me."[6] Wolf was
also stationed at Camp Gordon, Georgia, near the home of future God-
father of Soul James Brown, who as a boy often watched soldiers coming and going from the camp.

While stationed in Memphis in 1942, Wolf romanced a woman
named Lillie Alice Crudup who, amazingly, had married and quickly
separated from a man just the February before.[7] Wolf took her home to
meet his family during his Christmas furlough in 1942, and his father
thought they were married.[8] But it's unlikely they ever were married
legally; among other things, she never took Wolf's last name.[9] While
home for the holidays, Wolf played again with his pre-army partner
Floyd Jones.[10]

After Christmas, Crudup returned home to Tennessee while Wolf
was sent to the Pacific Northwest. He was transferred through Fort Law-

ton in Seattle, which had many jazz and R&B clubs in the 1940s, and arrived at Camp Murray, south of Tacoma.[11] By January 1943, Wolf was a Technician Fifth Grade in the Army Signal Corps, specializing in battlefield communications. Ironically, his inability to communicate caused him grief. Before the war, his stepsister Rosie was teaching him how to read and write, using J.D.'s schoolbooks. "Shortly after then he went to the army and he could write a letter back and we could understand it," she said.[12] Slowly writing letters to relatives, though, was not good enough for the army, so they sent him to school for lessons in reading and writing.[13] The lessons did not go well. He pretended not to know the alphabet until, he said, they "whupped" him. He then showed he could recite the letters from A to Z.[14]

The army's strict discipline affected Wolf badly. Maybe his reading and writing lessons, enforced by beatings, reminded him too much of childhood punishment at the hands of Will Young. Or perhaps he ran into a drill instructor who wanted to make a name for himself by breaking the spirit of the biggest, toughest man in camp. Whatever the reason, Wolf started suffering from spells of extreme nervousness and dizziness at Camp Murray. In August 1943, he was sent to a military hospital at Camp Adair, near Portland, Oregon. An army doctor wrote that during his spells, "he becomes extremely tense, cries freely & shows tendency to destroy furniture—on one occasion started kicking at steel gate (with size 16 feet); again, lifted a bed up into the air. During his agitated episodes he is fearful & begs to be allowed to go home to his father. . . . Has had nervous spells as long as he remembers. Gets nervous easily but doesn't know why he has spells. These do not sound like epilepsy."[15] The doctor's working diagnosis was that Wolf suffered from "possible syphilis" or "psychoneurosis."[16] In the racist army of the 1940s, the former may have been a favorite first diagnosis for any black man with unusual symptoms, while the latter was probably military medical code for "not cut out for us." The examining doctor said Wolf had a history of "injury to head by baseball bat several years ago—unconscious a short time." He also said Wolf "causes no trouble," but he was unsympathetic about Wolf's lack of education, describing him as a "mental defective."

The army sent a Red Cross worker to Parkin to talk to Dock about his son's troubles. The interviewer's notes say Wolf "suffered from bad tonsils and has poor teeth . . . is subject to severe headaches. He smoked cigarettes but did not drink . . . is a steady reliable boy with a strong sense of duty. He liked large groups and showed some leadership qualities. He was inclined to be high-strung. Is interested in music. He did not have pets but resented cruelty to animals. He liked girls, in his father's words, 'he shore liked them,' and preferred girls his own age . . . showed no unusual interest in religion. Farming was his main ambition."[17]

Wolf remained in the hospital at Camp Adair for two months, and his condition did not improve. By the end of October, the army had had enough of him, and he of them. He was transferred to Memphis, where he received an honorable discharge on November 3, 1943—almost two years before the end of the war—for "disability not in line of duty and not due to his own misconduct." The army rated his character as "excellent" but described his condition as "psychoneurosis, hysteria, anxiety type . . . soldier is not able to perform the drills, marches, and other duties required of enlisted men by reason [of] recurrent attack of hysteria and probability of future hospitalization. . . . Fraud is not involved." Wolf was not alone. More than 800,000 soldiers were inspected and then rejected by or ejected from the U.S. military during World War II.

Wolf later led friends and family to believe he'd been "shell shocked" in the army.[18] But he never went overseas and never got anywhere near combat.[19] He simply couldn't handle the stress of military discipline, and he was embarrassed to admit what had happened. After his discharge, he told his stepsister Sadie, "That army is hell! Don't you know that army is hell?"[20] He told an interviewer in 1970, "I stayed in the army three years. I done all my training, you know? I liked the army all right, but they put so much on a man, you know what I mean? My nerves couldn't take it, you know? They drilled us so hard it just naturally give me a nervous breakdown."[21] Wolf's military service helped him immensely at the end of his life, when he received free medical care at Veterans Administration hospitals around the country.

The experience Wolf received in the service was eye-opening. For the first time he was exposed to the country outside the Deep South. He may not have seen the bright lights of Paris, but he did see the lights of Seattle and other relatively progressive cities where black people weren't so viciously repressed. He told a friend that before the war, he was "lucky to be living, the things he had did in his life." The army, he said, was the best thing that ever happened to him. "When you get out, [it'll] change your way of living."[22] He already knew that he didn't want to work on a farm for the rest of his life.

Shortly after his discharge, Wolf moved with Lillie Crudup to a brick house on Sycamore Street in Lebanon, Tennessee, where at the end of November 1943, he got a Social Security card.[23] He didn't stay with Crudup for long.[24] Her family said the couple broke up because Crudup was "a Christian lady and the blues was the work of the devil."[25] But Crudup, like Wolf's mother, had mental problems characterized by extreme religiosity. In 1945, Crudup's own mother, also named Lillie Crudup, had her committed to a state mental hospital. She was later released, remarried, and spent much of the rest of her life serving as a volunteer counselor to people with mental and emotional problems.[26]

After leaving Lebanon and Crudup, Wolf returned home to the Phillips Plantation, where he teamed up again with Floyd Jones, and played around Arkansas for about six months.[27] Wolf also played with musician Lee Rodgers. Rodgers's son, Minneapolis bluesman Sonny Rodgers, said, "My daddy, Lee Rodgers, inspired me to get started. 'Fact, I got started playing his guitar. He was monkeying around with Howlin' Wolf in those back juke joints down south back in the 40s. This was before Wolf got real tight with the music. My daddy was playing those juke joints and he met Howlin' Wolf . . . [and] they just got together, y'know. This was before they had electric guitars and amplifiers; acoustic guitars was all they had."[28]

Wolf said, "After the war, I had gone back to farming, back to my father in Arkansas, out on the plantation they call Phillips' plantation — that's about 16 miles north of Parkin, Arkansas, on the St. Francis River. I stayed out there until after I figured I was grown enough to go for myself, and then I left there and went to Penton, Mississippi, and did some farming on my own for two years."[29]

Wolf developed an interest in a woman named Blanche Ship, who decided to return home to her mother in Penton, on the river about twenty-five miles south of Memphis. Wolf caught a ride across the Mississippi from a fisherman one Sunday afternoon to see her. Despite his pursuit, Wolf and Blanche soon parted ways, and Wolf started seeing a woman named Mamie — another relationship that didn't last.

Israel "Wink" Clark, a boyhood friend of Robert Johnson's who loved gambling and often traveled with Wolf around Penton, said, "Fellows at that time was worse than they is now. And I think it was more womens than it is now! He'd stay here with one two or three weeks and if she'd tell him he needs a bath, hell, he'd get his few clothes and go on to another one. He done had a wife near about everywhere he went. You could easily get you a woman. Stay in her house there oh, three or four months. You get tired of there or get tired of her and say, 'Hell, move on!' Find you another one! So that's just the way people lived in that days. Back in that time, you give a woman four or five dollars, you had done put her on top. They could take a dollar and buy 'em a pair of shoes, a dress for 75 cents. So everything was just real cheap, and women was the cheapest thing goin'."[30]

The constant in Wolf's life was music. While living at Penton, Wolf often played on the streets of nearby Robinsonville. Sitting on a bench with his guitar and a harp in a rack, he entertained passersby on Saturday nights.[31] Local resident Lonnie Bailey heard Wolf play on the streets of Tunica, Walls, and Lake Cormorant, and at parties.[32] Wink Clark said, "Everywhere in the neighborhood from here in Tunica to Dundee, Lula, Clarksdale, all out in the hills, back to Robinsonville — that was his stay-home and he would leave out from there. We'd always mostly would get off Friday evenin' or Saturday. And if he got off Friday evenin', he would go a long ways like Clarksdale and come in Sunday night or Monday morning. But now, we didn't have no special place to stay. We was women-struck, and they was givin' it to us and we was gettin' it halfway free!"[33]

They may have gotten it halfway free, but it again almost cost Wolf his life. He went home with a woman in Clarksdale who told him she was single. Undressed and in bed, they heard a key turning the door lock. The woman moaned, "Oh, my God — that's my husband!" Wolf grabbed his clothes and jumped out the second-story window. He was running away when he hit a strand of barbed wire, which wrapped around his neck. Thinking the husband had come to cut his throat, he yelled, "Oh, mister! Please don't kill me! Don't cut my throat! Please don't kill me — she told me she didn't have a husband! Mister, please don't kill me!" The husband yelled, "Who's that down there?" Wolf heard her say, "Some old drunk fool done got tangled up in that barbed wire down there and think somebody got a knife around his neck." Wolf saw red and felt the welt for days.[34]

Wolf often played at a juke in Robinsonville called the Oil Mill Quarters—the same juke where the young Robert Johnson tried to convince Son House and Willie Brown to teach him how to play guitar.[35] The owner, Nathaniel Richardson, Sr., sold homemade whiskey, plus sodas, hamburgers, and hot dogs. His son, Nathaniel Jr., said Wolf was the most popular musician around and loved to joke. Wolf usually played there solo, but was sometimes accompanied by Fiddlin' Joe Martin, who despite his nickname played guitar. Wolf received food and whiskey for a night's work there.[36] Wink Clark heard Wolf play with Fiddlin' Joe but doubted they were a regular team. "Fiddlin' Joe would probably sit in around with him because Fiddlin' Joe was too big a drunkard to try to play. He would get drunk all the time."[37]

Wolf and Fiddlin' Joe were closer than Clark knew. Joe's left hand was later severely injured when the gas tank on a tractor exploded, and he had to give up playing guitar. Wolf suggested his friend take up drums and even bought him a drum set. The two also made a pilgrimage down to Holly Ridge, Mississippi, to visit the grave of Charlie Patton—a three-hour drive each way in those days, which speaks volumes about Wolf's continuing admiration for his idol.[38]

Wolf also played with Woodrow Adams. Born in 1917 in Tchula, Mississippi, Adams met Wolf in Minter City, Mississippi, in the mid-1930s but didn't play with him until Wolf moved to Robinsonville in the 1940s.[39] Adams sometimes played with Wolf, Fiddlin' Joe, and Barber Parker, a one-legged drummer.[40] Adams made a handful of recordings, some in the style of the Wolf.

Dan Curry of Port Gibson, Mississippi, heard Wolf play at Clack's store in Lake Cormorant, where folklorist Alan Lomax recorded Son House, Willie Brown, Fiddlin' Joe Martin, and Leroy Williams in 1941 for the Library of Congress. Curry recalled how Wolf played the guitar behind his head and crawled on the floor. " 'Boogie! Come on, baby, boogie! Boogie for me!' That's what people wanted to hear. He played that more than he did anything," said Curry. "He had a bluesy way of playin'." Curry also heard Wolf play on the Watson Plantation, near Prichard, Mississippi, at a juke run by Willie Steele, a gambler in his forties who was unrelated to Wolf's later drummer of the same name.

"Willie Steele used to cuss him," Curry said. " 'That big, long-foot son of a bitch!' Wolf said, 'Yeah, may be, bud, but that's all right, that's all right. The guys tell me I got big feets—but I got a foundation to stand on!' " Curry thought someone had warned Wolf he'd be poisoned because he was always careful about where his whiskey came from.[41] More likely, Wolf remembered what bad whiskey had done to his step-mother and to his late friend Robert Johnson.

Chicago bass player Aron Burton as a child witnessed an unusual entrance by Wolf at his uncle's picnic in Senatobia, Mississippi. The huge bluesman came riding in on horseback while playing guitar and a harp in a rack! Burton recalled the excitement Wolf created in the pic-nic area, which was lit by beer bottles full of kerosene with rag wicks. "It'd be dusty and shit, and he would be playin', and you could hear the guitar, but you couldn't get up there because of all the old people be up there dancin'. Be a few women buckin' in there, and the little guys like us would be hangin' around the edges tryin' to get to see."[42]

Chicago bluesman Maxwell Street Jimmy Davis met Wolf during these years at a juke owned by Dave McGee near Drew, Mississippi. Wolf performed solo at McGee's Friday through Sunday night and drew crowds of one hundred to three hundred people a night.[43] Monroe Bur-nett also heard Wolf at McGee's. "He could get to singin' just like a guy preachin' or singin' spirituals and feel the spirit." Burnett marveled that Wolf could play guitar behind his head. "Wolf could play just as good that way as he could with it down in front of him."[44] Wolf sometimes played McGee's with Houston Stackhouse, a talented bluesman who had played with Tommy Johnson in the late 1920s, with Sonny Boy II on the King Biscuit radio show, and with Elmore James and Boyd Gilmore at McGee's in the late 1940s.[45] Wolf probably played with Elmore James at McGee's also.

Playing at night, Wolf worked days at various plantations. He and Wink Clark hauled hay together for the Abbay and Leatherman Planta-tion in Robinsonville.[46] Wolf also sharecropped on the Koehler Planta-tion at Penton and occasionally drove a tractor there: a prestigious job in the Delta, though Wolf didn't do it often.[47] Clark himself spent two years as a backup driver before he "got to be a professional."[48] Wolf held an even more important position: overseer for a farm owned by a Mem-phis lawyer.[49] Wolf also worked as a plantation's straw boss: in charge of hiring and firing.[50] Wolf eventually inherited a farm from his grandfather near Walls, Mississippi.[51]

Wolf's old Penton friends remember him with great fondness. "He treated you as nice as your mama," Clark said. "If he had anything you wanted, he would give it to you or divide with you: I can say that about him! Now, he didn't ill-treat nobody. He didn't steal or interfere or nothin'. When he wasn't workin', he was sittin' around home. You'd go by there, he'd have about a half-gallon of corn whiskey sittin' there. 'You better come on man. Yeah, you better come on here. Get you a drink of this stuff.' Me and him have drank many a time together. He was a good boy."[52] Curry and Wolf went coon hunting together with Wolf's big red untrained hound.[53] Curry recalled a car accident Wolf was in at Penton while driving his old Chevrolet one Sunday to take a friend to a funeral. Nobody in Wolf's car was hurt, but two people in another car were killed.[54]

Monroe Burnett was impressed by Wolf's speaking voice. "He could stand out there and make a good talk just like a preacher could," he said.[55] Wolf may have talked like a preacher, but his relationship with the church continued stormy. "I remember one night revival was goin' on at church," Clark said. "Me and Wolf had worked together that day. Went in and put the mules up, and his old lady and her mama was at church. We was over a mile from church with his guitar, and the people come out of church and they could hear Wolf, and they went down there. Church folks went down there and told Wolf, 'Don't do that no more.' They said, 'People can't return to church for you.' Preacher and the people, they just couldn't stand it!"[56]

"His old lady," as Monroe Burnett described Wolf's new girlfriend, was Katie Mae Johnson, a short, gorgeous woman with long hair and a mouthful of gold teeth. Katie Mae grew up in Quitman County in the northern Delta. On Saturday, May 3, 1947, when Wolf was thirty-six and Katie Mae was thirty-five, they were married in Penton.[57] Magnolia Frazier met Katie Mae soon after the wedding. "She was a beautiful woman," Magnolia said. "She looked like a doll. When she sat down, she'd have to reach and get her hair and bring it from behind."[58]

Newly married, Wolf continued to make music. Willie Johnson's girlfriend, Corrinia Wallace, used to sneak out of church in Horn Lake, Mississippi, to hear him entertain at baseball games across the street, perhaps at games where his father played. "He wasn't no blues singer, but he was a great ballplayer—country ballplayer," Wolf said.[59] "Wolf'd play the ballpark Sunday afternoons and at night he would move down farther to his brother-in-law's little country juke. . . . They were sellin' corn whiskey there and people were dancin' and Wolf was makin' the music. And I just liked music. Being young, I had never saw a person really playin' live music before. Believe me or not, from that time on, he had the same crowd all the way to his funeral. He carried a crowd *always*."[60]

Wolf's marital status changed his relationship with his female fans. When two women at a juke argued about who was going to spend the night with him, he said, "It ain't any use you cuttin' up, 'cause hell, I don't want none of you! I got my wife at home, man!"[61]

Now that he was married, Wolf decided he wanted to be a father to his only child, and he returned to Pace to pick up Floyd. Several years had passed since his narrow escape there, but he kept a low profile, staying with Elven's parents.[62] Willie Walker, Floyd's nine-year-old half-brother, awoke to noises one night. In the morning, he peered around a corner and saw Wolf and his mother, Elven, laughing as Wolf played guitar and harp. Walker was impressed by the size of Wolf's feet and by his name. "He was a big man and he had a big name," he said.[63]

Floyd was happy to get a chance to finally know his father, the famous bluesman. Floyd also became close to his new stepmother, who had no children of her own. "She was a very beautiful person," he said. "To be a stepmother, I couldn't ask for no better."

The new family lived on a plantation at Penton and then moved to another plantation near Lake Cormorant. Wolf was adamant that Floyd go to school. "I brung him some water out in the field," Floyd remembered, "and he told me, said, 'Son I want you to go get an education,' 'cause he didn't have no education. And he said, 'One day I want you to sit down and count my money.'"

Wolf's long-estranged mother, Gertrude Jones, entered his life again in the late 1940s. Living near Lake Cormorant, she learned that Wolf lived in nearby Penton and walked fifteen miles round-trip to visit him. Floyd liked his grandmother, describing her as a "beautiful person." Gertrude, a sanctified street minister, still didn't like the way her son lived. "She would always tell him that God sent her to tell him to quit playin' for the devil and play for Him," Floyd said. "But he didn't want to hear that. He would get mad. He didn't never cuss her out, but he would say things like he was a grown man and he was livin' his life the way he wanted to live it. He came up under pressure, and I guess he figured didn't nobody care nothin' about him.

"When he was real young, he didn't believe that God could do nothin' for him. That's the way he felt, because he wanted to play a guitar and he couldn't play the guitar. . . . I believe that he had a devil connection, because he had some evil in him, too!"[64]

Wolf told his son a bizarre story about how he'd *really* learned to play the blues. "It was a scary story, what he told me about it," Floyd recalled. "Said when he first learned how to play the guitar that he had went to this cemetery where somebody that he knew had died. And this old man told him to go to this cemetery and sit on this grave of somebody that he knew. And after twelve o'clock, somebody goin' to come there and learn him how to play the guitar. So he said he did it. Said he must've drank a half gallon of that old corn whiskey. . . . He was just so nervous and as much of that liquor he drank, he still couldn't feel nothin'. And like the man said, after twelve o'clock, something walked up to him—something like he said he ain't never seen in his life—and took the guitar out of his hands and chorded that guitar, and handed it back to him and told him, 'Play!' And said he played that guitar just like he had been playin' for twenty years. And he went that Friday night to that house where them fish fries was at. He told the guy, 'Well, I'm goin' to play tonight.' He had been saying that all the time, but he wasn't playin' nothin'. And the guy told him, 'Well, if you play tonight we're goin' to buy you all the fish you want to eat and all the whiskey you want to drink.' Said when he got to playin' that guitar, 'You could hear a rat piss on cotton!' And he was playin' it ever since."[65]

What to make of this story? Wolf always had a sense of drama. In the Delta, many people believe both in Christianity and in hoodoo, which is based on traditional African myths. Wolf had heard all the hoodoo stories about bluesmen like his late friend Robert Johnson who'd sold their souls to the devil. He elaborated on one of these stories to pull Floyd's leg.

But at some level, Wolf really did feel that he'd sold his soul to the devil. He sometimes told the story of how blues really came down to earth. God and Lucifer, he said, had a terrible fight up in heaven. They battled for days and days and finally God won and knocked Lucifer off his cloud. As Lucifer fell to earth, his tail hooked on to God's cloud and pulled some things down to earth with him: dice, cards, guitars and other stringed instruments, and harmonicas. God still had his horns up in heaven. That's why horns are played by the good people and why guitars and harmonicas are played by people like him, he said.[66]

Wolf wouldn't serve two masters. "A lot of people, they'd sing spirituals a while," he said, "then they'd try to sing blues a while, y'know, but I don't believe it. I just believe in serving one man."[67]

And if the Baptist God was on the side of the two people who hurt him most in life—his mother, the religious fanatic who cast him out, and his great-uncle, the church deacon who beat him with a whip—he didn't mind hinting that he worked for the other side. The scorned, abused boy had grown up into a man who believed in taking care of himself his own way.

The Wolf was a practical man who also understood the power of myth. The blues was his badge of shame because it made him a pariah and his fount of power because it made him self-sufficient in a culture that wanted to crush him. If that put him in league with someone's version of the devil, so be it.

Later in life, Wolf would come home, kneel down next to his bed, and say his prayers every night.[68] He also said grace before meals, even in public. Like many other great American musicians—Charlie Patton, Hank Williams, Son House, Skip James, Johnny Cash, and Elvis Presley come to mind immediately—Wolf was conflicted about religion. But he was sure about one thing: He wouldn't stand with the hypocrites he'd known who called themselves Christians and then did ungodly things.

5. House Rockin' Boogie

Wolf made a momentous decision in 1948. The Delta was rapidly changing with the widespread adoption of the mechanical cotton harvester, which threw sharecroppers out of work. That meant less money at the jukes. Though Wolf couldn't read, he could understand the handwriting on the wall. Like many Delta bluesmen, he pulled up stakes and lit out for better territory. He moved to West Memphis.

Founded in 1910 as a logging camp called Bragg's Spur, West Memphis was incorporated and renamed in 1927. By the early 1940s, it had a population of about 3,500.[1] When Wolf arrived, he took a job in a factory, but it was the clubs in the region that really grabbed him.[2] By the late 1940s, blues clubs were hard to find in Memphis, just across the river. Beale Street featured mostly jazz music, and few blues musicians still played in Handy Park. But West Memphis was wide open with booze, gambling, loose women, and other vices, or pleasures, depending on your point of view. As usual, the music followed the money.

The days when a bluesman could hold a crowd with an acoustic guitar or harp were ending. West Memphis was at the forefront of a dynamic new music, based on amplified instruments and full bands with guitars, pianos, drums, and horns. Electricity was spreading through the South, even in the Mississippi and Arkansas deltas. Money

was flowing freely in the good times after World War II, and black people were listening on their radios and record players to the new rhythm
& blues. Jukeboxes, more common than ever, blared out the latest R&B
hits in jukes, bars, clubs, and cafés. T-Bone Walker, Louis Jordan, Roy
Brown, Amos Milburn, Wynonie Harris, and Charles Brown were the
stars of the new genre. Even down-home bluesmen like Lightnin' Hopkins and John Lee Hooker were going electric (though Hooker's first
hit, "Boogie Chillen," featured an acoustic guitar). Wolf had been a
local celebrity in the old blues style, but he had ears and sense enough
to know he had to adapt to the new style if he expected to remain in the
game. Even before moving to West Memphis, he was experimenting
with electric instruments. "Long before them others I was playing electric," he said. "Yeah, man . . . it's true, you know? Used to run a wire
from the storefront to the boardwalk. It sure kicked things up down
there when the Wolf went electric. I always dug power, boy. I just don't
go too much on shit."3

Wolf assembled the finest musicians he could find and fused them
into a sensational unit—the hottest blues band West Memphis ever
heard. "It was there, in 1948, when I formed my first band and began to
follow music as a career," he said. "On guitars I had Willie Johnson and
M. T. Murphy; Junior Parker on harp, a piano player who was called
'Destruction'—he was from Memphis—and I had a drummer called
Willie Steele. . . . The band was using all electric, amplified instruments at that time. After I had come to West Memphis, I had gotten me
an electric guitar."4 Other musicians in the band were Pat Hare, born in
Cherry Valley, Arkansas, in 1930, and harp player James Cotton, born in
Tunica, Mississippi, in 1935.

Wolf said, "It was my dream come true, to have a stable band playing in its own proper style. Together, we developed a style along the
lines of the black tradition in West Memphis; that's a very wild and
rhythmic style. . . . We played as hard as we could, and the clubs were
always packed with people come to hear us."5

Wolf's band, the House Rockers, sounds like a blues lover's super-
group—Parker, Hare, Murphy, and Cotton—but they were all still
teenagers. Willie Johnson was slightly older, in his twenties. William
Johnson on piano, known as "Destruction," " 'Struction," or
" 'Strutcher," was closer to Wolf's age. Wolf, fast approaching forty, was

old enough to be the father of most of his band members, and treated them accordingly. Playing with Wolf was their first major gig, and Wolf clearly molded their playing. He knew exactly what sound he wanted, and he put together a talented group of musicians to help him create it.

The sound that Howlin' Wolf and the House Rockers created was electrified Delta blues with a dollop of R&B thrown in for good measure. A musicologist would describe it as "Chicago" blues, but West Memphis can make as strong a claim as the Windy City for gestating the genre. Everything that Muddy Waters and his band did in Chicago, Wolf's band did at the same time in West Memphis—and then some. Critic Robert Palmer wrote, "The personnel shifted somewhat, but between 1948 and 1950 Wolf molded his musicians into the most awesome electric blues band the Delta had seen. Muddy, Jimmy Rogers, and Little Walter were shaping their definitive ensemble sound during these years, and, as another amplified group playing updated versions of traditional Delta blues, Wolf's band, one would think, should have been comparable. In fact, it was both more primitive and more modern than Muddy's group, for while Wolf was moaning and screaming like Charley Patton and Son House and blowing unreconstructed country blues harmonica, his band featured heavily amplified single-string lead guitar by Willie Johnson and Destruction's rippling, jazz-influenced piano. The result was an unlikely but exceptionally powerful blend, and it perfectly mirrored the dialogue between tradition and innovation that was beginning to transform the Delta's music. Wolf and his group could sound exceptionally down-home . . . and they could swing, jump-blues fashion. But most of the time, Wolf strutted and howled, Willie Steele bashed relentlessly, and Willie Johnson, his amp turned up until his tone cracked, distorted, and fed back, hit violent power chords right on the beat. Wolf's band rocked."[6]

The key member of the band was guitarist Willie Johnson, who had already learned much of what he knew about blues guitar from Wolf. "Wolf was hell on a guitar," Johnson said. "He really didn't need a guitarist."[7] The two elevated their musical partnership to a new level. With his amp cranked up to 10, Johnson poured out an incendiary mixture of deep Delta blues, jazzy chords, and hornlike flourishes.[8] His solos were alternately fiery and distorted or tastefully delicate, with a hint of swing. Music critic Dave Rubin wrote, "Johnson played like a bull in a rut on these jumping jaunts, pounding out comp chords and molten lead lines. . . . One of Willie Johnson's many attributes was his ability to combine jazzy, dominant chords with basic blues licks. Like a good short-order cook, he tossed it all together with sizzling distortion, making seemingly disparate elements blend into a satisfying culinary stew for the ear."[9] British critic Charlie Gillett said Johnson's playing "sounded as if he was twanging baling wire with a six-inch nail."[10] Sunnyland Slim described Johnson's sound succinctly. "That's the man that made Wolf. That used to be a ass-wiper guitar player. That son of a bitch was a motherfucker. Him and Murphy was top of all of 'em."[11]

Matt "Guitar" Murphy, born in 1929 in Sunflower, Mississippi, was another sophisticated, bluesy guitarist whose ears were open to the new sounds bursting out of the radio and record machines. He said, "This guy came through and guess who it was. He was looking for a guitar player. Howlin' Wolf. But, it wasn't organized. It wasn't organized at all. It was just that he needed a guitar player. Actually, what I did is, I really put some structure into the band because these guys didn't know. . . . I knew about time. I knew about chords. I was a little young upstart, I thought I knew everything. And I didn't, of course. But anyway, I knew enough for these guys. They weren't very good anyway because they were actually making fun of them. It's just that people loved to hear him sing. He had a tremendous voice. His voice sounded like it was coming out of a brass pipe or something. He had a hell of a voice. I always marveled at his voice."[12]

Murphy's precocious knowledge of music helped Wolf focus on singing in a band setting. "Little Junior Parker and I helped Wolf a lot, because his timing was rather off," Murphy said. "While he was playing, a lot of times he would start to change at a certain point and I would just cut right on through—keep on playing it *right*. Every once in a while I'd overlook his mistakes and go along but not often, because at that time I was concentrating on my time, too, see? . . . I was concentrating on stuff like that, studying these books, see, and that's the reason why I was so critical of Wolf—you know, because I was working to get my stuff straight."[13]

Wolf worked to get his own stuff straight by taking music lessons from legendary Memphis jazz guitarist Calvin Newborn. After Newborn taught Wolf a C scale on guitar, Wolf threatened right away to fire his entire band, saying, "Y'all can't play my music. I'm goin' to Chicago and get some musicians can read my music."[14] St. Louis saxophonist Oliver Sain, who played with Wolf's band in West Memphis, said, "He would sit down and start playin' these chords for me. He'd show me what he had learned. . . . He was very proud of that. I mean that was a big thing to him. So he would sit down and he'd get that guitar, man, and it might be 'I'm in the Mood for Love' or somethin'. . . . And he would sit there, man: chomp, chomp, chomp, chomp, on the guitar. And I'd sit there and look at him and I'd say, 'Yeah, man, that's all right.' . . . He was very proud of even just to say 'I was goin' to school.' "[15]

The third member of Wolf's Holy Trinity of West Memphis guitarists was Auburn "Pat" Hare, whose family had moved in 1940 to a place near Parkin, where he met Wolf. Just a kid then, Hare already showed promise on the guitar. He refined his natural talent with lessons from blues guitarist Joe Willie Wilkins, a phenomenal Delta guitarist best known as one of Sonny Boy II's King Biscuit Boys. Hare's style was aggressive and intense with lots of distortion. His leads burned like a brushfire, threatening to sear everything in sight.[16] A teenager when he joined Wolf's band, Hare rode to and from practice in Wolf's car.[17] Hare's parents never knew that their boy's first gig with Wolf was at a West Memphis whorehouse.[18]

Junior Parker and James Cotton had unusual roles in the band. As harp players and singers in a band fronted by a powerful harp player and singer, they rarely performed at the same time as Wolf. Born in West Memphis in 1932, Parker learned harp from Sonny Boy II. Able to play and sing down-home Delta blues and urban R&B with equal skill, Parker was sometimes called "Baby Wolf"[19] or "Little Wolf."[20] Murphy said, "While I was playing with Wolf, Junior Parker used to come around and sit in with us. People started liking us together, so they almost demanded that we play together. This became a real nice little thing. Junior would play harmonica for an hour or so and then Wolf would take the harmonica. We'd get into contrasting styles: whereas Little Junior was like an idolizer of Roy Brown at that time, doing things like 'Corn Bread,' boogie things, and shuffles, when it came down to real low dirty blues, Wolf would take it. That made it really fill out."[21]

Wolf didn't even want Parker in the group. "[Parker] was just good, so he had to hire him," said Murphy. "Little Junior Parker would have a section and then Howlin' Wolf would have a section. That went on for a while."[22] Whatever their personal feelings, the group was one of the best Wolf ever had. Abu Talib (born Freddy Robinson), who later played with Wolf in Chicago, saw this band and many others while growing up. He said the lineup of Wolf, Murphy, Parker, and Steele "was one of the best groups goin' at the time that I heard."[23]

James Cotton also learned harp under the tutelage of Sonny Boy II, whom he met at the tender age of nine and lived with off and on for the next six years. "It was Sonny Boy introduced me to Wolf," Cotton said. "Wolf was really a quiet kind of guy who liked people to leave him alone, but if they gave him trouble he'd give 'em trouble back. Sometimes you had to be mean back then, the way everything was."[24] Cotton enjoyed playing with Wolf: "I thought he was a nice guy because he was the type of person who would work. When I'd be playing the harmonica, he'd be on the door selling tickets, and when he'd be playing the harmonica, I'd be on the door. So we kind of kept it going, which was good."[25]

Cotton also appreciated Wolf's competitive nature: "Soon as I got with Wolf he was electric, way before everybody 'cept Sonny Boy and his band," Cotton said. "See, round here there's so many musicians that it's real competitive and you're up against these big bands with the saxophones. Now Wolf would never let anybody outdo him onstage; that's where the tail dragging and everything came from, and the band was the same. No one was gonna cut us. . . . With the amplifiers and everything we could go up against a nine-piece band and blow the motherfuckers right off the stage. We annihilated them, man."[26]

'Struction Johnson, a tall, thin man with big feet, was a versatile pianist who'd already survived the vices of youth. "He wouldn't drink or mess around—he just did the womens all the time," said Ernestine Mitchell, wife of Memphis impresario and club owner Sunbeam Mitchell. "He always got somebody hemmed up in a corner somewhere."[27] Tot Randolph, a saxophone player from Memphis, said, " 'Struction was a good jazz musician. He could play! . . . 'Struction was about the best musician in the band."[28] Memphis bluesman Big Amos Patton, a nephew of Charlie Patton, said, "Anybody that wanted to cut a record or impress a crowd with a piano player would get 'Struction."[29]

With his band together, Wolf set out to get the group better known in 1949 by securing a spot on local radio station KWEM in West Memphis. Opened on February 23, 1947, KWEM had studios in the Merchants and Planters Bank at the corner of Broadway and 2nd (now the site of the Union Planters Bank). A 1,000 watt station, KWEM was at 990 AM on the radio dial and from 6:45 a.m. to 5:45 p.m. every day broadcast a combination of popular music, piano, Hawaiian, hillbilly, and Western—but no blues.[30] When Wolf asked for a spot in their lineup, KWEM's management was receptive because of the success of rival station WDIA in Memphis, which had gone to an all-black format in 1947.

Wolf said, "I was broadcasting, too, on a radio station in West Memphis, KWM. I went to a Helena station [KFFA] a time or two in Sonny Boy's place—Rice Miller—when he had to be away, he'd get me to blow harp with his little outfit. But I had a steady job on KWM. It came on at 3 o'clock in the evening. . . . I had been lucky enough to get a spot on KWM. I produced the show myself, went around and spoke to store owners to sponsor it, and I advertised shopping goods. Soon I commenced advertising grain, different seeds such as corn, oats, wheat, then tractors, tools, and plows. Sold the advertising myself, got my own sponsors."[31]

Wolf sold the advertising, but didn't actually read the ads on the air. "Howlin' Wolf couldn't read," Murphy explained. "I don't think he could read anything that good. So what happened was they tried Howlin' Wolf one time to do some commercial about some bread or something and he said something wrong and they took it off the air."[32] Despite his deficiencies as an advertising pitchman, Wolf's show was popular, and bluesmen Sonny Boy II, Willie Love, and Willie Nix soon got spots of their own on the station.[33]

Wolf's show was on for fifteen minutes. After Wolf played each song, announcer and program director Dick Stuart, known as Uncle Richard, read a commercial.[34] Wolf also announced where the band's next gig would be. The band often played requests sent in by listeners.

Guitarist Ronnie Smith, who later played with Elvis Presley and Jerry Lee Lewis, met Wolf at KWEM. "His guitar player was always dressed pretty sharp. . . . But Wolf looked like he got off work to make this thing. It would be a T-shirt and maybe work britches, and work shoes—what I mean is shoes that are run-down, scuffed. . . . He had a cigar box with maybe eight harmonicas in there in different keys."[35]

For Wolf, the benefit of doing the show was the exposure it gave to his band. Willie Johnson said, "We'd play different songs. A lot of people would turn us on, and Wolf would announce where we was gonna be that Friday night and Saturday night. People would be there waitin' on us when we get there, if they done heard us on the radio."[36] Honeyboy Edwards said, "Wolf was playing at different places in Memphis and out in the country. He got pretty popular at that time because he was broadcasting on the radio from KWEM in West Memphis, and that helped him a whole lot in the farming areas through there. They advertised feed and seed and farm implements, stuff like that. In Mississippi and across West Memphis, Arkansas, around Little Rock and Franklin and Marianna, the people would hear him on the radio, and the folks that had them country jukes, the bootleggers, they would get him to play."[37]

Paul Burlison, guitarist for the Rock and Roll Trio, often listened to Wolf's show as he drove home from his own show at KWEM. "He would holler like a wolf. 'Aooooh—this the Wolf comin' at you, baby! Oooh, this here's the Wolf comin' at you, baby!' Like that, see? He'd talk that way. 'This song right here, I'm goin' to do it for So-and-So and So-and-So.' "[38]

Burlison got to know Wolf well and even jammed with him once at KWEM. "There were two studios there at the radio station, and we played in the front and he played in the back," said Burlison. "He was standing outside the studio one day leaning up against the wall while we was playing some song. And he was looking in through the glass of the window then, and this gal was singing a song that had a little blues feel to it, so I played some blues on my guitar, and he gave me the okay sign, like 'That sounds good,' you know? So after we got through playing the show, I went out in the hallway and he says, 'Hey, I like the way you play guitar.' I said, 'Thanks.' He said, 'How about playin' some blues with me today?' I said, 'All right. I'd be glad to.' Smokey Joe Baugh, who had that song 'The Signifying Monkey,' he was there, and he said, 'Well, if you're going to go back there and play the guitar, I'm going to go back there and play the piano.' Wolf said, 'Well, come on man—the more the merrier!' So we went back there and he sat down and got his rhythm guitar out and he got a big old box of harmonicas out, and he took the harmonica and stuck it in his mouth long-ways, you know, and start doing one of these blues songs, 'Waaaa-waaaa-waaaa-waaaa-waaaa'— long-ways. And he was playing and I just repeat what he was doing on harmonica on the guitar, and Smokey just started playing 'Da-da-da-da-da-da!' I don't remember what song it was now. It was just a lot of old blues. I liked what he was doing and I liked playing the blues. So Wolf said, 'Are you goin' to be over here tomorrow?' And I said, 'Yeah, I'll be playing here every day.'

"That went on for about three months. One night he said, 'Come on over to the club and sit in with us.' He was playing over on 17th Street or 18th or 19th. I don't remember the name of the club now, but I went over there a few weeks later. It was on a Saturday night. I went around to the back and knocked on the door. They let me in, and I sat down beside the door right close to the bandstand. I was the only white person in the whole place. I listened to him play about three songs before they took a break. He called me up and I got to play. There was little Willie Johnson playing the guitar with him. And I got to sit in and play about three songs with him. Then they took a break. He walked me back out to my car out in the parking lot, slapped me on the back like that and said, 'Say, man, come back again sometime.' And I drove off and he stood right there until I got plumb out of sight."[39]

Rockabilly legend Ronnie Hawkins saw Wolf many times in West Memphis and always came away impressed. "Wolf had a hell of a voice," he said. "It was stronger than forty acres of crushed garlic, man! He didn't need a PA system. A guitar wide open couldn't get over his voice. . . . I'll tell you, nobody messed with him. I heard some stories. I don't know if it's true, but you know, he almost killed two or three cats that jumped on him in a fight one time? It was one of them fights over a woman. Somebody jumped him when they were leaving, and Wolf just nearly had a concussion. He hit them fuckers and like to broke their necks. . . . Another time somebody pulled a knife, and he took it and stuck it in him—with the guy's own hand. . . . Then there was the time outside the Cotton Club when he held up the whole back end of a car while they changed a flat."[40] As Hawkins said, those were stories— unconfirmed as of this writing.

Ernestine Mitchell recalled West Memphis with great fondness. "West Memphis used to be like Las Vegas," she said. "Eighth Street—that was the street. They had a joint in every little hole and stop through there—some kind of joint. On each side was gamblin' joints, and people would come far and near. I knew a man that would come from Texas, had oil wells and things. Put a rope around the table because they would have so much money stacked up, so you couldn't get near them or bother them. . . . My husband was a gamblin' fanatic. Wherever you dropped some cards or dice he was there."[41]

R&B pianist Roscoe Gordon also compared West Memphis to Las Vegas. "In every club, they had dice tables there," he said.[42] Sunnyland Slim said, "Everywhere you go in West Memphis, there was a gambling joint and honky-tonks. I used to play all them places. It used to be so muddy in the streets you had to carry hip boots to get around."[43]

Honeyboy Edwards said black gamblers from all over the country came to West Memphis lugging suitcases full of money.[44] James Cotton said, "Memphis was the quiet side, West Memphis was where they did all the gambling and whiskey drinking—everything worth naming was in West Memphis, right on 8th Street."[45] Memphis music legend and WDIA disc jockey Rufus Thomas said, "Now in West Memphis, across the bridge, you're talking the blues language. Howlin' Wolf was on the radio over there . . . 8th Street—it used to be the place in West Memphis. The Little Brown Jug—I used to go over there, boy. It was a joint. They did a lot of gamblin' and stuff over there. But it was the place. It was wide open."[46]

Chicago bluesman Alex "Easy Baby" Randle, born in Memphis in 1934, spent much of his youth across the river in West Memphis. "West Memphis was dusty, but it was beautiful," he said. "There were gamblin' houses, 8th Street, 9th, 10th, 12th, and 7th Street, too. Bands was all around there, Little Brown Jug and all. That was on 8th Street. . . . That's where I first seen Wolf."[47] Jack Brown ran the Little Brown Jug and had a few other clubs nearby. West Memphis also had the Be Bop Hall, Miss Annie's, and the Dinette Lounge.

Chicago bluesman Brewer Phillips, best known for his years with Hound Dog Taylor and the House Rockers, said, "They had a curfew time there in Memphis for black people. If they catch you on the streets after 11 o'clock, you went to jail. . . . But they had good blues in West

Memphis, Arkansas. . . . West Memphis wasn't nothin' but gravel and dirt. When the wind blow, you couldn't see down the streets 'cause it wasn't no pavement or nothin', you know, it was sand. And boy, they had a blues band in every joint—and gamblin'. It was a band here and a band there and a band there and dust and, heh heh, gamblin'. Boy, that was good times. . . . I'm tellin' you, man, from 8th Street back down to 16th Street, wasn't nothin' but night clubs, restaurants, and music too."[48] Tommy Williams, who worked for a bootlegger, said, "Music— you could hear it all out on the streets. People be out there dancin' out on the streets and inside, too. They was wide open over there back in the '50s."[49]

West Memphis was wide open largely because of the unstinting efforts of "Mr. Cuff"—C. C. Culp, West Memphis city marshal from 1932 to 1942, who winked at the town's wicked ways. West Memphis bluesman Sonny Blake described Culp's routine. "He'd go around them gamblin' clubs every Monday morning. Now what he was doin', didn't nobody ask him. Wasn't nobody goin' to sit and watch him, 'cause he would whup you—so help you, Jesus! White and black, woman and man, didn't make him no difference. He was just a tough guy."[50] "He would stop you on the highway and have your trial right there on the highway," Roscoe Gordon said. "He'd get X amount of dollars and then he'd let you go."[51] Ernestine Mitchell said matter-of-factly that clubs paid "Cuff" protection money.[52] Tommy Williams said that with Culp's blessings, no one bothered gamblers. "He had those people runnin' these clubs for him. He run that West Memphis!" Culp received cash tributes from the town's pleasure palaces even after he left his marshal's job to buy a shoe store.[53]

West of West Memphis about fifteen miles was Black Fish Lake, known for its catfish, crappie, bream, and bass fishing, and for its two clubs, which featured blues and gambling. The Top Hat, the larger club, attracted customers from all over the region and held several hundred people. It had music and dancing in the front and a big room in back for high-stakes gambling. Wolf, Sonny Boy, Joe Hill Louis, Joe Willie Wilkins, and B. B. King all played there. B. B. first met Wolf at the Top Hat, and he was floored by the older bluesman's passionate singing and playing. The two kept running into each other at clubs in the region, and they stayed in touch on the blues circuit for the next twenty-five years.[54]

Sonny Blake first heard Wolf at a club on 8th Street. "I see'd a big, old dude, hair stickin' straight up on his head. I said, 'Who's that big guy yonder?' They said, 'That's the Howlin' Wolf.' I said, 'No!' He had on some old brogan shoes and a pair of khakis. I didn't believe it. . . . Said he goin' to be at Black Fish. I went down to Black Fish to see the guy. Really was the Howlin' Wolf, by my surprise! What he was doin', he did it. Wasn't nobody else like him. The guy was awesome! I don't know where he come from; but when I saw him and heard him play things just went over me."[55]

Big Amos Patton said Wolf "had Black Fish Lake sewed up."[56] His popularity bothered some other bluesmen. "Sonny Boy was playin' down at King's Junction and somebody comes up and says, 'Hey, Sonny Boy! How about playin' "Goin' Upstairs Bring Me Down My Clothes" by the Howlin' Wolf?' He said, 'Goddamnit! The Howlin' Wolf is over yonder at Black Fish Lake.' Says, 'You want to hear "Goin' Upstairs," goddamn you, go over there where the Wolf is!' "[57]

Matt Murphy recalled, "We played a lot of places, like Black Fish Lake. That's the place where he would run out across the field with the money and hide it when they had a fight at the club, and pretend that he lost it and all that."[58] Wolf had several opportunities to pull this stunt because fights were common there. Matt's younger brother Floyd, also a talented guitarist, said Black Fish Lake had "lot of gamblin'. Lot of shootin'. Lot of problems."[59]

With a hot band, a popular radio show, and a solid base in West Memphis and Black Fish Lake, Wolf was soon busy playing all over. In Arkansas, he played clubs and jukes in Hughes, Brickeys, Twist, Marianna, Seyypel, Stuttgart, Osceola, Helena, Horseshoe Lake, and Brinkley. "He was packin' peoples in. Lot of peoples used to come in and see him everywhere he played at," said Chicago bluesman Little Mack Simmons, an Arkansas native.[60]

East St. Louis bluesman Little Cooper, born in Prattsville, Arkansas, in 1928, was a teenager when he first heard Wolf. "Wolf, he was playing in Woodson, Arkansas. That's the first time I come in contact with a professional blues player. There was a club they had in

Woodson called the Woodson Hall and he and his band come in there. He was in Arkansas awhile and he was doing a show there every Friday, Saturday, and Sunday night."[61]

Chicago blues singer Mary Lane often sat in with bands at the White Swan in Brinkley, which held two hundred people and had gambling in the back. Wolf's band was her favorite, and she sometimes sang with them before Wolf came onstage. Wolf liked Lane's sound and told her to keep singing the blues—and "never take any mess" from anyone. "The way I look at it, Wolf was a great person," she said.[62]

Bluesman Frank Frost, a fine harp player from Helena, also met Wolf at the White Swan. Too young to get into clubs, Frost would pedal his bicycle to a drugstore and buy Wolf a harp for 25¢, and Wolf would get him inside.[63] "I'd be singing, he'd be blowing, he told the people I was his son so they wouldn't bother me, they wouldn't throw me out," Frost said. "He was a fine person but he had a mean temper, a lot of temper!"[64]

Hubert Sumlin, Wolf's guitarist and musical alter ego for over twenty years, as a teenager met Wolf at a juke in Seyypel, Arkansas. "The first time I saw Wolf he was playing at this juke joint, this big old honky-tonk up on cement blocks, right down besides the Mississippi River called Silkhairs," Sumlin said. "You could crawl up under the pilings, man, and hear everything that was going on. . . . I knew he was playing there, but they didn't allow no youngsters in that club, 'cause they had booze and gambling going on in there. So, the first night I got up under the house, next to the band, where Wolf was playing. . . . I heard so much music that night, I couldn't believe it. . . . But this particular time I'm getting bold. I been over there long enough to know now, I said, 'I'm going over here and see these folks. I got to see the Wolf.' . . . I went around to the back of the club, where they had all these Coca-Cola cases piled up. I climbed up to the top of that stack to where I could see everything that was going on, 'cause there was a window, right behind the drums. Well, these Coke cases started to come unbalanced and I fell through the window into the club, in the middle of a song. Over on the old Wolf's head I landed—right on the dude's head. He said, 'Let him stay, let him stay. Bring him a chair.' . . . The lady brought me a chair. I sat between Willie Johnson, Pat Hare, and

Junior Parker, which he had at this time. He didn't buy me nothin'; he had the lady bring me a glass of water, and I sat there. I stayed with him that whole night and when the show was over he said, 'You live around here, boy?' and he took me home in his car. When he got there he made me wait in the car while he went in to see Momma. And he told her, 'Don't punish him, Mother, he just wants to hear the music.' That's the first time I saw the Wolf and I followed him ever since."[65]

One night at Brickeys, Wolf went to a juke to hear Sonny Blake and his band. Sonny Boy II was also there and during the evening Wolf and Sonny Boy took off their shoes and fell asleep. Both wore huge shoes, and Blake switched them around. Wolf woke up and said, "Hey, this ain't none of my goddamn shoes!" Sonny Boy said, "You got my shoes! You got my shoes!" Blake's drummer said, "Hey man! Old Blake swapped shoes with y'all." Wolf and Sonny Boy said, "Bring him here." "Shit—they weren't bringin' me over there!" Blake said, laughing. "Man, I cut out. Them two big guys wasn't goin' to get me. I liked to have got in a fight doin' that!"[66]

Tommy Bankhead, who saw Wolf at Lake Cormorant as a child, was introduced to Wolf at the State Line Club, on the border between Arkansas and Missouri, by his bandmate Woodrow Adams. "Wolf was tyin' handkerchiefs to the tail of his pants and would crawl around on the floor like a wolf or somethin'," Bankhead said. "I was kinda scared of him. He was such a big guy."[67] Dirty Jim Thomas, who later played in Ike Turner's Kings of Rhythm, also saw Wolf at the State Line Club. "My old man used to take me up there; in fact that's where I first saw Howlin' Wolf. He had a whole band, saxophones—he had everything. Them cats came from Memphis; they were professionals to us. They were really big guys. . . . Oh, man, he was big shit to us. That just goes to show you how low down the scale we were! We was on the floor, man. But it was great because them guys, they taught us a lot, they liked for us to come around and watch 'em, try to copy them, we never tried to copy mannerisms but voices and things. I think that is why I've got a versatile voice now . . . because I used to try and sing like Howlin' Wolf and all of 'em, man."[68]

Wolf sometimes played the Hole in the Wall club in Helena.[69] In Marianna, he played a club owned by a man called Slack Britches.[70] In

Osceola, he played the popular T-99 Club, which regularly featured B. B. King, Rufus Thomas, Albert King, Joe Hill Louis, and other well-known bluesmen, and had its own respected band, the In the Groove Boys.[71]

Arkansas was his main lair, but Wolf also played in Mississippi, Tennessee, and Louisiana. Bassist Willie Kent, who grew up in Shelby, Mississippi, heard Wolf in 1950 at a school dance in nearby Hushpuckena, and also at the Harlem Inn in Winstonville.[72] Wolf also returned to Pace with his band to play for the children at school.[73] Bluesman Smokey Wilson heard Wolf and his band play at a club in Rexburg, Mississippi. He recalled: "[Wolf], that's the only man really that I stood and looked at and every time he opened his mouth I could feel his voice inside of my skin, and looked like right in my chest, right in here, I could hear every word he was givin' me . . . and it stayed here in me. And that's why today I feel so good when I do his songs because I stood and looked at him."[74] Wolf played at three clubs in northern Mississippi owned by Harold "Hardface" Clanton, a local vice lord: one in Tunica, another at Moon Lake, and a third called the Barn in an old tractor shed out in the country.[75]

In south Memphis, Wolf played blues clubs such as Oliver Prince's Bungalow Inn, Baby Brother Gooch's Mona Lisa Club, and Jack Tampa's Ballpark, which had a baseball field, nightclub, and gambling house. Tommy Williams heard Wolf at all these clubs. "I think Wolf was more popular than B. B. King at that time. Wasn't nobody else as popular as he was. He could get the people's attention. He could hold you there all night long!" Wolf's shows usually started around eleven and went until three or four the next morning. Wolf didn't mingle or socialize with the crowd between sets, but gave it his all onstage. Wolf "would throw that microphone between his legs and rock it some kind of way, go down with it and come back up. He had them womens hollerin'!"[76] Amos Patton saw a battle of the bands between Joe Willie Wilkins's band, which he played for, and Wolf's band. Wolf stole the show by getting down on the floor and crawling and howling. "Wolf was a pretty good athlete," said Patton.[77]

Oliver Sain, who played drums and saxophone in Wolf's band in West Memphis, witnessed a memorable stunt by Wolf at a Memphis club. The band was onstage warming up the crowd while Wolf was taking up the money at the door. "All of a sudden there was a big commotion up at the front, and Wolf was pointing out, 'Went thataway!' So man, these guys was runnin' around, man, and runnin' out into a grassy area all around the joint, lookin' for this guy who had snatched the money off the gate. But Wolf had the money! He fell out. Wolf fell out in the ticket booth and started yellin', 'This guy snatched the money.' When we left there, shit, man, we got halfway back to where we were goin' and Wolf come up with this money. I don't know how the hell he done that!"[78] Sain figured Wolf, an honest man normally, heard the band was not going to be paid and decided to take matters into his own large hands.

Ernest Gatewood, Otis Rush's bass player in Chicago, heard Wolf's band at a country juke in Moscow, Tennessee, in 1951, where he'd gone with his gambling, bootlegging uncles. He heard Willie Johnson on guitar and saw Wolf crawl on the floor while singing and howling. This made a strong impression on the twelve-year-old, who later sat in with Wolf in Chicago.[79]

Tommy Bankhead had an unusual experience with Wolf at a gig in Bastrop, Louisiana, when pianist 'Struction got sick at the last minute. Bankhead said, "The contract was you had to have a certain amount of musicians. So he couldn't find a piano player and he said, 'What are you doin'?' I said, 'I don't know how to play no piano.' He said, 'That's all right. I'll work it out.' And I would find a key that sounded like them and I'd stay on that one key. He thought I was playin'. I wasn't doin' nothin'!"[80]

Since most of his band was young and wild, Wolf ruled them with a firm hand and physically intimidated them into doing what he wanted. Amos Patton said, "You either do it like the Wolf said do it, or then you had trouble. He was a straightforward type of guy. Wolf wasn't no rowdy type of guy. He may have been cruel to his players, but I never seen no violence."[81] "Wolf would be on the guys, you know," Mary Lane said. " 'Be on time! Play that music right!' And that was Wolf."[82]

Wolf wasn't above using his fists to maintain order. "He would whip Willie Johnson, Willie Steele, and them!" Sonny Blake said. "Yeah, he'd jump on them. They would mind him. Wolf was a big guy, man!

They weren't going to argue with Wolf."[83] Roscoe Gordon heard musicians say, "If they playin' wrong, said he would beat 'em up or punch 'em or somethin'. So I stayed clear of the Wolf." Gordon, who didn't know Wolf well, heard he was "mean as a junkyard dog!"[84]

Sax man Tot Randolph joined Wolf's band in 1950 while still in high school. "He wanted you to play your music," Randolph said. "He was a hard driver. He didn't know music as such, but he knew what he wanted, and he demanded it. . . . Be better to like him than not to like him!"[85] Randolph, who didn't drink, never had problems in Wolf's band. Nor did Oliver Sain, who defended Wolf's way of running the band. "Wolf didn't want to do nothin' to none of us, man," Sain said. "Wolf was a big, imposing man. I'm sure he could have done anything to us. He was a big guy, man! But he was a really nice man. He was quiet. . . . Wolf had that fatherly thing. He was older than everybody else in the band. Wolf was like my daddy, man! He was crazy about me."[86] Floyd Murphy, who often saw his brother Matt with Wolf's band and sat in with them himself, defended Wolf's leadership. "As long as you treated him all right, then he was all right with you. . . . But Wolf had to be the boss."[87]

Willie Johnson had big problems with Wolf. Small and highly combative when drinking—which was often—Johnson "had a bad temper when he was drinking, one that you wouldn't want to be bothered with," said Corrinia Wallace, Johnson's girlfriend.[88] "They got along all right until Willie started drinking," Sonny Blake said. Then Wolf would "carry him out the club and tear him up, and bring him back in there and say, 'You're the one that's goin' to play!' And he would play. Didn't have no more problems out of him that night."[89]

Eddie Snow of the In the Groove Boys witnessed a confrontation between Wolf and Johnson in West Memphis. "[Wolf] was kind of a cruel guy. I remember him having this boy with him on guitar, Willie Johnson. So Willie was late that night and him and Wolf exchanged words. And while he was setting up, Wolf grabbed his guitar and hit him in the back of the head, and knocked him out cold!"[90]

Wolf was not always the last man left standing after their fights. At the White Swan, Wolf and Johnson got into a fistfight in the parking lot. "Wolf fell under the car and he hurt his leg," Sain said. "He told Willie Johnson, 'Awww, you hurt my leg. Yeah, you're goin' to have it fixed, too, if I have to go to the doctor or somethin'.' "[91] Honeyboy Edwards saw a fight between Wolf and Johnson that could have turned fatal. "Howlin' Wolf was kind of a quiet type; he didn't raise no lot of hell," Honeyboy said. "He always just played his music and paid his boys alright, but he could be kind of mean if you make him mean. He didn't take too much shit. One time him and Willie Johnson got to arguing, and Willie went after Wolf with a knife. Little old Willie run him all around the room and then outside and down 16th Street in the dark. Wolf was running down the street. Then all of a sudden he stopped and turned. He had a pistol in his hand and he pointed it at Willie and said in that big old voice of his, 'Willie, I done got tired now.' "[92] Another time, Johnson pulled out a knife when Wolf told him his guitar was out of tune.[93]

Pat Hare could also turn aggressive when drinking. He once stood on a chair to punch the taller Wolf in the mouth. Wolf didn't punch him back, but did tell his parents what had happened and recommended that they give the fiery guitarist a solid whipping. Another time, Hare took a few shots at Wolf with a small-caliber handgun and laughed as the big man scrambled up and over a woodpile behind a juke.[94] The headstrong teenager chafed at Wolf's dictatorial style. Hare said, "I've never been a mean guy. I just never did back up off nothing or anybody. Oh, I would fight in about two seconds if somebody gave me a reason to, but nobody can say I went around looking for someone to jump on. It was somebody always around . . . that thought they could kick my ass. Then I would have to come unglued you dig? See, I just never afraid. And lots of people mistook that for meanness."[95] Hare's volatile temper when drinking proved disastrous when he killed his girlfriend and a police officer after a quarrel in Minneapolis in 1963. He spent the rest of his life in the state prison and died of cancer of the jaw in 1980.

Wolf's band toured in his brand-new, yellow-and-black DeSoto, which held twelve passengers and had "Howlin' Wolf" written on the side. Oliver Sain said, "Wolf didn't want you mouthing off to no white people or doin' anything, but now, he did it! We would drive up in this brand-new DeSoto. Man, we would roll up in this thing, and the guy would come out to put gas in the car and be some young white guy or something. Wolf would say, 'Well now, check that oil and that water and wipe them windshields off there!' You see what I'm sayin'? He did that! But he didn't want you to do it. I guess we being young, he didn't want us to get involved in nothin' like that."[96] Wolf did all the talking when, as often happened, police stopped the car. Once he offered to pull out his guitar and play to prove to the police that they were musicians.[97]

Gigging outside of West Memphis, the band usually left early to arrive by mid-afternoon. "We played Hughes, Arkansas, Little Rock, Arkansas," Murphy said. "It was so funny. It wouldn't be that long of a ride but if we had 50 or 60 miles to go, he would leave like 12 in the day-time goin' there. I hated that. We'd be there by 2 and wouldn't start play-ing till about 8. They would make a deal with you because what they would want you to do is work all night in some places. This is how we got extra money. Sometimes we would start playing around 9 and we would play until 5 the next morning, or whenever the daybreak. . . . I would be so sleepy and I would be sitting up there nodding off."[98]

But arriving hours early was effective advertising. Wolf would stop at local gas stations, stores, and restaurants where black people worked and traded to get the word out that he was in their town that night. Then he'd flirt with all the women he met and ask them to come to the show. "Meet as many women as you could so they would be there that night," Tot Randolph said, laughing.[99] Sonny Blake noted that wherever Wolf played in Arkansas, "Them gals would be there!"[100]

Wolf drew a large crowd in every town. Sain said, "Man, we were goin' down this little road, goin' to the club, and these people were run-ning alongside of this car. This one lady was hollerin', 'Hey! There he is right there. I know that's him drivin'. That's him! There he is!' That was so exciting to me. I couldn't understand that. . . . It was exciting, but it was strange!"[101] Sax player Robert "Fat Sonny" Williams had the same experience. "When we would go into one of these cities, we were like big-timers! Everybody would gather around the van."[102]

Wolf's band members got $8 a night for playing in West Memphis, but $25 a night for playing on the road, which they didn't like—except when they went to Laurel, Mississippi, where the club was next to a spe-cial hotel. "When he announced we were goin' to Laurel, everybody pepped up." Randolph said. "They had this hotel and a lot of chicks were there!"[103]

Wolf's horn section was unusual for a Delta blues band. "On his records he would just use a rhythm section," Randolph said. "He wouldn't use no horns on the records. But when he come in person, that's why people was surprised. He would have a big band . . . three horns. He wanted that big sound in them days. He wanted everything heavy." Wolf hired some of the best horn men in the region. Trombone player Walter "Tang" Smith played with Wolf.[104] Oliver Sain, who played drums for Wolf's band in 1948, played saxophone for the band in 1952, after he left the army.[105] Adolph "Billy" Duncan, the mentor of Wolf's future saxophonist Abb Locke, played with Wolf for a time. Wolf also picked up a trombone player nicknamed Big Jaw at the Be Bop Hall in West Memphis.[106]

Wolf carried a box of harmonicas onstage when he played. "He had one, seemed like, for every key on the piano," said Fat Sonny Williams. "He would play in so many different hard keys a saxophone player does not like to play in: B natural and C sharp and all of those. . . . That always kept me on my toes." Williams, who played for years in Phineas Newborn, Sr.'s, band the Red Tops, was impressed by Wolf's talent. "I thought he was very highly intelligent in what he did . . . close to being a genius."[107]

Trumpet player Willie Mitchell, later a respected producer at Hi Records in Memphis, worked with Wolf just once at a baseball game in Hughes, Arkansas. "He hired me and my brother and fired us when we first started playing. We probably got off about thirty seconds of it. Wolf said, 'Naw, I don't want that Ble Blop!' " Years later, Mitchell met Wolf at a sold-out show at Club Paradise in Memphis and asked for the $4 Wolf still owed him for the gig. "Wolf said, 'Man I don't owe you nothin'.' "[108]

Though Willie Steele was Wolf's regular drummer in West Memphis, Barber (sometimes called Bobby) Parker, the one-legged drummer who'd played with Wolf in Robinsonville, sometimes occupied the drum throne. St. Louis bluesman Arthur Williams said, "He wasn't what you call a fancy drummer. He was just a timekeeper."[109] When Parker left the band, Wolf's brother J.D., who'd learned to play drums just as Wolf did, by beating on tin cans as a child, took over and copied Parker's unique style. Matt Murphy said, "[J.D.] was just stumblin' along with the time and stuff. . . . He would play with his left leg on the bass drum like Bobby. I couldn't believe it! Because he didn't know: He thought that was the way it was supposed to go."[110] J.D. also played with Wolf at KWEM.[111] J.D., who idolized his brother, was thrilled to play with his band, though playing jukes was always an adventure. At a juke in Arkansas, someone fired a gun. Wolf grabbed his guitar and with J.D. slipped out the back door and ran across a field—where a bullet struck Wolf's guitar.[112]

Dock Burnett did not live to hear much of the musical success of his sons. He took sick one afternoon in March 1950 while working, made it back to the house, and told his family to call a doctor.[113] He died soon after from stomach cancer, and was buried where the Burnetts went to church, at the Shady Grove Baptist Church in Parkin.[114]

Wolf's relationship with his son and wife was troubled. "My daddy, he was the type of person he had to have his way," Floyd said. "Anybody else couldn't know no more than he did." They lived at the Anderson Motel on 11th Street in West Memphis, where Wolf's band rehearsed. Floyd would get up about 3:30 or 4:00 in the morning to get ready for school, and after school, he shined shoes. When Wolf wasn't rehearsing he was rarely home, so Floyd spent most of his time with Katie Mae, who was devoted to him. Wolf and Katie Mae fought constantly. Though Floyd never witnessed any physical abuse, he heard arguments where Wolf would yell at Katie Mae and tell her to shut up.

Once when Wolf caught Floyd stealing from a bag of change, he made him strip naked and whipped him with a fan belt from a car. Another time, he caught Floyd playing hooky and used a wet plow line to inflict the punishment, just as Will Young had used one on him. "He only whipped me twice, but I'll never forget them whippings because I played hooky from school and he beat me for that," Floyd said. "He just about killed me for that. Them two times now, buddy, he made my tail sore! And that was enough whippin' for me." Floyd was still bitter years later. "He beat me them couple of times and that was enough to make me hate a person." He added, "I think of him now as a father. I look at it that maybe them whuppings did me a little good, too."

Floyd said, "My daddy had a hell of a way!"[115] Wolf let Floyd smoke at the age of ten and even gave him liquor. Floyd never told his mother that when Wolf was supposedly out of town, his car was parked behind a stranger's house. Wolf never told his son that his grandparents had died within a week of each other, because he feared Floyd would go home and never return.[116] Katie Mae finally told Floyd his grandparents were dead after their funerals.

Wolf got a comeuppance, of sorts, one night after a gig in West Memphis when Wolf let Hubert and Willie Johnson use his station wagon. The next morning, Wolf was relieved to see it back in his yard. Katie Mae said, "Wolf, I want you to go to the store and get some food. I'll clean your car while you're gone." While Wolf shopped, Katie Mae cleaned the car and found some woman's panties on the back seat. Not knowing that the boys had used Wolf's car, she was incensed, and ran inside to get a 12-gauge shotgun. As Wolf returned with a bag of groceries, he sang, "I gots the d'matoes. I gots the d'tatoes." Katie Mae yelled out a window, "Yeah, you son of a bitch, and you got d'lead in your ass, too!" Wolf dropped the bag and ran—too late. It took a doctor two hours to pick all the buckshot out of his rear end.[117]

Floyd knew James Cotton and Junior Parker best from the band. The teenaged musicians would sit up late and play cards with the boy. "They didn't get along too well with Daddy," he said. He also knew Willie Johnson, whose Little Rock girlfriend stayed at the motel.[118]

Wolf had to deal with a major change in the band's lineup when Oliver Sain enticed Junior Parker and Matt Murphy to join Clarence Hinds's band. Murphy said, "Me and Little Junior Parker went down to Greenwood, Mississippi. We stayed down there 'bout 4 or 5 months thinking that we were doin' somethin'. With Little Junior Parker we were the Blue Flames. We were a co-op group at the time . . . everyone got the same money. That's what it was. And I named the group the Blue Flames. He [Parker] kept that name until he died."[119]

With Murphy gone, Willie Johnson and Pat Hare came to the fore in the band, and Cotton took over Parker's role. Cotton had been playing with his own band, which included Hubert Sumlin. Wolf heard them play at Twist and Seyppel, Arkansas, and was impressed by Hubert's playing. Thus began one of the great musical partnerships in blues history.[120]

Wolf was middle-aged now, had played music for more than twenty years, and had gained local and regional fame as a blues singer. But he had a wife and son to support and no prospects better than playing gambling palaces by night and, if he had to go back to it, farming by day. He didn't know it, but his big break was just around the corner. It would make him famous all over the country, and then around the world.

6. I'm the Wolf

Spinning his radio dial one afternoon in 1951, an aspiring young Memphis record producer named Sam Phillips heard the astonishing voice that changed his life. "A disc jockey from West Memphis told me about Chester Burnett's show on KWEM and I tuned him in," Phillips said. "When I heard Howlin' Wolf, I said, 'This is for me. This is where the soul of man never dies.' "[1]

Phillips was ideally prepared to appreciate Wolf's voice. Born in 1923 in Florence, Alabama, he grew up on a farm and was exposed at a young age to the sounds of black musicians and churches. When his father died in 1941, he had to leave high school to provide for his mother and a deaf-mute aunt. After working several jobs, he found his calling and first call letters when he got a job at radio station WLAY in Muscle Shoals, Alabama. Smitten by radio, he soon took courses in radio engineering. After working at several other Alabama stations, he got a job in June 1945 at WREC in Memphis, where he engineered live broadcasts of big bands from the Peabody Hotel—broadcasts that were carried nationally the next year on the CBS radio network.

In January 1950, Phillips opened his own recording studio in Memphis at 706 Union Avenue. "I opened the Memphis Recording Service with the intention of recording singers and musicians from Memphis and the locality who I felt had something that people should be able to hear. I'm talking about blues—both the country style and the rhythm style. . . . I feel strongly that a lot of the blues was a real true story. Unadulterated life, as it was. My aim was to try and record the blues and other music I liked and to prove whether I was right or wrong about this music. I knew, or I felt I knew, that there was a bigger audience for blues than just the black man of the mid-South. There were city markets to be reached, and I knew that whites listened to blues surreptitiously."[2] Phillips's recording studio boasted the slogan, "We Record Anything—Anywhere—Anytime." But his WREC co-workers often ridiculed him with comments like, "Well, you smell OK. I guess you haven't been hanging around those niggers today."[3] Phillips leased his blues recordings to the Bihari brothers of RPM Records and Modern Records in Los Angeles and the Chess brothers of Chess Records in Chicago. Within a few years, Phillips would start his own label—Sun Records—and revolutionize popular music by discovering and first recording Elvis Presley, Carl Perkins, Jerry Lee Lewis, Johnny Cash, Roy Orbison, and other early rock legends, earning him the nickname "The Father of Rock 'n' Roll." By early 1951, Phillips had also recorded sessions with bluesmen B. B. King, Joe Hill Louis, Walter Horton, Joe Willie Wilkins, Lost John Hunter, Roscoe Gordon. On March 5, Phillips cut what many experts consider to be the first rock 'n' roll record: "Rocket 88" by the Kings of Rhythm, Ike Turner's band, featuring vocalist–saxophone player Jackie Brenston.

Then Phillips heard the Wolf. Eager to record him, Phillips got word to him that he could come by the Memphis Recording Studio whenever he wanted. Perceptive when it came to dealing with musicians, Phillips knew that telling Wolf to come at his own convenience would help put the bluesman at ease.

Days later, Wolf appeared at the studio's tiny front office and asked office manager Marion Keisker if Phillips was in. Phillips led Wolf back into the studio, where they had a long talk. "The Wolf didn't say a hell of a lot, but then he said it in his quiet way," Phillips said. "It was no time until I picked up on his demeanor and manner and everything, and I was just impressed with Wolf when I talked with him just for a little while. . . . He came in and it was no time after I heard him open his mouth that I said, 'Oooooh, I've got something interesting here.' "[4] A few days later, Wolf and his band went to the studio and recorded demo versions of two songs that greatly impressed Phillips: "How Many More Years" and "Baby Ride with Me (Riding in the Moonlight)." "After I heard the first damn song—whatever it was that he sang—I just knew that I had something very, very intriguing and that I really wanted to work with him."[5]

Phillips said, "Wolf came over to the studio, and he was about six foot six, with the biggest feet I've ever seen on a human being. 'Big Foot Chester' is one name they used to call him. He would sit there with those feet planted wide apart, playing nothing but the French harp, and I tell you, the greatest thing you could see to this day would be Chester Burnett doing one of those sessions in my studio. God, what it would be worth to see the fervor in that man's face when he sang. He cut everything out of his mind and sang with his damn soul. I mean, his eyes would light up and you'd see the veins come out on the back of his neck. Awwwww . . . how different, how *good!* I would love to have recorded that man until the day he died. I never would have given up on him."[6]

Phillips sent Wolf's demos to the Chess brothers. Impressed, they asked Phillips to set up a full-blown recording session with Wolf as soon as possible. The Chess brothers remembered that Phillips had also sent them "Rocket 88" by Jackie Brenston and Ike Turner, which became a big hit. "Rocket 88" caused a rift between Phillips and the Bihari brothers, who, because of their long relationship with Phillips, felt they should have had first crack at Brenston and Turner's hit. Now the Biharis missed out on Wolf, too.

Phillips only recorded two songs at Wolf's first session in May or August 1951, but they were two of Wolf's most powerful: "Moanin' at Midnight" and "How Many More Years." The first opened with an unearthly, humming-like moan that seemed to emanate from some bottomless wellspring of suffering and sorrow. Then Willie Johnson's heavily amplified guitar charged into the mix, along with Wolf's powerful, country-style harp, playing in the key of E with an A harp, plus the relentless pounding of drummer Willie Steele. Wolf's lyrics were sparse and enigmatic, an anxious eruption about someone hounding him incessantly, and he sang them in a voice that threatened to overpower his deafening band:

Well, somebody knockin' on my door.
Well, I'm so worried, don't know where to go.

The sound was like nothing ever heard before: three minutes of pure, surreal worry. Phillips said, "I can take one damn record like 'Moanin' at Midnight' and forget every damn thing else that the man ever cut and that is a classic thing that nobody can improve upon!"[7]

Willie Johnson was equally excited about the record. "When I first heard 'Moanin' at Midnight' on the radio, I knowed who it was. But it was funny to me. I say to myself: 'Listen at me!' . . . Then all my friends and family heard it. Wolf went to gettin' bookings, oh man, all over then. We played in Little Rock a lot of times. McGehee, Arkansas. Now that was the best club for us. I forget the name of it, but it was in McGehee. I just liked the way the place was lined up. It was in the summertime. They had fresh air goin' through there and everything. The tables were sittin' way out, they wasn't backed up to the bandstand. Bandstand revolved, go around, and the lights come on. It was nice. It was a widow lady's place."[8]

The record's flip side, "How Many More Years," also proved popular. Many sources have identified the piano player on this rocking boogie as Ike Turner, but Phillips says Turner never recorded with Wolf at his studio, and this session would have left a lasting impression on Phillips, since it yielded Wolf's first hit.[9] Whoever the pianist was, he laid down a driving boogie beat that the rest of the band rode for all it was worth—particularly Johnson, who romped along with slithering guitar runs and crunchy, distorted power chords. Wolf's cross-harp playing, in the key of G with a C harp, was simple and tasteful, and his voice conveyed the pain of the rejection he'd felt so often, and the need to pack up and leave it behind just like he'd fled his childhood traumas:

I'm goin' upstairs, I'm gonna bring back down my clothes.
If anybody ask about me, just tell 'em I walked outdoors.

Willie Johnson claimed he wrote "How Many More Years" on the way to the studio.[10] "I'm the one written out the first number for him. I printed it, and put the words in his mouth. He couldn't hardly read. He didn't have too much schoolin' and I didn't either. I got a tablet, taken a pencil and printed the first number that Wolf made. He could make the letters out. He just went to singin' it and playin' it. Later he went and had it printed, you know, on a machine, and copyrighted."[11] But Johnson also told another story about the origins of the song. "So we would rehearsal this number 'How Many More Years,' " he said. "We'd rehearsal that on the bandstand. We'd play that particular number a few times in a two-hour show. Then we'd play Friday night, Saturday night, Sunday night. So we'd do that and it become a tight, together thing, you know."[12] Wolf said, " 'How Many More Years' . . . now that's an original of mine."[13]

Released in September 1951 as Chess 78 1479, "Moanin' at Midnight" and "How Many More Years" was a double-sided hit. By the middle of October, the record was on the *Cash Box* hot chart in Dallas. It was number 1 in Dallas from November 17 to December 1, 1951, and it entered *Billboard*'s national R&B Top 10 chart in November.[14] In the next few months, the record also charted in Atlanta, New Orleans, Milwaukee, Newark, and Opelousas, Louisiana.[15]

Excited by the sales, Leonard Chess in September 1951 signed what he thought was an exclusive contract with Wolf, saying, "Business is better than ever."[16] But Wolf's contract wasn't as exclusive as Chess thought. The same month, the Biharis reported they had signed Wolf to "a term disk contract" on their Modern label for release on their subsidiary label RPM.[17] The controversy over which set of brothers legally owned Wolf's services would rage for months.

The Biharis had heard about Wolf from their Memphis talent scout Ike Turner.[18] Little Junior Parker introduced Turner to Wolf at a club in 1950. Soon, Turner was playing with Wolf's band, which included Matt Murphy and Willie Nix, around West Memphis.[19] Turner also played in Wolf's band at times with Willie Johnson and Willie Steele.[20] His last gig with Wolf was at a West Memphis club on 11th Street, where Wolf refused to pay him for playing, causing Turner to swing at the outsized singer with a mop.[21] But Turner knew talent when he heard it, and he recommended Wolf to the Biharis for recording.

The Biharis sent Wolf a contract and money and set up a first recording session in West Memphis at KWEM in September 1951.[22] Joe Bihari flew all the way from Los Angeles for the session.[23] Using a portable recorder, he made sure the band was properly miked and left the rest up to Wolf. "I liked Wolf very much as a blues singer and har-monica player—very good," Bihari recalls. "We went in and did one take on those things and paid him right there, and that was it. That's the way it was done in those days, anyway." Bihari said he paid Wolf $25 per side and Wolf's sidemen $15 a side.[24] Turner says the artists also got a bottle of whiskey.[25]

The Biharis' first session yielded four songs, though only two were released at the time. "Morning at Midnight," a thinly disguised remake of "Moanin' at Midnight," featured guitar by Tommy Bankhead. "I had to do a session with Howlin' Wolf in West Memphis," Bankhead explained. "His second guitar player was sick and I did a session with him, 'Moanin' at Midnight.' "[26] "Riding in the Moonlight," which Wolf had cut for Phillips as a demo called "Baby Ride with Me," was the ses-sion's hit—"probably the best seller of the bunch," said Bihari.[27] A writer at *Billboard* magazine described it: "Old-fashioned Southern style chanter knocks out a fragmentary blues vocal, as guitars and har-monica make medium fast buck dance beat in back. Okay for rural market."[28]

The Biharis released "Morning at Midnight" and "Riding in the Moonlight" as RPM 333. The two songs not released from the session were "Dog Me Around"—a version of "How Many More Years" as good as the one released on Chess—and "Keep What You Got," a fast rocker featuring Wolf's dynamic harp plus a torrid guitar solo that threatened to blow the roof off the studio. Wolf's lyrics warned his woman to stop flirting and throwing his money at other men—a recurring theme for Wolf.

Wolf also recorded his next sessions for the Biharis' RPM label. "Crying at Daybreak" was the first version of a tune that Wolf would later cut as "Smokestack Lightnin'." A lurching, country blues based on a Charlie Patton song, "Crying at Daybreak" featured a delicate vocal from Wolf punctuated by falsetto-like howls and down-home harp. The band, including Ike Turner on piano, was terrific. "Passing by Blues," which was coupled with "Crying at Daybreak" as RPM 340, was a relaxed shuffle that featured another fine Wolf vocal and jazzy guitar playing from Willie Johnson. RPM 347 paired "My Baby Stole Off," a song about Wolf's woman leaving him for another man, with "I Want Your Picture," a beautiful, slow blues where Wolf asked his woman for her picture to take to Chicago—a couple of years before he was to make that move.

Recorded but not released was "House Rockin' Boogie," also known as "House Rockers." Over a rocking boogie beat, Wolf exhorted listeners to come see him in their town. A remarkable performance, it captured the joy that Wolf felt for his new career as a recording artist:

> Good evenin', everybody. The Wolf is comin' into town.
> You haven't never see'd the Wolf.
> Play that guitar, Willie Johnson, 'til it smoke!
> Look out, piano man! Whup that ivory there!

By December 1, 1951, "Crying at Daybreak" was on the *Cash Box* hot chart in Oakland.[29] "Riding in the Moonlight" was also selling well in the South, Chicago, and Detroit.[30] "He was red-hot, man," said Roscoe Gordon.[31] The Chess-RPM battle for Wolf's services kept heating up. On December 15, a music scribe wrote, "The revolving battle between the Chess brothers, of Chess-Aristocrat here, and the Bihari clan, of Modern-RPM waxeries, has broken out again over yet another artist's contract. Latest round was touched off when Phil and Leonard Chess staked a claim on Howlin' Wolf, who has cut sides for both the Biharis and Chess, with the latter fraters claiming him exclusively this week. The Wolf, otherwise known as Chester Burnett, a farmer from West Memphis, Ark., was signed into Local 208, the Negro chapter of the American Federation of Musicians here, and duked a musician's recording pact with Chess. Currently Howlin' Wolf has *How Many More Years* on Chess listed among the top 10 on the r&b charts."[32]

Phillips was simply wild about the Wolf in the studio. "When I got the Wolf in there, I just fell in love with the sound that I heard from him," he said. "And I can say to this day there is nobody that I enjoyed recording more." He was especially impressed by Wolf's commitment to what he was singing: "When Wolf sat down in that little old chair with his big feet sticking out and began to sing, this guy didn't know anything was around him! I mean, he was singing to exactly the thing that we all want to make contact with—and that is the ears of the world. Maybe that's one person; maybe it is everybody on the globe. But Wolf had nothing in mind but just to make sure that he conveyed everything that was in his mind, and in his heart, and in his soul when he opened his mouth to sing. . . . He was, boy, pouring out his soul, and you could just see it, in addition to feel it. . . . He sung his ass off—and that was a big ass!"[33] Phillips, like Johnny Shines, sometimes spoke of Wolf as more than a mere mortal. "He wasn't just a blues singer," Phillips said. "I mean he was a commander of your soul and he got hold of you with the blues. The Wolf was a hypnotizer—he hypnotized himself when he opened that mouth and let it loose."[34]

Phillips was also impressed by Wolf's intelligence. "He was a very bright man. There was nothing about the Wolf that was dumb! He was silent at times when somebody'd be running their mouth. That might make you think that he didn't understand. Bullshoot! He understood and he just didn't want to bother with that right then. . . . He was going to take that home and think about it. . . . There ain't no way that guy was dumb or thick! . . . He had a lot of damn street sense!" Always suspicious of people's motivations, Wolf kept quiet. "Wolf had that, I think, to a degree, and maybe it went beyond what was good for him—that healthy skepticism about him," Phillips said.

In the studio, Phillips made sure everybody was miked properly and the recording levels were correct. He also tried to create an atmosphere where the artist felt comfortable expressing everything he had to give. Other than that, Wolf was "totally in charge of his band," Phillips said. "He had one person in the band that he would work off of. . . . Willie Johnson was the guy he worked off of, 'cause he knew if Willie was right, the others would fall in line. . . . He depended on Willie a lot and Willie was somebody that thought a lot like Wolf."[35]

Wolf said, "On those early records, even the ones for RPM, I was the one told the guys what to play, how the music was to go. Now, the bass patterns on those records, they are mine—that's my bass. Some of those numbers are just one chord. There's no changes to them; that's something I got from the old music. But the music, the songs, the sound—they are mine all the way out, from coming up playing guitar. I always tried to play a different sound from the other fellow."[36]

Phillips loved Wolf's harp playing. "Wolf's harmonica playing was always the right amount," he said. "He would never do anything on the harmonica that would detract from you waiting to get back to Wolf's voice. . . . There is a certain lonesomeness about the harmonica that just fit the Wolf's character in voice, in song, in lyric; and he played that just enough to titillate things he was going to do next with his voice." Phillips noted that Wolf would usually lay off the top end of the harp and play from the middle reeds on down in a raw, open style.[37]

Wolf was not a virtuoso harp player like Little Walter, Big Walter, or the two Sonny Boys, but he had a distinctive sound with an amazing sense of rhythm and a massive tone. He excelled at playing second-position harmonica, often called "cross-harp"—using a harp in the key of the subdominant of the song, a fourth interval above the keynote. For a song in E major, for example—one of Wolf's favorite keys—he used an A harp; for a song in G, a C harp, and so on. An alternative way of playing often used in country and folk music is "first position" or "straight harp"—using a harp in the same key as the song: an E harp in the key of E, for example. Playing cross-harp allows the player to bend and slur into the flatted third and seventh "blue notes" that are essential to the blues scale. Wolf always played cross-harp on his recordings and rarely, if ever, played straight harp or third- or fourth-position harp (with a harp a whole tone or two whole tones below the tonic, respectively) in performance.

Wolf's harp style was heavily influenced by both Sonny Boys—John Lee Williamson and Rice Miller. Jerry Portnoy, harp veteran of the Muddy Waters and Eric Clapton bands and creator of a popular blues harp instructional method, said, "I actually hear more of John Lee Williamson than Rice Miller in Wolf's playing. John Lee Williamson was the guy who made second-position playing the primary way to play the instrument. Everybody really came out of his bag. . . . I'm a great fan of anyone who can do one thing extremely well. Better to do one thing well than a whole bunch of things badly. Wolf had certain signatures to his playing that were just killer. First of all, he had that big, deep vibrato. He had a big tone. He also used his rhythm chords really effectively. He could be a very driving kind of player. . . . People who put his harp playing down don't know what the hell they're talking about. He's really underestimated."[38]

Kim Field, author of *Harmonicas, Harps, and Heavy Breathers*, a history of the harp's greatest players, said, "Wolf and Sonny Boy both played in a kind of down-home style that reflected where they came from and was based on nice, simple patterns that were slightly distinctive for each song. But what the Wolf brought to it that made him distinct from Sonny Boy was the kind of pneumatic approach that he got from his singing. He totally filled that harp with air and made it vibrate. His throat vibrato is really powerful, which is not surprising when you listen to him sing. . . . He had really good technique. He wasn't a virtuoso, but he was clean and powerful. Like all great blues players, it sounds much simpler than it was. He was underrated as a harp player probably because most people focus on his voice."[39]

Blues scholar Dick Shurman wrote, "What musical instrument wouldn't be overshadowed by That Voice? But [Wolf's] harp work brought a great deal of passion and nuance to [his] music and was a fully realized vehicle for his musical message and soul. On a slow blues, he would tease, warble and bend notes with a huge tone and the elegant simplicity which Rice Miller came as close to perfecting as anyone. On Wolf's ferocious up-tempo workouts, he maintained his mix of relentless intensity and admirable dynamics through rhythm more than melody. His toe-to-toe eighth-note romps with guitarist Willie Johnson are archetypal."[40]

Marion Keisker had fond memories of Wolf until her death and even rescued his rejected acetates from the trash for her own collection.[41] Wolf gave her quite a scare, though, one night when she was alone in the studio, painting the floor. Wolf came by unannounced and when he entered, Marion had her back to him. Hearing him, she turned around suddenly and saw his gigantic shoes. Looking up, she saw Wolf standing there quietly. Startled, she made nervous small talk while Wolf said little. He left after a few minutes. He had been courteous, but because of his size and the racial climate of the time, it was a tense situation for Marion. She told Phillips about the incident and when Wolf was next at the studio, Phillips chided him in a goodnatured way.[42] After what had happened in Pace, Wolf was probably as scared as Marion.

Wolf went back into the studio with Sam Phillips to record for the Chess brothers on December 18, 1951. Two songs were released as Chess 1497 — "The Wolf Is at Your Door," a terrific slow blues in the key of D in which Wolf cajoled his woman to treat him right, and "Howlin' Wolf Boogie," a fast romp in G. Wolf also recorded two unreleased songs about the Golden State — "California Boogie," a ragged, uptempo piece, and "California Blues," a slow blues in which Wolf sang about moving to "Beverland Hill." "Look-a-Here Baby," a rocker with a spoken Wolf vocal, included excellent guitar work by Willie Johnson and nice tenor sax by an unidentified musician. Best of the unreleased songs was "Smile at Me," a medium-tempo rocker in which Wolf again sang about problems with his woman.

Phillips produced Wolf's next session on January 23, 1952, for Chess, though the Chicago label again issued only two songs. "Getting Old and Grey," a slow blues about Wolf's imagined old age, featured sensitive guitar by Willie Johnson. The flip side on Chess 1510 was "Mr. Highway Man," an automobile song in the style of though not derivative of Jackie Brenston's "Rocket 88." With a hard-driving band accompaniment and the support of his energetic harp playing, Wolf sang about watching out for the law on the road. It's hard to know whether in the heat of recording he made a mistake about traffic signals — "green light said stop; red light said go" — or was merely cracking a joke.

Three songs from the session were not released. "My Baby Walked Off," an archaic Delta blues, featured a powerful vocal and bizarre lyrics about a woman walking off and dying. "My Troubles and Me," a nice, slow blues, featured a solid vocal and mellow harp playing by Wolf and inventive guitar by Johnson. "Chocolate Drop," a medium-tempo shuffle, had Wolf praising the edible glories of a chocolate-colored woman.

Wolf had played the small clubs in south Memphis and busked on Beale with his guitar. Ernestine Mitchell said, "He'd stop and play a few minutes and get a crowd and getcha laughin' and talkin'. And you'd find a trail behind him up and down Beale Street."[43] Wolf also hung out at a barbershop at 4th and Beale owned by a former umpire in the Negro Baseball League.[44] After his recording success, Wolf was ready to play Beale's better clubs. In February 1952, he played the Hippodrome, a large club on Beale that Sunbeam Mitchell managed.[45]

Wolf recorded his last session for RPM on February 12, 1952, producing several good cuts, though none were released at the time. The eponymous "I'm the Wolf," a slow blues that Wolf rerecorded better in Chicago, featured a field holler vocal, lots of howls, and a lurching, rhythmic accompaniment. In "Worried About My Baby," a rocker in the vein of "Keep What You Got," Wolf gave his woman all his money but she did him wrong anyway. "Driving This Highway," another take on "Mr. Highway Man," was equal to the original with blistering performances by Wolf and Johnson plus knockout piano by Ike Turner. "The Sun Is Rising," a beautiful Delta blues in the style of Charlie Patton or Tommy Johnson, featured a tender Wolf vocal with howls and sympathetic band backing. "My Friends," a medium-tempo ditty, ran down Wolf's no-good, mooching friends—a theme he would return to in "Neighbors." "Brown Skin Woman" redid "Chocolate Drop."

Soon after, the Biharis settled with the Chess brothers over Wolf. A trade reporter wrote, "The Biharis turned over exclusive pact to Howling Wolf to the Chess Fraters, while Chess brothers gave four Roscoe Gordon masters to Modern."[46] Like Wolf, Gordon had recorded for both Chess and RPM, and had a hit on both labels with his tune "Booted." "I was about sixteen or seventeen when I went into this business," Gordon said, "and I didn't know right from wrong—I mean, as far as recording for this one and that one. So I recorded for everybody at the same time. . . . for Chess in the beginning and then I recorded for RPM and also for Duke."[47] Joe Bihari said, "We had a contract on Wolf and they had a contract on Wolf. We had some disputes with them, even though Leonard Chess was a very good friend of ours. We had some disputes with him back in those early days. He'd record the same artists that we recorded and we'd record the same artists that he had. Finally, we settled everything out, we gave him Wolf and we kept the sides that we recorded, and then he got Wolf under contract."[48]

The Chess and Bihari brothers fought over Wolf because of the success of electrified down-home blues on the national R&B charts and because Wolf was racking up impressive sales in the Deep South and in Northern cities like Chicago, Detroit, and Milwaukee. One trade reporter wrote, "Before this latest trend began, a wide gulf sometimes existed between the sophisticated-type city blues and good-rocking novelties waxed for the Northern market, and the country or Delta blues that were popular in the South. Gradually the two forms intermingled and the country blues tune, now dressed up in arrangements palatable to both Northern and Southern tastes, have been appearing on disks of all r&b labels. Although it is true that the largest market for the country blues is still in the South and West, especially in places like Dallas, Memphis, Atlanta, New Orleans and Los Angeles, even Northern cities such as Detroit and others have felt their influence. . . . Along with this country kick some exclusively country artists have achieved popularity of late, including Howlin' Wolf, B.B. King, Muddy Waters and others."[49] That B. B. King, early in his career, could be compared to Wolf and Waters shows how much the various blues styles had converged.

With his contractual problems solved, Wolf was back in the studio again with Sam Phillips to record more songs on April 17, 1952. "Saddle My Pony," a Charlie Patton tune that was the first song Wolf ever learned, was released as half of Chess 1515. Wolf played guitar on it and James Cotton played tentative harp—no big surprise, since it was his first record and he was just sixteen years old. "Saddle My Pony" had the sound of a field recording and for many years blues scholars thought it was Wolf's first recording. The flip side was "Worried All the Time," probably recorded at a later session. A boogie closely related to "How Many More Years," it was not up to the level of the earlier song, but featured exciting guitar work by Johnson and upbeat singing and harp by Wolf.

Some of the unreleased songs from the session were better than those released. "(Well) That's All Right," a raw, ragged rocker, featured Wolf's jumping harp and wonderful voice, again singing about mistreatment by a woman. "Bluebird," originally recorded by John Lee "Sonny Boy" Williamson in 1937, was a fine, slow blues with a heartfelt vocal. Wolf reworked its lyrics for "Mr. Airplane Man" in 1959. "Decoration Day," another slow blues from the Sonny Boy I canon, depicted Wolf promising to bring a dying woman flowers every Decoration Day. "Everybody's in the Mood," a jumping blues version of Glenn Miller's "In the Mood," was propelled by Wolf's terrific vocal and harp. "Color and Kind" was a superb Delta blues in which Wolf powerfully conveyed the pain of a heart broken by another no-good woman. "Dorothy Mae," a down-home Delta blues, again featured James Cotton on harp. "Sweet Woman" was a slow blues in which Wolf sang the praises of his woman.

Phillips saw something special in Wolf that he thought could appeal to young listeners of all races. "I think that he had that honest sound and that heartfelt feeling that he gave with that unbelievably different, totally different voice that the young people that I was looking for that didn't have anything they could call their own would have heard this man and said, 'Man, he is . . . telling it like it is,' " Phillips said. "The freedom that he gave you and the truth that he told and felt in his songs were something to hear. And then to hear the way that he sang 'em, it is something that I just wish everybody could hear right now."[50] Black buyers of blues, particularly in the South, did hear the honesty and emotional intensity of Wolf's music. In mid-August, "Worried All the Time" was selling well in Dallas[51] and by the end of that month "Saddle My Pony" was doing the same in Memphis.[52]

On October 7, 1952, Wolf returned to the studio. Only four songs were recorded, but they were all good performances. "Oh Red," originally done by the Harlem Hamfats in 1936, was a jumping tune that prominently featured Walter "Tang" Smith on trombone and Charles Taylor on tenor sax. It was probably recorded in tribute to Katie Mae, whose complexion was red.[53] On the flip side of Chess 1528 was "My Last Affair," a slow, downhearted blues featuring a beautiful harp solo by Wolf and plenty of Johnson's jazzy guitar. Two songs were not released at the time: "Drinkin' CV Wine," an upbeat blues about Wolf's drink of choice, and "Come Back Home," a shuffle with another fine Wolf vocal, solid harp, vamping horns, and terrific band ensemble work.

Some songs from another session are in the same Memphis style but sound somewhat different, leading a few discographers to believe Wolf recorded them in Chicago.[54] But it's quite likely they were recorded in Memphis after all. At the start of the unreleased (at the time) "Just My Kind," a rhythmic Delta-style romp, someone said, "Howlin' Wolf, recorded in Memphis." "All Night Boogie" from the same session was a furious boogie featuring Johnson's blistering guitar.[55] Wolf's lyrics, sung in his toughest style, were once again about a woman doing him wrong. On its flip side on Chess 1557 was "I Love My Baby," a slow blues in which Wolf sang regretfully about a woman leaving him because he mistreated her. Another excellent unreleased number was "Work for Your Money," a jazzy blues with mournful lyrics that seemed to come straight from Wolf's heart and past, as he sang, "Well, my Momma, she don't love me, Daddy don't love me no more. / I might leave this town and I ain't comin' back no more."

"I've Got a Woman" again had Wolf's woman leaving him. "Mama Died and Left Me" was an ancient-sounding country blues with acrid lyrics about Wolf's mother dying and his father driving him away. The lyrics were not autobiographically accurate but close enough that the anger Wolf felt about his childhood was reflected in the song. "Streamline Woman" was a tough, slow blues about a woman built for speed. "Crazy About You Baby" was a fast-paced rocker with torrid harp and vocal from Wolf and hot guitar from Johnson. In "I'm Not Joking," Wolf pleaded with his woman to believe what he said. "Highway My Friend," another slow blues, featured especially fine guitar by Johnson. "Hold Your Money" was a fast-paced bit of advice from Wolf about holding on to your money because you will need it one day. Oddly, it had a long drum solo in the middle of the song. "California Blues #2" was another paean to the Golden State. "Stay Here Till My Baby Comes Back" was a jumping blues with a shouted vocal and terrific harp.

Wolf's Memphis and West Memphis recordings are some of the most powerful in blues history. Researchers Colin Escott and Martin Hawkins wrote, "The bizarre, haunting images that populated Wolf's songs, the quality of his voice, and his frightening energy were the marks of a true original. His music ran the gamut, from purest evil to heartbreaking tenderness. There was an emotional greatness to Howlin' Wolf, a greatness that Phillips was the first to capture."[56] Dick Shurman wrote, "The Memphis sides recorded by Sam Phillips for Chess . . . were characterized by an almost demonic, overpowering outpouring of self on vocals and harp, Willie Johnson's blasting, hyperkinetic, wildly distorted electric guitar, boogie piano and Willie Steele's drumming with all the subtlety of a jackhammer—which Wolf and his band would have probably drowned out. . . . The results were a simply marvelous mixture of the primeval and the progressive."[57] "Wolf's best records came on like three-minute race riots," wrote Greil Marcus. "The drums, bass, piano, and harp converged on the beat, hammering, shoving; for a moment they let the beat take the song, let you think you had the sides sorted out and the picture clear, and then the guitarist leaped in, heaved himself through the crowd like a tornado, and the crowd paid no attention and went right on fighting."[58]

With a profitable recording artist in Wolf, the Chess brothers moved to further secure their claim by encouraging him to move north to Chicago to record for them. "I came here in the winter of '52, before Christmas, I came here to cut the records, and I've been going ever since in the business," Wolf said. "I left the other guys back in West Memphis and came up to Chicago by myself—they was afraid to take the chance."[59] In another interview, Wolf elaborated. "Leonard Chess kept worryin' me to come to Chicago. They talked me the notion to give up my business and come. I turned my farming business over to my brother-in-law, my grandfather's farm that he left me. I moved to Chicago in 1952 or 1953. I had a four thousand dollar car and $3900 in my pocket. I'm the onliest one drove out of the South like a gentle-man."[60]

Wolf's move north came at great personal cost. Katie Mae did not go with him, and their marriage, which had been rocky, came to an end. She went to Chicago once to visit Wolf, but returned to West Memphis.[61] In 1953, she was diagnosed with breast cancer, had a mas-tectomy, and died of cancer a few years later.

Shortly before Wolf left town, his son went to visit his mother in Mississippi. Floyd did not return to his father. He wouldn't see Wolf again for twenty years.[62]

Sam Phillips was devastated when Wolf left town. "When Leonard Chess came down here and promised him the moon it broke my heart," he said. "This was one of the things that made me want to start my own label."[63] Phillips was unimpressed by how the Chess brothers handled Wolf's career. "I do not think that the Chess boys—and I am certainly not putting anybody down—I don't think they heard in the Wolf what I heard," Phillips said. "I believed in him so much that I would have worked hard toward that end that he was heard by a lot more people than he was heard by. . . . I don't think that anybody in the world could come close to getting out of the Wolf what I could have gotten out of the Wolf had I had the opportunity to work with him over a long period of time, because nobody had any more belief in what this man conveyed in his music than I did. . . . The world missed a lot by not hearing the Wolf."[64] Who knows what Phillips could've done to spin Wolf's talent into gold, given the racial climate of the time? It's one of the great what-ifs in pop music history. Phillips says, "It's unfortunate that I didn't get to record the Wolf a lot longer because he would have been my entirely different approach to rock 'n' roll."[65]

Despite Phillips's misgivings, Wolf lit out for new territory. In Chicago he would create his most famous records and influence a generation of blues and rock musicians while establishing himself as a giant of American music.

7. Smokestack Lightnin'

"Hog Butcher for the World," Carl Sandburg called it. By the 1950s, Chicago was also the blues Mecca for the world. As early as 1936, Robert Johnson had celebrated the city in his "Sweet Home Chicago"; Chicago also figured in songs by Bessie Smith, Roosevelt Sykes, Big Joe Williams, Honeyboy Edwards, Arthur Crudup, Tampa Red, Memphis Slim, and many other blues artists. To black people in the rural South, Chicago wasn't exactly heaven, but you could see it from there. In 1940, 49 percent of black Americans lived in the rural South. More than five million of them fled the South between 1940 and 1970 to find a better life in Northern cities like Chicago—one of the largest peacetime migrations of people in history.[1] They brought with them their customs, religion, and music: especially the blues. From 1940 to 1950 alone, the population of black people in Chicago nearly doubled, from 277,731 to 492,265.[2]

Chicago was the home of the *Chicago Defender*, a crusading black-owned newspaper that was widely and surreptitiously distributed throughout the South. In the *Defender*, black people read positive stories about life up North, in contrast with the outrages they experienced every day in the South. The newspaper encouraged them to leave for a better life in Chicago, often comparing it to the biblical flight of the Jews from bondage in Egypt to the promised land of milk and honey.

The Illinois Central Railroad, which ran from New Orleans through the Mississippi Delta to Chicago, made the city a natural destination for people heading north. Chicago provided high-paying jobs in steel mills, stockyards, food-processing plants, and other industries—most of them easier by far than planting, chopping, and picking cotton with calloused hands in the scorching sun. The shortage of labor in Chicago became acute during World War I, causing a huge influx of black people from the South. They put down roots in the city, which encouraged later immigrants, many of them relatives, to head north.

More proof of the marvels waiting in the North was seen in the pages of the Chicago-based Sears, Roebuck and Montgomery Ward catalogues, which were widely distributed in the rural South. Many items in the catalogues were beyond the economic reach of people laboring in farm jobs, but were affordable with better paying city jobs in Chicago.[3]

Legal segregation in Chicago forced black people to live in the city's South Side, where black-owned businesses grew to serve them. Centered on State Street, the South Side began just south of the Loop—Chicago's central business district—and expanded south, over the years, from just a few blocks to almost fifteen miles.

In the 1920s, Paramount Records maintained its recording studio in Chicago, where it created hits by major blues artists such as Blind Lemon Jefferson, Ma Rainey, Blind Blake, and Ida Cox. In the 1930s and 1940s, the South Side attracted artists such as Tampa Red, Big Bill Broonzy, Washboard Sam, John Lee "Sonny Boy" Williamson, Memphis Minnie, and Lonnie Johnson. All of them recorded for the Bluebird label, founded by Lester Melrose, and often played on each other's records, creating a sound known as the "Bluebird Beat."

During World War II, rationing of shellac caused a lull in recording across the United States, aggravated by a recording ban imposed by J. C. Petrillo, head of the American Federation of Musicians, who feared that jukeboxes were putting live musicians out of work. Almost no blues records were released for two years, and dozens of record labels went out of business or became hopelessly out of step with current musical tastes among the black buying public. Many independent record labels emerged to take their place in recording and promoting new music—especially the dynamic sound of electric "city blues."

In Chicago, the most important of the new independents was Chess Records, owned by Leonard Chess (born Lejzor Czyz in Motele, Poland, on March 12, 1917), and his younger brother Phil (born Fiszel Czyz in Motele in 1921). Their father, Joseph, had immigrated to the United States in 1922 by himself and settled in Chicago, where he had family. In 1928, Joseph sent for his wife, Celia, and children, Leonard, Phil, and daughter Mae. The hardworking Chess brothers adjusted quickly to their adopted country, but the Depression brought tough times and the family struggled to get by. As an adult, Leonard worked as a shoe salesman and with Phil in his father's junk store before going into the liquor business on his own.

In 1946, Leonard opened the Macomba Lounge on the South Side. Phil returned to Chicago soon after his discharge from the army to help with the club. The brothers got into the record business when Leonard persuaded Aristocrat Records, a fledgling local independent, to record Andrew Tibbs, who performed at the Macomba. Leonard started working for Aristocrat as a salesman. In 1948, he became a partner in the label, and in December 1949, he bought it. Phil soon joined his brother in the company and they renamed it Chess Records in 1950 and created a blue-and-white company logo that would become recognizable to blues fans worldwide.[4]

Boxing promoter Don King said he'd never want to be in the record business. "Too dirty," he called it. The 1950s were especially rough-and-tumble times for independent labels like Chess. Leonard and Phil worked hard to keep their company afloat, logging thousands of miles on the road to get their product out to jukebox operators and record stores. They dropped in constantly on radio stations to offer disc jockeys cash incentives—payola—to play their records, a common practice at the time. Through hard work and smart deals, the brothers built up a network of distributors, record shops, and radio stations across the country. An astute businessman, Leonard led the company, with his younger brother playing a supporting role. Though many of Leonard's artists claimed he had an ear made out of some kind of base metal, Leonard took a lead role in the studio, producing records that defined the Chicago blues sound during the 1950s.

In 1953, Muddy Waters was the star of the Chess studio. Born

McKinley Morganfield in Jug's Corner, Mississippi, in 1913, Muddy worked as a sharecropper while honing his craft as a bluesman.[5] His main musical influences were Delta legends Son House, with whom he played at various jukes, and Robert Johnson, whose records he admired, though he never played with him. Waters developed a subtle, declamatory singing voice and a powerful acoustic bottleneck guitar style. He played professionally with a local string band that included fiddler Henry "Son" Simms, who had recorded with Wolf's mentor, Charlie Patton. In 1941, at the age of twenty-six, Muddy recorded at his home on Stovall Plantation, near Clarksdale, Mississippi, for folklorist Alan Lomax, who was making field recordings for the Library of Congress Archive of Folk Song. In 1942, Muddy recorded again for Lomax with the Son Simms Four. Encouraged by Lomax's interest in his music and tired of Mississippi, Muddy moved north to Chicago in 1943. Switching to electric guitar, he developed his biting slide tone and rich Delta baritone voice and put together a blues lover's dream band: harp genius Marion "Little Walter" Jacobs, singer-songwriter-guitarist Jimmy Rogers, who usually played second guitar but sometimes switched to harp, and pianist extraordinaire Otis Spann—three of the greatest Chicago bluesmen ever. The Headcutters, they called themselves; to advertise their gigs, they'd hit a bar, ask to sit in with the house band, blow them off the stage—"cut heads," in blues parlance—and mention their own upcoming shows across town or down the street.

By 1953, Muddy had recorded a string of blues hits for Aristocrat and Chess. Everyone with ears considered him and his band the reigning kings of Chicago blues. He was about to meet the main rival to his throne for the next twenty years.

Wolf drove up to Chicago in his two-tone DeSoto with serious folding money in his pocket. It was a matter of intense pride for Wolf that he didn't have to take a bus, hop a freight train, or hitch a ride to move up north in a desperate flight to salvation in Sweet Home Chicago. Moving to Chicago for Wolf was simply a smart business decision to enhance his music career. "I had a four thousand dollar car and $3900 in my pocket. I'm the onliest one drove out of the South like a gentleman," he said.[6] But the gentleman had no place to stay. He spent several months living with his sister Sadie in Gary, Indiana, and even worked briefly in a Gary steel mill. Then he crossed the state line into Chicago, where, surprisingly, Muddy took him in and made him feel right at home.

Wolf and Muddy had never met, but they knew each other's records and reputations. Leonard Chess, who had just signed Wolf's record contract, asked Muddy to take Wolf in, and Muddy, unlike Wolf, was always inclined to do exactly as the boss man said. "When he first came to Chicago, he drove his car up here and I kept him with me until we got him on his feet working," Muddy said.[7]

Muddy didn't offer room and board for free, though; Wolf paid him. "He took me in and I respect him for it today," Wolf said. "But whiles I was there, I paid for every mouthful of food I ate and every night I slept there. He didn't do it for nothin'."[8] Muddy remembered it differently. "No, he wanted to go to a motel and I just said, 'Well, no; I'll make room for you until you get yourself together, and get you a job, and then you can find you a place to go, you know.' So, no, he didn't ask to, he wanted to probably . . . stay in a hotel. Even if it ain't but $10 a day, man, there. The five days is fifty bucks, you know."[9]

Muddy also introduced Wolf around at the clubs where he played: Silvio's, the Zanzibar, and the 708. "I was playing seven nights a week and matinees, and I taken him every night with me and let the peoples know him," he said. "The Zanzibar had two taverns, two clubs. They put him in the small club up on Paulina and I was playing in the big one on Ashland & 13th street."[10] When Muddy went on the road, Wolf took over for him in the clubs and picked up musicians because he didn't yet have his own band.[11] Wolf broke into the local club scene quickly. "After moving to Chicago, I found it easy to get into those clubs, playing my music," he said. " 'Cause the people had heard about me before I come: the records were out before I came to Chicago. Then I went to stretching out all across town. After people found I was there, they commenced giving me jobs. I only played at one house-rent party here. They tore up all my instruments, and I said to myself that I wasn't ever gonna play for no more of them."[12]

Competitive and driven, Wolf started to put together a killer band. "After my arrival in Chicago, I tried to put together another band in the West Memphis style," he said. "I wanted to have a regular lineup, so the musicians would have time to get used to each other."[13] Wolf hired a hot

young guitarist from West Memphis whom he had known for years—
Hubert Sumlin. Born in Greenwood, Mississippi, in 1931 and raised in
Arkansas, Hubert learned to play guitar through a down-home method
so common it's become a cliché. "My brother A.D., who was about 10
years older than me, he played the guitar," Hubert said. "He made him
a one-string, upside the wall, with a snuff bottle in it. These brooms
used to have this baling wire, wrapped around the straws, and cost, at
that time, I guess about 35 cents. We had three or four of 'em. So my
brother taken that broom, unwind the damn wire off it, and drove him
a nail in the wall, put another at the bottom and tied that wire up to the
wall. Stuck my momma's snuff bottle in there and pulled it down 'til he
got this tone off the wire. When he got ready to change the tone he
raised the bottle up, get back to C, raise it up to G, and only one fuckin'
string."

Hubert's mother, Annie, bought A.D. a guitar for $8—a week's pay
for her. Hubert, then seven or eight years old, became the one-string
master of the family but had bigger ambitions. One day he asked his
brother to teach him a song on guitar. A.D. told him to stick to his one-
string. Hubert was still crying when his mother came home, and he
blubbered out what had happened.[14]

Within a few weeks, Annie had saved enough money from her job
at a funeral home to buy Hubert his own $8 guitar. Hubert became so
fond of it that he used to bring it to work with him in the fields. One
day, he was playing guitar when he should've been working, and his
boss caught him and broke the guitar against the wheel of a tractor.
Annie confronted the man and forced him to buy Hubert another one.
But when Hubert was in his teens, she came to regret ever buying him
a guitar in the first place.

"My mama, she was so sanctified: Holy Sanctified, man—that's a
religion," Hubert said. "So she goes to church, the Church of Jesus
Christ. So I used to go to church. I played with the best musicians in the
world in church. They come from all over the plantations. Every weekend, they have different musicians come to church. So I got up there,
and I hit a couple blues notes. I tore a couple of those musicians' asses
up in church. They knows I'm bad, man. I could look at 'em and tell.

"Mama said, 'Do you know what you just did?' I said, 'Mama, what
I did?' 'You don't know?' I saw them eyes, man. My mama had eyes, and

I knowed when she was angry. . . . She said, 'You playing the blues. I heard you, son. You're up there playing Charlie Patton and everybody.' I said, 'Mama, how'd you know that I was playing Charlie Pa——' I didn't get "Patton" out. Pow! Upside my head! Then she pointed to the door. All them folks sitting there looking at me. She done whupped my ass in the church.

"I went home. When I got there, church was out, here she come. . . . She said, 'Look, go to the devil. You ain't gonna play in church no more.' I said, 'Yes, ma'am. Thank you, Mama.' She made me get out on account of the music that I was playing, 'cause she didn't believe in it."[15]

Hubert's first professional gig was with a band in West Memphis led by harmonica player James Cotton. Wolf saw them and was impressed with Hubert's playing, and even let him play with his band on a couple of short tours. "These guys he had working with him, such as Willie Johnson, was his regular band," Hubert said. "I didn't know at the time that they was quitting. My first night of playing with him was in New Orleans. Then we played another job, still with his same old band, down south in Mississippi. We stayed in Memphis and then went through Tennessee."[16]

Before heading to Chicago, Wolf called Hubert and asked him to join his new band. "Wolf was already established, and I was just this little old boy checking him out. Scared me to death, he did. Then one day I'm staying with Cotton at this old hotel and I get this call from Wolf. He said, 'Hubert, I'm putting this band down and I'm going to Chicago and forming me a new group, 'cause these guys, they think they're too good, they don't wanna play, and this and that.' I said, 'OK,' like that. I didn't believe him—I really didn't. So Cotton said, 'Hey man, you know he meant what he said?' I said, 'Hey, I sure hope so.' Sure enough, two weeks later he calls up the hotel, tells me, 'The train leaves at so and so time and you are going to be met by Otis Spann,' Muddy Waters' piano player. And that's what happened. I packed my little suitcase, gets on the train and finally arrives at the big ol' Illinois Station on 12th Street. Otis Spann met me, man. I got to see all these big lights, and I got scared, so we went straight back to Leonard Chess's daddy's apartment building. Wolf had his own apartment there. He got me an apartment there and had done got my union card and everything. So the second

ABOVE LEFT: Howlin' Wolf's father, Leon "Dock" Burnett
ABOVE RIGHT: Wolf's stepmother, Ivory Crowley
BELOW LEFT: Wolf in the army in 1941
BELOW RIGHT: Wolf's half sister, Dorothy Burnett Clay

(Photographs © Dorothy Burnett Clay, courtesy of Elizabeth Clay)

ABOVE LEFT: Howlin' Wolf's son, Floyd
Frazier *(Photograph © Floyd Frazier)*
ABOVE RIGHT: Elven Frazier, mother of
Floyd Frazier *(Photograph © Floyd Frazier)*
RIGHT: Wolf at the opening of a grocery
store in West Memphis in 1948 *(Photograph
© Ernest C. Withers, courtesy of Panopticon Gallery,
Waltham, Massachusetts)*

ABOVE, LEFT TO RIGHT: Wolf, Jody Williams, Earl Phillips, and Hubert Sumlin at the 708 Club in 1954 *(Photograph © Jody Williams)*
BELOW: Wolf and band at the 708 Club in December 1957. *Left to right:* S. P. Leary, Alfred Elkins, Wolf, Abb Locke, Hosea Lee Kennard (at piano), and Hubert Sumlin *(Photograph © Yannick Bruynoghe, courtesy of Margo Bruynoghe)*

ABOVE, LEFT TO RIGHT: Howlin' Wolf, Hosea Lee Kennard, and Tampa Red (Hudson Whitaker) with Abb Locke and Alfred Elkins in the background at the 708 Club in December 1957 *(Photograph © Yannick Bruynoghe, courtesy of Margo Bruynoghe)* BELOW, LEFT TO RIGHT: Wolf, Hubert Sumlin, Abb Locke, and Willie Johnson at the Big Squeeze Club in Chicago, summer 1959 *(Photograph © Jacques Demêtre/Soul Bag Archives)*

ABOVE: Wolf with old White Station friends at Silvio's. *Left to right:* Wolf, Jonas and Mary Swift Quinn, Johnny and Millie Anne Swift, and Louis and Priscilla Swift Henderson *(Photograph © Priscilla Henderson)*

BELOW, LEFT TO RIGHT: Wolf, Jimmy Rogers, David Hervey, and Marilyn Childs at the Delta Kappa Epsilon ("Deke") fraternity homecoming party at the University of Mississippi in October 1961 *(Photograph © David Hervey)*

ABOVE: Sam Lay, Wolf, and Jimmy Rogers at the Grand Terrace club in Birmingham, Alabama, in 1961. *(Photograph © Sam Lay)*
BELOW: Wolf greets a fan from the passenger side of a Ford Anglia while pianist Ian McLagan smiles in the backseat after a show at the Corn Exchange in Chelmsford, Essex, United Kingdom, in 1964. *(Photograph © David Hatfield)*

ABOVE: The American Folk Blues Festival in the United Kingdom in 1964. *Left to right:* Sunnyland Slim, Wolf, Willie Dixon, Clifton James, and Hubert Sumlin *(Photograph © Sylvia Pitcher)*
BELOW: Johnny Jones, Wolf, and Andrew McMahon at Silvio's nightclub in 1964 *(Photograph © Raeburn Flerlage, courtesy of Clifford Radix)*

ABOVE: Lillie Burnett and her husband in 1968 *(Photograph © Sandy Guy Schoenfeld at www.howlingwolfphotos.com)*

BELOW LEFT: Wolf and one of his prize hunting dogs *(Photograph © Sandy Guy Schoenfeld at www.howlingwolfphotos.com)*

BELOW RIGHT: Wolf's stepdaughters, Bettye and Barbra *(Photograph © Sandy Guy Schoenfeld at www.howlingwolfphotos.com)*

day, me and Wolf, we done had lunch, and he starts to telling me how this worked, how that worked, and we're sitting around the apartment going over the numbers and hey, I got to like that old man. I was kind of scared of him at first. He was so big and huge, you know what I'm talking about? But that didn't last long. He was just like a little baby if anybody knowed him, man."[17]

Chicago was exciting for Hubert. "In Memphis, you had one street, the main street, this is where the music was at, but in Chicago you had the South Side, North Side, East Side, West Side. When I got to Chicago, you could go out of one tenement so fast and get to another band, it wouldn't take you two minutes out the door into another door," he said. "When all the musicians came from the South, we made Chicago. We made it 'cause we had more music than anybody. But it was just a big old city, man; people played everywhere. 'Big lights, big city,' like Jimmy Reed said. I heard so much about Chicago before I even got there, you know how it is? People who had been up there come back and say, 'Hey man, it is too bad up there, people shooting one another, they doing this, doing that—watch yourself.' I said, 'Well, I am going anyway.' So hey, I go to Chicago—and they learnt me fast. My first paycheck, the first week that I worked there, I got stuck up."[18]

Also in Wolf's new band was guitarist Jody Williams. Born in 1935 in Mobile, Alabama, Joseph Leon Williams was raised in Chicago from the age of five. His first instrument was harmonica, but he switched to guitar as a teenager. "I was doing a talent show and that's how I met Bo Diddley," he said. "I'd never seen him before, and he was playing guitar and he had Roosevelt Jackson playing the washtub, and it was really art. . . . So we got together backstage. That's when I became interested in that guitar. So I asked him, if I got one, would he teach me how to play it? And he said yeah, because it was just the two of them together. About two weeks later, I spotted a guitar at a pawnshop: an electric Silvertone. And I told my mother about it. She was the type of woman that as long as I was interested in something, well, she'd back me up. . . . So I told her I was interested in that guitar and she bought it for me. And the following weekend I was out on the corner with Bo Diddley. We had two guitars and a washtub. He taught how to do the bass line and tune, and that's how we got started."

Williams progressed quickly on the guitar and formed his own group with Otis Spann on piano and Henry "Pot" Strong on harp. "He got his name from smoking weed," Williams said, laughing. "Pot is another name for reefer. I never smoked any of that stuff myself," he added. "You're not going to find a better piano playin' blues and shuffles and that kind of stuff than Otis Spann." This group broke up when Strong and Spann left to play for Muddy Waters. Williams's friendship with Spann helped him find session work with Chess Records, where he met Wolf, with whom he would work for the next two years, an experience he recalled fondly. "Most of the time he was easy to work with," he said. "He got a little temperamental from time to time. But I enjoyed it for the time I was with him."[19]

On drums, Wolf first tried to get Willie Steele to come to Chicago. "In West Memphis I had been using Willie Steele on drums, but he didn't come up here; at the time I sent for him he had to go into the Army, and he decided to make a career of it," Wolf said.[20] For his new drummer, Wolf hired an experienced musician: Earl Phillips. Born in 1920 in New York City, Phillips moved in 1940 to Chicago, where he played with various jazz and blues groups. He was playing at a club at Paulina and Madison when Muddy Waters approached him about joining Wolf. "I had that little old joint around the corner and Muddy came by there one evenin' where we was in there," Phillips recalled. "And Muddy says to me, 'How about getting with my man and help him, and I can go somewhere.' Just like that—Muddy did. And so I said, 'Yeah, where is he?' So, Muddy told me where he was. . . . And after I went over there to see him he got talkin' and everything, and he decided to take me on. He wanted me to work with him. Well, I'd been playin' swing, jazz, and what have you. I been playin' the whole thing, in and out, in and out, you know. Didn't none of it seem hard to me. So we started our first rehearsin' in Howlin' Wolf's basement. Well, we used to practice in Muddy Waters' basement, too, 'cause Spann used to be with us sometimes."[21] Despite being crippled—one of his legs was shorter than the other—Phillips brought a subtlety and versatility to Wolf's music that had been missing in the thunderous playing of Willie Steele.

Wolf, who didn't have a regular piano player, used Spann whenever he wasn't engaged with Muddy, but soon sent word back to Memphis for Hosea Lee Kennard to head north.[22] Kennard brought youthful energy and talent to the bandstand, plus a soft, subtle voice that sounded a bit like Nat "King" Cole's. Williams said, "We nicknamed him 'Yak' because he'd talk so much. Now, he was a hell of a singer. He wanted to be another Nat Cole."[23]

Kennard's veneration of Nat Cole got on Wolf's nerves when the band drove to New York to play the famous Apollo Theater. "Hosea and I were runnin' our mouths about Nat King Cole," said Oliver Sain. "Man, that was his idol, I think as much as a piano player as a singer. . . . Yeah, boy, he would be talkin' about that. So Wolf made a statement. We were just kind of rollin' along on the turnpike and Wolf said, 'Well, you know, everybody's daddy can chin the moon, but when they gets through, they bes right here with the Wolf.' It got quiet in there then."[24]

Floyd Jones, Wolf's old Arkansas playing partner who'd moved to Chicago, almost joined the band as well. "See, I was going to do an audition for him for the job," he said. "His boys, he had 'em, but one of the boys was too young. He had to get him in the Union and whatnot, and somebody, his parents had to sign for Wolf to use him, y'know, 'cause he was only eighteen years old—Hubert [Sumlin].[25] So we parked, went in—this is the Rock Bottom—it's on Madison right off Madison and Paulina—and I done lost my guitar too. He said, 'Well you won't have to use nothing, Mr. Jones—you use our stuff.' Then he said, 'No, you have to have your guitar.' So I went back to get my guitar and they broke in there and stole my amplifiers and everything—they got 'em then."[26] Wolf also had his first union gig in Chicago at the Rock Bottom: an open-ended engagement, with the contract submitted on April 1, 1954.[27]

Having assembled his band, Wolf quickly made his outsized presence felt on the local blues scene. "The first week that we went to work—the first month—Wolf had Chicago sewed up in the palm of his hand," Sumlin said. "That's how hot he was."[28]

Wolf quickly took over Muddy's gig at the Zanzibar at 254 South Ashland Avenue on the West Side, which caused tension with Muddy.[29] "That place was crowded seven nights a week, and then we moved Muddy out!" recalled Sumlin with a laugh. "And that's when the feudin' really started and they feuded all the way up!"[30]

Wolf's popularity at the Zanzibar resulted from his over-the-top showmanship. Most Chicago blues musicians sat down while performing. Not Wolf. "If you went into someplace where Muddy Waters was playing," said Williams, "and you looked up on the stage, you'd think somebody was giving a whole church sermon up there. It looked like a Baptist pulpit. Everybody had a chair—a high-backed chair." Wolf's style was far more flamboyant—more like a street riot than a church service. "Wolf had a long cord on his microphone," Williams said. "He had at least a seventy-five or hundred-foot cord. In the Zanzibar, there was a long, oval-shaped bar that was the length of the club, and Wolf would be singing. The bandstand was at the back of the club with the men's washroom on one side and the women's on the other, and the place would be jumpin', and Wolf would climb the bar!" At the 708 Club on the South Side, Wolf walked more than the bar. "Wolf would start playing the blues or a shuffle or somethin', and he'd be walkin' the bar whoopin' and hollerin'," said Williams. "So one night he just walked out the door on 47th Street all down to the corner. The 708 Club was at 708 East 47th Street. It was a couple of doors from the corner. So he went out the door all down to the corner, whoopin' and hollerin' with his harmonica and singing—and the police run him back there! Oh, that place was jumpin'! They loved him!"[31]

"Wolf always was an explosive type of fellow," said bluesman Lacy Gibson. "He'd get on the bandstand and start playing and moanin' and yellin' and goin' on, and he'd have the whole house upset!"[32] Bluesman Dusty Brown said, "He was the only one was performing on the floor then. He was the best in the performance. He'd dance all around the floor."[33]

More important was Wolf's astounding singing. "Wolf's voice was so unique and so powerful and so distinct that it made him famous," said Billy Boy Arnold, a gifted blues singer and harp player himself. "Wolf was born with a unique voice. That was his gift from God—to have a voice like that."[34] Wolf's voice also impressed his young guitarist. "I been around a lot of different blues singers and everything else," Williams said. "Wolf had a very unusual voice. He had one of them gravel-type voices, but he could also hit some high notes if he wanted to. But it was just his voice, period. That was his natural voice. . . . If you tried to sing like Wolf, you'd have a sore throat!"[35]

Wolf was no slouch on harp, either. "When Wolf come to Chicago he made it with that harp. He cut a right-of-way with that!" said Honeyboy Edwards.[36] Dave Myers, on the other hand, who with his brother

Louis formed the Aces and backed Little Walter—probably the greatest blues harp player ever—claimed that Wolf had it easy because bluesmen like himself had already created the modern Chicago blues sound. "Wolf come when he found the wagon was carrying a load," said Myers. "He didn't create anything with the harp. He just blew!"[37]

Wolf and Muddy had radically different philosophies about how long to let their bands warm up a crowd—and how hard to work in a club. Call it ego or ambition, but Wolf wanted to work hard with his band every song every night. Billy Boy Arnold said, "Wolf was aggressive onstage. The people really liked it 'cause he worked hard every time he got onstage. . . . He didn't lay down on the job like Muddy Waters did. He didn't turn his band over and his music over to the rest of the guys and sit at a table and try to get by. He gave peoples their money's worth at all times."[38] Retired bluesman and working minister Little Hudson Showers said, "Whenever he worked in the clubs someplace, the manager or the owner, they got out of him what he said he'd give. Wolf would be the first up on there and the last one to leave off. . . . Nobody was as outstanding as Wolf was for an entertainer. No, no. Even as great as Muddy Waters and them was, they didn't even come close to him for an entertainer."[39]

Muddy, by contrast, would often sit with one of his girlfriends while his band played most of a set. Showers said, "He was saying, 'My name is big enough I don't need to do that.' " Muddy hinted that he left his band onstage to let them enjoy the spotlight. "I know Wolf, 'cause we've been playing together at clubs here in town," Muddy said. "I let my band play up there half an hour before I go up there. But as soon as his band plays the theme song he's on his way. Ha, ha, ha. You can't take everything with you, you know. You have to get your little bit and give somebody else some of it."[40] Even Muddy acknowledged that Wolf worked hard. "Some singers they's cool," Muddy said. "You know, they sing the words: 'I'm broke and hungry blee-blah-doo.' They sing the words but it don't mean nothin'. They too *nice* to sweat! But Howling Wolf now, he *works*. He puts everything he's got into his blues. And when he's finished, man, he's sweatin'! Feel my shirt, it's soaked ain't it? When Wolf finishes his jacket's like my shirt! He's a big man and he's a real blues singer."[41]

Sumlin wasn't confident playing in public yet. "I played a couple of weeks with my back turned to the public, but the Wolf got me out of that," he recalled. "He got tired of it and one night he said, 'Ladies and gentlemen, let's give the drummer a nice round of applause.' And he introduced the whole band—piano player, bass, and I knew he was saving me for something. So he said, 'Now this is my guitar player, this is Hubert. Let's give him a nice round of applause for playing with his butt turned to the people.' And everybody there fell down screaming and carrying on; you should have seen me turn around. He sure fixed me, man. But I come to thank him for it. He shamed me out of my nervousness—sometimes you have to do people that way."[42]

Sumlin learned a lot from Williams. "[Wolf] said, 'Well, you's just a little ole' boy. Jody, show him something.' That was Jody Williams, the other little guitar player that joined him. So, Jody taught me a few things about my time, and so forth."[43] Wolf also made Sumlin take musical lessons at the Chicago Conservatory of Music. "Sometimes I'd mess up on changes and things, 'cause I was new with the band, and Wolf, he got tired of it," Sumlin said. "One day he sent me to school just to learn my keyboards and scales, and so forth, so I could know what I was doin'. The man I studied under was 66 years old and he played opera guitar. But he could play anything, the blues, and I got to love the man. So after he passed, I just quit and said, 'Well, I know enough anyway.' "[44]

Wolf had other problems with his drummer. "I remember one night, we was playing over at the Zanzibar, and they had this oval-shaped bar," Williams remembered, laughing. "We up on the stage there and Wolf, he got a shuffle or something goin' and he sittin' there stompin' his feet and singing the blues. And all of a sudden the tempo started slowin' up. We had this drummer Earl Phillips, we used to call him Stovepipe: everybody had a nickname, I guess. Wolf's stompin', trying to keep the tempo goin', singing—and the shuffle kept getting slower and slower.

"So he turned 'round and looked back at the drummer to see what the drummer's doin'. And the drummer, he done fell off the drums! And Wolf's stompin' his feet tryin' to keep the tempo goin', and the bass drum has stopped, and he's fallin' down toward the floor, and he's holding his stomach with one hand, and hittin' the cymbal with the other trying to keep things goin'. Then he starts missin' the cymbal, and started hittin' on the bass drum with his sticks. Wolf got mad! I said, 'What's the matter with him?' Somebody said, 'He's sick!' Wolf said, 'Naw—the motherfucker DRUNK!' "[45]

"Lockwood and Earl's old lady, they loved one another," Hubert said. "So Earl Phillips come off the drums one night in the club Zanzibar with this goddamn .38. All them folks sitting there, they opened up that goddamn place down there, 'cause Earl had the goddamn gun. Robert Jr. Lockwood—the only thing I could see of him was his bald head going out the place! Wolf said, 'Hey, man—what the fuck's going on here?' Earl Phillips said, 'I'm gonna kill him! I'm gonna kill him!'

"Robert told us the next day in the studio, 'You know what, Hubert? That was my old lady before she was your drummer's, goddamn it! This motherfucker—I didn't do nothing. . . . I'm sorry I caused all this commotion.' I said, 'You ain't caused nothing, man. You all get together and try to work things out.' He said, 'Not as long as you got that goddamn Earl Phillips. That motherfucker's crazy!'

"So Wolf bought the gun! He offered Earl $15 for the gun, said, 'Earl, you ain't got no business with no goddamn gun in the first place.' Wolf taken the goddamn gun and throwed it in Lake Michigan, man! I went with him! He said, 'Hubert, watch this motherfucker.' Whoosh! 'Now if I catch you with a goddamn gun, I'm going to do the same fucking thing, man. This is my band. You're the greatest guys in the world. You don't know that. You're the greatest guys in the world. We don't want to have a reputation that we done shot somebody, we done did this and that.' I said, 'You're right. I understand.' He said, 'No, you don't understand yet. But you will!' "[46]

The contrast between the loud, brash Wolf onstage and the serious, businesslike bandleader offstage was startling. "Music was a business to him," said bluesman Little Arthur Duncan. "A lot of musician men out here, music ain't no business to them—it's just a hobby. Wolf was business all the way with his music. And when he played someplace he always carried hisself where he could be booked back there." Wolf was different from most other Chicago musicians in that he didn't much like to mingle with people at the clubs. "He sort of kept to hisself when he came off on intermission," Duncan stated. "Anybody wanted to talk to him, they had to go to him. They didn't have to worry about him at their table. So I think that was a nice thing. All musicians should be like that."[47] Billy Boy Arnold described Wolf as a "very classy, dignified man . . . a gentleman in every sense of the word . . . a man with high character . . . and an asset to the blues."[48]

But even a gentleman's life was dangerous if he played the blues, as Wolf learned from several incidents. Bluesman Sleepy Otis Hunt remembered one that almost ended in violence. "My wife started goin' around taverns. She was messin' around Silvio's over there with some of her girlfriends. She met Wolf. Wolf started goin' with my wife. . . . Little Walter was playin' one night in the Zanzibar. He was goin' with my sister, and me and my sister was both there. Like I said, I had seen and heard about Wolf but I didn't know too much about him. So my wife come around there, talkin' to me about the kids. They were little bitty things then, couldn't even walk. I told her, 'What you doin' out here? I know you ain't got no money to pay no babysitter. Who got the kids?' 'Don't worry about it,' she said. I finally told her, 'Go on home and beat it, girl.' She went back around where Wolf was and set down on the stool near him. I got up and went around: 'I thought I told you to go.' He got off the stool, Wolf did, and he stood up. He said, 'She ain't got to go nowhere, little old boy.' I said, 'Who you talkin' to?' He said, 'I'm talkin' to *you*.' I looked up. He had a pistol in his hand down beside him but I didn't see it. I said, 'No, you ain't talkin' to me.' And I made a step or two. He said, 'Don't come up on me.' Little Walter was playin' a long time up there on the bandstand. He seen what was happening and jumped down there on the floor between me and Wolf. He told Wolf, 'You shoot that boy and you'll have to shoot him right through me.' I said, 'Shoot?' I looked around Walter then and I seen that pistol in his hand. Here I was gonna hit him if I got close enough on him—and he mighta shot me! I went home and got my shotgun and come back. Walter told Wolf, 'You better get your big black butt outa here. That young boy gonna blow your head off, man. That's that boy's wife.' So when I got back there he was gone."

Weeks later, the pugnacious Little Walter, of all people, played peacemaker at Silvio's. Hunt said, "I went over there with him. They come down on intermission and come over. Walter and me was settin' at a table. Walter said, 'Wolf, you probably don't remember this guy. . . . This is the boy you drawed that pistol on that night. He just wanna make friends.' Wolf said, 'Yeah, I apologize.' So he apologized with me and, behind that . . . he seems like my father, Wolf did. I liked him just that well. And he liked me. He'd say, 'Come on up and blow some for me, son.' " A harp player himself, Hunt was impressed with Wolf's style. "Now I used to could blow a harp funny like my daddy used to blow it. But when I seen Wolf, I said, '*Shee-it.*' I wanted to learn to blow harp like him."[49]

At Silvio's one night, three of Wolf's girlfriends in the house watched him crawl through the crowd. "He had this particular girlfriend," Lacy Gibson said, "and he was playing and he was hollerin' and shakin' his ass and everything. She stuck him in the leg with a butcher knife! And he kept on singin', and went straight on out the door to the hospital, and never even said a word! Everybody cracked up about that. That's one of the damnedest things, I can tell you."[50]

Williams said, "You know, he was quite a character! One night we was heading for the West Side. Right on the corner of 47th and Ellis was a funeral parlor. It was snowing, and the windows were all fogged up. Wolf had a yellow-and-black DeSoto. So he turned the corner there, and the windows are all foggin' up and he's trying to drive and wipe the windshield at the same time. And I felt a little bump, and I'm trying to see out the window 'cause it's all fogged up and I can see something red reflected. And he had the blowers on and the radio was on, too. And I'm lookin' there, and I say, 'Wolf, I think there's a woman out there on the hood!' And he said, 'Where?' I said, 'You done hit a woman—out there kickin' and screamin'!' He hit the brakes, and sure enough, a woman fell off the hood of the car to right down in front! She wasn't hurt. I guess she was more scared than hurt, because it was wintertime and he wasn't moving fast when he turned the corner and he didn't see her. And the woman just come from a funeral! She come out of the funeral parlor and almost went to her own! So we were late gettin' to work that night."

Wolf had other problems just finding his way around by car. "Wolf was not an educated man," said Williams. "When I first met him, he couldn't hardly read or write. So we was driving down the street one day and he was trying to read off billboards. He looked up and spotted this sign and said, 'B-R-E-A-K-F-A-S-T. Break FAST!' I said, 'No, Wolf, that's *breakfast.*' "[51]

But Wolf didn't have to read to draw a crowd. Chicago drummer

Robert Plunkett said, "I would go around and hear him all the time down at Silvio's. At that time he had Jody Williams, and the crippled drummer, Earl Phillips. . . . Jody was *good*. He had a big sound, had a pretty soundin' guitar. Sang good too: Wolf let him sing. The Wolf? Oh man, he was great. Wolf was a showman. He did all kind of funny things like bug his eyes out, crawl around on the floor—called that 'draggin' his tail.' He was a good singer, would blow the harp and he would play the guitar. . . . Silvio's was a big club, had lots of people *all* the time. It was a lot of fun."[52]

Billy Boy Arnold was impressed by how far and fast Williams had progressed. "I went over to the Zanzibar one night," he said, "and Jody and Hubert was playing with Wolf and I thought that was Hubert. . . . 'Cause when I knew Jody with Bo Diddley he couldn't play nothing but little riffs, chords. And I went over there one night and somebody was ringing that guitar and I thought it was Hubert. 'Cause the Zanzibar was a long club, from the front you couldn't see the band—I just saw Jody there but I knew that wasn't Jody, I walked back there and there was Jody, I mean cooking rice, man! Cleaning up! And I looked at him and I asked him that night, 'How did you learn to play so fast and good?' "[53]

Despite his hot young band, Wolf went into his first recording session in Chicago in March 1954 with just his drummer Phillips and the Chess session players: Lee Cooper on guitar, Otis Spann on piano, and Willie Dixon on bass. Dixon had played bass on some of the earliest Aristocrat sessions in 1948. By March 1954, his role in Chess Records had grown dramatically after he wrote hits for Eddie Boyd ("Third Degree") and Muddy Waters ("Hoochie Coochie Man"). Though Dixon's relationship with Wolf was often tense, he would write some of Wolf's greatest hits. No one squeezed more emotion out of a Dixon song than Wolf.

Wolf recorded five songs at his first session. "No Place to Go" was a patented one-chord Wolf vamp in E featuring lockstep piano by Spann, primal guitar by Lee Cooper, pulsating harp by Wolf, and a sizzling, lockstep beat by Phillips. "So that 'No Place to Go'—that was my beat, and Wolf was crazy about it," Phillips said. "We was sittin' up there just bull crappin' around and that beat I gave him—boo-ba-boom, ba-boom—he fell in love with it. He got on that little piece of harp of his and I thought he was gonna swallow it, you know?"[54] The lyrics were a variation on "How Many More Years," but this version was even more elemental—less a blues tune than a plea for mercy. With the studio's ad hoc echo chamber—built from a concrete drainage pipe—lending his voice a timeless timbre, Wolf sobbed out his tale of an aging, rejected lover with startling conviction, singing, "I'm old and gray—got no place to go. You got yourself a youngster, and you can't stand me no more."

It was an auspicious debut in Chicago. *Cash Box* said, "The Howlin' Wolf comes up with a strong Southern blues chanted in the style that spells s-a-l-e-s."[55] Chess combined "No Place to Go" with another cut from the session, "Rockin' Daddy," as Chess 1566. "Rockin' Daddy," a swinging, up-tempo rocker, included the usual stellar vocals by Wolf, with a funny spoken aside about walking down 8th Street in West Memphis. Fantastic boogie piano from Spann and jazzy guitar from Cooper in the best Willie Johnson style helped propel the song, which was full of ribald lyrics like, "I can rock you easy, don't want you to hesitate. / I can let you down easy, like-a jelly on a plate."

The three cuts not released were just as good. Wolf recorded an alternate take of "No Place to Go" called "You Gonna Wreck My Life," released years later as Chess 1744, which differed significantly from the first song. Wolf's vocal was even stronger on this take as Cooper laid down a skittering solo and Phillips pounded home the beat. The other cut, "I'm the Wolf," was a deep, slow blues in E that Wolf had previously recorded in West Memphis for the Biharis. Spann's piano work was powerful, with flashy treble runs adding dashes of color. Wolf's cross-harp playing was some of the best he ever recorded, and his vocal was by turns aching and threatening as he complained about a woman who was spending his fortune and wrecking his life.

"Neighbors" was a romping shuffle with sizzling, distorted licks by the underrated Cooper, excellent piano by Spann, and hard-driving bass by Dixon. Thematically, it was, like "I'm the Wolf," all about money, in this case, freeloading neighbors instead of a spendthrift woman. References to money abound in Wolf's songs; others just to this point in his career could be found in "Keep What You Got," "Worried About My Baby," "My Friends," "Work for Your Money," and "Hold Your Money." "He was mostly about money," said bluesman Sam Myers, who met Wolf at Silvio's. "He conserved his money and he was always singing about money. . . . I don't think I've ever seen him broke. . . . He really was into that money thing and he had some money!"[56] Wolf's ability to gather and hold on to money distinguished him from many of his raffish blues-playing contemporaries, who spent their money as fast as they made it. Down-to-earth and frugal, Wolf rarely spent money ostentatiously. "Anything I put my hand on turn to gold," Wolf bragged. "I don't have to worry about no money."[57]

In May 1954, Leonard Chess and Memphis wildman deejay Dewey Phillips co-sponsored a show at the Hippodrome in Memphis featuring Chess's three hottest blues acts: Wolf, Muddy Waters, and Little Walter.[58] Wolf, in particular, was enjoying great success in Memphis with his single "No Place to Go," which first appeared on the *Cash Box* hot chart for Memphis in the middle of May and stayed there until July 10.[59] The show was a homecoming for Wolf, and he made the most of it. Big Amos Patton remembered Wolf doing his best crowd-pleasing antics. "He'd get down on his knees and crawl around onstage and howl," Patton said. "He could howl—ooooooh! And that set off a lots of people. . . . Wolf was a heck of an entertainer." After the show, Patton asked Wolf why he put on such a physical show. Wolf said, "Hell, they paid for it!"[60]

At the end of May, Wolf went back into the studio to cut two sides, accompanied by Jody Williams and Hubert Sumlin—Hubert's first session—plus the rest of the band from the session before: Spann, Dixon, and Phillips. Sumlin's first recording made him nervous. "I got beside Wolf in the studio. He knew what was goin' on, 'cause Chess and them, they call you and they sack you in a minute! And Wolf—he kinda protected me."[61] Sumlin needed Wolf's protection. "We got in there and I heard this guy screaming at me. 'He didn't do that right. Take it again.' I said, 'What's this? I ain't gonna like this guy.' Wolf said, 'That's the man. He's up in the booth behind the glass.' That was how I first met Phil Chess. Wolf told him right from the beginning, 'Don't talk to him no more. You want something done, you ask me. I'll tell him what has to be doing.' From then on, he always asked Wolf. He didn't speak to me no more."[62]

Williams said, "Leonard had his own studio that he'd built on the corner of 48th and Cottage. We used Universal [Recording Studios] downtown from time to time. We used the same studios as Nat Cole and a lot of big orchestras used. But you're in those studios and the longer you're in there, the more it's goin' to cost. But Leonard was a smart man, even though he ripped us off a lot—he was pretty smart. He built his own little studio there and made his records in back. We'd go into the studio and work on it until we got it right. . . . We'd record and then we'd listen to how the tape sounds, and see what needs to be changed and what they want to keep."[63] Leonard's perfectionism made for long, difficult sessions, but the results were usually worth it. Chess Records released one great record after another in the 1950s.

The session yielded two more solid songs. "Baby How Long" (not the blues standard by Leroy Carr, with which it shared only the refrain) was a speedy shuffle in the key of G. Backed by heavy harp with tons of vibrato, sensational piano by Spann, hard-charging drums by Phillips, and tasteful lead guitar by Williams, an incensed Wolf begged his woman to come back.

Much darker was the stop-rhythm number "Evil Is Going On (Evil)"—the first and one of the best of many tunes that Dixon wrote for Wolf. In an unusual vocal, Wolf shouted out the first lines of each verse in a constricted voice and then sang the last lines in a different voice. The result was a call-and-response pattern between the singer and himself—a trick Wolf picked up from Charlie Patton. The song was a warning about infidelity on the home front, something Wolf worried about obsessively:

> Well, if you call her on the telephone, and she answers awful slow,
> Grab the first thing smokin' if you have to hobo:
> That's evil, evil is goin' on wrong.
> I am warnin' ya brother, you better watch your happy home.

Musically, the song was striking—driven by Phillips's unusual stop-time drum pattern. The band clicked like a well-tuned engine, with Spann's fast runs on the upper keys playing off against the twin guitars superbly, all while Wolf screamed the sinister lyrics, propelled his vibrato-heavy harp, and muttered dark asides à la Charlie Patton.

The two songs were released as Chess 1575 and "Evil" became a hit. From the end of August through the end of November, it appeared on the *Cash Box* hot charts in Memphis, Detroit, Atlanta, and even in country capital Nashville, where it charted from September 4 to November 27.[64] A columnist for *Billboard* wrote, "Gathering momentum in the Middle Western and Southern territories, where he has always had a good following, Howling Wolf stands a good chance to break out into a larger national market on this one. Now appearing on the Detroit, St. Louis, and Atlanta territorial charts, this etching is also reported selling unusually well in Cleveland, Chicago, Nashville and Durham."[65]

Wolf's band witnessed evil firsthand as their new hit was rocketing up the charts. Wolf was hollering the first words of "Evil" at a club one night when shots rang out, and a man in front of the stage lurched forward onto Sumlin and his guitar. "I'm pushing him, man, and every time I push him . . . he's dead, he's dead! This guy lighted him up, man. The first [dead] guy I ever seen, man. I had a Gibson guitar, I'll never forget it. The guitar went this way, the neck went this way, and I went that way, man." Badly shaken, Hubert fell to his hands and knees and crawled through the kitchen to a back bedroom, where he hid under a bed until the police arrived.[66]

On October 16, 1954, Wolf appeared at the Madison Rink in Chicago along with Guitar Slim, Willie Mabon, and the El Dorados in "Jam with Sam," a dance party organized by WGES deejay Sam Evans.[67] Also in October, Wolf went back into the studio with the same personnel as on the last session. The results were again stellar: "I'll Be Around" and "Forty Four," released together as Chess 1584. "I'll Be Around" was as tough a blues as Wolf ever built. His vocal was so powerful that it threatened to overpower the band and literally blow out the microphone. As usual, Wolf blew cross-harp, this time with a C harp played in the key of G. The band was menacing, with funereal drums by Phillips and blistering guitars by Jody and Hubert. Wolf sang from the point of view of a psychotically jealous or possibly even dead man, raving that he'd be watching his woman to see if she was running around on him.

"Forty Four" was equally hard-boiled. It had been a piano standard for decades, known as " '44' Blues" by Roosevelt Sykes and as "Vicksburg Blues" by Little Brother Montgomery. Wolf's version was different from either in its powerful emphasis on the beat, created partly by Spann's brilliant keyboard work and mostly by Phillips's use of a martial shuffle on snare plus a bass drum that slammed down like an industrial punch-press on the first beat of every measure. Phillips's extra-heavy accent on the bass drum was partly due to his handicap. "He had had one leg shorter than the other," Hubert said. "That's the reason when you hear 'Forty Four' and all these we made, you hear 'Bam du du du, Bam du du du!' 'Cause he couldn't get that short leg down on the bass drum! He had to put a goddurn block up under so he could reach the bass drum!"[68] The interplay between Williams and Sumlin was subtle; their different styles meshed perfectly. Wolf's vocal was incendiary, and his country-style harp in the key of F added just the right rhythmic touches and color. The lyrics were minimal and malevolent, as Wolf shrieked about wearing his pistol so long that it made his shoulder sore.

The session was memorable also for a special visitor to the studio. "I was recording with Wolf at the time," said Williams. "Naturally, when someone comes in, they're quiet in the studio. So he come in and he didn't say anything. I'm sitting there and I'm just squeezin' those strings—playing B. B. King! So I look over and this guy's lookin' at me. I'm thinking maybe he's trying to steal some of this stuff, you know? But we were having a ball! So we would stop to listen to the playback. So Wolf got up, put his harmonica down and put his mike and everything down, and he said, 'I want you to come over here and meet an old friend of mine.' So I went over there to see what was goin' on, so he says, 'I want you to meet a friend of mine: B. B. King.' Oh, man! I almost fell through the floor! I was playing all his stuff, just squeezin' out that stuff and the man's sitting there lookin' at me!"[69] Williams ended up cutting a tune with B.B. the same day.

By the end of 1954, Wolf had an exciting band with Williams, one of the city's most creative guitarists, at its core, and he regularly played some of the city's top clubs. His dynamic stage presence was drawing large crowds wherever he played. His records were selling well not just in the Deep South, but in Chicago, Detroit, and other Northern cities.

Wolf got off to a good start in 1955 as well. "Forty Four" was on the *Cash Box* hot chart in Memphis for most of February and appeared on the chart in New Orleans, too.[70] Wolf was still holding down his regular gig at the Zanzibar—billed as Howling Wolf and his "Evil Going On" Combo.[71] In March, Wolf went back to the studio to cut his only session of the year. The lineup was the same as on the previous session with one notable change—Henry Gray on piano. Born in Kenner, Louisiana, in

1925, Gray started playing piano as a child. After serving in the army (and injuring his hip) in World War II, Gray moved in 1946 to Chicago, where he was influenced by Big Maceo Merriweather, for whom he sometimes played the left hand on the piano after Big Maceo had a stroke. Over the next few years, Gray worked with the Red Devil Trio, Morris Pejoe, and Dusty Brown, and he did session work with Jimmy Rogers for Chess and Morris Pejoe for Checker, another label owned by the Chess brothers. Gray's studio work got him on this session. He soon joined Wolf's band and played with him off and on for twelve years.

Wolf recorded four songs at the March 1955 session. "Who Will Be Next" was the highlight of the session, with a clever, syncopated stop-time snare figure by Phillips, a spiky guitar solo by Williams, and powerful piano by Gray. The theme was Wolf's favorite—a woman doin' him wrong. By the end of the song, Wolf was almost sobbing as he begged her to return. Wolf might as well have been speaking directly to his mother as he cried, "Who will you hurt next? How will you start? / Who'll be the next one, baby, you tear apart?"

"I Have a Little Girl," not nearly as original as "Who Will Be Next," was a shuffle with fine guitar from Jody and a solo from Gray featuring rolls and staccato notes. The two songs were released as Chess 1593.

Two other songs were recorded at the session and released as Chess 1607. "Don't Mess with My Baby" was a deep, slow blues with terrific guitar by Williams, nice piano, thumping drums, and splashes of harp. Wolf's vocal was strong, with some howling thrown into the mix. "Come to Me Baby" was a nice but nondescript shuffle.

Chess sent Wolf on tour in Louisiana with Bo Diddley in March. Billy Boy Arnold, who was playing with Bo Diddley, said, "We went to New Orleans, stayed about I guess ten days. . . . Howling Wolf took Jody Williams, which was his guitar player. Wolf wouldn't go with us—Wolf flew, 'cause Wolf said he wasn't going to be flying up and down the road in a coffee-pot; he called Bo Diddley's car a coffee-pot!"[72] The first gig was less than encouraging. "We played in Houma, Louisiana," Arnold said, "and Bo Diddley's record ["Bo Diddley"] was just breaking real hot and at this club we played at the people just—Wolf did all his tactics and everything, the people just stood there and looked at us. They didn't know what to make of us. . . . We played in New Orleans the next day and it was a pretty good reception, but it wasn't what we thought it would be."[73]

Not long after this trip, Jody Williams quit the band. "Wolf was coming up short on the money," he said. "As an example, let's say the scale was $18, and the leader got a little bit more. But he was coming up short on that. I mean $18—well, I guess back then it was a nice piece of change for working a club as a sideman. But when you start short-changing a sideman out of $18 and say, well, you got $12 here or something like that, that's not right! That's not right. As long as somebody can do something and get away with it—nobody said anything—it's goin' to continue, and it'll get worse and worse down the line. But I just put my foot down and I told someone, 'If Wolf don't pay me all my money tonight, I'm quittin'.' Because I had Memphis Slim and other people asking me to play with them because they liked my playing, but I said, 'No, I'm goin' to stick right here with Wolf.' Matter of fact, if he'd wanted to go, I even had a job for Hubert, but Hubert didn't want to go. But Wolf, last time he messed up with the money, it was a Monday night at Silvio's. We got paid on Sunday night, but he messed up with the money, so I said, 'I'm not goin' to put up with this shit any-more.' . . . So I left the band that night. I haven't talked to him since."[74]

The abrupt departure of Williams left Wolf without a lead guitarist; Hubert wasn't quite ready for the position. Needing a replacement fast, Wolf drove down to West Memphis and hired Willie Johnson. "Wolf came back down and got me," Johnson said. "Brought me here, and we was playin' at the 708 Club on 47th Street. We played there that Saturday night."[75] Hiring Johnson was a desperate move by Wolf. Their relationship had grown increasingly antagonistic before Wolf moved to Chicago. Muddy Waters said: "Then he had Willie and Hubert and he had two *bad* boys up there, too, boy. *Two bad boys*."[76] An amazing guitarist, Johnson could, alas, be very difficult to deal with, especially if he'd been drinking. But onstage, the old magic with Wolf was still there. Bluesman Jimmie Lee Robinson, a Chicago native, thought Wolf's band with Johnson was the best. "In those days, Wolf had more of a blues sound than he did in his later years," he said.[77]

Although he'd never lived anywhere bigger than West Memphis, Johnson adjusted quickly to playing in Chicago. "It wasn't hard gettin' used to city life," he said. "I'll tell you one thing: I was more interested in my music when I got here in Chicago than I was all the time before. 'Cause I had more music people to meet, and jobs were regular. . . . With Wolf in the '50s, we used to play the Green Door on 63rd, at Silvio's on Kedzie and Lake, at Walton's Corner on Roosevelt and Fairfield. Oh, a lot of places we used to play, Blue Monday parties or whatever. Out of town too. St. Louis, Rockford, back down South. Everywhere he went, I was there. Never did get too much sleep at that kind of playin'. You'd have to be up all the time. And he'd entertain 'em. He'd crawl around on the bandstand or the bar with his harp, blowin' and singin'."[78]

In early 1955, Wolf and Muddy had a dispute about a gig. Muddy had subcontracted Wolf to take his place at Silvio's whenever he was on the road. After hearing that Muddy would be touring throughout April, Wolf turned down a two-week tour himself to play at Silvio's. Wolf was furious when he learned the club had already booked another band for April and he was without a gig. Wolf filed a complaint with the local musicians union against Muddy to get paid for the road gigs he'd turned down. Muddy told the union he was no longer under contract to play at Silvio's, so his subcontract with Wolf was no longer valid. Silvio Corroza, the club's owner, was called as a witness and confirmed Muddy's story. The union ruled against Wolf.[79] The dispute didn't adversely affect Wolf's relationship with Corroza, but it added to Wolf's growing rivalry with Muddy.

In November 1955, Wolf and his band drove to Cleveland for a stint at Gleason's Bar, one of their favorite out-of-town clubs. Two young singers came in to watch their show. James Brown was about to cut his first hit for the Cleveland-based King label. Called "Please, Please, Please," it would be produced by Ralph Bass, who would later work with Wolf. Brown's friend, Little Richard Penniman, was riding the success of hits like "Tutti Frutti," "Long Tall Sally," and "Good Golly, Miss Molly." Wolf called them onstage that evening. "Little Richard sung 'Tutti Frutti' behind us," said Hubert. "He got on that piano, man! We didn't know how to play it!" Then Brown sang and jumped offstage, crawled up to several women and teased them by begging, "Please, please, please!" as he grabbed and shook the fronts of their skirts.

According to Hubert, Wolf had stern advice for Brown after the show. "Wolf said to James Brown, 'Young man, I would advise you, if you want to live, don't crawl up under these women's dresses singing 'Please, Please.' 'Cause you ain't gonna be able to please nobody if you go on doing that! You gonna get yourself killed. I'm telling you, man.' James Brown looked at him and said, 'Yes, sir.' James cut that shit out, man!"[80]

The next week, Wolf and the band drove to New York's Apollo Theater for a show so successful that it garnered a long write-up. "Frank Schiffman, owner of the theater, said, 'I haven't seen anything like it in my thirty years with the Apollo.' The line began forming at 7 a.m. on Election Day and continued throughout without a letup. . . . The crowd outside grew to such proportions that the police were called to keep order and NBC-TV shot its cameras over to 125th Street to cover the event. . . . Talent booked for the show included Howling Wolf, Bo Diddley, the Flamingos, the Jacks, the Harptones, the Heartbeats, Dakota Staton, Etta James, Bill Doggett's trio and Willis Jackson's band."[81]

Oliver Sain, who played the Apollo with Wolf's band, laughed about two incidents offstage. Wolf sent a love note to Etta James, who was just seventeen, and was rebuffed. "Oh man, she went off!" Sain said. "She confronted him backstage. Called him 'an old country man!' It was embarrassing, you know."[82] Hubert witnessed the incident at close quarters. "Etta James was tailor-made at that time," he said with a laugh. "She wasn't too big, she wasn't too fat—she was just built like a Coca-Cola bottle, like the three girls that worked with her, Peaches. Wolf give me a note to give to her. Had somebody to write the note. I don't know who it was, but I knowed Wolf couldn't write. So I said, 'Wolf, you wrote this note?' 'Just give it to her!' I opened this note before I give it to her. I saw it wasn't his handwriting. He told her he loved her and he wanted to see her.

"That night after we get through rehearsing, everybody want to have dinner with us. She wrote a note and give it back to me and says, 'Hubert, tell that motherfucker: Fuck him!' I give him the note! He said, 'Read it to me.' I say, 'You motherfucker: Fuck you!' So he gets mad with me!

"He said, 'I'll tell you what, Hubert. Write this: "Kiss my ass!" ' I said, 'I ain't going back there. I ain't going to give this woman that goddamn note! I already fucked up with that first one. I ain't carrying nobody's goddamn messages!' He said, 'Well, I'll tell you what. Fuck her. She think she own the world. Fuck her, man. But she sure do look good!' "[83]

Sain was mortified by Wolf's rehearsal in the basement of the Apollo. "The bandleader Reuben Phillips was down there gettin' the band together for people who didn't have a band," Sain said. "So Reuben said to Wolf, 'Man, you don't need to rehearse. You've got your own band. We need to get this stuff together for these guys.' Wolf said, 'Well, I want to go through mine, too.' So Reuben just said, 'Well, okay, man.' We started playin' and Wolf went right through his act right there: crawling on the floor and howling. And these musicians, man, I swear to God—there was a bunch of old chairs and a bunch of stuff down in the basement of the Apollo—guys were fallin' down behind those chairs! You could see feet stickin' up! People were laughin'! I mean guys layin' out, man: fallin' over chairs, legs stickin' up in the air, man! They'd never seen nothin' like this. These were all the orchestra guys in the Apollo band. I said, 'Oh, my God!' I was so embarrassed. See, when you're young you're embarrassed by things like that. Now, that would just be Wolf. I would not find it embarrassing at all."[84]

For Wolf, 1955 had been another good year. He'd been to the studio just once, but made *Cash Box*'s list of the top twenty-five male R&B vocalists of the year.[85] He'd recovered from the departure of Jody Williams, his right hand musically for two years. And his popularity in Chicago was unrivaled except by Muddy Waters. He was also hugely popular in the South and, as the Apollo Theater show proved, increasingly popular elsewhere.

In January 1956, Wolf went back into the Chess studio to record with Johnson and Sumlin on guitar, Dixon on bass, Phillips on drums, and Hosea Lee Kennard, a studio virgin, on piano. They cut only two songs, but both were terrific. "You Can't Be Beat," an uptempo number in the key of G, featured guitar by Johnson at his jazzy, fiery best, swinging drums by Phillips, and stunning harp by Wolf.

The next cut was Wolf's masterpiece. "Smokestack Lightnin' " had been part of his repertoire as far back as the early 1930s. Its lyrics were inspired, in part, by Charlie Patton's "Moon Going Down." Wolf had already recorded a version of it for RPM as "Crying at Daybreak." Wolf said with characteristic understatement, "Well, Smokestack Lightnin' means it's a train . . . that, uh, runs on the rails, you know."[86] Saying "Smokestack Lightnin' " was a song about a train is like saying *Citizen Kane* was a movie about a sled. It was Wolf's single greatest recording, distilling into one unforgettable performance everything that made him unique. A propulsive one-chord vamp, nominally in E major but with the flatted blue notes that make it sound like E minor, it was a pastiche of ancient blues lines and train references, timeless and evocative, as American as could be. It wasn't so much a song as a mood: insubstantial as a smoke ring melodically and lyrically, yet gigantic as a gathering storm in rhythm and power. Wolf's voice, harp, conviction, and band made it one of the great songs of the '50s—and it might just as well have been the 1850s.

Over a hypnotic guitar figure and a driving rhythm that subtly accelerates like a locomotive, Wolf sang a field holler vocal, interspersed with falsetto howls like a dread lupine beast just down the road at midnight. The lyrics, pared to the bone, were dark and cryptic, conveying a mood of metaphysical agony. Small wonder. The song was carved from his own past, reminding him of his dark childhood near the train tracks in White Station, Mississippi, as he sang, "Well, who been here, baby, since I been gone? / Little bitty boy, derby on. A woo-hooo."

The beloved English poet Philip Larkin, in one of his music reviews, perceptively described the otherworldly power of the song. "Howlin' Wolf's 'Smoke Stack Lightenin' ' is an amazing performance, a piece of pure jazz Gothic, creating with no more properties than an echo chamber and his own remarkable voice an impression of Coleridge's demon love wailing for his woman."[87]

Billboard described the song as "a hard-driving, primitive chant, with a fascinating rhythm and a solid beat."[88] *Cash Box* wrote: "Howling Wolf wails and howls on a middle beat rhythmic effort, *Smokestack Lightnin'* and comes through with an unusual sound adorning a solid beat. Deck has that stop and listen quality. It has already created excitement in the Chicago area and, from the sound of it, will be spreading to other markets in short order. Watch it very closely."[89] "Smokestack Lightnin' " first appeared on the *Cash Box* hot chart in Chicago on February 18 and stayed there until early April. It peaked in Chicago at number 2 for two weeks in March. The record also charted in Memphis, St. Louis, and Cleveland during these weeks, and was on the national chart from March 24 to April 7, peaking at number 11 on March 31.[90] "Smoke-stack Lightnin' " also reached number 11 on *Billboard*'s rhythm & blues chart in 1956.[91]

Despite the brilliance of "Smokestack Lightnin', " Wolf and Willie Johnson soon fell out again. In 1954, bluesman Mighty Joe Young, who lived in Milwaukee, went to see Wolf at the Zanzibar after hearing the show advertised on the radio. Mighty Joe brought his guitar, and Wolf let him sit in with the band. In 1956, Mighty Joe visited Chicago again and went to see Wolf at the 708 Club. "As I walked into the club, he seen me when I came in, and he says to the audience, 'Give my young friend a hand of applause, from Milwaukee, Wisconsin,' " he recalled. "And when he taken a break he taken me into the washroom and asked me how I had been doin' and did I want to work. I said, 'Oh, yeah!' And so what he did was he went back out and got his guitar player, which at that time was Willie Johnson, and brought Willie Johnson into the washroom. I'm standin' there, and he says to Willie, 'Willie, I'm firin' you and I'm goin' to hire this man.' So, I could have melted! I could've went through the floor, because I wanted the gig, but I didn't want it like that. . . . So Willie threw up his hands and said, 'Don't worry about it man!' . . . I told the Wolf, I said, 'Wait a minute!' . . . He said, 'Look, you be quiet! You want to work? You just be quiet!' And so he said that and walked on out and then Willie told me, 'Hey, don't worry about it man! He just mad with me 'cause I pulled a knife on him last night!' Which I think was Sunday night at another club somewhere."[92]

"[Willie] would drink and he would just get to the point, I guess, that Wolf couldn't take it any longer," Corrinia Wallace said. "Wolf had to be strict with his sidemen because those guys would get drunk and they would go crazy. So if he wasn't strict, he wouldn't have any music. I've seen Willie get drunk, just set his guitar down and walk off the bandstand. When he had been fired for a long time and had just come back into Wolf's band, he'd be okay for a few weeks. But it didn't last long."[93] "Wolf was a very strict guy," Johnson affirmed. "He didn't want no smokin' on the bandstand, and he didn't want no drinkin' on the bandstand. But when you come down on intermission, you could smoke. We'd come down. We'd sneak in a drink anyway. He'd be laughin' and talkin' with somebody else. We'd be tastin', you know. But he'd rather for you to wait 'til you get off work. He'd *buy* it for you. He'd buy it for you when you get off work. Me and Hubert played together with him a long time, and Earl Phillips. They would fight Wolf. He'd just get mad and go to cussin' and doin' about. I seen him slap Earl Phillips for drinkin', gettin' drunk and messin' up his music. I would stand up there lookin' at them, 'cause he knowed not to hit me! One time the union put a $1,000 fine on [Wolf]. He stopped his fightin'. . . . Then he started fining his men. That's what they talked to him about. They told him, said, 'When your mens do wrong, fine 'em.' And he would give you some days off from playin' too. That hurt badder than anything, you know. That hurt badder than hittin' you and all that kind of stuff. You'd miss that money."[94]

Many times after Wolf fired him, Johnson would go back to Memphis. "Willie Johnson and Wolf would have some ups and downs," Easy Baby Randle said. "Willie Johnson would leave Chicago and come back to Memphis; and Willie Johnson have played with me quite a few times when he come back to Memphis."[95]

While waiting for Wolf to hire him back, Johnson would play with other Chicago musicians, including Dusty Brown. "Willie Johnson: a beautiful guy until he get somethin' to drink," Brown said. "Get somethin' to drink, then he want to do it his way. . . . I'll say it like this. I had lots of different boys play with me and I never had a fight with nobody but Willie Johnson! . . . Get somethin' to drink he go crazy!"[96] Johnson played briefly with Muddy Waters, too. "I *loved* the way he played," Muddy said. "He did play two or three weeks for me or something, I remember him doin' that. He's a good guitar player, but his head was *baaad*, like come out he got, what you call it, evil? He wanted to fight and that kinda thing. I don't like the band fightin'."[97] Billy Boy Arnold said, "Willie Johnson was an alcoholic and a crazy guy and everything else, so anybody can understand why Wolf couldn't get along with him."[98]

Although he didn't play with Wolf for long, Mighty Joe Young enjoyed his time in the band. "It was a highlight of my life to play with him a couple of months 'cause it was a top-flight professional job to play for the Howlin' Wolf," Mighty Joe said. "He always liked a drivin' band. He liked a very aggressive band. He didn't like no down band. . . . He liked the fire!"

Among the clubs Young played with Wolf were the 708 Club and the Club Alibi. Wolf was enjoying tremendous popularity in Chicago because of his two recent hits—"Evil" and "Smokestack Lightnin'." Mighty Joe had a hard time learning "Smokestack Lightnin'" until Wolf showed him how to play it. "He wasn't doin' anything any different from what I was doin'," he said. "Only thing was, it was his timing and the way he was feelin'." Mighty Joe was also impressed with Wolf's showmanship. "He would get on the bar and he would crawl and man, he could put on a show. And he had so much charisma! He could wreck a house!" Wolf was particularly popular with his female fans and his act always had a strong sexual component. "He put a Coke bottle in his pants and all that shit," Mighty Joe said. "The Wolf was the man." (The Coke bottle trick was also one of Muddy's favorites. Wolf would shake up a bottle, stick it down the front of his pants, saunter up to the microphone, tantalizingly unzip his fly, pop the bottle top, and "accidentally" spray the crowd. This use of the soft drink has never been officially endorsed by the Coca-Cola Company.) Mighty Joe got along with Wolf while in the band. "I had no problem with him. . . . He treated me real well and with a lot of respect."

Mighty Joe quit the band when Wolf told him they were going on tour in the South. "He got teed off with me 'cause I wouldn't go on the road with him down to Atlanta, Georgia, and everything, but he got over that," Mighty Joe said. "He didn't like the idea but later on . . . he got over it and we came to be friends again." This took some time, though, as Mighty Joe found out when he met Wolf at Big Bill Hill's radio show three months later. "He tell Bill, said, 'Yeah, I give that young man a job there, and he turned me down.' He told me, said, 'You was my boy there, and you messed me around!' I said, 'No, I didn't mess you around. . . . I just didn't want to go back out on the road.'" Mighty Joe saw through Wolf's tough exterior. "He liked to try to intimidate you, if he could, with your fines and with his size and everything. . . . And he was the Wolf and everything, but deep down inside he was a pretty nice guy."[99] The nice guy was about to lose his most important band member to his biggest rival.

8. I Better Go Now

Wolf was hurt when Mighty Joe Young quit. He was devastated when Hubert Sumlin left to play for Muddy Waters. Sumlin simply felt Wolf didn't appreciate him enough. "He would try to talk to me and keep me from getting a swelled head," Sumlin said. "He would say, 'Look here, Hubert, I think you're good. I like you, but you ain't great. Don't never let nobody tell you that you are the best in the world, 'cause, in my book, you all right, but guitar players are a dime a dozen with me. You know that, don't you?' I said, 'Yeah, well I know that.' I said it but I didn't believe it. I thought now he really done got down to the nitty-gritty with me. I be the next one to go. Now at this time, I could get anything, anybody I want, I made my name in that town; I was very famous. That's what I thought."[1] Wolf and Sumlin also disagreed about the band's sound. "You know how musicians is," Sumlin said. "They have their little faults. I thought I had done got good enough to play what I want to play. And so Wolf was tryin' to help me all the time by telling me, 'No, you ain't—don't think you are the greatest, don't do this and don't do that.' "[2]

Word of Sumlin's problems with Wolf got back to Muddy, who took advantage of them. "I went to Muddy on account of Muddy offered me more money," Hubert said. "He tripled the money that Wolf was giving me. He sent his chauffeur over from Silvio's to the Zanzibar and got me, with this big roll of money. Hey, I looked at this money, I thought about it. I said, I believe I'll change. I believe I'll leave and go and make this money. I figured it was just going to be three or four days. They tripled the money that Wolf was giving me, 'cause we was only making $14 a night. And I taken my guitar down and I went to take my amp down, and James Triplett, the chauffeur that Muddy done sent over from Silvio's, took my amp down because I was too nervous and scared of Wolf. I'm scared of what he going to say or what he may do. Wolf caught onto it, man. He knowed something was wrong and he saw James Triplett talking to me, and he knowed he wasn't up to no good. Told me, man, before James Triplett took the amp down, said, 'Hey, come here.' Man, I said, 'Oh, shucks! Wolf done smelled a rat here. Somebody done told him something.' So I went to go in the bathroom, and this bathroom didn't hold but one somebody, and especially a big person like Wolf, he had the bathroom full. So I went to open the door. He just cracked the door open and stuck his big finger through there and beckoned for me. So I went to open the door and he's standing up there. He says, 'Yeah, take your shit down, man. Don't come back. I know where you going. Hey, I brought you here.' I say, 'Well, I'm . . .' 'Don't tell me nothing. Just get the shit and get on out of here.' Hey, man, James Triplett ain't scared of nobody, but he ended up being scared of Wolf. Wolf looked like a giant up on this guy. This guy got the amp, took it on out, put it in the car, and my guitar. I went straight to Silvio's where they's playing and played that night. Man, let me tell you, I was nervous that night. I was so nervous up there playing that but hey, man, I knowed I'm going to wake up with all this money and every-thing. Muddy, after we got off that night, well, I tell you what, Muddy sent his guitar player back to Wolf. And that's when this whole thing about them falling out started."[3]

With Muddy's band, Sumlin spent most of his time on the road. "Sometimes we'd drive a thousand miles to make it to the next gig," Sumlin said. "Get off at three, four o'clock in the morning. Get right in the car and start to driving." Going on the road with Muddy was differ-ent from touring with Wolf. Muddy traveled in a car driven by a chauf-feur, while the rest of the band was in another car. Wolf and his band all rode together in Wolf's car, with Wolf often behind the wheel. The hard touring with Muddy was too much for Sumlin. "Finally, we had this set of one-nighters—40 one-night stands in a row," he said. "Then when we had just finished, we drove all the way back to Chicago, and had to open up at the 708 Club the next night: after all these 40 one-nighters. That night I was playing on the bandstand, Muddy had got him a fifth of Old Grand Dad, and he was sitting out front with this young girl. Now we done played a whole set, Muddy hadn't been to the bandstand yet; when he did come, he sang two songs and it was time for intermission. Now we had this fan to keep us cool sitting right in front of me. I had my hand on the guitar and I pushed the steel fan with my other hand. Fire come from my mouth; I couldn't turn it loose. So at intermission I told Muddy I couldn't play out the night. He got mad at me, called me all kind of things, and raised his foot to kick me. I grabbed him. Here come [Otis] Spann with a trace chain, gonna whip me about Muddy. I had a-hold of Muddy, and every time Spann tried to get me with that chain, I put Muddy next to him. Every time he hit Muddy, I said, 'Man, when you get right, I'll turn you loose.' So, finally, I turned him loose and jumped back; we went on to the bandstand and I played the night out."

The altercation with Muddy was the final straw. Sumlin called Wolf the same night from the 708 Club to demand his job back in Wolf's band. "I said, 'Hey, man, that's it. Whoever you got in there, they got to go. I'm coming back.' He said, 'No problem.' After the gig, he met us at Muddy's house. He told Muddy, 'Next time you do that, man, I'll kill you over him.' Muddy didn't speak to me in a year, but we finally came back to being friends. Things were never right between him and Wolf, though. Ever since Wolf come to Chicago and started to taking over, Muddy didn't like him too well. A kind of rivalry started up between them about who was the boss of the blues. After I went with Muddy, Wolf didn't speak to him no more."[4]

Muddy attributed their rivalry to Wolf's jealousy, but it was clear that it cut both ways. "The onliest thing that was between me and Wolf was jealousy," Muddy said. "Friend, yeah, but Wolf wasn't really a friend if you better than him, as good as him. He couldn't understand it. And that's what me and him always used to be. No, I know the peoples thought we hated one another, but we didn't, but Wolf wanted to be the best and I wasn't gonna let him come up here and take over the best.

And he used to tell his people, 'That Muddy Waters' band ain't good as mine.' I'd tell the people, 'Wolf's band ain't good as mine.' . . . So that's the way that was there. We never did have no guns at one another. Wolf was jealous—anybody that could play good or sing good as him. And then I did all this for him. I could have set him up in Chicago, he still figured that he should be better than I am, or Wolf thought he shoulda been better than anybody. And that's a good mind to have, but don't show it, you know."[5]

Oliver Sain witnessed Muddy's pettiness firsthand at Silvio's. Sain, sitting at the bar, was trying to talk to an attractive woman, with another woman sitting between them—unknown to him, one of Muddy's many girlfriends. Muddy thought Sain was trying to make time with her. "Muddy was mad about it and he had told a couple of people . . . about shootin' me or beatin' me up or somethin', you know," Sain recalled. "He didn't say anything to me. And Wolf got ahold of it some kind of way and went and confronted that guy, man. I wasn't around when he did it. . . . As a matter of fact, I went over to a joint on Ashland, I think it was. And I was sittin' up in the front eatin' some chili and Wolf came in and started tellin' me about it. . . . He said, 'I'm goin' back there and straighten that out there.' Hell, I didn't know what he was talkin' about. I didn't do nothin'. And he actually went and confronted Muddy and straightened it out. . . . He said, 'Ah, you leave that boy alone there, then.' So Wolf had a certain influence now. . . . People respected Wolf."[6]

When Sumlin left to play with Muddy, Wolf replaced him with Willie Johnson—whom Wolf soon had to fire again. Then Wolf hired guitarist L. D. McGhee, who had played with some of his band members in West Memphis. Easy Baby Randle, who played with McGhee in West Memphis, said of his guitar playing, "L.D. was bad, man!"[7] Sumlin said, "L.D. was a nice guitar player, but he was quite a guy. He stayed with Wolf all the time I had gone to Muddy." When Sumlin rejoined Wolf, McGhee left to play with Muddy.[8]

Tired of touring, Sumlin nonetheless went on the road again. "After I returned to Wolf we went out on the road, out of Chicago back to Mississippi to play," he said. "Wolf always used a station wagon and we tied the stuff on top of the car on a rack. One time we lost $6000 worth of equipment, just flew off, the whole thing. We was going across the Mississippi River, you know . . . and the wind just took the racking off. We got out to look and there was our stuff going down river, all the instruments! Wolf was mad but when we got to Memphis he just bought new instruments and kept going. We never did see that stuff no more . . . drums, upright bass, everything, just kept floating down river."[9]

Wolf maintained his popularity in the South by touring often there. Monroe Burnett heard Wolf at Tutwiler and Webb, Mississippi, in the late 1950s. In Webb, Wolf played a place known colorfully as Poor Whore's Canyon, where rooms could be rented for $2 for trysts.[10] Alabama bluesman Little Whit Wells vividly recalled seeing Wolf on tour. "Howlin' Wolf, whenever he came through town I'd be up on stage with him, not playing, but I'd be up there watching and trying to get as close as possible and hanging out with him on breaks. I loved the Wolf! To hear a guy on record that you like and then to hear him just brings out everything. He was a great performer! Yes sir, he'd get down on them knees and his hands would be trembling while he was singing. Man, he would crawl from here to your mailbox and back! Boy, he could go! Yes sir!"[11] Earl Phillips recalled one Southern trip. "I was in Florida—it wasn't but about 40 miles out of Miami. This club is indoor and outdoor. He had it so he could close it over and it be indoor, and open it and it be a grove. Well, one night the Wolf was just a-howlin'. I'm just beatin' away there and my pegs on that slick floor, they just lost their hold and they started movin'. And here I am, skis blowin', and they thought I was part of the show. They tried to start out, 'Whoo-woo-woo! Whoo-woo-woo!' They go, 'Do that number again.' Man, I hurtin' all up in here."[12]

Wolf didn't see his mother much when he toured the South. Lost in a world of religious delusion and paranoia, she refused to talk to her son. At a commodity store in Ruleville, Mississippi, in the 1950s, Dorothy Spencer saw Gertrude Burnett holding a picture of a nicely dressed Wolf. "She said to me, 'This is my son. But he ain't like me. I'm Jesus' child, but he's not.' I said, 'Where did you get that picture?' 'Oh, I've been having this a long time. Do you know this man?' I said, 'I sure do!' 'Could you tell me where he is?' I said, 'Now, last time I heard from him he was in Chicago.' 'Where?' I said, 'Well now, I really don't know.' But I didn't. . . . She was crazy. She was really nuts."[13]

Oliver Sain enjoyed touring with Wolf because he was so unpredictable. "You never knowed what he was goin' to do," he said. "He would come tippin' out onstage and lookin' weird with his eyes bucked or somethin'. . . . One time he just came out of the wings of this theater, man, real slow and he had his eyes bucked. And the audience was quiet man! I guess they didn't know what to expect! And he walked really slow all the way to that microphone, man. Yeah, he was strange sometimes." Sain never knew what Wolf might say. "One time in Cleveland [Ohio], he said, 'Well, I'm the Wolf and these is the Little Wolves. I'm the man that drags his tracks out with his tail as he go along.' He said, 'I come to play the blues. I'm a bluesman! And if you don't like the way I play the blues, don't order me no more.' He made it sound like you just kind of ordered him right out of a catalogue or somethin'."

Cleveland was memorable for an incident back at the hotel. "Wolf met this good-lookin' woman," Sain said. "You know, Wolf liked kinda heavy women and light-skinned women. So this kinda heavy, light-skinned gal, man—she was a good-lookin' woman—I had seen her goin' into the hotel with us once or twice, then I didn't see her anymore. So Wolf was kinda like our daddy. We were asking him, 'Wolf, what happened to that woman, man—that good-lookin' woman?' Wolf said, 'Grrrrrrr!' So he mumbled somethin', you know, and then he said, 'Naw, I didn't want to put up with that no more. I woke up and she was down *there!*' I said, 'Down there? Down where?' 'When I woke up.' You know what he was talkin' about. Wolf didn't understand that! That was the end of that right there!"[14]

Popular as he was on the road, Wolf played most often in Chicago, including a big birthday party for Elmore James at Silvio's on January 18, 1956, advertised as "The Broom Dusters and the Howling Wolf and his Little Wolf, also Sunnyland Slim and his Trio, the Red Devil Trio, and Big Bill Bromzie [sic]—many, many other Outstanding Musicians are giving Elmore James The 'Old Man' Broom Duster the biggest 'BIRTHDAY PARTY' that ever hit the Middle West."[15] In April 1956, the Club Alibi put an ad in the *Chicago Defender*: "Florine & Bob want you to know that the Howling Wolf is back week ends."[16] Wolf's main Chicago gig was at Silvio's, where he often appeared along with Muddy on Friday, Saturday, and Sunday. Jimmy Reed was added on July 8, 1956, for a special Sunday "Cocktail Party."[17] "One weekend over there they had Jimmy Reed, Jimmy Rogers, Muddy Waters and his band, Howling Wolf and his band," said Billy Boy Arnold. "Jimmy Rogers and his band and Jimmy Reed worked with my band. This was a big weekend at Silvio's, and they advertised on the radio 'The greatest blues artists in the city,' and I felt proud that I was in that group. I was working with these guys—guys that I admired and looked up to."[18] In September 1956, Wolf appeared at a club called (pre–House of Blues) the House of Rock 'n' Roll.[19] In December 1956, Wolf was at the Casa Blanca, where J. B. Lenoir often played.[20]

Wolf was back in the studio again on July 19, 1956. The lineup was the same as the previous session with one exception: Otis "Big Smokey" Smothers replaced Willie Johnson on guitar. Born in Lexington, Mississippi, in 1929, Smothers learned guitar as a child after being inspired by his aunt's playing. In 1946, he moved to Chicago, where he met many of the city's leading bluesmen and further developed his skills. In the mid-1950s, Smothers formed his own band, known as the Muddy Waters Junior Band, because they often filled in for Muddy at clubs when he was out of town. When this group broke up, Smothers joined Wolf's band.

Wolf recorded four songs at this session. "I Asked for Water," based loosely on Tommy Johnson's 1928 "Cool Drink of Water Blues," was as traditional as Wolf ever got in Chicago. Over a funereal beat with guitars tolling like death bells, Wolf laid down a darkly menacing vocal, complete with falsetto embellishments. The autobiographical lyrics, again about a woman mistreating him, were as morose as the music, as Wolf sang, "Oh-ohhh, I asked her for water; oh-ohhh, she brought me gasoline. / That's the terriblest woman ooohhh, that I ever see-eeen."

Billboard said, "Artist sings this Southern-style blues with feeling and his usual impact."[21] "So Glad" was a fast, stop-time shuffle with excellent guitar and another strong Wolf vocal with harp. The two were released as Chess 1632.

"The Natchez Burnin' " was a down-home blues about a fire at the Rhythm Club in Natchez, Mississippi, in April 1940 that killed more than two hundred people, including most of the Walter Barnes Orchestra.[22] Wolf wasn't there that night, and other blues singers had already recorded songs about the disaster. Over a minimalist backing, including acoustic guitar (" 'The Natchez Burning,' that's me playin' that little lonesome guitar," Smothers said[23]), Wolf personalized the event by calling out the names of people who died when "the whole building done tumbled down."

The song was unreleased until 1959, when it was coupled with "You Gonna Wreck My Life" as Chess 1744. "Break of Day," also unreleased at the time, was a driving shuffle featuring lyrics that would be reworked in the better "Killing Floor."

In September, the music press reported on Wolf's newest song, but garbled the title. "The Howlin' Wolf hittin' 'em hard on his Midwest tour with a new long-titled shot called 'She Gave Me Water When I Asked for Gasoline.' "[24] This mix-up was corrected as soon as the record began to sell well. By September 22, "I Asked for Water" was on the *Cash Box* hot chart in Cleveland and stayed there until November 17, reaching as high as number 2. It also charted in Atlanta, St. Louis, Newark, and Memphis.[25]

In December, Wolf went into the studio to cut four more songs with Willie Johnson and Smokey Smothers on guitar. Alfred Elkins, a talented musician who had played on Chicago blues sessions since the early 1940s, played bass. Adolph "Billy" Duncan, whom Wolf knew in West Memphis, was on tenor sax. Earl Phillips and Hosea Kennard were on drums and piano as usual.

"Going Back Home" from the session, a slow blues rumba in the unusual key of B-flat minor, featured heartfelt harp and moans plus downbeat lyrics about going back home because "Everybody know you treat me wrong. . . . Got somebody there make you leave me alone." Sonically and thematically, it was a precursor to the equally autobiographical "Who's Been Talking?," which Wolf would record the next summer. *Cash Box* said, "The deck that seems to have it made is 'Going Back Home.' Wolf, of course, is strongest in the southern markets—but the side has an appeal that could grab hold in all markets if it gets the exposure."[26] "My Life" was a return to the West Memphis sound of records like "Moanin' at Midnight," with a shouted Wolf vocal (including howls) and terrific country-style harp. These two were released as Chess 1648. "Bluebird" was another version of the John Lee "Sonny Boy" Williamson song that Wolf recorded in Memphis. It was a fine, slow blues with beautiful vocal and harp by Wolf and jazzy guitar by Johnson. "You Ought to Know" was another throwback to Wolf's West

Memphis sound, with terrific right-hand work by Kennard and more jazzy guitar from Johnson. These two were not released at the time.

In February 1957, a music reporter wrote, "Our get-well wishes this week go to Len Chess, who is in Michael Reese Hospital. He suffered a heart attack and will be forced to take it easy for at least another six weeks. With brother Len out of the office, Phil Chess is wishing he could grow three more sets of arms and two more heads to handle all the orders and phone calls coming in on Howlin' Wolf's brand new Chess deck, 'I'm Going Home' [sic]."[27] Released in early February, "Going Back Home" showed up on the hot chart for Memphis on February 23. It stayed there until early April and peaked at number 5 in early March. Meanwhile, the flip side, "My Life," charted in St. Louis and Atlanta.[28]

Bluesman Bobby Rush, who first saw Wolf in Pine Bluff, Arkansas, in 1955, befriended the older bluesman in 1957. Wolf gave advice to Rush whether he wanted it or not. "Wolf used to tell me, 'Hey, youngster! You know, if you listen to old Pops, he'll tell you somethin'.' . . . He would always tell you: You shouldn't do this, you shouldn't do that. I said, 'Wolf, before you tell me anything, just don't tell me to leave the ladies alone!' I said that jokingly, but I respected his opinion about a lot of things, and I didn't want him to tell me bad about the girls because I was kind of wild at the time." Wolf also talked with Rush about his career. "Wolf told me one time, 'Son, if you got somethin' workin', don't change it even if they get tired of it. Change towns. . . . Because if you see me tomorrow, I'm gonna howl. If you see me next week, I'm gonna howl. I was howlin' when I come to Chicago and I'll be howlin' when I leave. I'm a Howlin' Wolf!' And he didn't change things."[29]

Chicago bluesman Luther Allison, born in Mayflower, Arkansas, in 1939, also had fond memories of Wolf. "Wolf was a sweetheart. Wolf had his thing. Up the ladder, he played guitar more than he did harp, which is obvious because he was getting older, the harp take a lot more wind. But, in these days, people were sitting down. Wolf, Muddy, Little Walter, everybody was sitting down. Us, we was sitting down. And the audience was sitting down. There was dance space in the front of the stage. Wolf had this long chord. . . . And he would crawl on the floor . . . with the tablecloths over the tables, the ladies sitting there with their nice dresses; he'd crawl up under the table blowing the harmonica, and freak 'em out, and stuff like this. But, it was nothing to it; it was entertainment. He was a big man. You could look at him and get scared. . . . He would tell you, 'OK, you boys wanna play? You respect *me*. Respect *yourself*. This is not B. B. King. This is the Howlin' Wolf. I don't wanna hear no B. B. King notes. You gonna play with Howlin' Wolf, you learn Howlin' Wolf stuff.' That's what he would say. You know, it was like, 'OK?' But, he loved you, man. You could see him with a smile on his face when you played some things he liked. Then he'd say . . . 'That's my boy, ladies and gentlemen.' They're the ones to tell you to stay away from drugs, stay finishing on the whiskey bottle, watch the women. Be careful. They would tell you that."[30]

Billy Boy Arnold also got to know Wolf well. "I remember one time I was playing at Silvio's and M. T. [Matt] Murphy and Jody Williams was considered the greatest guitar players on the scene. Jody was my regular guitar player, and once every now and then when Memphis Slim wouldn't be working, I'd use M.T. So I had Jody Williams and M. T. Murphy on guitars and they were considered like during the Western days—the great gunfighters. So when Howling Wolf's band came in, somebody came in first—like Howling Wolf's stooge, which carried his equipment—he came in and saw M. T. Murphy and Jody Williams on the bandstand, and he broke back out there to tell Wolf and the boys, 'M. T. Murphy and Jody Williams in there.' Everybody came in quiet looking: Uh-uh, it gonna be a hell of a night! Wolf would stand around and look at my band. See, I was full of life. I would sing John Lee Hooker songs, all of Muddy Waters if Muddy wasn't there, all of Little Walter's stuff—and I would sing a little more upbeat blues. I could sing a variety of stuff and my band was steady drivin'. And Howling Wolf used to get on his boys. He used to tell 'em, 'You gotta work tonight.' "[31]

Billy Boy's band played at Silvio's for nine months in 1957, sharing weekends there with Wolf and Muddy, which allowed Billy Boy to observe the two top bands in Chicago for a long time. He formed distinct impressions. "Muddy Waters didn't necessarily have his own sound, 'cause his sound was built around Little Walter, Jimmy Rogers, and Spann and those people like that. When you took them away from Muddy, Muddy's sound was gone. But Wolf had his own sound and he would have been the Howlin' Wolf whether he went to California or anywhere else in the world. His sound would have been there 'cause his sound was the Wolf—his harp playin' and his singin', and he was strong, aggressive, and dominating on the stage. He wasn't a weakling at all! . . . He was unique in every sense of the word. . . . He was truly an artist."[32]

Louisiana bluesman Phillip Walker met Wolf in 1957 while in Chicago to record with Clifton Chenier, the King of Zydeco, for the Checker label. "I used to go down on 51st and State. I used to catch all these blues guys," Walker said. "We used to go down and jam 'til three or four o'clock in the morning with people like Muddy Waters, Howling Wolf. They was young artists in those days. Wolf was quite a guy. He was a humorous guy to work with and he was just a real blues guy. I mean if you were talking the blues and drinking some whiskey, Wolf was there with ya!"[33]

Wolf went back into the studio to cut four more tracks on June 24, 1957, with the personnel from the previous session. "Somebody in My Home" was another hypnotic, Howlin' Wolf one-chord mood piece in E major, complete with dirgelike guitars by Johnson and Smothers and an arresting, dampened drum sound by Phillips. Wolf's powerful vocals were beefed up by adding lots of echo to the mix. *Cash Box* said, "Howlin' Wolf 'howls' out a slow beat blues with a big voice and mournful, tricky, reading."[34] On "Nature," an upbeat vamp in D major distinguished by Kennard's hard-charging boogie piano, Wolf had problems finding the groove. After take six, he lit into the band. "You all acting like this is some damn plaything. This ain't no goddamn plaything! I work my motherfucking ass off and you motherfuckers standing around bullshitting." "We doin' what they asked," said a band member. "I don't care what they *asked* you to do," Wolf sneered. "I don't give a damn thing what happens. Shit."[35] Tearing into the song, Wolf sang that it's his nature to cheat—not his fault. "Nature" and "Somebody in My Home" were released as Chess 1668, which charted in Memphis from the end of August to the middle of September.[36]

"Who's Been Talking?" remade "Going Back Home" in the key of E minor, with better lyrics and a bravura performance by Wolf on vocal and harp, plus an odd horn line on melodica by Billy Duncan and Phillips's muffled drumming. Wolf no doubt was thinking about his own flight via train from White Station while he sang:

My baby caught the train, left me all alone. (2x)
She knows I love her; she doin' me wrong.

The powerful shuffle "Tell Me" included another standout Wolf vocal. Thematically, the song was about trouble at the Wolf's door. It was released with "Who's Been Talking?" as Chess 1750—the last recording Willie Johnson made with Wolf, though he would play with his band off and on for a few more years. While most of Johnson's recorded work in Chicago didn't match the burning intensity of his Memphis and West Memphis sides with Wolf, his loss in the studio was significant.

The session was notable not only for the fine recording but because it was Wolf's first in the new Chess company headquarters at 2120 South Michigan Avenue—an address revered by blues fans. (The Rolling Stones cut an instrumental titled "2120 South Michigan Avenue.") Built in 1911, the run-down building had housed a furniture slipcover manufacturer and a tire company by the time Leonard and Phil Chess bought and renovated it as their new headquarters. They installed a new recording studio with state-of-the-art technology in a room about twenty feet wide by thirty-seven feet long, with two inches of cork and a layer of concrete over the original wood floor. The studio walls were built for maximum soundproofing; one had nine adjustable panels that opened to absorb sound better. They also built two echo chambers by running wires from the studio down to the basement, where the wires attached to microphones and speakers on both sides of the room. The sound waves from the studio slapped around nicely in the basement to create an echo. The control room at the east end of the studio had a special twelve-channel console, and the rest of the studio equipment was as good as at any other independent studio.[37]

Wolf entered the new studio again in December 1957 for another session, memorable because for the first time Sumlin was alone on guitar, foreshadowing the band's new sound as he became Wolf's musical alter ego. The session also included Kennard on piano, Elkins on bass, and Phillips on drums. Wolf was in a nostalgic mood, recording several songs that reached back into his past. "Poor Boy" was a Delta blues standard that he had played solo for years. Ably supported by his band, Wolf sang and played it with stunning intensity because he knew exactly what it was like to be a poor boy a long way from home. He intoned the last line of the song repeatedly like a prayer: "And the world, it can't do me no harm."

"Sittin' on Top of the World," another old Delta standard, was first recorded by the Mississippi Sheiks in 1930 and became a huge hit for the popular black string band, a basis for the Robert Johnson song "Come on in My Kitchen," and a country and bluegrass standard recorded by Bob Wills, the Carter family, Bill Monroe, Doc Watson and Clarence Ashley, Earl Scruggs, and many others. Wolf's version was magnificent; the song is usually identified with him. Sumlin showed flashes of his growing guitar greatness, Kennard filled in with high-energy yet tasteful piano trills, and Phillips maintained a sledgeham-mer beat. Wolf played sensitive cross-harp with a B flat harp in the key of F major and brought out all the bitter irony of the lyrics—mournfully singing the superficially triumphant "Now she's gone, but I don't worry 'cause I'm sittin' on top of the world." As with so many of the songs he picked, this one had deep personal resonance for Wolf, specifically to his White Station childhood: "Going down to the freight yard, gonna catch me a freight train. I'm gonna leave this town—work done got hard." "Poor Boy" and "Sittin' on Top of the World" were released as Chess 1679.

Two other songs recorded went unreleased at the time. "Walk to Camp Hall" was a tough, slow blues in compound time featuring sparse but biting guitar embellishments by Sumlin. Wolf redid the song in 1965 as "I Walked from Dallas." "My Baby Told Me" was another prim-itive one-chord vamp, this time in the key of F, on which Sumlin did his best Willie Johnson guitar licks while Wolf provided rhythmic harp and a passel of powerful howls.

Belgian blues scholar Yannick Bruynoghe, who helped Big Bill Broonzy write his autobiography, *Big Bill Blues*, visited Chicago with his wife, Margo, in December 1957. After a party at Big Bill's house, Bill took them out to hear music. "Around midnight, Bill drove us, with Tampa Red, to the 708 Club, where we were greeted by Howlin' Wolf," Bruynoghe wrote. "I had previously heard some of Wolf's records—especially 'I Want Your Picture,' which was one of Bill's favorites—but hearing him live, so lively, so rough, so wild, was of course very impres-sive. As a first night in a Chicago blues joint at that time it was a real shock! We went back there quite often and still regret today that this powerful singer was never properly recorded. Wolf's band at the 708 included Abb Locke (tenor sax), Hosea Kennard (piano), Hubert Sumlin (guitar), Alfred Elkins (bass) and S. P. Leary (drums)."[38] Bruynoghe's visit was a harbinger of things to come. Wolf soon became well known to blues fans across Europe.

In 1958, Malcolm Chisholm came to work at Chess as chief recording engineer. He had already worked on many Chess sessions while an engineer at Universal Recording Studios across town. A man of strong opinions, Chisholm liked and admired Leonard Chess, but also recognized his flaws. "He was a businessman and a very good one," Chisholm stated. "He was an absolutely first-class businessman. . . . He was a lot smarter than most of the people that he dealt with. But probably his chief flaw was that he thought he was a lot smarter than everybody!" In an industry where fair dealing was rare, Leonard was better than most. "Leonard was as good a schemer as anybody," Chisholm said. "But on the other hand, if you were straight with Leonard, he was very straight with you. And he ran Chess like a Jewish delicatessen. He took care of his people. . . . He was just an incredibly clever, devious, and so forth man when the necessity arose. He didn't do it for fun."

Chisholm was under no illusions about Leonard's musical knowledge. "Leonard knew very little of music, but a great deal about merchandising," he said. "Leonard rarely interfered with sessions. He did every once in a while, and usually mucked it up somewhat. His brother, Phil, occasionally did the same thing, with even poorer results." Leonard usually left the music to the musicians, and he often recorded people based on the recommendation of musicians he trusted. He also understood that the success of Chess was based more on consistency of product and steady sales than on pursuing the next big hit. "Leonard's immortal saying was, 'Fuck hits! Give me thirty thousand on everything I release.' " This helped artists like Wolf, whose records always sold steadily, even if he no longer hit the national R&B charts.

Chisholm said, "Phil was a classic younger brother." He was not as bright or focused as Leonard, and he didn't have his brother's huge ego. Often forced to do the dirty work such as firing people so Leonard could play the good guy, Phil was a decent, likable man who realized his role in the company. Chisholm summed up by saying, "Phil made a wonderful vice president of everything!"[39] Stan Lewis, an important record distributer in Shreveport, Louisiana, knew the Chess brothers well, having met Leonard in 1948 when he was pushing a record by a new artist named Muddy Waters. The two quickly became close. "Leonard was like a father to me," Lewis said. He also got to know Phil Chess well and had a higher opinion of him than Chisholm did. "Phil was the younger and he just . . . kind of took a back seat, but don't sell Phil Chess short, either. They were both great in their own way."[40]

"Leonard was a businessman all the way," Jimmy Rogers said. "Phil is more open and a gentle guy and a much easier fella to deal with. He just didn't live for himself, like Leonard did. Phil would understand people and was more lenient. Neither one of them knew nothing about the blues."[41] Both Chess brothers had a paternalistic attitude toward the bluesmen who recorded for them. Phil Chess said about Wolf, "We got along in or out of the studio. He was a very, very nice man. He was one of those old-time blacks. He was always very polite around whites. He was not like the young ones. He was older and he was very, very smart. Not too educated, but a very smart man."[42]

Malcolm Chisholm had a different opinion. "Wolf . . . was two steps ahead of an idiot," he said. "Wolf looked like the kind of fellow . . . who wears caps and works in alleys." He also thought Wolf was "vaguely menacing," "very black," "pretty ugly," and "had the paranoia of the very stupid." But even Chisholm recognized Wolf's abilities as a musician. "He was an unbelievable talent! Frankly, he was more talented than Muddy. It's just that Muddy was a more civilized man." Chisholm thought Wolf's chief talent was his ability to distill his total essence into his music. "What Wolf did was, I think, extremely sophisticated blues in that there wasn't anything in it except Wolf. Most one-man acts don't make it, but Wolf had enough going for him so that his one-man act worked extremely well." Chisholm also had the highest praise for Wolf as a singer, saying that Frank Sinatra "was not half as good a singer as Wolf." He also said Wolf was a better guitarist than most people knew and a solid harmonica player who never tried to show off. "He was essential blues!" Chisholm said.[43]

Wolf's next recording session was on April 3, 1958, with the same lineup on the previous session plus Abb Locke on tenor sax.[44] Only two songs were recorded. "I Didn't Know" was a driving shuffle with nice cross-harp in G, with lyrics about Wolf discovering what his woman did the night before, much to his dismay.

"Moaning for My Baby," a powerful one-chord workout in the tradition of "Moanin' at Midnight," featured a strong Wolf vocal with howls and harp. The two songs were released as Chess 1695. Also recorded but not released at the time was "Midnight Blues," a fine alternate take of "Moaning for My Baby."

This session was the first for sax player Locke. Born in Cotton Plant, Arkansas, in 1934, Locke saw Wolf around West Memphis in the early 1950s but never played with him. After moving to Chicago in 1957, Locke sat in with Wolf's band a few times at the 708 Club while watching Billy Duncan, an old friend from West Memphis. Guitarist Earl Zebedee Hooker heard Locke play at the 708 and asked him to join his band. Locke later moved on to other Chicago bands before joining Wolf's band in late 1957.

Soon after joining Wolf's band, Locke went on the road for the first time in his life with a long tour through Florida, Georgia, Alabama, Mississippi, Tennessee, and Arkansas. Locke enjoyed touring with Wolf, though the places they played were sometimes primitive. At a juke in a cotton field outside Greenwood, Mississippi, Locke saw frogs jumping all over the floor when the band came down for intermission! Touring in the South was also tough because of the racial discrimination of the time. The band often had to go to the back doors of restaurants to find something to eat, and had to stay in black-only hotels or people's homes. Even finding a bathroom was difficult. In Mississippi the band stopped at a Shell station to get gas and Wolf asked the attendant if they had a restroom. The man said they didn't have one for "niggers." Wolf told the man to stop pumping gas, paid him, and drove off.[45] In the tense times of the late 1950s, this simple act of defiance could have cost Wolf his life.

The band toured in Wolf's new green Pontiac station wagon. Locke, who didn't drink or smoke, often did the driving while the rest of the band drank. Wolf wouldn't get drunk, but often complained that his back hurt after driving only ten miles. Locke told Wolf that he should be paid extra for doing most of the driving, so Wolf gave him an extra $5 or

$10 a week.[46] The sidemen were getting $10 a night to play on the road, except in Hallandale, Florida, where they got $25.

Back in Chicago, the band played three or four nights a week at the 708, Silvio's, and other clubs. Onstage, they wore tuxedos. "We was the best-dressed band," Locke remembered. "We had the best band, I think, in the city."[47] Pianist Henry Gray also took pride in the band's appearance. "Wolf was about business. . . . You didn't come on Wolf's bandstand with no shorts or blue jeans on, looking like a damn fool. If your shoes weren't shined, he would fine you. He bought the band uniforms, so you damn well had to wear one. I had six different suits when I played with Wolf. Some musicians didn't like Wolf telling them what to do and what to wear. But if your name was out there, would you want a band behind you with their asses hanging out? I'm the same way with my band. Wolf was a professional and taught me a lot. I loved him for that."[48] Willie Johnson resented wearing a tuxedo. "For a while he had us wearin' a tux," Johnson said. "Yeah, we was wearin' tuxedos. And if you wore the wrong color tux for a night, you got fined for that, too."[49]

Wolf impressed Locke as a performer. "He'd buck his eyes and wink and go on," he said. "He'd be winkin' at them women and grinding." Locke admired Wolf's showmanship, especially when Wolf would howl, walk the bar, and crawl on the floor. "I used to laugh at him," Locke said. "It tickled me." The reaction that Wolf's antics evoked in his many female fans often amazed Locke. "Sometimes women would jump on his back and ride him while he was crawlin'," he said. "I seen three women on his back at one time."[50] Gray also remembered the excitement that Wolf's performances generated. "He would crawl around on the stage on his hands and knees like a real wolf and drive the audience crazy. People would throw money on the bandstand and women would fall out in a faint."[51] The sexual energy generated by Wolf's performances benefited the other guys in the band as well. Years later Locke remembered with great fondness all the women he had while playing with Wolf, which was fine with Wolf as long as it didn't interfere with the band. Wolf would encourage the guys in his band to learn their instruments. " 'Leave them women alone and get on your instrument' — he always preached that," said Locke.

Less positive were the arguments Wolf had with band members.

Locke, who had no bad habits, was on time for his gigs, but others who liked to drink often showed up late. One night Wolf cussed the entire band out for being late. When Locke protested that he was on time, Wolf cut him off with a curt, "I'm talkin'!" Locke then started showing up late, too. His problems were minor compared to the others. Sumlin in particular often earned Wolf's wrath. On the bandstand, he'd turn up his amp too loud, and when Wolf told him to turn it down, he'd turn it down so low that Wolf couldn't hear him.

Things came to a head one night after the band played in Arkansas and were driving to Memphis. Wolf and Sumlin began arguing and Wolf told him to stop the car. They jumped out, and Sumlin started swinging, missing with a right uppercut that Wolf slipped by backing up. Wolf slapped Sumlin, knocking him to the ground for a ten-count and this night retired undefeated. The other guys picked Sumlin up, put him back into the car, and drove on to Memphis.

Round two started the next day as the band left Memphis for a show in Mississippi. Drummer S. P. Leary, drunk in the back seat, whistled at a white woman walking on a sidewalk. Wolf waited until they crossed the state line and stopped the car. Knowing what was up, Leary jumped out, ran across the road, and fell into a ditch. Wolf walked across the road, pulled out a pistol, and said, "I'm goin' to kill you now because you are goin' to get us all killed." Fortunately, Wolf didn't pull the trigger.[52]

Born in Carthage, Texas, in 1930, S. P. Leary learned to play drums in his school marching band and orchestra, and was playing in local nightclubs by his early teens, backing up well-known bluesmen such as T-Bone Walker and Lowell Fulson. He went into the army for five years, where he played in a band with jazzmen Cannonball and Nat Adderley. He then went to business school for two years before moving to Maywood, Illinois, where his sister lived. Leary was about to go home to Dallas when Sonny Boy Williamson II heard him practicing one day and asked him to join his band. Leary went on to play with many other Chicago blues greats such as Johnny Shines, Robert Lockwood, Jr., and Jimmy Rogers. Right before joining Wolf's band, he was playing with the talented young West Side bluesman Magic Sam.[53] Wolf had asked S.P., also known as Kelly, to play with him once before, when he was working with Elmore James. "Kelly, how 'bout comin' to work for me?" Wolf asked. Leary was surprised. "Wolf, I thought you and Elmore was best friends!" Wolf replied, "Yeah, man, but in this business, it's dog eat dog."[54]

Leary joined the band when Wolf's regular drummer Earl Phillips quit in a fit of pique. Phillips had played on every Wolf session since May 1954, providing the beat on blues classics such as "Smokestack Lightnin'," "Forty Four," and "Who's Been Talking?" Wolf had many other talented drummers in Chicago, but none had a greater impact on record than Phillips.

Leary enjoyed playing with Wolf, but butted heads with him off-stage. "I was doin' things that he didn't like," Leary said. "I used to drink too much, I did, and he didn't like for you to drink. . . . He didn't care anything about what you drinkin'. He just didn't want you drinkin' too much so that you couldn't do your job. . . . Now that man had struggled for years and years to get to his position, and he didn't want no fool to come up there and tear the thing down that he had done built up for hisself in the position that he was in." Wolf also wouldn't tolerate any-one being late. "He wanted you to hit on time and he wanted you to stop on time," S.P. said. "And you'd better not be late. If you were late, you were in trouble—big trouble! He'd fine you! He'd charge you. . . . You just had to follow his rules; that's all he asked of you."

Like Abb Locke, Leary did his first tour of the South with Wolf. "He knew about the situation down South," he said, "and he would always school us before we ever went thataway, because me, in particular, I never had toured the South and I really had to listen to him, man." (Given what happened while leaving Memphis, Leary apparently wasn't a good listener.) Leary had to adjust to the discrimination in the South, brought vividly home by a stop in Elvis Presley's birthplace, Tupelo, Mississippi. "We stopped off to get a bite to eat and I looked up and I saw the sign there that said 'Men's Room,' but it didn't mean me—for whites only! You had to go outside in the outhouse, which was sittin' out there in a great big puddle of water, man, and it was *cold*, so I couldn't go. No, I couldn't make it."

Leary was amazed by how well Wolf knew his way around the South. "We'd get to some towns that he knowed just like he did the palm of his hand. . . . Wherever he had been, he had never forgotten it. Naturally he knew all about the Southern states because he came up down South there: Mississippi, Alabama, Georgia. Aw, he just knew his way around. He was a godsend, man! He could take us through towns like Money, Greenville, Greenwood, and Belzoni, and boy, he knowed the back trails and stuff going through them places."[55]

Wolf was back in the studio in September 1958 with Sumlin and L. D. McGhee on guitar, Kennard on piano, and Leary on drums. It was Leary's first recording for Chess, and it came as a shock. "Aw, they called each other all kinds of names," he laughed. "Sometimes I thought they were goin' to fight: Wolf and Leonard. . . . I ran up in the pit box up there where they was doing the taping. . . . I had to have me a couple of words, too, until Wolf got me out of there. That's right! Sure did. Yeah, they had to talk to me—Hubert, all the boys. I said, 'Shit! Ya'll better tell me something.' Because I didn't know." Leary soon appreciated the Chess brothers' abilities. "They knew what they was doin'. They knew how to get it out of you, too! They knew how to get the best out of him—Wolf and all his musicians there."[56]

"I'm Leavin' You" from this session was a hard-driving shuffle in G with splendid harp and guitar. Its lyrics were on perennial Wolf themes—romantic betrayal and abandonment.

On "Change My Way," a powerful, slow blues with heavily echo-chambered vocals and classic blues harp, a remorseful Wolf promised to change his evil ways. The two songs were released as Chess 1712, which became a regional hit in Atlanta, where it charted from late December 1958 through late January 1959. *Cash Box* stopped publishing regional R&B charts in 1959.[57]

"I Better Go Now" featured terrific guitar from Sumlin and solid playing from the rest of the band, including saxophonist Abb Locke. It was another menacing song that dealt with Wolf's favorite topics: romantic betrayal, money, and violence.

"Howlin' Blues," loosely based structurally on "Sittin' on Top of the World," was a slow, atmospheric blues that made heavy use of the studio's new echo chamber. The band never quite jelled on it, despite Wolf's impassioned vocal. "Howlin' Blues" and "I Better Go Now" may actually date from a session earlier in 1958. The two were released as Chess 1726. *Cash Box* said, "Wolf's in top blues form on both ends. His fans'll dig this pairing."[58]

Two songs recorded at the September 1958 session were not released. "You Can't Put Me Out" was a one-chord, up-tempo blues based on the "Moanin' at Midnight" riff and vocal line, here in the key of F major. Kennard added dynamite piano as Wolf sang another tune about his devastating childhood trauma:

> *This is my house. You can't put me out . . .*
> *If you try to put me out, I'll tell what I'll do.*
> *We'll get to fighting, then I'll knock you out.*
> *I'm so glad you can't put me out.*

"Getting Late" featured tighter band backing, a harp solo with stunning vibrato, and a vocal on which the mighty Wolf crooned the last lines with great tenderness. Neither song was near the best of Wolf's recorded work, though.

Wolf had successfully made the transition to Chicago, establishing himself as a dominant force on the local club scene while maintaining his traditional fan base in the South. He'd also enjoyed many hits on the regional and national R&B charts. But despite his professional successes, there was one huge area of his life that was incomplete. That would change one night when someone special walked through the door of Silvio's Lounge.

9. Howlin' for My Darling

By 1957, Wolf had been married and divorced once and had had at least five long-term girlfriends, including one his father thought he had married and another who was the mother of his son. He was about to meet the great love of his life—the woman who would do her best to fill the gaping hole left in his soul when his mother put him out to fend for himself.

Lillie Handley was born to Square and Annie Handley in Livingston, Alabama, on August 12, 1925. Lillie's father died when she was two, so Annie moved with Lillie to the large farm and orchard of her father, Harry Sledge, in Sumter County, where many of her relatives owned farms. Lillie grew up in an atmosphere of love and financial stability and got a good education, graduating from high school and briefly attending college.

In 1945, Lillie married local farmer Nathaniel Jones, and the next year they were blessed with a daughter, Bettye. In 1947, Lillie and Nate separated, and she moved to Chicago, staying with her sister. Big-city life didn't appeal to her at first, so she came home a few months later to reconcile with her husband. Their daughter Barbra was born in 1950. The couple soon separated again, and Lillie moved back to Chicago, where she stayed with a cousin and started working in the dietary department of a hospital. In 1952, Nate Jones died.

As a young, attractive widow, Lillie had many admirers. Her boyfriend at the time, though, was none other than Wolf's old harp man, James Cotton, who'd been seeing her for several years. Hubert Sumlin said, "Cotton was going with her way before Wolf."[1] One night, Lillie's brother and a cousin from New York suggested they go down to Silvio's to see Wolf, Muddy, and Elmore James. They called another cousin from Chicago to join them.

Silvio's was jammed because of the stellar lineup. "Wolf was on the bandstand when we got there," Lillie said, "and he was just doing his show. Now this is the first time I had ever saw him, but heard him [on the radio] so many a time. . . . He peeked at me when we walked in and this cousin that lives here says, 'Oh, he got his eye for you, cousin.' . . . Wolf was still doing his thing on the bandstand, but he kept cutting his eye at me. And I sat between this cousin and my brother, and the rest of 'em was all around — my cousin's wife, she was there, too — all of us just having a nice time. When Wolf came down off the bandstand, he sat over in a corner. . . . I looked and he would look, and he nodded his head for me to come to him."[2]

Many women would have jumped at the invitation. Not Lillie. "He begged for me with a hand sign. My cousin was watching, too. He said, 'He begged for you.' I said, 'I'm not going over there because I'm not going to get my head cut by all these ladies.' "[3]

Wolf approached her. "He says, 'What's your name?' And I told him. I said, 'Why?' He said, 'You look like a cousin of mine.' I said, 'What was her name?' He said, 'Cookie.' I said, 'Oh, no.' She lived in Louisiana or someplace like that, you know? He was lying. I said, 'Well, no, no, no, no.' And he says, 'Who are these people?' . . . I said, 'My cousin, my brother': I was just naming everybody that was at the table. He said, 'Oh, I've heard that before.' I said, 'Well, you have?' 'Yeah! Brothers, cousins . . .' and he just went on down. I said, 'Well, I'm telling the truth.' So he says, 'Waitress, come over: Give them whatever they want!' Well, I wasn't drinking. I don't drink. My brother and all — he set up the table for them. And he says, 'When I come back down, I really want to talk to you!' I said, 'You want to talk to your little cousin?' We laughed."

While Wolf performed, Lillie's Chicago cousin encouraged her to speak to him again. "My cousin—he always was a devil—said, 'Cousin . . . you better talk to him.' I said, 'Now, will I talk to him and get my throat cut?' 'Cause I said, 'You know what musicians is?' . . . I said, 'These womens.' I said, 'I don't know him and he don't know me and I'm not going to get hurt.' He said, 'Oh, you ain't going to get hurt.' He said, 'We with you.' . . . Then my cousin said, 'Talk to him! Talk to him!' I said, 'No, I'm not either.' So finally he come down again. Then he came over to the table where we were and he got him a chair and he sat there and he talked. He wanted to know if I was married. I said, 'No.' . . . He asked me where did I live. I told him exactly. I said, 'I live at 44th and University.' He said, 'I'm at 46th and Greenwood.' That was just like two blocks over and two down." (Wolf was living at 4554 South Greenwood Avenue, the building managed by Joseph Chess, Leonard's and Phil's father.)

"So he says, 'How about me taking you home tonight?' I said, 'Oh no, you can't do that.' He said, 'I wouldn't do anything but drop you off.' He said, 'I wouldn't dare think of . . . going in because I know a good-looking woman like you got 'em standing around.' . . . I said, 'Yeah. And I bet a guy like you got 'em standing around, too.' We talked and . . . when he went up again I told my cousin what he had said. My cousin said, 'Don't worry.' He said, "We'll trail you.' I said, 'No, no, no, no. I'm not going.' He said, 'Go on! We'll trail you. We'll trail you.' "[4]

"I think he was really wanting to find out that I lived where I said I lived," Lillie said with a laugh. "And sure enough, he drove me home and my cousin and brother and them were right behind him. He says, 'Who is this with the bright light just right behind me?' So we got there and he asked me for my phone number. Of course, I gave him the wrong number. And I thought maybe I'd never see him again."[5]

The next day, Hubert told Wolf that Lillie's boyfriend was their old buddy Cotton. Wolf said, "Fuck Cotton! He ain't got what I got!"[6] Not long after, Lillie ran into Wolf on 43rd Street and he confronted her about giving him the wrong phone number. She denied that she had, but Wolf didn't believe her. Here the matter may have ended except for the visit of another cousin and a return trip to Silvio's for another night out on the town. "My cousin's boyfriend was from Greenville, Mississippi, and she had told him about Wolf was talking to me . . . and he says to me, 'You better talk to that guy! He's a guy that don't play.' . . . And I told my cousin's friend, 'You know, I gave him the wrong phone number and I'm ashamed.' He said, 'Well, I tell you what if he asks you for it again you better give it to him, because that's a man!' He knew him from down in Mississippi. . . . So when he [Wolf] come down he shook hands with this guy and they were talking. He said, 'Yeah, I tried to get this little girl's phone number, but she gave me the wrong one!' I said, 'I don't know why you keep saying that.' I said, 'I gave you the right number, but I will give it to you again.' And I gave him the right number after talking to my cousin's boyfriend. And oh, boy, we talked and he set up the table whatever we wanted, so we stayed for a while. And all the way home this guy would say, 'If Wolf talking to you, you better talk to him.' I couldn't see it, but I just went along with them. And finally he called me." Then Wolf had to leap another hurdle. Lillie had her brother and nephew, who were staying with her at the time, answer the phone whenever Wolf called to tell him she was not at home.

Wolf was not easily deterred, though, and she finally told him he could come by to see her. They started dating. One day he found evidence of a back-door man at her place. "Wolf liked to caught Cotton!" said Hubert. "He almost did at Lillie's apartment, 'cause Cotton left one shoe on the porch. . . . Cotton went out the back door to keep from facing Wolf!" Cotton knew Wolf was smitten by Lillie. A legendary babe magnet, "Big Red," as Cotton was called by his band mates, figured he could find another woman soon enough. Maybe the thought of facing two hundred and fifty pounds of fighting Wolf made him uneasy, too. Game over: Wolf 1, Big Red 0.

Besides being beautiful and well educated, Lillie was well-to-do. According to Hubert, she owned properties in Livingston, Alabama, and on the West Side of Chicago. "Lillie had money and she didn't have to work," he said.[7]

Just as Wolf and Lillie were getting close, Lillie's mother took sick, and Lillie had to return to Alabama. Wolf called Lillie and asked her not to leave until they could talk in person. He came by after his gig one night and asked her to marry him. She promised to give him an answer when she got back from her trip, and Wolf suggested that they move her belongings to his apartment. She reluctantly agreed.

Back in Alabama, Lillie told her mother, who was quite religious, that she would have a new address when she returned to Chicago, but she didn't explain why. "I came from back home and here I am shacking with a man," she said. "This was 1958." Guilty about not telling her mother, she finally wrote to her to explain her new living arrangements. She was relieved when her mother wrote back that it was fine with her as long as Wolf was good to her. Lillie eventually asked Wolf why he'd been so nice to her when she had repeatedly discouraged him. He said, "I know if I didn't do it, somebody damn sure would!"[8]

Meanwhile, another band member was finding romance. Born in 1937 and raised in Arkansas, Evelyn Cowans first saw Wolf when his band played a teenage dance in Pine Bluff, Arkansas, in the early 1950s. After moving to Chicago, she saw Wolf's band many times because her sister Geraldine was dating Willie Johnson. The guys in the band were always trying to set Evelyn up with someone. The natural candidate was Hubert, but his shyness was an obstacle. Evelyn remembered, "Hubert would not talk. And this particular night, someone had pushed him up to ask me if he could bring me home. And he did. And from then on, we would do our talking, but he was very shy, and so was I. But things got a little bit better and a little bit better. And he was living on the South Side, and when men live by themselves, they don't really take care of themselves. I'm going from the West Side to the South Side all the time, and one time he said, 'Well, how about me coming over to live with you?' And I said, 'I don't want anybody to live with me.' And my brother-in-law said, 'Why not? If you all going to see each other all the time, you might as well put your money together.' And that's how we started." Evelyn and Hubert ended up married for twelve years.

It was Hubert's second marriage. In Mississippi when he was just sixteen, he married a young woman named Alberta, fourteen, in a private ceremony arranged by their parents—not a legal marriage. Hubert promised Alberta's mother he'd never mistreat the girl. They were together only ten months. Hubert suspected she was playing around on him, and he returned her to her mother, who was mystified. "Hubert, what's wrong with you-all?" she asked. "Can't you-all work things out?" "No, ma'am," Hubert said. "You told me 'fore I whup her to bring her home. Here she is." A decade later, Alberta showed up at a Chicago club where Hubert was playing and tried to reclaim him, even displaying her invalid wedding license to Evelyn.[9] Hubert made Alberta return to Mississippi empty-handed.

Evelyn became the band's official photographer and secretary, from which position she saw the inner workings of the band. "Wolf came here inexperienced," she said. "He knew what he wanted and went about trying to get it. He pushed himself a lot, but he got what he wanted. He lived the life he wanted to live. He didn't like a fast life. And he got a woman who was down-to-earth just like he was, so his life was beautiful."[10]

Romance was not the only thing on the band members' minds. They had to play the shows to pay the bills. In early 1958, the band went on tour in Florida for three months with R&B singer Big Maybelle, who had recorded an impressive string of hits for the OKeh and Savoy labels. Her 1956 recording of the pop chestnut "Candy," in particular, was as tasty as its title. Hubert said, "She was really nice and she really hated to leave us. Nothing I can tell you about her, except she's a large lady, and boy, when she's singing, everything she's got shakes!"[11]

Joining the band in 1958 was Abraham "Little Smokey" Smothers, younger brother of Wolf guitar alumnus Otis "Big Smokey" Smothers. Born in 1939 in Tchula, Mississippi, Little Smokey was a talented young guitarist whose style was more modern than his brother's. He learned much of his technique from hot young West Side guitarist Magic Sam, who was cutting seminal, modern Chicago blues for the Cobra label. Little Smokey got to know Wolf when Big Smokey was in the band, and continued to see Wolf play even after his brother left it. Seeing Little Smokey in the crowd one night, Wolf offered him a job as long as he didn't play too loud or cop any B. B. King or Muddy Waters licks, because the Wolf wanted to have his own sound. "I don't remember what I played," Smothers said. "I was scared!" Whatever he played satisfied the Wolf, who hired him.

Little Smokey had few problems with his new boss, but was witness to many disputes between Wolf and the other guys in the band. "I'd wait and let him and S.P. get it on, S.P. or either Hubert. That was nightly! Wolf never did mess with me or Hosea Kennard or Abb Locke. Them other guys used to quit and come back so fast. Willie Johnson, he'd quit and come back. The only guy would stick was Hubert—and he quit, too! One'd quit, then [Wolf] would get the other one in there. They'd come backwards and forwards."¹²

Musicians who played for Wolf were expected to carry themselves professionally just as he did, which meant being on time, dressing properly, and not smoking or drinking onstage. "He was a gin drinker," Smothers said. "Yeah, he was drinkin' once in a while, but as long as he was workin', he wouldn't drink." When someone violated a band rule, Wolf would call everyone on the carpet. "He would hold meetings, you know," Smothers said. "If one messed up, everybody got to go to the meeting."

Some of Wolf's rules applied offstage. He had strict rules about how the musicians should behave while touring in his green Pontiac station wagon. Nobody in the band could drink in his car. "Hubert would have a bottle in his pocket," Smothers said with a laugh. "And one time we was going out of town and he brought a half pint of whiskey in his pocket. We all were sitting in the back seat. . . . So Hubert opened him a 100 proof and got him a big swallow of it, and you could smell it all over the car. [Wolf] raised up and said, 'Somebody in here been drinking.' He reached over in the back seat and slapped Hubert! Then he said, 'Stop the car—stop the car!' Everybody got out of the car. Hubert, he had the Wolf [try to] throw a big headlock on him and missed it, and fell all the way down the hill off the highway. Climbed back up the hill and got in the car and said, 'Let's go, y'all.' Yeah, he and Hubert, they would do that."

Another source of amusement on the road was Wolf's limited education. "Just like we'd be riding down the highway, he'd see signs on the side of the road," Smothers said, "and he'd be spelling the words, and he'd get it wrong and everybody be laughing in the car. He'd get mad about that shit. He'd see a sign on the side of the highway; he'd be mouthing the words wrong."¹³ Wolf may not have been as educated as the guys in his band (many of whom were barely literate themselves), but when it came to mother wit, there was little doubt who hauled the heaviest load.

Wolf had another rule forbidding his band members from hanging out with Muddy's. "He want you to act like you was mad with those guys," Smothers said. "I used to be with 'em all the time, so he just had to fine me. Me and Pat [Hare] and Otis [Spann] and James Cotton and all us, the only thing that would break us up is death, because we was just friends like that. We used to all get together down at Ricky's Show Lounge and Smitty's Corner and on the West Side at the Zanzibar, get a great big jug and drink it up. Oh, boy—we had a lot of fun!"[14] Bass player Jimmy Lee Morris of Muddy's band said, "All of us was drinking. Everybody would be drunk. They'd call us the Muddy Waters Drunken Ass Band. Shit man, when you're playing blues all night long, that's life man."[15] In Wolf's eyes, that kind of blues life was no way to run a professional band. "Wolf didn't want us to hang with them guys," Smothers said. "He didn't want us to go out there and drink with them. He would say they would stay drunk all the time."[16]

Wolf often used his massive size to physically cow those around him. Little Smokey saw only one man who could physically intimidate Wolf—Sylvester Washington, a renegade cop and bartender who ran vice on the South Side through coercion and violence and was known as "Two-Gun Pete." "Abb Locke was livin' upstairs over Two-Gun Pete's bar, the Hilltop Inn on Oakwood Boulevard," Smothers said. "Wolf used to come there and pick Abb Locke up. He'd be scared 'cause Pete'd make him drink. He'd say, 'What kind of whiskey you drink?' Wolf would say, 'When I drink, I drink a little gin but I'm not . . .' He'd set the gin bottle up there on the bar, say, 'Drink!' and touch his pistol like that. Wolf'd grumble, 'Well, I'll take a little.' After a while, Wolf used to send me in to get Abb Locke out. He'd stay in the car."[17]

No one intimidated Wolf when it came to singing and performing. "He was great, you know," Smothers said, "because couldn't nobody do his thing. He wasn't never worried about nobody trying to take his music. He just sung. Because they couldn't do it. Nobody had that voice, and he knew this. He was the only Howlin' Wolf. The rest of them guys running around calling themselves the Howlin' Wolf, Jr., and all that—he said he ain't worried about them. 'Let them go! They'll never be me!' "[18] Smothers also enjoyed Wolf's active stage style. "It was great to see a big guy like that who weigh 300-and-some-pounds get down on the floor, start crawlin' on his knees and on his back, then get up there on the bar and crawl down there. I'd get my guitar, get right behind him down on the floor."

When the blues struck him, Wolf would make up songs on the spot about what was happening in the club. "Sometimes he'd sit down, look up there in the lights and start singin' 'Ooh I See My Baby Settin' Right There on the Bar,'" Smothers said. "Lotta times he just make that stuff up as he go."[19] Wolf would also say wild things onstage, often with hilarious results. In a show in Milwaukee at the American Legion Hall, Wolf told the audience that he had a tail like a real wolf. Amazingly, several members of the audience believed him and tried to get backstage after the show to get a peek at the anatomical wonder.[20]

Lee "Shot" Williams, a cousin of the blues-playing Smothers brothers, often heard Wolf's records on Nashville's WLAC radio while growing up in Mississippi. Williams moved to Chicago in the late 1950s and started going out to the clubs to get started as a blues singer. Wolf liked the young man and would call him up onstage to sing a couple of numbers with the band. Williams said, "He'd tell me, 'Boy, I like you. You're tryin' to learn. I like the way you carry yourself. You come up there tonight. I'm goin' to call you up.'" Wolf didn't extend the courtesy to singers he didn't like, Williams said. Wolf would tell them, "The people didn't come to hear you. They come to hear me."[21]

Another Smothers cousin, Lester "Mad Dog" Davenport, was a part-time drummer with Wolf's group. He first sat in with the band one night at Silvio's when Earl Phillips was too drunk to play. Best known for having played harp on some of Bo Diddley's records, Davenport dared not refuse when Wolf barked, "C'mon man! Get on the drums and hold a beat for me."[22] Passing this test under fire, Davenport played with Wolf in Chicago off and on over the next few years. But he had a full-time day job, so he only did out-of-town gigs if they were nearby.

Davenport liked Wolf personally but chafed at all of his restrictions. "That what make it hard playin' with Wolf. In his band, he wanted to be the father. Not just the music, but your own personal life." At gigs, Davenport avoided Wolf so he could sneak a drink or two. One night, Davenport and Sumlin sneaked some alcohol into the bathroom at Silvio's and agreed to take turns as lookouts outside. But Sumlin got distracted by a woman. Davenport was startled when Wolf walked in and caught him red-handed. Wolf fined him $10—a heavy penalty, since his pay for the night was just $12.50. Davenport finally quit the band so that he could remain friendly with Wolf yet drink as much as he wished. He got S. P. Leary to take his place.

Wolf had paternal feelings toward Hubert and the other guys in the band, with all the love and tension inherent in such a relationship. Davenport watched this dynamic at work between Wolf and Sumlin. "They were close like father and son! And I think that's why they got along so bad sometimes, because Wolf wanted Hubert to be like a son. . . . He wanted that kind of respect from Hubert like he was his father. Sometimes Hubert wouldn't go along with that, you know? Hubert would turn around, 'I'm grown! I'm a man! . . . You can't tell me what to do!' That's how they would get into it from one word to another, arguing about respect."[23]

Wolf saw Hubert as a younger version of himself—all alone in the world with no one to protect him. But Wolf went too far in trying to watch out for his "son." Hubert said, "I figured he was too protective with me at times. I mean, God knows, I couldn't do this, I couldn't do that. . . . But I found out by growing up and being with him so long, he was just trying to take care of me. I was his son, you know what I'm talkin' 'bout? That's the way I see it, and he did, too. . . . He make me mad at times for asking these things, but I'd say he meant well for my interests and his'n. So hey, I loved him."[24]

In July 1959, Wolf went back into the studio. The first tune he cut was "I've Been Abused," a storming blues shuffle with Leary laying down a rock-solid beat, Kennard throwing in wild flourishes on piano, and Abb Locke honking along rhythmically. Unusually, Hubert played bass by laying down a driving pattern on the bottom strings of his guitar. Freddie King, who was at the studio for a session with Etta James, sat in on guitar and came up with the distinctive rhythm lick that drove the song.[25] Wolf's lyrics were patently autobiographical—right out of his Dickensian childhood and hard luck youth—and he screamed them with blistering anger, accompanied by powerful cross-harp in the key of D.

> *All my life I've caught it hard.* (2×)
> *I've been abused and I've been scorned.*
>
> *I feel so bad; this ain't gonna last.* (2×)
> *I've been scorned and I've been kicked out.*

I've been abused; I've been talked about. (2×)
I've been scorned sure as you're born.

I'm so mad I can shout. (2×)
I've been abused and I've been kicked out.

The second tune of the session, "Mr. Airplane Man," featured the one-chord vamp from "Smokestack Lightnin' " coupled with lyrics from Wolf's version of "Bluebird," substituting an airplane for a bluebird to carry his message down South to his woman. Despite the musical hodgepodge, the song worked well, with a great groove and atmospheric howls. As always, Leonard Chess was tough to please. Before recording it, he said, "Hey Wolf, I'm recording this one, so moan in this son-of-a-bitch, will ya?" On take 1, Wolf and the band were cooking along nicely as Wolf sang, "Mr. Airplane Man, sail down to Jackson, Mississippi, with me." But Wolf forgot that he was doing a new song and inserted a line from "Bluebird." "Goddamn!" he swore as the take stopped. "That's OK, baby," Leonard said. "We'll do it again. Don't worry about it. You made a mistake on the other one, anyway. Uh, Wolf, an airplane man *flies,* he don't *sail*—MOTHERFUCKER!"[26]

The standout track cut that day was "Howlin' for My Darling," and its genesis is a good example of the recording process at Chess. It started out as a variation on "49 Highway Blues" by Big Joe Williams, which Wolf had sung for more than twenty-five years. Though Wolf and Willie Dixon both received credit for writing the new song, Leonard Chess clearly helped mold it. On take 1, the band launched into a wobbly shuffle and Wolf immediately started singing, "Melvina my sweet woman, she lives on Highway 49." Leonard stopped them and said "Wolf, go about three times and then come in." Take 2: Leonard stopped them and said to Leary, "Hey drummer, if you could get a solid beat and stay there—don't go up and don't go down. You're rushing it. When you go up, you're rushing it. I want that 2-4 real heavy, man." Take 3: Leonard stopped them and said, "That beat ain't right. The drummer ain't right." Take 4: Leary double-timed the beat, but the rest of the band had problems locking on to it. Leonard stopped them and sang the melody to show exactly how he wanted it accented: "Da-da-da-da-da DUH-daaaa." Then he had Wolf sing the same accents to the band. By take 7, Leary had slowed the beat considerably, and the band was clicking in one of the most heavily syncopated dance grooves in blues history, playing off against each other like a Dixieland band jolted by electricity. Later that day, Dixon came in with new lyrics. "Howlin' for My Darling" was a strutting, joyous celebration of love and lust. Wolf sang it with obvious delight—his newfound happiness with Lillie undoubtedly on his mind.

> *Hmm-hmm-hmm! Pretty baby!*
> *Hee-hee-hee-hee, hee-hee-hee-hee! Come on home! I love you!*
> *If you hear me howlin', calling on my darlin'.*
> *Hoo, hoo, hoo, weee!*
>
> *She's hot like red pepper, sweet like sherry wine.*
> *I'm so glad she love me, love me all the time.*
> *She's my little baby, sweet as she can be.*
> *All this love she got, do belongs to me.*
> *If you hear me howlin', calling on my darlin'.*
> *Hoo, hoo, hoo, weee!*

Also recorded that day but not released was "My People's Gone," a tough little blues shuffle in D major, done in the West Memphis style. Lyrically the song is again right out of Wolf's past, as he bemoans being all alone in the world: "Why should I walk? My people is gone. I won't start to walkin'; I'm just alone." Musically, though, the song never quite came together. "Wolf in the Mood" was an inferior, instrumental remake of "Everybody's in the Mood."

This session was Little Smokey's first time recording at Chess, and like Sumlin and Leary, his experience was less than positive. "We went down at Chess Studio and got screamed at all day long. Man, them guys get on the microphone, turn it up loud as they could, hollerin' out, 'What the hell is you doin'?' 'Youuu!' 'Play it by your own goddamn self!' They shake you up so bad. Them guys was terrible. I prob'ly coulda had plenty of recordin's, but the way them guys used to shake me up, they practically scared me away from the studio." Little Smokey wasn't the only one Leonard yelled at. "Oh, shit! He'd get on Wolf, too. They'd have a cussin' match for a hour there. I mean a *real* cussin' match, knock down and drag 'em out. Leonard'll be the one to back down. He'll go out of the studio slammin' the door. Wham! He'll say, 'Y'all do it your own goddamn way!' "[27]

By the late 1950s, recording technology was changing. Singles were still the choice of many music buyers, but a growing number of educated, affluent music fans wanted more musical bang for their buck. Chess started releasing the new twelve-inch long-playing album format, first with their jazz artists—a more sophisticated audience open to technological change. When these jazz albums made money, Chess branched out, releasing albums by Chuck Berry, Muddy Waters, Little Walter, Dale Hawkins, and the Moonglows. These weren't as successful at first as the jazz LPs, but Chess was in the album market to stay.

In 1959, Chess released Wolf's first album: *Moanin' in the Moonlight*. Its cover set the tone for the dark contents inside. In a barren and desolate landscape, a wolf howls forlornly at the moon, with a shattered tree on a distant hill in the background. Compiled from singles Wolf had recorded from his first session with Sam Phillips all the way up to recent sessions, the album served up some of the deepest, darkest blues ever recorded, including "Smokestack Lightnin'," "Evil," "Moanin' at Midnight," "Forty Four," "I Asked for Water," and "I'm Leaving You." The liner notes played fast and loose with the facts by portraying Wolf as a folk artist. "Howlin' Wolf . . . is still a man of the soil. He was born in West Memphis, Arkansas, and in that country, where he lives with his wife, he works a cotton patch of over twenty acres. He has several mules and jackasses to help him with his plowing and other farm chores."[28]

In the fall of 1959, Jacques Demêtre and Marcel Chauvard, two French blues enthusiasts who wrote for the magazine *Le Jazz Hot*, traveled to the United States and visited Chicago after earlier stops in New York and Detroit. While visiting Little Brother Montgomery, a fine old-style blues pianist, they asked if any other bluesmen lived nearby. Montgomery said Wolf did and took them to see him at his new home at 4220 South Berkeley Avenue. "We went into a house and pressed a doorbell, underneath which was written 'Chester Burnett,' the real name of Howlin' Wolf. After a few minutes a gigantic figure of a man answered the door. 'Wolf,' said Montgomery, 'these two people are from Paris and they'd like to see you.' We explained to Howlin' Wolf the purpose of our visit and as we told him he screwed his face up into a mask of distrust.

'My dear young people,' he said, 'you want to make yourselves rich at my expense? I'm not going to tell you anything.' Little Brother tried his best on our behalf, but it was no good, although Howlin' Wolf, every inch the host, ordered tea and cake for us. After a while, the general atmosphere warmed slightly. . . . He stopped for a moment, then said, 'O.K. You seem genuine people. Ask me questions, then keep your ears open!' "[29]

The two young enthusiasts asked Wolf about his life and music. "Right now my band is well broken in," Wolf said. "We've been playing together a long time and we play often, so we understand each other well. . . . To have a good blues band, it is very helpful if the musicians come from the same place . . . regional distinctions are very important in black popular music. As far as I am concerned, you can say that to some extent I represent the style of West Memphis. Obviously, all the different styles are found in Chicago, where in turn a new style of blues has been created, to which I belong."[30]

Wolf invited the Frenchmen to hear him at the Big Squeeze Club the next night. "This club is situated in the western sector of the town," one wrote. "The atmosphere in this quarter was much more sinister and dirty than on the South Side. Men were walking about with bottles either in their hands or raised to their mouths. It was obvious that we would be better off in some club or other. The doorkeeper at the Big Squeeze Club wouldn't let us in, despite our references. One of us managed to get his head in the door and make frantic signs to Howlin' Wolf, who immediately hollered from the stage 'Let them in!' "

Safely inside, Demêtre and Chauvard settled down to enjoy the show. "Howlin' Wolf sang excellently in a strange voice well suited to his name. He alternated his harmonica playing with some guitar playing. The rest of his band was very good and the two guitars [Willie Johnson and Hubert Sumlin] afforded some interesting harmonies. Compared with the Muddy Waters band, this group sounded slightly monotonous, due in a way to the uniformity of tempos, which were always medium-paced. But despite that, we had a very enjoyable evening. By now extremely friendly towards us, Wolf introduced us to the audience— ordinary working people who had come to forget their daily routines and listen to their own folk music."

After the show, Wolf took his new friends out for an early morning meal. Pleased by the respect shown by two foreign journalists, Wolf decried his anonymity in his own country. "I'm not happy here in America. . . . We Negroes don't mean anything in this country. Nobody takes any notice of us. Have you seen my name mentioned in any of the papers here? It's all the young white people who get the credit. No. I'm tired of all of this. . . . As far as I'm concerned I'd rather go back and live in Africa. That's the country of my ancestors and there no-one questions the color of your skin."[31]

Willie Johnson hadn't been in the studio with Wolf in more than two years, but Wolf said, "My main guitar player is still Willie Johnson, who understands all my vocal intonations and accompanies them very well with his instrument."[32] Despite his admiration for Willie's guitar playing, Wolf was tired of his drinking. One night at a club, Abb Locke laughed while Wolf yelled at Willie about drinking. After Wolf left, Willie chased Locke around a table with a knife in his hand, screaming, "What you laughing at?"[33] Another knife incident got Willie cut from the band for the last time. Wolf caught Willie drinking and slapped him, so Willie chased Wolf and cut his back up.[34] Wolf must've been thinking about all the running mileage he put in with Willie when he later said, "I didn't mind the fighting, but he wouldn't give me no rest!"[35]

Wolf soon hired guitarist Freddy Robinson (later known as Abu Talib), who was born in Memphis in 1939, raised in Arkansas, and started playing guitar at age nine. As a child, Robinson saw Wolf perform several times and once stole some of Wolf's harps from a storage building at a club. In 1956, Robinson moved to Chicago and started playing around town with Birmingham Jones, Little Willie Anderson, and, most importantly, Little Walter. Walter's musical star was starting to fade when Robinson joined his band in 1958, but Robinson learned a lot while playing with him, picking up guitar licks from Luther Tucker and Robert Lockwood, Jr. He also started incorporating jazz into his playing while studying at the Chicago School of Music. His jazz leanings caused conflict with Wolf. "I worked with Wolf very briefly, because he's the only guy throughout the course of my entire career that I couldn't get along with too well. . . . He didn't realize that I really did love his music and had always loved it because he's one of the guys I used to see on the plantation. He thought just because I was studying that I didn't want to play the blues. Now ironically, he was studying also. He was taking lessons from Reginald Boyd. He was trying to learn how to read [music], and all this kind of stuff. His favorite quote every night when we'd get off the job, he'd tell me, 'Now, Mr. Fred, you come in here tomorrow night, don't bring me none of that Dizzy Gillespie music.' "[36]

Reggie Boyd, the talented musician Wolf took music lessons from, played bass and guitar on many Chicago blues sessions with Little Walter, Jimmy Rogers, Buddy Guy, Junior Wells, Earl Hooker, and Otis Rush. Many Chicago guitarists were knocked out by Boyd's playing. Robert Lockwood, who doesn't hand out compliments lightly, said, "Reggie Boyd was one of the best guitar players I ever seen. He'd play Charlie Parker shit note for note on the guitar! He was incredible! I used to try to teach him to play the blues. The cat was too fast for the blues." Lockwood and Boyd went to Lyon & Healy's music store in Chicago one afternoon and saw Les Paul and Alvino Rey, two legendary guitarists who were instrumental in the development of the electric guitar, in the store on business for the Gibson guitar company. "They were sitting in there messing around with the guitars," said Lockwood. "And then the two of them started to playing some, and Reggie picked up a guitar, and Reggie was playing the melody—in chords. At that time Reggie was about twenty or twenty-one. So Les Paul and Alvino Rey, both of them stopped playing and sat there and looked at him. And Alvino Rey said, 'Where'd you learn to play like that?' Reggie said, 'Oh, I fool around with the guitar a little bit.' Reggie was teaching across the street: guitar and piano. He'd play all of Parker's stuff. He was playing horn parts on guitar 'cause his wife was an alto player, and she was crazy about Parker."[37] (Boyd's wife, Josephine, was the alto sax player for the International Sweethearts of Rhythm and Eddie Durham's All-Star Girl Orchestra. She was reputedly a fabulous player and used to jam with Dizzy Gillespie in the years when he and a few other players were inventing bebop.)

Wolf's teacher obviously knew his stuff. "Reggie was teaching Wolf how to read music and writing out solos for him and going over it note for note with him and everything," Robinson said. "And he used to practice on the gig all the time, trying to play the stuff Reggie wrote for him."[38] Producer Ralph Bass came across Wolf one day at the Chess studio playing his guitar while reading sheet music. Shocked, Bass asked what Wolf was doing. "Wolf said, 'I'm trying to learn to read music.' I said, 'Wolf, don't do that, man! You're going to lose your thing.' "[39] Wolf didn't always see eye to eye with his guitar teacher. He once waved a thousand-dollar bill at Boyd while complaining that he couldn't make that kind of money playing the "progressive shit" Boyd was trying to teach him.[40]

Robinson got along well with the band's other guitarist. "Hubert always had that really friendly, adolescent-type personality," he observed. "I learned a lot from Hubert while playing with Wolf."[41] Less friendly was Wolf's drummer Junior Blackmon (also spelled Blackman). Born in 1933 in Leland, Mississippi, Blackmon had played with Charlie Booker in the Delta before moving to Chicago in 1954. In Chicago, he played with Muddy Waters and Magic Sam before joining Wolf.[42] Robinson said, "Junior Blackmon didn't have much to do with anybody."

Henry Gray also seemed cold to Robinson. "I don't think he really was exactly in love with me," he said, "but I didn't have any problems with him. He was too busy having problems with Wolf." Once, Robinson said, Wolf went out of town and left his band behind to play a South Side gig. "While he was gone Henry . . . was on the bandstand drunk, and he had a big pistol stuck down in his pants . . . and his coat kept flyin' open and everything." Wolf also heard about a fight Gray had with his wife just outside the club. "So when he got back," said Robinson, "he was more or less chastising Henry Gray and . . . he put a big fine on him and everything. And Henry . . . was trying to tell him that the hassle that he had with his wife wasn't in the club—it was outside of the club. . . . And then Wolf told him, said, 'Yeah, but you see, Mr. Henry, you're scandalizin' my name!' He said, 'First thing people say Wolf's boys whup their old lady's ass outside the club.' "

Wolf paid Robinson $15 a night for shows in Chicago and $25 a night for shows on the road in Cleveland, Detroit, and, unusually, outdoors at the St. Louis Blues Festival in Maryland Heights, Missouri, on July 31, 1960.[43] The festival also featured E. Rodney Jones (who later became a prominent deejay) and headliner Elmore James, all for the amazing price of one dollar.[44]

In June 1960, Wolf was back in the studio, where he recorded three songs that became Chicago blues classics and established the pattern for his records for years. With him were Hubert Sumlin and Freddy Robinson on guitars, Otis Spann on piano, Willie Dixon on bass, and Fred Below on drums. Wolf only sang on this session, but his vocals were so strong that his harp wasn't missed much. All three songs recorded were credited to Dixon, but like many Dixon songs, some had earlier sources. Dixon had a hard time pitching songs to Wolf, who preferred to record his own compositions, so Dixon resorted to devious stratagems. "Every song I'd give to Wolf, he'd say, 'Man, you're giving Muddy the best songs.' The songs I'd give to Muddy, he'd say, 'Man, you're giving Wolf the best songs.' A lot of times you have to use backward psychology on these guys. I'd say this is a song for Muddy if I wanted Wolf to do it. He would be glad to get in on it by him thinking it was somebody else's, especially Muddy's. They seemed to have had a little thing going on between them so I used that backwards psychology."[45]

"Spoonful," the first tune recorded that day, was loosely based on Charlie Patton's "A Spoonful Blues," about cocaine addiction. Dixon's version dealt candidly with sexual desire and jealousy. Like Patton, Wolf dropped the word "spoonful" from the end of many lines, letting Dixon's thumping bass substitute for the word. Robinson provided spooky lead guitar (often mistakenly credited to Freddie King), while Sumlin added bass lines on his guitar. Spann as usual was brilliant on piano. Wolf's vocal oozed lust and menace:

> It could be a spoonful of diamonds. It could be a spoonful of gold.
> Just a little spoon of your precious love satisfy my soul.

"Wang Dang Doodle" was based on a song popular with lesbians called the "Bull Daggers Ball," with "Fast Talkin' Fannie," for example, replacing "Fast Fuckin' Fannie."[46] With its roster of odd characters— Butcher-Knife Totin' Annie, Abyssinian Ned, and Pistol Pete—and its colorful description of a party where "when the fish scent fill the air . . . snuff juice everywhere," "Wang Dang Doodle" was a celebration of Saturday night fish fries down South. " 'Wang Dang Doodle' meant a good time, especially if a guy came in from the South," Dixon explained. "A wang-dang meant having a ball and a lot of dancing, they called it a rocking style, so that's what it meant to wang dang doodle."[47]

Wolf hated the song. Dixon said, "He hated that 'Tell Automatic Slim and Razor-Toting Jim.' He'd say, 'Man that's too old-timey, sound like some old levee camp number.' "[48] Nevertheless, Wolf sang the song with gusto as the band laid down a torrid sound. *Billboard* said, "Howlin' Wolf wraps up a primitive blues chant in solid, emotional delivery."[49] Koko Taylor redid it in 1966, and her version reached number 4 on *Billboard*'s R&B chart.

"Back Door Man" was a paean to the ultimate midnight creeper, the world champion pleaser of other men's wives, Jodie, the bogeyman of army marching calls, as Superman. Wolf's phrasing made the lyrics delightful. Partly because of his limited education, he never sang Dixon's lyrics exactly as written. Chess recording engineer Ron Malo said, "Wolf was funny. He was one of the ones that couldn't read, so Willie would have to yell in his ear the next lyric line on a new song. Wolf didn't know how to count so he didn't know where to come in. Wolf was a natural singer and performer but he learned things one way and that was it. He had to learn and memorize it and if we changed the introduction from what Wolf had learned, he'd be completely lost and Willie would have to cue him in."

Dixon thought Wolf was too stubborn to learn his songs. "Wolf didn't ever want to do none of the songs that I wrote for him but he finally would after a discussion with Leonard," he said. "A lot of times he would never learn the song. He couldn't read so he'd have to learn the words by heart but he really wouldn't be thinking about the song because I'd still have to whisper them into his ear after six months of training. Sometimes we'd have a good cut all the way down and right at the end he'd turn around and say, 'Oh, man, I didn't hear what you said,' and mess up the whole damn thing. A lot of times you whispered so loud they'd pick it up on the tape machine."[50]

Underrated as a songwriter, Wolf resented having to record Dixon's tunes. Wolf's songs weren't full of commercial hooks like Dixon's or unforgettable imagery and wry humor like Sonny Boy II's. Instead, they were like Wolf himself: simple, direct, honest, and powerful. "I can do my own songs better, but, you see, they won't let me," Wolf said. "They'll let Dixon give me songs to do, that's to keep me out of being the writer."[51] The songwriter's royalty was only one penny per record sold, but Wolf always saw the bottom line and knew those pennies added up.

But Wolf injected his full personality even into Dixon's tunes. "Back Door Man" was a prime example, as he transformed the trite-and-true into a chest-thumping ode to back door double-dealing. In Southern culture, a "back door man" made whoopie with your wife and then stole away out your back door while you came in the front. Wolf's hasty departure out a woman's back window in Clarksdale as her husband unlocked her front door personalized this song all too well for him, as did the reference to Wolf's favorite food: "I eats mo' chicken any man seen!" He became Back Door Man personified by dropping the indefinite article "a" from many lines in the song. Picture Wolf in cape and tights with a "B" emblazoned across his chest, his band strutting behind him, as he sang:

> *I am . . . back door man. I am a back door man.*
> *Well the men don't know, but little girls understand.*
>
> *They take me to the doctor shot full of holes.*
> *Nurse cried, "Please save his soul!"*
> *Accused him for murder—first degree.*
> *Judge wife cried, "Let the man go free!"*

Wolf got off to a roaring start in the 1960s with this session. "Spoonful" was released with "Howlin' For My Darling" from the previous session as Chess 1762, a two-sided hit. "Wang Dang Doodle" was released with "Back Door Man" as Chess 1777. It also became a two-sided blues hit. Over the next few years, Wolf would record one blues classic after another, most written by Willie Dixon, and he'd keep his core audience in Chicago and the Deep South while capturing the growing taste for blues among the young at home and abroad. He was, at last, the three-hundred-pound champ of the Chicago blues.

10. Three Hundred Pounds of Joy

One musician holds the key in any electric blues band. The drummer must keep solid time while using dynamics to propel the band—subtly shifting the tempo, adding color, and accenting notes and whole passages by changing the volume. A great drummer takes charge of your autonomic nervous system and makes your foot tap uncontrollably. The drummer's pulse is like your heartbeat, invisible but vital. You don't notice it when it's steady, but if it's irregular, the band dies. Willie Steele, Earl Phillips, and S. P. Leary—all great drummers—shaped Wolf's sound with their distinctive rhythms. In the fall of 1960, Wolf hired another great drummer: Sam Lay.

Born in Birmingham, Alabama, in 1935, Lay was just a toddler when his father died. His mother raised him. "As far as I'm concerned, Momma was the mother and the father," Sam said. Being religious, she wouldn't let him listen to the blues. "It was devil's music as far as she was concerned," he said.[1] One day at church with his mother, Sam heard the rhythm that would inspire his distinctive contribution to blues drumming: the double shuffle.

"It was an idea that stemmed from a church I used to attend in 1952 in Alabama, where they had tambourines and hand clapping. If you go in a sanctified church, it's like you and me and somebody else is clapping at the same time. It's so close that you hear a quick echo or two. I imitated that by playing a triplet with my left hand, so they should call it the 'triple shuffle.' The longest I played it on record is with the Corky Siegel Band on a Muddy Waters tune called 'Got My Mojo Working.' You'll also hear it on the *Fathers and Sons* album I recorded with Muddy. The closest thing to it is on a record called 'Folsom Prison.'[2] Whoever that drummer is is the closest I've heard. It don't exactly match it, but it's close. He scared me when I first heard it. I thought somebody done copped my style. Now I gotta go another route!"[3]

Sam got his first set of drums as a teenager. "I was just 17 or 18 and didn't play. I just thought it would be really nice to have a set of drums. There was this place downtown that sold on credit, so for a small down payment I could own a set of drums and that is what I did. I was quite a sight pulling a red Radio Flyer wagon all loaded with my drum kit from downtown to home. At first I let a fellow across the street come over and play my drums just so I could learn a little. After a while it started getting into me. I remember in high school sitting in the classroom when the band came marching by, I'd start pecking at my desk in rhythm with the band and get the whole class attention—and the teacher's attention!"[4] Smitten by the beat, Sam took drum lessons as a teenager from W. C. Handy, Jr., the son of the famous composer.

In 1954, Sam moved to Cleveland, Ohio, where he played with the jazz group Moon Dog Combo. In 1957, he joined the Thunderbirds, which featured Tommy O'Neil on harp. The Thunderbirds played blues and R&B and were a good training ground for the young drummer.

In February 1960, Sam and his wife, Liz, who was expecting a baby, moved to Chicago, where Sam got a job playing with Little Walter. The young couple stayed with the fiery harp genius, whose skills were being dissipated in a haze of alcohol and marijuana.[5] As Liz's due date grew near, Sam knew he needed a steadier source of income. Fate intervened when Wolf's drummer, Cassell Burrow, stepped on a nail, making his foot swell so badly that he couldn't play. Sam got a call that Wolf needed a drummer for a gig at the Playhouse on 43rd Street. Sam jumped at the opportunity and Wolf was so impressed with his drumming that he offered him a steady job.

Little Walter was livid when he saw the new paint job on Sam's bass drum: "I had wrote Howlin' Wolf on it because I'd promised the Wolf to stay on with him because he was working regular. But Walter would come in maybe and work a job this week and wouldn't work no more for three weeks. See, he was just happy-go-lucky, running wherever he wanted to. So I joined up with Wolf. And Walter asked me, 'How come you puttin' "Howlin' Wolf" on them drums and you play with me?' I said, 'Walter, I'm goin' to be playin' with Wolf.' And he got mad about it. He was ready to put me out right then, but I kept that name Howlin' Wolf on it. So I stayed with Wolf for six years."

Sam and his wife moved out of Walter's place and into their own apartment, near where Wolf and Lillie lived. Sam quickly grew close to Wolf. "To be honest, Wolf was like a father, man," Sam recalled. "I don't care what nobody say: I know what he was to me. And he treated my wife the same way. When you needed him, he was there. I don't care what you needed him for, he was there. He was just really a big pet. . . . I would go so far (hey, I'm not funny or nothing—don't get me wrong) and say he was one of the sweetest people you ever saw in your life. But you had to get to know him. If you just darted right in and out and seen him, around him for a few minutes, you might say, 'Man, this cat, I think he's Ricky the Dragon or somethin'. Fire goin' to come out his nose!' He wasn't like that. Man, he'd threaten to chop your head off with a double-bladed axe, but I betcha wouldn't nobody else threaten you in his presence. If you did, then you had to whip him, too."[6]

Chess producer Ralph Bass also recognized the dichotomy between Wolf's outer and inner worlds. "Now Wolf, his exterior personality, the one that he showed to everybody, was grrrrrrrrrr!" Bass said. "He was a bad guy! Don't mess with him! But inside, he was the softest cat in the world. He was so different inside."[7] Seemingly threatening to those who knew him only casually, Wolf was a sensitive and deeply caring man whose feelings were easily hurt. Suspicious and wary, he was slow to make friends, but once he did, he was warmly generous. The musicians in his band either made peace with both sides of his personality or didn't stay with him long.

Wolf took care of his band members by taking out both Social Security and unemployment insurance from their wages—unheard of for a Chicago blues band then and probably even today. "If you played in his band and you got fired or were laid off, you could draw unemployment compensation just like you would if you worked in a factory," Billy Boy Arnold said. "No other musician did anything like that."[8] Wolf hired a bookkeeper to check the band's finances and teach Lillie how to take out the right taxes. "If it was five hundred dollars, Wolf had to put up five hundred," she said. "Wolf had to match whatever he took out for those boys. Wolf had to match that out of his money. I'm telling you because I did it. . . . He wanted to shoot straight with them."[9]

Evelyn Sumlin helped Lillie with the band's bookkeeping: "She did the figuring and she would send the books to me, and I would do the rest. I did his income tax and so on. I'd get all the figures and things together, the things that we needed for his income tax man to figure out how much he owed or how much he was goin' to get back—I did that. . . . If you come into the band and you were going to be there to stay, then you were going to get Social Security taken out. He would always think about one day you gonna be older and you not gonna be able to do the things that you're doin' now, so you want to have something you can fall back on."[10] Hubert Sumlin and other band members get Social Security today because Wolf and Lillie had the foresight to take out the payments for them decades ago.

For gigs with Wolf in Chicago, Sam got $15 a night, but took home $12 after taxes.[11] In 1966, while playing with James Cotton, Sam accidentally blew off one of his testicles when a loaded pistol discharged in his pants pocket during some particularly vigorous drumming. Sam was wearing the pistol on the bandstand to protect Cotton from a jealous rival.[12] Because of Wolf's foresight, Sam drew unemployment for several months while recuperating. "Everything he had took out, I got it with no problem at all," Sam said. "He didn't try to hold it back. I knowed he wasn't stealing it . . . that's out of the question."[13]

Another musician who became a mainstay in Wolf's band was tenor saxophonist Eddie Shaw. Born in Stringtown, Mississippi, in 1937, Eddie played in his high school marching band in Greenville. On the weekends, he gigged with local blues musicians Charlie Booker, Oliver Sain, Ike Turner, and Little Milton. His big break came in the late 1950s when he sat in with Muddy Waters, who was touring through the area. Muddy hired him for the rest of his Southern tour. At the end of the tour, Muddy offered Shaw a job with his band in Chicago. Shaw accepted, and within weeks was in Chicago with his wife and two small children.

Eddie liked playing with Muddy, but didn't like how his band drank. "One night, we were playing in Chicago at Mel's Hideaway on Loomis and Roosevelt Road. Just a little before show time, we were all sitting outside in the station wagon. At about 9:00 p.m., Pat [Hare], Mojo Buford, and Otis Spann, who had all been drinking, started arguing and fighting. I jumped out of the car and said, 'Hey you niggers! Quit fighting! I'm tired of all your bullshit!' Before Muddy got to the club, I had quit the band.

"I left, walking west on Roosevelt Road. When I got to Damen Avenue, I saw a sign that said: 'Tonight! Howlin' Wolf!' I said to myself I might as well go in here and sit in with Wolf. . . . I went in and sat down. Hubert Sumlin saw me from the bandstand and said 'Ladies and gents, let's see can we get Eddie Shaw to sit in with the band.' Sam Lay was on the drums, Jerome Arnold on bass, and Henry Gray was playing piano.

"I sat in with the band, and when we came down, Howlin' Wolf said to me, 'Hey, man, you are blowing good. But I thought you was down there working with Muddy.' 'I was, but I quit.' 'Well, don't you want a job working for me?' 'Yes, man, I want to work. Do I start tomorrow?' 'No,' Wolf said, 'You start tonight.' Man, it was my lucky day: out of a band with Muddy Waters and into the band with Howlin' Wolf, all in the same night. Wow!

"Wolf was a big black man, standing 6'-5" tall, and weighing 260 pounds. He was also meaner than a junkyard dog. . . . I did fourteen years with Wolf, and came to love him very much.

"While playing that first night with Wolf, some had told Muddy that I was down the street, playing with Howlin' Wolf. About midnight, I looked down from the bandstand, and there sat Muddy Waters. 'Hey, man,' he said, 'What happened? They told me you quit, so I came to see why.' 'Well, Muddy, I got tired of the band fighting all the time. So I quit.' 'You should have waited until I got there and straightened it out. But that's okay. So now you are going to work for Wolf.' 'Yes,' I said.

'Well, give me my $20 you owe me.' 'Muddy, I don't have it now.' Wolf came up to us. 'Here's your $20, man. Now leave my musician alone.'

"Muddy took the twenty dollars and left. He didn't like me for a long time after that. About five years later, we became friends again."[14] Shaw played with Wolf for the next two years, then with Magic Sam, Otis Rush, Freddie King, and others until coming back to Wolf in the late 1960s.

Shaw got along well with the Wolf. "With many people he was difficult to get along with, but I found Wolf one of the most truest, straightforward fellas in the business," he said. "If the musician had a reason to not like Wolf, it was mostly because of the musician, instead of Wolf, because maybe the musician drank too much, his ability to play the right notes in the right place wasn't right, and Wolf would let you know right then to get it together. He didn't pull no punches. If you were wrong—you could be Leonard Chess—you were wrong!"[15] Shaw came to admire Wolf's hard-nosed honesty. "I think in the long run, that's the way to be. You have to love that, man, because he didn't lie for nobody, and if you was wrong, he let you know. That's the kind of guy he was."[16]

Jimmy Rogers, best known for his work with Muddy and his own fine recordings for Chess, joined Wolf's band for a few months in 1961 and could knowledgeably compare Wolf and Muddy as bandleaders. "Muddy wanted to be the big bear, Wolf wanted to be big—nobody was getting too close to Chess but they was thinking one would outdo the other one. Chess would get Muddy cars every two years, and take it off his royalties. Wolf would get his own car, wouldn't let Chess buy one for him. . . . Really, Wolf was better managing a bunch of people than Muddy was. Muddy would go along with the company, Wolf would speak up for himself. And when you speak up for himself, you automatically gonna speak up for the band, because if you don't agree to record, there's no recording. It was more of a business thing with Wolf."[17]

Muddy had a plantation mentality when it came to Chess Records. Leonard was the boss and Muddy did as the bossman said. Smart but unlettered, Muddy knew he could get what he wanted out of Leonard, and he flaunted it in the new cars he rode and the flashy clothes he wore. But Wolf was a rebel who'd left the plantation behind. All his life, he strove to be his own man. He bought his own car (a new Pontiac station wagon every other year) and dressed well, but not flashy. "He liked to have on his khaki pants, or whatsoever—this was his style," Evelyn said. "But if he had to get dressed, he could."[18] For Wolf, Chess Records was just a place where he worked, no more and no less. While Leonard respected Wolf, he didn't have a close relationship with him like he did with Muddy.

In May 1961, Wolf cut two more songs, both credited to Willie Dixon. Born in Vicksburg, Mississippi, in 1915, Dixon was a big man (over six feet tall and three hundred pounds) with a talent for songwriting and self-promotion. At Chess, he did everything short of scrubbing toilets: songwriting, bass playing, organizing, singing, and producing. Resented by some musicians, who felt he was too close to Leonard Chess, Dixon was a shrewd operator who knew how to look out for his own interests. His reputation as a songwriter is well deserved, but there was dross among his gold. A skilled lyricist with a talent for writing memorable hooks, Dixon often left the arrangements to others. "Everybody wants to credit Willie Dixon as the composer, but he was the lyricist," drummer Francis Clay said. "He wrote the lyrics, not the music."[19]

The studio band on the May 1961 session included Hubert Sumlin and Jimmy Rogers on guitar, Willie Dixon on bass, Sam Lay on drums, and Johnny Jones on piano. Born in 1924 in Jackson, Mississippi, Jones was a fantastic blues pianist who had played with Elmore James and the Broomdusters from the early- to mid-1950s. An exciting performer who loved to drink and have a good time, Jones was already suffering from serious health problems when he joined Wolf's band. He would play intermittently with Wolf until his early death from lung cancer in 1964.

"Little Baby" was a medium-paced rocker with tongue-in-cheek lyrics about how Wolf would look after his woman: "You bet the horses and I'll pick up the dough." Wolf sang this comedic confection with total conviction. Part of the credit goes to producer Ralph Bass. More interested in feel than technique, he strove to get the very best out of singers. "When I would produce Wolf or Muddy or Sonny [Boy] or whatever, I wouldn't stay in the control room. . . . Being in the studio was cold! I had to make them feel they had to give everything they had from inside and I would stay on top of them—right in front of them. And I would go, 'Come on! Come on!' The more I did that—they would really blow their asses off! Sang the shit out of the song!"[20]

"Down in the Bottom" was a driving Delta blues in the style of Willie Newbern's "Roll and Tumble Blues." Wolf had been singing variations on it as far back as the 1930s.[21] The band laid down a rhythm like a team of runaway mules as Wolf lathered jangly, down-home slide guitar on top. "On the record Wolf played slide guitar, bottleneck," Sumlin said. "Broke off a big ole bottleneck 'cause he couldn't find a slide."[22] Wolf bawled the autobiographical lyrics country blues style:

> *Well now, meet me in the bottom, bring me my runnin' shoes. (2×)*
> *When I come out the window, I won't have time to lose.*

Guitarist Sumlin started reaching his full potential on this session. Shy and unassuming, he had heretofore played largely in the background, lending sympathetic support to the other guitarists on Wolf's records. With guitarists as hot as Willie Johnson and Jody Williams, this wasn't a problem. By the early 1960s, though, Wolf wanted Hubert to develop his own sound and take over the lead guitar spot in the band.

Wolf publicly humiliated Sumlin to motivate him.[23] "Wolf told me to sit down—in front of about five hundred peoples," Sumlin said. "I never will forget it: the Key Largo, man, on Roosevelt Road there in Chicago. And hey, he fired me, and all them folks sitting up there looking at me. And he told me to come sit down and then called for another guitar player was in the audience. Told them I didn't know nothing about how to play no guitar at all. He said, 'Hey, go home. Take my advice. You go home. You get that shit straight. You know what I'm talking about? Put that pick down. You think I'm scolding you? You a grown man, Hubert—listen to me!' "[24]

Sumlin found the sound he needed late that night. "I went home, man. I went to my basement. And I'm going to tell you something: I couldn't sleep. I was thinking about what Wolf said. He said, 'Hey, put the picks down.' I put the picks down, man. I put the picks down and I started using all five fingers, you know what I mean? This is what happened."[25]

Sumlin had his sound, but he still needed Wolf's approval. "I put the picks down and I come back the next night and he helped me to play the last song. He called me, he said, 'Are you ready to play, old man?' I said, 'I ain't an old man! You an old man!' We always messing with the other! And he said, OK!' I never will forget it: 'I Asked for Water and She Brought Me Gasoline.' I could see that look in his eye, looking at me and then turning around so I think he ain't looking at me. He said one thing to me. 'Hubert, so you put the picks down.' And I said, 'Well, I like it.' He said, 'Yeah, you love it? I told you. You ain't even got my sound. You got your sound.' I said, 'You're darned tootin'!' And so from then on, man, that was it."[26]

Blues guitarist Bob Margolin said, "Hubert makes his own tone by the way he plays with his fingers, no matter what kind of guitar he uses. He brings out expressive harmonics and percussive accents, yelping slides up and kamikaze slides down. If you watch his fingers, they constantly go all over the neck, but he only actually picks a few notes—just the perfect ones. When he solos, he conceives lines and melodies rather than just stringing licks together. He's adventurous, humorous, and when he wants to be, heartbreakingly bluesy."[27]

With his guitar style blossoming, Sumlin's relationship with Wolf grew closer, musically and personally. "I found out I was closer to Wolf than a lot of musicians are to each other," Hubert observed. "I was by him like Spann was to Muddy Waters. I said, 'Hey, this is the man's voice, this is me.' The music and the voice. We got to be so close, like father and son, the way Eddie Taylor was with Jimmy Reed. Hubert was Wolf, Wolf was Hubert. That's the way we had it, that's the way it was. I got to where I knew what he wanted before he asked for it, because I could feel the man. I just did what came natural and it seemed to fit."[28] "I became the only one in the group he didn't come right down on and say, 'You didn't do this right,' because I could feel the man. Like we knowed what the other was going to do, what the other one was thinking. I never would get far away from him where I couldn't watch him, and we got to communicate so well that I knew what he was gonna do before he did. That's the way we were."[29]

The synergy between Wolf's voice and Hubert's guitar was magical, their teamwork unbeatable. Music writer Dan Forte wrote, "On electric guitar Sumlin's staccato attacks, extroverted slides, and unique style of playing fills, bass lines, and repeated riffs interspersed with only an occasional chord were perfect complements to Howlin' Wolf's rhythmic style and penchant for songs with no chord changes at all. Wolf's gravelly, demonic growl coupled with Sumlin's hypnotic riffs and occasional solo outbursts could only be described as haunting."[30] Comparing Hubert's playing to Willie Johnson's, Dick Shurman wrote, "Where Johnson brought fat, sustained swing chords and fluid single note work and buzzed like a chain saw, Sumlin was more like a whip, playing his leads in almost totally unconventional bursts and his chords in choppy patterns."[31] Luther Allison spoke for many Chicago blues guitarists when he said, "Hubert Sumlin . . . was behind Howlin' Wolf. And we, the guitar players, were all going, like, 'Wow!' when we see Hubert play, 'Wow!' 'Listen at this, man!' This guy was great."[32]

In June, Wolf was back in the studio with the same lineup as the month before. Once again he recorded just two songs, both credited to Dixon and both keepers. "Shake for Me" was a fast rocker that featured an angular guitar solo by Hubert, announcing once and for all that he was Wolf's lead guitarist—nobody else need apply. "I remember when we made 'Shake It for Me,'" Hubert said. "This was a number that really, I said, now, I had it. . . . This is the Wolf. This is the voice, hear the music."[33] Sam Lay pushes the song along by vigorously beating out a rhythm on a cowbell. Wolf lustily shouts out the lyrics, encouraging his baby to shake her ample charms. "Shake It for Me" got the ladies out on the dance floor in droves, whether Wolf played it in a Chicago club or a backwoods Mississippi juke joint.

Even better was "The Red Rooster," a slow, sly country blues with Wolf on acoustic slide guitar and Hubert on electric. Though the song was credited to Dixon, Charlie Patton cut "Banty Rooster Blues" in 1929 and white bluesman Cliff Carlisle "Shanghai Rooster Yodel" in 1931, both of which influenced Dixon's song. Wolf's stepsister Sadie remembered Wolf playing something like "The Red Rooster" in the 1930s.[34] Evelyn Sumlin said, "A bunch of the songs that Willie Dixon did over, Wolf had already did. But Willie Dixon took the credit for them."[35] Wolf's vocal is one of his best as he wrings everything out of the song's barnyard metaphor for desire:

> *I have a little red rooster, too lazy to crow for day.* (2×)
> *Keep everything in the barnyard, upset in every way.*

Both Sam Cooke and the Rolling Stones covered "The Red Rooster." Neither version packed quite the ribald wallop of Wolf's.

With hits on jukebox and radio, Wolf maintained an active schedule of live shows in Chicago and on the road. He often played the Key Largo on the West Side. Sam Lay said, "That was next door to a place that I didn't care to be next door to—the National Casket Factory." Wolf also played the Castle Rock and the Playhouse on the South Side.[36]

On the North Side, bluesman Little Hudson Showers had a run-in with Wolf at a club where they were both appearing. Showers got an enthusiastic response when he sang some of Wolf's songs such as "How Many More Years." "The crowd upgraded me so high that Wolf told me don't come back to his bandstand no more," said Showers. "He was a big man and I was a small man so I had to take him at his word, 'cause I couldn't whup him. I had to outrun him. And I had to kind of listen to what he had to say, so I just stayed away." Word of what Wolf did spread and attendance dropped off at the club for a few weeks. "They cared more for me because I was better-looking than he was," Showers said. "A couple of weeks later, he sent for me and told me I could come back and play anything I wanted to play."[37]

Silvio's remained the band's main club. Evelyn Sumlin, who worked at Silvio's whenever Wolf played there, knew the club's owner, Silvio Corroza. "He was real nice. I don't know what nationality he was, but he was just a real good guy. I worked for him when he was on Oakland and Lake, and I worked for him after he come to Kedzie and Lake, like I took pictures in the places and I worked the bar. I had a regular job. First, I was on night shift and I would work from ten till two o'clock or from ten until they closed. Then I got on day shift, and I had to sort of cut my hours and things. But he was always nice."

Silvio let Evelyn and Lillie use his place to raise money for their social club the Seven Vandellas, later called the Sophisticated Ladies. "My mom was a part of that, and Lillie, and—it was seven of us," Evelyn said. "This was like a Christmas saving club. We would go to the dog races. We'd get a bus and we'd charge so much to go to the dog races over in Wisconsin and to the casinos. The profits that came out—this was our Christmas money. At Christmas time, we would divide the money up and we would do our shopping." The ladies held special cocktail parties at Silvio's before Thanksgiving and Mother's Day to raise money. "So what he would do, he would pay half of the band. Wolf never would charge him, but we had to pay the band. So he would pay the half for the band, because that would bring him in revenue, and we would pay the other part. And he would give us all up until from the time we started until everything was over that night. And then he would put out all the publicity and then he would also have the tickets made. So he just a nice, outgoing guy."[38]

Wolf's prime touring territory outside of Chicago was still down South. He played a big show in Memphis: the WDIA Goodwill Revue at Ellis Auditorium, with B. B. King, Muddy Waters, and Ivory Joe Hunter also on the bill, a show to help raise money for the WDIA-sponsored black Little League. The crowd was full of children—not a typical Wolf audience. "Spoonful" was Wolf's big hit, and Sam Lay had bought a large soup spoon at a flea market for Wolf to use as a phallic symbol while doing the song.[39] Famed Memphis photographer Ernest Withers recalled what happened. "Well, he did that 'Spoonful' in a vulgar fashion, which was not apropos to a kid audience. Of course, now you get the same vulgarity on television all day long. But then, it just wasn't tolerated. They closed the curtains on him in order to discipline him. That was the only way to stop him because he got vulgar with the spoon."[40]

One crowd that loved Wolf no matter what he did was the Delta Kappa Epsilon fraternity at the University of Mississippi. The Dekes were the undefeated, untied, unscored-upon Goliaths of fraternity parties at Ole Miss and were well known for their love of black music. Little Milton, Irma Thomas, Muddy Waters, Slim Harpo, Jesse Hill, and King Mose and the Royal Rockers with Sam Myers all played for the Ole Miss Dekes in the early 1960s. Howlin' Wolf, though, had a special place in their hearts. "I guess out of everybody we ever booked, the Wolf was always the favorite there," said former Deke David Hervey. "And they would steal his harmonicas. I don't know how he could play the next gig 'cause they would always steal his harmonicas."[41]

Hervey grew up listening to black music on radio WESY in Leland, Mississippi, and often went to the station to meet the musicians his deejay friend, Rockin' Eddie Williams, interviewed. That's where Hervey met Wolf in 1960. A fan since hearing "Smokestack Lightnin' " on the radio, Hervey had never seen a picture of Wolf and was awed by his physical presence. "I was amazed by his size, and his head and his hands were so big. I was always amazed that he could play musical instruments with hands that big." He discovered how to book Wolf through Joe Glaser's Associated Booking Corporation, one of the largest bookers of black talent in the country.[42] Wolf agreed to play the Deke House for $375 a night if he was guaranteed three nights' work within driving distance. Hervey asked Rockin' Eddie to set up a show for Wolf in Greenville, Mississippi, and arranged a third night at the Flamingo Club in Tallulah, Louisiana, run by a man who called himself Po' Boy and had illegal slot machines.[43]

Wolf played in Greenville at the Elks Club. Perry Payton, who later owned the Flowing Fountain on Nelson Street, booked him. "He had a number out during that time called 'Spoonful,' " Payton said. "And he'd have his big, old spoon shaking it! Then he'd get on his knees with his mike and crawl all under the tables. Everybody go to hollerin'." Payton said Wolf outdrew B. B. King and Muddy Waters in Greenville. "Women loved the Wolf—really!"[44]

Ole Miss was strictly segregated when Wolf played the Deke House, and tensions were running high as James Meredith sought through the federal courts to become the first black student there. A bastion of Southern tradition in the quiet town of Oxford, Ole Miss had a football team called the Rebels, a mascot called Colonel Reb, and Confederate flags waving at its games as the school band played "Dixie." That blues bands like Wolf's were welcome at Ole Miss speaks to the complexity of Southern attitudes about race and to the true rebel spirit of the Dekes. Fraternity president Bill Morris, who grew up listening to black music on WOKJ in Jackson, Mississippi, said, "Yeah, we liked to heckle the campus. That was the nature of the Dekes—that we always were wanting to pull something that sort of shocked people and all."[45]

Wolf played for the Dekes after the Ole Miss homecoming football game on October 27, 1961, and again for a rush party at the Vicksburg Hotel in Vicksburg. Sam Lay, who played both gigs, said, "They rolled out the red carpet for us there."[46] The frat brothers would clear all the furniture out of the bottom floor for dancing at Deke shows. Admittance was by invitation only; the house held three hundred to four hundred revelers. One weekend the frat hired five bands to play—two at a time, one on the bottom floor and one on the roof.

Wolf's band members were treated well, and Wolf received special attention as Hervey's friend. "David was the son of a Delta planter, and

times, he'd even call Wolf's home at three or four o'clock in the morning. "If he was there, he would get up and talk to us," he said. "I remember one time his wife said, 'Well, he's gone squirrel hunting,' and we missed him." In the summer of 1963, Hervey hitchhiked across Europe with a folksinger friend and discovered that Wolf was well known in Europe: "In London numerous people asked me had I ever heard of Howlin' Wolf. And it blew their mind when I told them in the past year, we had booked him several times."[50] In a few years, many of these music fans, inspired by Wolf and other bluesmen, would revolutionize popular music in the Beat Boom—called the British Invasion in the United States.

Wolf's Southern gigs weren't all as cushy as at the Deke House. Many were in primitive backwoods jukes. One of the roughest was in Bastrop, Louisiana. "That was all black there," Lay said. "What tickled me—some of 'em come up on mules. And I had never been in a place where you go in there to use the washroom, and there's a lady on the commode, and here's two or three guys rollin' dice on the floor by the stool and the lady sittin' there on the toilet." (Talk about shooting craps!) In Mississippi, the band played for the door at a juke and made just 50 cents each because it was bitterly cold outside. Lay said, "Henry Gray—well, he's the first piano player I ever seen could sit up and play with an overcoat and mitts on."

Lay was delighted when he played for family and friends in Birmingham at a big show that also featured Muddy Waters. The next night, in Montgomery, Muddy's band failed to show, and the disappointed crowd grew hostile when Wolf refused to let a local deejay sit in on harp. Some men broke the tops off quart beer bottles and threatened the band. The band was about to beat a retreat when a lone white cop with a wad of tobacco in his mouth sauntered in and said, "What the hell goin' on in here?" Lay said, "You ain't heard a sound. If anybody's stomach had growled, you would've heard it. The place cleared out just like when Moses walked out and God made the Red Sea part.

"The policeman said, 'You boys get your stuff loaded up. I'll stay right here with you. Don't worry about a thing.' 'Yes sir,' we said. And we got the stuff loaded up and he stood there when we come out behind the club. They had us over in a yard and had the gate locked. Somebody went out there and unlocked the gate and let the station wagon out. He

he came to Ole Miss in a Corvette, and he didn't make good-enough grades," Morris said, laughing. "His daddy punished him and gave him a red Buick convertible. David had a bar in the back seat set up in sort of a console kind of thing."[47] Hervey had fun with the staid sensibilities at Ole Miss. "I remember one time the Wolf was coming through, and we had him for homecoming. I had a 1960 Buick convertible, and I put the Wolf in the back seat with his guitar player, and we had the top down and I gave him a tour of the campus there. Of course, all the alumni were there and here was this guy, three hundred pounds with a giant head, sitting in the back. They couldn't believe it! They didn't know what was going on. When I was riding him through the Grove up there before the homecoming game, I would see some of 'em with a piece of chicken almost to their mouth and they'd just pause when they saw him come by. Who'd ever seen a three-hundred-pound black guy, back before integration, and some white dude chauffeuring him around in a convertible?"

The alumni were even more shocked when they attended an afternoon tea dance at the Deke House after the game. "First time I saw him, he brought out that big cooking spoon that he had when he would sing 'Spoonful,' " Hervey said. "And all the alumni and their wives were over there at the house and Wolf was singing 'Spoonful' and he got that spoon down there around his private parts, waving it at 'em. The alumni literally couldn't believe it. They had never seen anything like it!"[48] That Wolf would perform a suggestive song in front of white women in Mississippi in 1961 was either breathtakingly reckless or insanely courageous. Just five years earlier, Emmett Till, age fourteen, was brutally murdered for saying, "Bye, baby!" to a white woman in the state.

The danger of playing for white folks was all too apparent to Wolf's band. At the Vicksburg Hotel show, they were warming up the crowd with Ray Charles's "What'd I Say" when a drunk woman sat down on the piano bench next to Gray. "It just scared that poor boy to death!" Lay said. "I said, 'Uh-oh, this poor boy fixin' to have a heart attack.' " Trying to play without touching her, Gray slid over as far as he could on the bench, sweat pouring off his brow, though the room was air-conditioned. Fortunately for the future of blues piano, the woman's boyfriend pulled her away to dance as if nothing had happened.[49]

After he left Ole Miss, Hervey stayed in contact with Wolf. Some-

said, 'See you boys.' Ain't nobody touched us. That one old policeman come in there, man, I don't know—he must have been Matt Dillon or somethin' around that town."[51]

In December 1961, Wolf recorded four songs—three written by Dixon—at one of his best sessions ever. The band was the same as on the previous session except for Henry Gray on piano. "You'll Be Mine" was a fast rocker driven by Gray's excellent keyboard work, Lay's rapid-fire drumming, and Sumlin's spiky guitar solo. Wolf declares his love for his baby with utter abandon.

Even better was Wolf's version of St. Louis Jimmy Oden's "Goin' Down Slow," a mournful blues first recorded in 1941. The lyrics were deeply personal. Wolf's voice sounded anguished as he begged his mother to forgive him. Comic spoken interludes by Dixon contrasted with Wolf's tormented singing, their difference in timbre adding to the surreal tone of the tragic tune. Gray jabbed at the keys in staccato bursts as Sumlin added spooky guitar cries and whispers to counterpoint Wolf's grief-stricken pleas:

> *Please write my mama.*
> *Tell her the shape I'm in.*
> . . . .
>
> *Tell her to pray for me:*
> *Forgive me for my sin.*

"Just Like I Treat You" was a stomping Delta blues in the style of "Down in the Bottom." Wolf shouted his vocals lustily over a swaggering rhythm by Gray and Lay, accompanying himself on acoustic slide guitar. Darting all over the neck of his guitar, Sumlin added accents, flourishes, and bursts of notes. "I Ain't Superstitious" was a slow stop-time blues, typical of Dixon, with a repeated rhythm riff and a strong Wolf vocal. The lyrics, full of fear and mojo, were ideal for Wolf:

> *Well, I ain't superstitious, black cat just cross my trail.* (2×)
> *Don't sweep me with no broom, I might get put in jail.*
> *When my right hand itches, I get some money for sure.* (2×)
> *But when my left eye jump, somebody got to go.*

On January 11, 1962, Chess released Wolf's second album, titled simply *Howlin' Wolf*—better known as "The Rocking Chair Album" because its cover showed a cheap acoustic guitar leaning against a rocking chair. The plain cover didn't hint at the riches within. Composed mostly of Wolf's hits from the previous few years ("Spoonful," "The Red Rooster," "Shake for Me," and "Goin' Down Slow," among others), the album has been hailed by blues fans and critics as one of the greatest blues albums ever released.[52] This album, of all of Wolf's work, most influenced the rock generation of the 1960s.

In the liner notes, Ralph Bass wrote that Secretary of State Dean Rusk had recently asked Wolf to perform at the First International Jazz Festival in Washington, D.C. The lineup for this festival at the Washington Coliseum on June 1, 1962, included Lionel Hampton, Cannonball Adderley, Sonny Rollins, Dinah Washington, Marion Williams, the Staple Singers, and Wolf—the only bluesman on the bill. It led to the often repeated but erroneous story that Wolf once played at the White House for President John F. Kennedy.

In the sweltering heat of the Coliseum, Wolf performed in his usual over-the-top style for the well-dressed crowd, even using the big spoon the way Lay intended.[53] His performance came as a shock to many. Most of the crowd didn't know his music, and he was hampered by a bad sound system.[54] Blues fan Dick Lillard said, "I can still see in my mind's eye the Wolf leaping on stage, seemingly on all fours . . . and his band working their butts off. He was the reason I had come, but many in the audience seemed genuinely taken aback and lots of tuxedoed and gowned people (no joke) got up and walked off. I ran over to where the Wolf stood perspiring off stage just after he did his last number and told him how great I thought he was. He seemed somewhat upset and wanted reassurance that he'd gone over OK. I could be wrong, but I thought I sensed a hurt look in his eye."[55]

After the show, Wolf and the band drove back to Chicago for another series of home gigs. As always, the band's personnel was changing. Francis Clay drummed for Wolf briefly. An erudite man and a sophisticated drummer, Clay had played with Muddy since 1957, but Muddy fired him—partly because of Wolf. "It's pretty widely known that Wolf and Little Walter got Muddy to fire me," Clay said, laughing. "They kept telling Muddy that I wasn't a blues drummer, that I didn't like the blues, so why doesn't he get rid of me? So they kept it up until Muddy fired me. But as soon as Muddy fired me, they both sent for me to play with their bands!"

Clay enjoyed the couple of months he played for Wolf. "It was great," he said. "I liked the cats in the band and I liked the way they played. Matter of fact, he gave me more freedom than Muddy did. Whatever I felt, he was happy whenever I'd throw him something different. He'd smile. He liked it. I guess if I did something distasteful, he would've hollered, but no, we got along fine. . . . He was always calm and soft-spoken, in my book. Sometimes he'd get loud. I mean, he sang loud and he talked loud with that big voice of his. But I never saw him get rowdy or angry."[56]

Bassist Nick Charles met Wolf in the fall of 1961 at a club in Greenville, Mississippi. Nick hung out with Wolf's band when they came to town. Wolf heard about him and one night invited him to sit in. For the teenaged musician, it was a huge thrill. "The first time I played with him," Nick said, "he'd just put you in a trance the way he'd be singing and moanin', playing. And that voice! This guy, he just had that—that moanin', I mean: Like a preacher! You could feel that through the floor, especially with those wooden floors."

Nick's excitement increased when he got to spend time with Wolf after the show. "When I first met him, I was kind of scared to go to his room. Sam Lay said, 'Come on—let's meet the Wolf.' I got his autograph, too, on one of the posters I took off the door. Oh, I was happy then! I kept telling everybody, 'Look, the Wolf—I went to his room.' 'Yeah, right.' But the next day, everybody in Greenville knew I played with him. I heard them talk about it, even on the radio."

In February 1962, Eddie Shaw called to offer Nick a job with Wolf's band. Nervous about moving to Chicago, Nick reluctantly agreed, but stayed only until the end of March; the bitter winter weather was too much for him. Wolf treated Nick like a son, but also made clear who was in charge. "He meant business," Nick stated. "When it was show time, you gonna be there in uniform. If you come and didn't have your tie on, he'd say, 'Well son—you're goin' to buy the band a drink tonight, huh?' 'I couldn't find it.' 'That's all right. Thanks for looking out for the band!' If you making $35, he might take $20 or $10. You might say, 'What's this for?' He'd say, 'You tell me now. You come in late?' 'Oh.'

He'd be there like, say, an hour before, get a good chair and sit down or get by the bar and talk. If you come in late, just sit up there if you can and he don't say nothin' about it. But you would know about it at the end of the night!"[57]

Wolf's regular bass player at this time was Jerome Arnold, the younger brother of Billy Boy. Jerome was talented but nasty. "The trouble with Jerome was Jerome," Lay said. "He was just a plain trouble-maker. If there was any way he could squeeze a dollar out of you, he would try it. He felt he was more than he really was. Anybody he could make a fool out of or say somethin' to hurt somebody, he would do it and it did him all the good in the world to see it. . . . If I had Jerome Arnold, I'd trade him for a dog—and I'd kill that dog."[58]

Born in Chicago in 1936, Jerome got his start playing in Billy Boy's band before playing for Otis Rush. Wolf lured Jerome away from Rush by offering him steadier work. Playing with Wolf was the big time in blues, but Jerome chafed at his rules. "He's a hard taskmaster and fines the band for anything that might occur to him, for dress, for playing wrong notes or socializing with the opposite sex too much in public," Jerome said of Wolf. "You can't push musicians, who are often neurotic and sensitive, around like that, especially these days."[59]

But Jerome's brother defended Wolf's leadership. "See, Wolf wasn't one of those guys like Little Walter—spaced out, drunk, falling out himself, and he didn't tolerate that in none of his musicians," said Billy Boy. "If you wanted a job with Wolf, you had to be on your toes, and do the right thing! All he asked you to do was come to work and play—and that's what he was paying you for."[60] Evelyn Sumlin agreed. "Wolf was a man that what he said, he meant it. . . . He didn't allow drinking on his bandstand. He didn't allow women up to his bandstand. He was just down-to-earth. He was a businessman. He did his job, and he didn't want people to go out and say, 'Well, Wolf was here, his band was drunk.' He didn't want people to say, 'Well, Wolf was here, but women was all over him.' He didn't allow that. That's the kind of man he was."[61]

Typical of Wolf's no-nonsense work ethic was his passion for self-education. "He was a man that believed in advancing himself," said Billy Boy. Still barely literate and numerate in the 1950s, Wolf confronted the problem in his direct way: He took adult education classes in reading, writing, and arithmetic. During the late 1950s and early 1960s, he attended adult classes at Crane High School on the West Side. During the mid-1960s, he attended Wendell Phillips High School on the South Side, and during the late 1960s and early 1970s, he went to Jones Commercial Evening School in the Loop. He achieved a sixth-grade reading and writing proficiency and was able to do basic math, which helped him tremendously on the road.[62]

As with his music lessons, Wolf took his 3Rs very seriously. During intermissions at Silvio's, Billy Boy often saw him sitting at a table with his schoolbooks, doing his homework. "When he put on his glasses, he looked like a professor," said Billy Boy. S. P. Leary said, "He was funny, man, when he was learning how to read. He'd have you read something to him as we traveled up and down the road, and you reading so fast, he would stop and say, 'Now what did you get out of that?' He wants to know if you learned anything from the passage that you read. Yeah, you better come up with something, too! That's right! 'Cause he'd say, 'What, are you educated? Read somethin' and you reading fast as light-nin' and then you can't explain what you mean. What was the conver-sation about? What was the text of the story?' " Eddie Shaw often helped Wolf read. "If we leaving here driving to Boston, he'd have a book and I got one," said Shaw. "Hubert be driving and I'd be teaching him. We'd be spelling words and I'd go to sleep and he'd cuss me out and wake me up. Raise hell with me, but he was always my friend, man."[63]

On September 28, 1962, Wolf cut four more songs written by Dixon, but this time, they were definitely a mixed bag. With the exception of Sumlin and Gray, the band was different from the previous session — Arnold on bass, Junior Blackmon on drums, and J. T. Brown and an unknown musician on tenor saxes. "Mama's Baby" was a forgettable novelty tune with banal lyrics like "You're mama's baby but your daddy's maybe." Wolf did his best, but even he couldn't float this sinking ship. "Do the Do" seemed just as inconsequential lyrically, but through some alchemy its elements coalesced to produce a primitive, tongue-in-cheek delight. Over belching saxophones, tom-tom drumming, and Sumlin's brilliantly off-kilter guitar, Wolf sang its bawdy lyrics with fervor enough to make anyone want to grab hold and enjoy the ride.

"Long Green Stuff" was about a favorite Wolf topic — money. But where most of Wolf's songs about money were powerful statements about the impact of money on relationships, "Long Green Stuff" was a novelty song. Thankfully for Wolf, it was not released at the time.

The highlight of the session was "Tail Dragger," a slow, sonic burlesque full of bleating saxes, twittering piano, squawking guitar, and a snare drum dragging along way behind the beat like a snake in late November. "Tail Dragger" was the perfect soundtrack for the onstage antics of the prowling Wolf. He sang and winked his way through the bucolic lyrics, a sly bestiary of rustic references to chicks and fish and cooters (a variety of painted turtle found in the South):

> A cooter drags his tail in the sand. A fish wiggles his tail in the water.
> When the mighty Wolf come along draggin' his tail, he done stole
>   somebody's daughter.

Brilliantly suited to him though the song was, Wolf had a hard time getting its words right. "Wolf was kind of hard-headed," Gray said. "Once he set his mind to doing something one way, it was hard to get him to do it any other way. . . . He kept singing 'I'm a tail dragger, I swipes out my tracks.' That drove Leonard crazy. He kept stopping us and yelling, 'Damn Wolf. You don't swipe out your tracks. You *wipe* out your tracks!' It took us over a dozen takes before Wolf got the words right."[64]

One of Wolf's closest friends was Chicago deejay Big Bill Hill. A native of Arkansas, Hill was well known for broadcasting live from blues clubs over radio station WOPA. He also booked Wolf's band through his Colt .45 agency.[65] One Sunday night at a club, Hill used his friendship with Wolf to get back at Sam Lay, whom he thought was pursuing his girlfriend. "I didn't want his woman 'cause his woman looked like he did," Sam said. Earlier that day, Lay had played a matinee gig with Little Smokey Smothers at the Blue Flame. While leaving, he tore his black tuxedo pants on a trash can. Hurrying home, he put on some suit pants that lacked a black stripe down the side but otherwise looked the same. Lay went to his gig with Wolf at the Key Largo and hoped to get by unnoticed.

Everything seemed to go well until it came time to get paid. Wolf told Lay he was out of uniform and fined him $10. "He let me sit up

there all night and play and didn't tell me," Lay said. "Okay if you goin'
to pay me $12.50 and take $10 of it, let me play for a few minutes and
give me $2.50 and then you keep the ten, I'll go on home. Don't make
me sit there and play all night and pay me half of my money. Why you
ain't goin' to pay me all my money, but I did all of your work? No, we
don't play that!"

Getting Lay angry was unwise, since he packed a snub-nosed .38.
Wolf, too, carried a pistol but didn't hold on to it at gigs. "When he
come in, what Wolf would do is open the cylinder, take the bullets and
stick 'em in his pocket, and hand the gun to the club owner," Lay said.
"He didn't want it in his possession while he was there."

Encouraged by Hill, Wolf exchanged heated words with Lay about
the fine. "He jumps all up and bangs on the table," Lay said. "So when
he did, I just stepped back from him a couple of steps. Then Bill Hill
stood up, too. And I looked behind, and there's Hubert standin' there,
and then there's Hubert's wife. They all would take up for Wolf. I didn't
know nothing else to do. I just whipped that snub out and cocked that
hammer back. Everybody broke and run. There was a little curtain with
a thing looked like a window. They climbed up on the table, him and
Wolf both, and when they opened the curtains, weren't nothin' but a
brick wall there. It was just decoration. I said, 'Where you goin' to run to
now?' They were huggin' each other and one was tryin' to hide behind
the other. And my money and stuff was still layin' there on the table, so
I reached down there and got my other $10 and I left. A couple of days
later, I went back and got my drums."

Lay played with Magic Sam for a few months until Wolf came to
see him at his apartment building one day. The two talked in the lobby
and Wolf told him how much he liked him and his drumming. "He
didn't ask me, 'You want to come back and play with me?' You know
what he asked me? He tells me, 'You got a clean white shirt and still got
your uniform?' I said, 'Yeah, Wolf. I still got it. I didn't have no reason to
get rid of it.' " Lay was back in the band.[66]

In July 1963, Wolf recorded live at Big Bill's Copa Cabana club.
Backed by Buddy Guy's band, Wolf did two songs that Chess released
on its Argo album *Folk Festival of the Blues*.[67] Guy, a hot young guitarist
who recorded for Chess and played in the West Side style, provided

stinging guitar on "Sugar Mama" and "May I Have a Talk with You." Wolf's vocals on both were powerful and "Sugar Mama" showed off his harp on record for the first time in years.

Wolf was back in the studio on August 14 to cut four more songs written by Dixon—the last time they would collaborate on new material. Besides Sumlin, the band included Lay on drums, Buddy Guy on bass, Lafayette Leake on piano, J. T. Brown on tenor sax, and Donald Hankins on baritone sax.

Dixon provided great songs for the session. "Built for Comfort" was a medium-paced shuffle about the benefits of loving a man of size. Lay's drumming was beautifully restrained but driving, Wolf's vocal was wonderfully funny, and Hubert added impish guitar—another example of his playing brilliance.

Even better was "Three Hundred Pounds of Joy," which was coupled with "Built for Comfort" as Chess 1870. Dixon wrote both for himself, but they were ideally suited to Wolf.[68] Over barking saxes and Lay's clever rhythm, Wolf turned the song into a roaring delight—the sonic equivalent of hippos sashaying around in pink tutus. Sumlin skittered across the strings as Wolf sang about being the big man of every woman's dreams.

"Hidden Charms," first recorded by Charles Clarke, was a clever pop tune on which Wolf recounted his woman's invisible but ample graces with obvious relish. With a tricky off-beat that would've stumped a lesser singer plus Sumlin's spectacular guitar, the charms of this cut were manifest. The highpoint? Wolf yelled, "Get it!" and Sumlin launched into one of the wildest solos of his or any bluesman's career. Playing a careening, hyperspeed solo full of hiccups and glissandos against an already zippy beat, he arrived back in time for an accented chop-chord before a half-note rest at the exact same instant as the band—leaving any listener with ears gasping in astonishment.

"Joy to My Soul" was a light pop tune that, unlike "Hidden Charms," never quite gelled, though Sumlin's guitar was again terrific. The song was not released at the time.

Wolf's musical relationship with Dixon was often testy, but the records they co-created became the classics that are remembered first when one thinks of either man. Sumlin was at his peak as a guitarist, creating one amazing solo after another, each unique and perfectly suited to the song. By the early 1960s, Wolf's popularity in Chicago clubs and Southern jukes alike was unrivaled, especially by Muddy Waters.

"The people, the crowd liked Wolf," said Billy Boy Arnold. "He was working when Muddy Waters couldn't even get a job around Chicago. . . . Wolf played on the South Side in clubs like on 63rd that were a little more sophisticated. Wolf could play there but Muddy couldn't get a gig out there because the type of music Muddy was playing was mostly slow. But Wolf played upbeat music and he was aggressive, his band was a more swinging band. And when Muddy stopped recording 78s and 45s, Wolf kept recording. That's when he made all those hits with Hubert—'Spoonful' and all that stuff, 'The Red Rooster'—all those were hits. Muddy had stopped making hits for some years then."[69] Soon people across the ocean would discover what Chicago and the South knew: Wolf was sitting on top of the blues world.

11. Sittin' on Top of the World

Johnny Littlejohn never recorded with Howlin' Wolf, but he was a vital member of Wolf's band for years. A dazzling slide guitarist heavily influenced by Elmore James, Littlejohn could also pick the blues with the best of them. His versatility and professionalism made him popular on the Chicago blues scene. Wolf's new bass player, Andrew "Blueblood" McMahon, told Wolf about Littlejohn's guitar skills, and Wolf went to see him about filling in for Hubert. "Wolf come where I was playing at one night somewhere down on Michigan," Littlejohn recalled. "He said, 'Well, I don't think I can hire you full time, 'cause I see you got your own little thing, but I'd like to use you. I've got a pretty good old guitar player, but he has a fucked-up mind sometimes—can't get along. See, I've been in the army and I'm shell-shocked and I'm nervous. . . . As long as you do what I ask you to do, you'll never have no problem out of me.' "

Hubert resented Littlejohn for taking his place. "He would get mad because when he quit, I'd go and help Wolf out," Littlejohn said. "I told him, 'Man, the man's music got to go on. He ain't goin' to let you stop him. That ain't no way to act, man! You can't play with him, let somebody else play with him, motherfucker! You look like a fool gettin' mad with me!' " Littlejohn wasn't unhappy that he didn't get to record with Wolf. "That would've looked like I had been rooting Hubert out."[1]

Like most musicians who played with Wolf, Littlejohn grew to admire him. "Wolf was one of the nicest black men I ever worked for in my life, but you just had to understand his ways. You know he was a country boy. . . . He tried to treat you as best as he could. Anything he had, he would let me have it if I made like I wanted it."[2]

But Littlejohn had to follow Wolf's rules. "He'd tell you, 'Say look man, I know you're goin' to have you a drink, but don't let me see it! Don't let the public see it! Get you a bottle and put it in your pocket. Go somewhere and sit down. Go out there to the van or somewhere like that and go get you a drink. But this staggering all over the tables and stuff like that with the parties and drinkin' with dancers—naw, that ain't goin' to work.' He'd tell 'em this before they started playing, and they do what he don't want them to do and it would make him angry."[3]

When Wolf got angry, he could be harsh verbally and physically, in public or private. Littlejohn witnessed an incident at the Castle Rock in Chicago when Henry Gray, nicknamed "Birdbreath" because his chest was round like a robin's breast, got too drunk to play. "Birdbreath liked to drink. He started tasting off that bottle. So Wolf say, 'Man, I want you to finish the night. I don't want you setting up there getting drunk and all the people looking at you.' Birdbreath say, 'Well, I'll just tell you, Wolf: I'll just get my shit and go home.' Wolf said, 'You can go home,' and he walked over and unplugged Birdbreath's mike. So Wolf watched Birdbreath fold his piano up and everything and waited 'til he got to the door. He had everybody watching. Birdbreath fell when he got near the door 'cause that piano was heavy. Wolf said into the mike, 'Look over yonder, y'all. There goes one of my slick new uniforms out the door. When he come drifting to me, he was raggedy as a flea-loft. And look at him now, all dressed up nice.' Boy, that house went apart laughing."[4]

Sam Lay also felt Wolf's stinging tongue. "Wolf could say things sometimes, and you'd think, 'Jesus Christ! If this man opens his mouth again, the walls of Jericho will tumble down.' " Lay recalled a particularly harsh tongue-lashing from Wolf. "I'm sitting there, tears streaming down my face. Wolf was puttin' me in the dozen about my mama. He was mad about something, and I wouldn't open my mouth and say nothin' back. I wasn't scared of him, but I just respected him. . . . But Henry Gray took it up and told him, 'Wolf, I don't like to dip in your business, but you ought to be ashamed of yourself.' Birdbreath did, 'cause he was used to Wolf cussin' him out. And Wolf lit in on him, too. And I kept hitting him, telling him, 'Man, shut up! Don't say nothin'! Don't say nothin'!' " Getting in trouble with Wolf didn't bother the taciturn Gray. "If I had the money that Wolf done fined Birdbreath, I would be rich," Lay said with a laugh. "I'd be the Howlin' Wolf!"[5]

Littlejohn also witnessed an altercation between Wolf and drummer Junior Blackmon. Wolf had his huge hand raised to hit Blackmon, who begged, "Mr. Wolf, don't hit me now! Don't you hit me now, Mr. Wolf!" In mid-swing, Blackmon pulled out a .22 caliber pistol he'd bought that very day, and Wolf's hand froze in midair. Wolf said, "Oh boy, I was just playin' with you." Littlejohn said, "Wolf talked nice that night because he found out Junior had that pistol."[6]

Guns were common on the Chicago blues scene, and many members of Wolf's band carried them. Lay had an unusual fondness for pistols, even after accidentally blowing off one of his testicles with one. Wolf sent Henry home early one night at a West Side club for being drunk. Lay, who'd also been drinking, feared he'd be next, so he slammed his pistol down on a table, causing it to fire.

Wolf said, "Man, what you got a gun on you for?" Then he turned to Littlejohn, who carried a .38 automatic in his guitar case, and said, "I ain't got no gun, man. I want you to shoot him in the chest! I'll get you out of jail. Don't try to kill him. Just wing him!" That got Lay's attention. "So Sam settled down," Littlejohn said. "Wolf told him that he got to find him another job. 'I don't work with guys that got a gun on 'em.' So Sam Lay and his old lady begged me [to help get Lay's job back]. Said he don't know what made him get a drink that night. And from that day to this one I never seen him take a drink—clean Sam Lay. . . . I'd've shot him. I wouldn't've tried to kill him. I would've shot him in the arm or leg or somewhere."[7]

Wolf also got into a fight with bluesman Albert King, a burly left-handed guitarist who was almost as physically imposing as the Wolf. A master at bending strings to get his unique sound, King was, like Wolf, a tough bandleader who took no guff. The two respected each other.

"He and Albert King was always in cahoots," Evelyn Sumlin said.

"They loved to play against each other. To me, they were more of the lovely type together than any blues band I saw. Because he played with a lot of blues bands, but a lot of them would kind of do things to get his band's attention and drinking so that they could steal his show. But Albert King was just a different person from that. He'd always tell Wolf, 'I'm gonna cut your head tonight, Wolf. I'm gonna cut your head tonight!' Wolf say, 'Oh, man. I wanna see that!' And Wolf would end up taking his show. Albert would end up saying, 'Well, wait till I get to Chicago. When I get to Chicago, I'm gonna cut your head.' But he knows that he could never do that because Wolf knew what he was doing."[8]

Their normally good-natured rivalry turned to violence one night at a club in East St. Louis. "Wolf was hitting at Albert King," Littlejohn said. "Man, them two guys looked like dinosaurs together! Me and Sam Lay, we done got 'em apart. Wolf hit him but he skated me on the shoulder goin' across me to him. It jerked a knot in my neck. . . . I had to leave and go to the hospital." As for Albert, "He hit that floor, man! He hit the floor! He got up. Shook his head. 'Huh!' And he flew back into him. Wolf knocked him down again. Then when Wolf knocked him down, he rolled over and grabbed Wolf. And him and Wolf fought like two dinosaurs, man. Tore each other's clothes off. We got 'em together and then got 'em apart."[9]

Life was a bit calmer for Wolf at home. Wolf and Lillie lived happily together for seven years before deciding to marry. "Wolf and I, we got along real good and then in '64, we got lawfully married," Lillie said. "It took a long time."[10] On March 14, 1964, Judge James C. Soper joined Wolf and Lillie in a simple civil ceremony, chosen to keep their marriage private, though the news soon leaked to the newspapers.[11] Lillie said, "I married him to help him, because that is what he needed, and I'm so happy I did. . . . Wolf always said, 'I wished I had had you the first day I ever howled.' "[12]

Evelyn said, "The years that Lillie and he was together, he got a chance to really enjoy his life and know what life was about. He didn't have to stay in a broke-down house. He didn't have to wear something that he didn't want to wear. He had whatever he wanted to wear if he wanted to wear it. He had whatever he wanted to eat. And he could go where he wanted to go. That was left up to him. And he had somebody there to really enjoy his life with. Because she was much younger than he was, but deep down within, she took good care of him. She took really good care of him. And vice versa, he took good care of her. She could come and go just like he did. Not in the streets, but goin' back and forth to see her family and so forth and so on. When her mother got sick she didn't have to worry about money to get there because he was goin' to see that she had money to do what she had to do."[13]

"Wolf wouldn't have had anybody that wasn't first-class," Billy Boy Arnold said. "She was a very first-class lady. All of the musicians liked her and respected her."[14] Producer Ralph Bass admired Wolf for being one of the few blues musicians he worked with who was a good family man. Bass felt closer to Wolf than to any of the other bluesmen at Chess.[15]

In 1963, Wolf bought a lot at 829 East 88th Street on the South Side, where he had a stylish new brick bungalow built for Lillie. "He wanted her to have a house," Evelyn said. "So they went out and looked around and picked a spot where she wanted to have it built, and he had it built."[16] Wolf got the idea for a furnished basement from Reggie Boyd's home. Down in his den, he could listen to music, practice his guitar, take a nap, entertain friends at the built-in bar, or just be by himself. Lillie said, "He wanted to be to himself, which he needed at times."

The house cost $30,000, a lot of money in 1964, and the couple signed a thirty-year mortgage. A year after they moved in, Wolf asked Lillie why they were making a monthly house payment. He insisted that they pay off the mortgage as soon as possible, which they did the next year.

Leonard Chess learned that they'd paid off their house note and asked Lillie why they hadn't come to him for help. "He said, 'Why didn't you let me know? I would've bought it for you.' I said, 'Wolf didn't need you to buy it for him.' " Wolf shrewdly figured that if Leonard had bought his house, he'd pay for it for years from his record royalties—perhaps long after the original amount with interest had been paid.

Wolf was too proud to ask for advances from the Chess brothers. Lillie talked to the head secretary at Chess when she and Wolf went to see where he recorded. "She says, 'Why, look who's coming! You know what, Mrs. Wolf? He's the only man that I'll be glad to see come through that door out of all the musicians. You know why? When I look up and see him, I know he's not coming to beg.' "

Wolf didn't go begging with hat in hand, but he always had money for friends and even rivals in need. Wolf helped pay for Little Walter's funeral in 1968, though he'd been disgusted by Walter's drinking and drug use. Wolf also helped Muddy Waters, who was anything but thrifty. "Muddy would have to come to Wolf for money," Lillie said. "Oh yes! I'm a living witness. I know." Wolf even helped Muddy pay for the funeral of his wife, Geneva, in 1973.[17]

Though Wolf never lived ostentatiously, Lillie also deserved credit for managing their finances wisely. Wolf would bring money home from club dates and tell Lillie to pay the bills, take some out for herself, and put the rest in the bank, where it would draw interest. The money she kept was hers to do with as she pleased. Geneva Morganfield told Lillie she wished Muddy treated her half as well.[18]

"Wolf was the type that wanted me to have what I wanted," Lillie said. "I'd say sometimes, 'I want something—so and so.' He'd say, 'I don't even know what you're talking about, but you get it.' If I needed something done around the house, he'd say, 'Call someone.' They'd come and I'd say, 'Wolf, the guy's here.' He'd say, 'Baby, you just pay attention.' . . . That's just the way he was. He wanted me to learn about what had to be done around the house because he stayed gone a lot." Wolf also wanted to make sure that no other man came snooping around his door. "I never had to ask him for anything and didn't get it," Lillie said. "He always said, 'Well, if I don't do it, I know damn well somebody else will!' "[19]

Wolf had other faults as a husband, though. "He was very jealous," Lillie said. "I couldn't go out with him for a long, long time because every time we'd go out together he'd see more than I'd see. He'd say, 'I know he was looking at you,' and I'd say, 'Aw, I didn't see anything.' He'd say things like 'Lillie, look like you going to get away from me in spite of it all.' "[20]

Blues harpist Little Arthur Duncan said, "Over on Wentworth one night, some guy kept on appealing on his wife. Wolf got up and wiped his guitar off and told him, 'Come here, buddy! Now I'm Mr. Wolf, and that's Mrs. Wolf. Two things I ain't never had enough of, and that's ass and sweet potatoes. Now you keep on fuckin' with Mrs. Wolf, I'm goin' to get one of the two. If you ain't got no sweet potatoes, I'm goin' to get that ass!' And that guy went on and sat down."[21] Another night at a club, Wolf knocked a man out for getting fresh with Lillie.[22]

Blues singer Koko Taylor saw Wolf's better side when she met him in the early 1960s. Born in Memphis in 1935, Taylor was working as a maid in Chicago when her husband approached Wolf one night at Silvio's. "I happened to go in this particular night where Howlin' Wolf was at playing with his band, and my husband said to him, 'My wife can sing. She loves to sing.' Howlin' Wolf said, 'Well, let her come on up here. Come up here, gal, and do a tune with us.' And that's what I did. Got on up there and did a song with the Howlin' Wolf and his band. Yeah, an old song by Tina Turner called 'I Idolize You.' And the other one was an old song by Brook Benton: 'Make Me Feel Good Kiddio.' Those were the first two songs I ever sung onstage."

Wolf was an inspiration to the novice blues chanteuse. "I loved him," Taylor said. "Howlin' Wolf and Muddy Waters was my biggest influence and my idols. All through the years, they was my number one idols. . . . Wolf was a lot of inspiration to me. He'd always say, 'Gal, you know you could sing!' He was very encouraging. . . . His music was always first for him. He wanted to make sure it was right. He wanted to make sure the musicians was on top of what they was supposed to do and how they was supposed to do. . . . I learned a lot from being around him, listening to him talk and the way he do his shows. His audience, his fans always came first. They were first on the list. When I say I got a lot of tips from him that's what I meant. Because right today my fans is number one with me. That's what I learned from Howlin' Wolf."[23] The undisputed Queen of Chicago Blues learned her lessons well.

Drummer Robert "Huckleberry Hound" Wright played with Wolf for a month in 1964, getting the gig with the help of pianist Johnny Jones, who'd played with Wright in Magic Sam's band. Wright admired Wolf, but didn't get to know him well. "He stuck to himself until we got our instruments out," Wright said. "I was young, and I was a ladies' man, and when he went to the bandstand, if you were talkin' to some lady and you didn't come onstage when he wanted you to, he'd say, 'Come on, man, quit gettin' your romance on the gigs. Get your romance after the gig.' Other than that, he was cool."

Wright enjoyed watching Wolf from behind the drum kit. "Well, he'd freak you out. He bug his eyes, roll in the floor, lay on his back, crawl on the floor, imitate a crawlin' king snake while he was blowin' the harp and singing. He'd make you laugh while he was playing." Wright saw a particularly memorable performance. "One time they were playing during a blues festival out on the West Side and they were lookin' for Wolf—calling for him to be onstage. Well, they started hearing his harp blowin', but they couldn't see him and they didn't know where he was. He had climbed up in a tree, and he was blowin' his harp as he climbed down. That freaked everybody out! They had never seen nothin' like that before. He tore 'em up that day."[24]

In August 1964, British blues fan Frank Scott traveled to Chicago, meeting Bob Koester, owner of the Jazz Record Mart and Delmark Records, who took him out to the clubs. Their first stop was Pepper's Lounge to see Junior Wells and Fenton Robinson. At midnight, they went across town to Silvio's to catch Wolf's last set. Scott wrote, "His act was certainly something to see, he's one whale of a performer. His band, apart from Hubert Sumlin, was pretty bad, but Wolf's singing was as good as ever on such numbers as 'Shake for Me,' 'I Ain't Superstitious,' '300 Pounds of Joy' and, obviously one of his most popular numbers, 'Goin' Down Slow.' His guitar-playing was almost non-existent but he had a great laugh pretending he could play—and the audience loved every minute of it! Though I felt he was probably overdoing the acting at the expense of blues feeling, as this is what his audience wants, who am I to complain? It was a most enjoyable evening and I was very sorry when it ended."[25]

The same month, Wolf went back into the studio and cut four classic songs with Hubert, Sam Lay on drums, Andrew McMahon on bass, Lafayette Leake on piano, Arnold Rogers on tenor sax, and Donald Hankins on baritone sax. All four songs were credited to Wolf as composer, though only one was entirely original. The session was one of Wolf's best—one of the best in the history of Chicago blues, in fact: a magical night in the studio where everything clicked and everyone played with special intensity.

"Love Me Darlin'," a souped-up version of "May I Have a Talk with You" from the live *Folk Festival of the Blues* album, was a remake of "Pleadin' for Love" by Larry Birdsong from 1956. Wolf's version was incendiary as he pleaded with his woman to have a "little talk" and tell him if she loved him. Hubert's guitar was simply ferocious—slashing, sliding, and sobbing all around the beat, with startling attack, especially for a guitarist who played with bare fingers instead of a flat pick. Sam Lay slammed down a sledgehammer rhythm accented by triplets on two drums at once while Leake's piano tinkled madly away in the background and the dual horns honked on the beat, all of them building an unstoppable momentum. If hard rock had a grandfather, this was it. Hubert's guitar solo on "Love Me Darlin' " was copied almost note for note in a 1989 remake by Stevie Ray Vaughan.

"My Country Sugar Mama," also recorded for the *Folk Festival* album, was based on a 1937 record by John Lee "Sonny Boy" Williamson I. A majestic slow blues, "My Country Sugar Mama" was highlighted by Wolf's marvelous vocal and, for the first time in years in the studio, his powerful harp playing, which showcased his gargantuan tone and demonstrated the dictum "less is more." The "sugar" of the title was a metaphor for sex. Sobbing saxes, superb piano, and dazzling drumming propelled the track. "Louise" was a stately remake of a Johnnie Temple hit from 1936, later remade by Bill Broonzy. It featured another primal vocal from Wolf, powerhouse drumming by Lay, great horn work by Rogers and Hankins, magnificent piano by Leake, and more of Hubert's subtle soloing.

The most powerful song of the session was "Killing Floor," released with "Louise" as Chess 1923. The "killing floor" is the blood-splattered platform in a slaughterhouse where animals are killed before being cut up. The term "killing floor" was used in 1930 by Son House in "Dry Spell Blues" and again in 1931 by Skip James in "Hard Time Killing Floor Blues." Another phrase from Wolf's song—"If I had-a followed my second mind"—also came from House, who used it in his 1941 recording "Camp Hollers." Chicago's slaughterhouses were infamous in the early twentieth century when Upton Sinclair used them as the backdrop for his great muckraking novel *The Jungle*. They employed many of the city's black residents, so for a Chicago crowd, Wolf's imagery hit close to home as he sang that his woman had him down on the "killing floor." The image also hit close to home for Wolf. In a fight in the Delta, after all, he'd allegedly whacked a man across the head with a hoe and had seen his body drop, killed instantly, onto a porch floor.

Musically, the song was marked by a distinctive ascending riff played in unison by two guitars plus the bass and accentuated by Lay's tricky high-hat work. The song was not easy to record. Buddy Guy, who played second guitar on it, said, "Wolf was in the studio for almost two days doing 'Killing Floor.' And they called me that morning around seven, they said, 'Come down here, I want you to play a lick. Leonard is humming something, and can't no guitar players feel it or hear it.' I said, 'Yeah, I can play it.' And we cut the tune within 20 minutes."[26] With Guy scratching out the riff, Hubert's blistering glissandos propelled the song into the stratosphere as Leake added keyboard flourishes.

In September, Wolf and Hubert traveled to Europe as part of the 1964 American Folk Blues Festival. Started in 1962 by German music promoters Horst Lippmann and Fritz Rau, the AFBF was a showcase for the best blues talent America had to offer. When such a tour was unthinkable in the United States, the AFBF tapped into and helped create a growing European audience for blues. Neither Wolf nor Hubert had ever been overseas, and the trip revealed the widespread appeal of their music.

Lippmann hired Willie Dixon as a consultant on the tour. "Willie was my guide to all the clubs and most of the people," Lippmann said. "I'd go to all the main clubs where Muddy played and Wolf's place Silvio's and then little clubs on the corner you'd get in and suddenly there was Magic Sam playing . . . and another West Side club where Otis Rush was playing. These were not famous clubs but Willie knew them. At that time, Chicago was full of blues music, especially on the South Side."[27]

When Hubert met Lippmann, he thought he was one of the many bullshitters common to the music business. "So this guy, Horst Lippmann, he came over to Silvio's where we was playing . . . and he asked Wolf, 'How would you like to go to Europe?' Wolf took his contract and studied on it and finally he agreed. Then he came to me and asked me would I like to go? I said, 'Sure, why not.' But I didn't pay him no mind. People used to ask you all kinds of funny things late at night in the club. . . . So when he left, he waved at me and said, 'So long, Hubert, I'll see you in Europe.' I waved, 'See you.' I never thought I'd see him again, though."[28]

Joining Wolf and Hubert was an impressive tour lineup: Willie

Dixon, Sunnyland Slim, Clifton James, Lightnin' Hopkins, John Henry Barbee, Sugar Pie DeSanto, Sleepy John Estes with Hammie Nixon, plus Sonny Boy Williamson II, the star of the previous year's tour. Hubert's first adventure began with the flight over. "Wolf and I got on that plane," he said. "It was my first plane ride. I just knowed good and well that was it. I put Wolf in the window seat, and I just prayed that we'd make it."[29]

The plane touched down at Rhein-Main Airport in Frankfurt, Germany, on September 27. The first tour stop was at Baden-Baden, where a show for German TV was filmed over several days. All the performers did one song each except Sugar Pie DeSanto, who hadn't yet arrived, Sonny Boy, who opened the show with two numbers, and Wolf, who closed it with three.

Wolf's performance was dramatic as he gesticulated and contorted his face to convey his message. He sang with passion and played rhythm guitar, expertly accompanied by Hubert, Sunnyland Slim, Willie Dixon, and Clifton James. During "Shake for Me," the group laid down an infectious groove as Wolf lurched out of his chair to shake his hips. The tempo slowed for Wolf's second number, a deep blues; and he closed his set with a dramatic reading of his new single "Love Me Darlin'." For German TV viewers, the sight of Wolf in all his glory must have been quite a shock.

Bob Koester, who accompanied Delmark recording artist Sleepy John Estes on the trip, heard praise of Wolf from an unusual source one night outside the studio. "We're waiting to go back to the hotel, and Sonny Boy is in the back seat. I'm in the front seat. Wolf is pacing up and down. . . . He was just enjoying the night air, and he didn't really feel like sitting down, because he worked sitting down. And Sonny Boy looked out of the back seat and said, 'That man's got a whole lot of soul!' That was unusual. Sonny Boy didn't often say nice things about people."[30]

After completing the TV show, the musicians traveled across Europe performing concerts. "We went to Germany, France, and all over while we's there," Hubert said. "England. We did everything. . . . I enjoyed it. This was new to me."[31] The show on October 9 at the Musikhalle in Hamburg, Germany, was recorded and an album released on the Fontana label. Wolf had one number on the album—a hard-driving version of the blues classic "Dust My Broom." Years later Wolf's portion of the concert in Bremen, Germany, was released on the Sundown label as *Live in Europe 1964*. The show featured such Wolf standards as "Goin' Down Slow," "Howlin' for My Darling," and "Forty Four." It also included "Rockin' the Blues," an instrumental shuffle that Wolf never recorded elsewhere.

Chris Strachwitz, owner of Arhoolie Records, who traveled over with Lightnin' Hopkins, was not impressed with Wolf as a performer. "Howlin' Wolf to me was much more of a carnival-type performer," he said. "He would come out of these concerts and say, 'Well, these people, they don't know what the hell dust my broom means.' So he went out there with his overalls on and a broom in his hand. That was dust my broom. I mean, bullshit. . . . He said, 'People love bullshit and I'm going to give it to 'em.' I'm pretty sure he said that to me. He certainly put it out there."[32]

Willie Dixon also had problems with Wolf clowning around onstage. "I used to have to get Wolf off the stage and take him back in the alley and talk to him," Dixon said. "I've threatened him and I even had him in the collar a couple of times but I don't remember actually coming to blows with Wolf. Sometimes, guys can be so illiterate by inexperience and all like that you have to take them off to the side and talk to them. If they won't act right, you threaten to send them home or something like that."[33]

Wolf's relationship with Hubert also bothered Strachwitz: "Wolf seemed to be really kind of an insecure man, and you could tell by his little power trips that he had with Hubert Sumlin who played beautiful guitar behind him. But he figured it was show biz and you got to do what you can, and he knew he had this weird voice, and people just loved it. And when he came on, he'd try to play a little guitar and the spotlight was always on him, but you could hear Hubert over in the corner doing all the playing. He would never let them even have the spotlight go on him when he would play his solos. He would always be in it himself, banging away on the damn acoustic guitar, which you couldn't hear. And, well, maybe it was Hubert's fault. He was sort of his puppy dog."[34]

Spirits were high on the tour as the musicians were treated like stars. Sugar Pie DeSanto appreciated Horst Lippmann. "He believed in all of us blues characters and he just really put the mat out for you . . . nice accommodations . . . good food."[35] The European audiences were universally receptive and friendly, which for some of the musicians came as a shock. "This totally different audience spooked most of them out," Strachwitz said. "All of these white folks who'd usually been kicking their ass around, all of a sudden there were tons of them and they couldn't speak the same language, but they simply loved their stuff. It was just a phenomenon for most of them."[36]

Wherever they traveled by bus, the musicians would pass around Willie Dixon's acoustic guitar. Koester said, "John Estes would play it sometimes and used it on all his shows. But John was not a guy to play a lot just to kill time. Wolf would sit in the back and play. And he would do Charlie Patton tunes. He seemed to be better on acoustic than he was on electric! The shit just seemed to work better."[37]

Sonny Boy was often at the center of these impromptu concerts. "Sometimes Sonny Boy would get up over the PA system while everyone was trying to get some sleep and blow his harp," Hubert said. "Pretty soon they'd all be jammin' and carryin' on."[38] "Sonny Boy was the guy that I thought was the real character," Strachwitz said. "Jesus, I heard him play that fucking harmonica on that intercom on the bus driving from the airport to downtown Munich, and he was just, he did the filthiest version of 'Dirty Dozens' you will ever hear in your life! . . . Sugar Pie was the only woman in the bus. We were just roaring. That was one time I wish I had a tape recorder. I had never heard a filthy version of 'The Dirty Dozens,' and it went on and on. It was just absolutely hilarious."[39]

An attractive woman of Filipino and black ancestry, Sugar Pie was unfazed by anything Sonny Boy sang. As the only woman on the tour, "Everybody was trying to reach for Sugar Pie!" she recalled with a laugh. "I turned them all down." The only musician on the tour who didn't flirt with her was the newly married Wolf. "He was just a friendly person . . . like a big old baby," Sugar Pie said. "He never did say too much, but when he said it you heard him!"[40]

Groupies were everywhere on the tour and for some of the musicians it must have been a shock to have white women chasing after them in Europe. Wolf didn't seem to notice them. "He apparently wasn't making it with any of the groupies who were running around, most of whom were not all that young, I might add," Koester said. "He said once as the plane was taking off, he was in the seat across the aisle from me, he said, 'The trouble with Europe is, you can't get your balls off!' If I had his wife—she was a good-looking lady—I'd be true to her."[41]

An attractive younger wife can be a blessing and a curse. Wolf tried to stay in touch with Lillie back home to make sure no other mules were trying to kick in his stall. "I never will forget," Lillie said, "I belonged to my ladies club, and this particular time, it was ten o'clock here, so Wolf thought—he'd been calling me all night. So when he finally got me, he said, 'Where have you been? Staying out all night?' I said, 'Wolf, I didn't stay out all night. It's ten o'clock here.' 'Oh no—it's six o'clock in the morning.' He had forgot about the time. The interpreter that was traveling with him was named Georgie. I said, 'Put Georgie on the phone.' So I said to Georgie, 'Please explain to Wolf that it's only ten o'clock here.' Georgie explained to Wolf, and Wolf got back on the phone and said, 'Ah, now I can sleep!' That's just the way he was."[42]

A highlight of the tour was when Wolf and some other musicians went behind the Iron Curtain to perform. "The first tour behind the Iron Curtain was in 1964, and that was only five or six people I took, namely Wolf, Hubert Sumlin, Willie Dixon, Sunnyland Slim, and one or two more," Horst Lippmann said. "We toured East Germany, Poland, and Czechoslovakia. We recorded all of that session in East Berlin for Amiga (Hubert's first studio recordings as a leader), the East German company, and Hubert Sumlin played some guitar solos. Wolf wasn't on that session because of his contract with Chess but Willie, Sunnyland Slim, Hubert, and Clifton James were on that session released by me on my L&R record label."

One of the shows in Poland was in South Galicia, a backwoods region. "The people came with the horses and the wagons behind . . . real countryside people that never saw any black people in their lives nor heard anything about blues or American music," Lippmann said. "They had been very, very astonished, so there was not very much applause. Wolf said, 'I'm going to get them,' so he went on his knees and played a tango. It was a very, very strange thing."

Lippmann had an unexpected problem in paying Wolf for the shows in Eastern Europe. "When we played Poland and East Germany, he got the salary paid partly in dollars but we had to take 50% in local currency, which is not convertible, so we had to spend it in the country. Willie bought himself a mink hat, which was stolen, Hubert Sumlin bought some jewels and stuff, and Wolf didn't know what to buy so he said, 'Give it to the YMCA.' I said, 'But, Wolf, there is no YMCA. This is a communist country.' He said, 'The YMCA is everywhere.' "[43]

After touring continental Europe, the AFBF traveled to Great Britain, where the language was familiar but the accent strange. The British audiences were warm and enthusiastic. Wolf was already well known in England with a recent chart hit after Pye International (Chess's British distributor) issued "Smokestack Lightnin' " in June 1964. The song rose to number 42 on the British charts. "To many, Wolf was the great hero," English bluesman Long John Baldry said. "He was known from radio. 'Smokestack Lightnin' ' — you couldn't escape that song. He had an enormous advantage coming there with a hit song."[44]

The British music press eagerly awaited Wolf's arrival. In August 1964, both *R&B Monthly* and *R 'N' B Scene* published biographical profiles of him, reflecting what little was known about his life and career. The most prophetic line came from *R&B Monthly*. "From reports, his act is essentially visual, and it will be another hallmark in British blues appreciation to see this massive bluesman roar his blues."[45] Neil Slaven, who attended the tour's opening show at Fairfield Halls in Croydon, wrote, "The final spot was saved for Howlin' Wolf, whose massive bulk instantly commanded everybody's attention. On this opening show, Wolf confined himself to the guitar, which he only played during instrumental breaks, playing rhythm to Hubert Sumlin's lead. On later shows, he also featured the harmonica. As with Otis Spann and Muddy Waters, it was clear that Hubert was Wolf's man. Now we heard some of his best most distinctive work. Wolf sang 'Shake for Me' . . . 'Going Down Slow' (yes yes) and 'I Didn't Mean to Hurt Your Feelings.' A rousing end to a rousing show."[46]

A correspondent for *Melody Maker* who caught the AFBF show at Manchester's Free Trade Hall was struck by the physicality of Wolf's performance. "He pads around the stage like a caged animal, fixes his baleful stare, makes a violent movement of his hands, then belts out the blues with such power and effect that the whole of his massive frame shakes. Literally a giant of a man, and certainly a giant among today's folk artists. This, then, is the almost legendary Howlin' Wolf, the man we've waited years to see."[47] Charles Keil, who saw a show in London, was not so positive in his appraisal. "Howlin' Wolf's performance style—stalking around, rolling his eyes, lunging to and from the microphone—so appropriate to the boisterous atmosphere of a Chicago lounge, made him look like an awkward Uncle Tom."[48]

Simon Napier gave a more balanced review of Wolf in *Blues Unlimited*: "The Wolf's act varied from day to day somewhat as to content, quality and power; some days he played harp, others not at all; sometimes he got over very well, at others he was less effective. At this particular show he was superb. He began with his recent 'hit' in Britain, 'Smokestack Lightning' . . . and the effect of the man was astonishing. Roughly the same build as Big Willie [Dixon], but rather straighter, Wolf approaches the mike with an almost timid air. Once into 'Smokestack' though and the strength of the man was quite apparent. His voice, as powerful as always, forced its way through this, one of his greatest songs. Next he gave out with 'Dust My Broom' complete with simple but blasting harmonica, quite finely accompanied by Hubert Sumlin and Sunnyland Slim. . . . Then came 'Tell Me' and the show was brought to a complete climax on 'Shake for Me.' . . . Wolf . . . was absolutely great."[49]

For budding British bluesmen, a visit by blues giants like Wolf, Sonny Boy, and Willie Dixon was a major cultural event. "I'll never forget—it was an afternoon about four o'clock," said Giorgio Gomelsky, who ran the famous Crawdaddy Club in London and managed several bands. "There was Howlin' Wolf, Sonny Boy, and Willie Dixon, the three of them sitting on this sofa I had in my living room. Willie was huge, Wolf wasn't exactly small, and Sonny Boy was very towering and lean. These three grand viziers were sitting on this thing and there's like Jimmy Page, Eric Clapton and everybody sitting at their feet."[50]

Tony McPhee, guitarist for British blues band the Groundhogs, attended one of the AFBF shows and met Wolf outside afterward. "Wolf was steaming like a horse," McPhee said. "There was steam rising over his head. He was bigger than even I imagined. And my bass player, Pete Cruickshank, is five foot six and he came up to Wolf and looked up to him and said, 'Mr. Burnett, we're a band called the Groundhogs and we play your songs.' Wolf looked down at him and then looked over him and down at me and said, 'Is this another little groundhog?' I thought that was great. Anyway we got invited back to the hotel. Wolf got an acoustic and he started playing 'Down in the Bottom' and I couldn't believe the way he did it because he does it with such an attack on the album, and he was doing it exactly the same way on acoustic."[51]

Wolf basked in all the attention, telling *Melody Maker*: "The folks over here are so friendly. They take you out, they show you around. I've never had such a good warm feeling in months."[52] For Wolf and Hubert, the warm feelings continued as they stayed on in England after the AFBF tour was over to play for several weeks on their own. Backed by various English blues bands, Wolf and Hubert played smaller, more intimate venues.

Their first English club appearance was at the Marquee, and John Broven wrote of it for *Blues Unlimited*. "Accompanied by Hubert Sumlin and Chris Barber's band, Wolf came on well after 9:30, and apologies were made to the effect that Wolf had been detained by the BBC for filming *Beat Room*, but this is no encouragement to fans at the Marquee. Such thoughts loomed up again as Wolf departed after four numbers. Admittedly these took the best part of half an hour and were superbly done. 'Smokestack Lightnin',' 'Can I Have a Talk with You,' 'Dust My Broom' and one unknown . . . were all fine with Wolf performing the kind of blues never seen in a European club. If only Muddy, [John Lee] Hooker and the rest would realize Europeans can take the blues the hard way. . . . The second set started where the first left off. . . . Wolf did a whole string of unbelievably brilliant numbers many of which were new to me—a refreshing change from the 'hits only' policy of some—and including a harmonica instrumental with odd verses to the order of 'Who's that kissin' over there'; and a version to end all versions of 'I Asked for Water.' . . . Here was the modern blues at its very, very best. Thank you, Howlin' Wolf."[53]

In addition to appearing on *Beat Room*, Wolf played for the BBC radio show *Saturday Club*, accompanied by Chris Barber's band. Wolf also appeared on the TV show *Juke Box Jury*, where he was the week's mystery guest. A panel of judges including British skiffle legend Lonnie Donegan listened to part of "Love Me Darlin' " and had to vote it a hit or a miss. They called it a miss and then had to sit uncomfortably as an imposing Wolf came out and shook their hands.

Jazz trombonist and bandleader Chris Barber had already played with visiting blues musicians and considered Wolf unique. "He was a very nice man, a very gentle man. But he was a strange and alarming-looking guy onstage. He would kind of pace round about the stage. And the thing is, in the London Zoo there's a gorilla called Guy who looked exactly like him and walked around his cage the same way. The other thing that was interesting about his character was that we had a lot of guests from Big Bill Broonzy in '55, Sonny and Brownie, Champion Jack Dupree, gospel singers, and all kinds of people through the years. And we'd invite them up to the house for dinner. And the only one guest in the whole lot who said grace before he ate was Wolf. The only one! The gospel singers were too busy saying, 'Where's the whiskey?' "[54]

Blues singer Baldry, whose band backed Wolf on a few shows, said, "It's so strange. I mean, he was the most ferocious-looking person, but what a sweetheart—a really wonderful guy! Despite being so huge, he was actually a really dainty person. He was an exceptional dancer— amazingly lively and agile for such a huge man. You wouldn't believe that such a big person would be able to dance so gracefully. And it was just magic watching him."

Baldry was equally impressed by Hubert. "Hubert Sumlin was the first guitarist I ever saw that would go on with his guitar totally out of tune, yet he was able to play it into tune, if you follow what I mean, by note bending. It might truly be absolutely out of tune and yet his playing was never out of tune because he was always able to bend those notes from wherever and put them into the right context."[55]

Wolf did at least a dozen shows in the U.K. with young R&B band the T-Bones, whose debut single was a cover of "How Many More Times." The T-Bones got on well with the visiting bluesmen after a brief rehearsal with them at London's Marquee Club. "Wolf and Hubert couldn't have been more helpful," said Winston Weatherall, the T-Bones' guitarist. "They were a couple of nice guys. We also played with Sonny Boy. He was just the opposite of Wolf. He was very cantankerous, was Sonny Boy. No, I found Wolf to be a very genuine bloke."[56] Andy McKechnie, the T-Bones' other guitarist and harp player, said, "The Wolf Man, as we used to call him, really was a gentle giant with seemingly no hang-ups at all. He was a professional in every way, unlike Sonny Boy, of whom we had the so-called pleasure of being his backing band after the Yardbirds had done their stint with him."[57] The T-Bones, themselves fairly bibulous, were shocked by Sonny Boy's drinking. "He drank a phenomenal amount of whiskey," said Weatherall. "I'd never seen anyone drink like that. And he didn't bother to eat. He just lived on whiskey—two or three bottles a day. Wolf definitely told us that he didn't like Sonny Boy because he'd treated his sister badly."[58]

The T-Bones backed Wolf and Hubert at gigs such as one at Liverpool's infamous Cavern Club, where the Beatles got their start. A hot, dank, subterranean dive, the Cavern was the kind of venue where the T-Bones hit the bar early and often. "Wolf, bless his heart, drank Coca-Cola all night," said McKechnie. "He didn't touch a drop of booze until we got back to our hotel, whereupon he consumed the best part of a bottle of whiskey and entertained us with stories of his past good and bad times. What that man had to offer to a very young bunch of boys was so very touching—not just in the music field, but heart-to-heart father-like instructions for a good life. He was a great man and we admired him so much."[59] T-Bones bass player Stuart Parkes said, "Wolf was never much of a drinker. He was pretty much a gentleman. He was a nice guy, a really friendly guy."[60] Parkes wrote to Wolf after the tour, and Wolf wrote back to invite him and his friends to visit the Burnetts in Chicago. Wolf's letter also asked if Parkes could procure some "perfume, cologne, and those French stockings, the thin, sheer tan color . . . and the price." Wolf had help writing the letter; it's in Lillie's hand.

Wolf loved to show off his dramatic flair wherever he went. The T-Bones' manager, Giorgio Gomelsky, had a movie camera and filmed comic scenes with Wolf and Hubert. In one, Wolf sauntered along like a visiting movie star while Hubert struggled behind him under a load of guitars and amps. In another, Wolf howled at the moon. Wolf and the T-Bones stopped for gas one day on the way to a gig. A knot of people rushed up to stare at Wolf, thinking he was the British professional wrestler Prince Kumali.

Hubert's simple interests surprised the young U.K. bluesmen. "He couldn't wait to get back to the States to play with his train set!" said Parkes.[61] Hubert's guitar was a shock. "It was really sort of cheap and nasty," said Weatherall. "It was made of all sorts of pearl and plastic, with about six pickups on it—as many pickups as you could squeeze on a guitar! I think it might've been Italian or something, and the action was almost unplayable. It was the sort of thing you'd throw in the dustbin."[62] The T-Bones introduced Hubert to two new pastimes. They spent a lot of time with him plinking various objects with a BB gun, and when he left for home, he filled his suitcase with bottles of his favorite new refreshment: Guinness beer.

Blues fan Dave Hatfield attended one of Wolf's club appearances and met two of his heroes. "December '64 we found that Wolf was on tour and was actually doing a show in a town called Chelmsford in Essex, and that's where I lived at the time. So I and my brother and a few friends set off for that concert, and we got to the show, and the first thing we did was to go find the cloakroom to get rid of our coats. And we just looked around the corner of these racks of coats and we couldn't believe it—the Howlin' Wolf actually sat there in this room, and Hubert was there as well! There was no such thing as a plush artist's dressing room. They were just shoved in a corner behind the coats. So we immediately pounced on them and asked for autographs and everything like that. But they were such nice people. The Wolf was a wonderful guy. And his reputation before then in the press was this incredibly fierce guy was coming over to England. But the opposite was true. They were having an absolute ball on that tour."[63]

Wolf's backup band for the show in Essex was the Muleskinners. Pianist Ian McLagan, later of the Small Faces, the Stones, Bonnie Raitt's group, and many other bands, recalled his first meeting with Wolf. "We're all anticipating this scary, big man, and the doors open and he turned up in this huge greatcoat, a big overcoat down to the floor. He put his arms out, and we were up at the other end onstage, and he was right at the other end of the hall. 'My boys!' he yelled. I mean, five little white kids—we were anything but his boys, but we were so happy to be called that. And Hubert was kind of peeping around him . . . Wolf was so sweet. We just went up to meet him, and he put his arms around the five of us and just hugged us. 'My boys!' He just made us feel so special."

The Muleskinners returned the compliment by seeing Wolf and Hubert off at the airport just before Christmas. "Strangely, we were the only people there—just the band, all of us, the whole mob turned up at the airport to say goodbye. It was just him and Hubert; nobody else was around. It was really sad. And he said he was thrilled to see us, and he gave me a hundred-dollar bill and he said, 'Hey, go get me some bourbon.' I said, 'Okay.' There was no way to get bourbon in England then. I wandered around and there was a bar there and I asked them if they had any bourbon. 'No bourbon here, mate.' And I went back and had to hand him his hundred-dollar bill. It was sad."[64] Sad or not, Wolf's trip to Europe had been a smashing success and an eye-opening experience for him, Hubert, and the thousands of fans who got to see them in the flesh for the first time.

As Wolf's audience was growing in Europe, it was changing back in the States. It was shrinking among Wolf's core audience as young African-Americans abandoned the "old-fashioned" blues of their parents and grandparents for the new soul sounds put out by Motown, Atlantic, and Stax. To young African-Americans, soul was progressive and up-to-date—reflecting the changes of the civil rights movement and associated with black pride culturally and politically. Wolf weathered changing tastes better than most blues artists, retaining much of his audience in Chicago (especially on the West Side) and in the Deep South. The high quality of his 1960s recordings and his over-the-top live performances helped him hold on to his audience.

While Wolf's black audience was slowly shrinking, white fans in small numbers were starting to come to his shows on the South and West sides, having heard of him through black radio, the folk movement, and British rock 'n' roll. These early explorers of the ghetto scene, many of them aspiring musicians who wanted to soak up the music and the culture, were the first of a growing audience of white American blues fans throughout the decade.

One of the aspiring musicians was blues harp great Charlie Musselwhite. Born in Mississippi and raised in Memphis, Charlie grew up near Beale Street, where he hung out as a teenager with blues legends Will Shade and Furry Lewis. In the early 1960s, Charlie moved to Chicago to look for work as a laborer. Soon he was hanging out at Silvio's, where he first saw Wolf. "Man, it was such a thrill to walk in and see Howlin' Wolf for the first time," Musselwhite said. "The power that he emanated was just awesome, and the band was just . . . I was just slack-jawed. I couldn't even drink my drink."[65]

Already a talented blues harpist, Musselwhite was impressed with

Wolf's style on the Mississippi saxophone. "He had a tremendous tone," he said. "He was like one of those guys who didn't really need to play much. He could just hit that tone and it just said it all. He had that huge, big, fat tone.... The tone comes from your diaphragm. I think he just played real deep. A lot of people play just from their mouth, or even from the front of their mouth, which gives the thinnest tone. The further back and down you can play—you have to think about it in a Zen kind of way. You mentally place the source back and down and that's where it comes from, and it gives it a deeper sound. He used to play the harp without his hands. He'd put it in his mouth like a cigar."

Outgoing and observant, Musselwhite got to know some of the guys in Wolf's band and watched how they got along with their boss. "He was real strict," Musselwhite said. "You had to wear a white shirt and a tie. Everybody had to dress right, and he would fine you if anything was wrong, if he didn't like anything you did.... Sam Lay told me about one time they were in Jackson, Mississippi, and he didn't wear the right color tie. They were staying in different rooming houses or something. Wolf said, 'I'll be by tomorrow morning to pick up my fine.' And Sam just went out on the front porch and sat there cleaning his pistol. Wolf came walking down the street and all he said was, 'Good morning.' Saw that pistol and never even brought up the fine at all."

Musselwhite got to know Wolf a bit. "I remember when [President] Kennedy got shot. We were standing next to each other at the urinal. He said, 'That was really a shame they shot him. That was an awful thing.' ... I never had any real long conversations with him—just small talk. He was a real guarded person. I don't think he said anything without thinking about it first." Wolf was anything but guarded onstage. "He was holding the microphone down by his crotch as if he was masturbating, and kind of making his eyes really roll around and laughing, and everybody was cracking up," Musselwhite said, laughing. "He could get silly like that when he was performing. But when you were talking to him, he was never silly."[66]

As a poor Southerner, Musselwhite was unusual among the white musicians hanging out in the blues clubs. Most were from the Chicago suburbs and relatively well-to-do. Typical was guitarist Michael Bloomfield, who grew up in the affluent Jewish suburb of Glencoe, Illinois. Exposed to blues by a family maid who listened to Leonard Chess's radio station, WVON, Bloomfield was visiting blues clubs on the South Side with his friends by the age of fourteen. The talented guitarist started sitting in with his idols such as Muddy Waters.

Bloomfield soon ventured out to the more dangerous West Side to see Wolf at Silvio's. Roy Ruby, Bloomfield's boyhood friend, remembered the attention they got from Wolf. "He'd say, 'I want to do this one for my white friends. I've got some white friends here tonight. Put the spotlight on them.'" Another friend, Fred Glaser, added, "He'd say, 'Stand up, white people. Here they are—give them a big hand. They're right at this table, right here. Now I want all you people to be nice to these white people out here in the audience."[67] Sometimes Wolf would yell, "Look at this white boy in from the suboibs!"

Another aspiring young white bluesman was Elvin Bishop, originally from Oklahoma, who was attending the University of Chicago on a scholarship and learning to play guitar. Bishop heard Wolf attempt a B. B. King–style single-note solo, and he wondered how, with his huge hands, Wolf could even find a single guitar string. Bishop was more impressed by Wolf's slide playing, which he compared to his harp style: "a swash of sound."[68]

Another young musician who was hitting the blues clubs in the early 1960s was blues harpist Paul Butterfield. A native of Chicago who grew up in Hyde Park, Butterfield was exposed to the Chicago blues scene while hanging out with Nick Gravenites, who was slightly older and already known on the blues scene. Considered arrogant by some, Butterfield sat in and paid his dues with various bluesmen, including Wolf at Silvio's.[69] Charlie Musselwhite and Michael Bloomfield also sat in with Wolf's band on occasion.

Pianist Barry Goldberg, later a member of the Electric Flag with Bloomfield, remembers the first time he sat in with Wolf. "Michael Bloomfield and I had been playing together since high school. He was always going down to the blues clubs like Silvio's and Pepper's, striking up relationships since he was fifteen. He was known as an oddity for it. He would do anything for Muddy, like baby-sit for his grandkids—anything to get close to these people to learn about them and the music. So he said to me, 'C'mon, we're going to the West Side.' I got really, really nervous because it was my first time. We took his mother's car and drove down there—Michael, me, and Roy Ruby. We pulled right up on the curb so we only had about five steps to get in the front door. Michael said, 'Listen to me and don't say anything. Look straight ahead. Don't look to the left or right. Just follow me.'

"We walked in and it was like the movie *Adventures in Babysitting*, where they walk in the wrong door and all of a sudden they're onstage in the baddest blues club in the whole world. These women are wearing stiletto heels—the sharper the better, Nick Gravenites said, in case a fight breaks out. God knows what else was in the club: probably an arsenal. It was a real blues club, not some sort of plush place. As soon as we walk in the door, everyone sort of freezes. We can't be inconspicuous. It's like, 'Look at these little weirdo kids.' And Wolf starts laughing and he says, 'We got some white boys in the house tonight.' And everyone's looking at us, as if they didn't know we were there already. I'm frozen and I start to shake. This is baptism by fire, okay? This is the real deal.

"Wolf says, 'C'mon up and play with us.' So Michael and I get up there, and there's a hushed silence in the crowd. They must sense that we're totally out of our minds—just insane—or our reverence for the music is profound, beyond fear. And the band launches into 'Killing Floor,' and I play the piano and Michael plays rhythm guitar, doing that riff: Da duh da, da da da duh, da duh da. Wolf looks like he's six feet eight inches tall and at least three hundred pounds. I look up and he's wearing a white shirt and a tie, and he's smiling, and Hubert is smiling with no teeth and we get a standing ovation. That was my rite of passage into the blues world.

"My God, man: to be playing that song with Wolf onstage! It was my first time ever playing with a blues master. It was like playing baseball in Yankee stadium with the Yankees. Just to have the balls to get up there and play 'Killing Floor' with Wolf was something I will never forget. We later cut that with the Electric Flag out of reverence for him. Fearsome as he looked, he was a really sweet man."[70]

Goldberg was lucky he was with Bloomfield, whom Wolf knew. Singer Tracy Nelson saw what happened when a guitarist from out of town tried to sit in with Wolf's band at Silvio's. "He walked up to Hubert first. It was a big, high stage, and it was hard to get up to. So he kind of climbed up a little platform and then he was going to go up to the next level. And he got to the first level and was talking to Hubert about sitting in, and Hubert started to give him his guitar. And Wolf came over and said, 'Leave my guitar man alone!' and just bapped him right off the stage! Knocked him on his ass off the stage! It was the funniest thing I've ever seen in my life!"[71]

Wolf started getting gigs on the North Side through Bloomfield and Musselwhite, who said, "Mike and I would tell the owners of the clubs, 'Man you ought to hire this guy Howlin' Wolf.' 'Who?' they asked, 'Howlin' Wolf? Never heard of him.' 'Yeah he's great.' Eventually they'd agree, 'Well, we'll give it a try.' Before long, every night of the week there'd be Muddy Waters, Howlin' Wolf, Otis Rush, or Magic Sam in this one bar. It was flourishing."[72]

Big John's club on North Wells was the first North Side club to book black Chicago blues bands. "Butterfield played there Thursday, Friday, and Saturday, and on Sundays and Mondays they would have other bands in from the West Side or the South Side," Gravenites explained. "Wolf had a regular Monday night gig there. It was very homey. He actually had a rocking chair and a little table, blues harmonicas and whatever. He'd sit there and he'd smoke a big meerschaum pipe. He'd sit there in the chair like it was his living room and play his songs. It was the beginning of the blues clubs on the North Side, which is now where they all are. Once they started to play there, a lot of the black bands felt real comfortable there. I know they felt safe there. They got paid real good money to play there compared to what they were making.

"He really felt at home there at that club, even though it was a white club. He played real nice there. He'd do the same riff over and over and over and over again for fifteen fucking minutes, and every time, it was a little bit different, a little more interesting. . . . He had such an intense, perfect rhythm sense—his band, too—that he could make that interesting for fifteen minutes, playing the same thing over and over. It was almost like you never wanted it to end. You knew if it ended, some other beat would come and you wouldn't hear this one anymore.

"Wolf's music was always very impressive. I mean, it was so far out. The sound of his voice was far out. The tone of his guitar was far out. The depth of his passion was far out. His rhythms were beyond primitive. Some of his rhythms I still haven't figured out yet!

"Wolf was the consummate bluesman. Anybody who was in the blues loved the Wolf because he personified the genre. And of course, there's nothing bad you can say about him in terms of representing the genre. This is what a bluesman does: He supersedes whatever society tells him isn't what's happening, and through strength of will, projection of personality, he makes something happen. Wolf was that way; he had a powerful drive. Sometimes it was malevolent. A lot of his communication was just looking at you. . . . He was the kind of guy who would scare the shit out of you! He was the Howlin' Wolf, and the Wolf ain't no socialite. Yeah, he was an extraordinary character: extraordinarily talented, but a scary guy, too. . . . He was a consummate, perfect musician. He had it in his blood."[73]

Wolf was back in the studio on April 15, 1965, cutting four more songs. Many discographies list Sam Lay on this session, but Billy Davenport, later of the Butterfield Blues Band, actually played drums on this session. "Wolf was playing at a club and he told me to come down and play a night with him to see how it went," Davenport said. "I ended up playing a couple of nights with him. Then next week we went into the studio, the Chess studio. We did four sides, two records at that time."[74]

"Tell Me What I've Done" was a sad, languid blues in which Wolf begs his woman to forgive him for hurting her feelings. Wolf's vocal is heartrending and Hubert's guitar cries and sighs like a wounded animal. "Ooh Baby" starts with a "Killing Floor" groove but never quite gels as Wolf praises his baby's charms. "I Walked from Dallas" was a solid remake of the unreleased 1957 "Walk to Camp Hall," with an infectious Delta groove built around the twin guitars of Hubert and Buddy Guy.

In "Don't Laugh at Me," Wolf begged his baby not to make fun of his looks. It was a potentially good song cluttered by too many guitars playing the same busy "Killing Floor" lick. Wolf sang, "Please don't laugh at me. I didn't make myself." Musselwhite said, "He was real paranoid. He thought people were making funny looks at him. He had real big feet, and he thought people were looking at his feet, and he would make comments to the audience. 'I seen you making eyes at me out there. I know who you are. You want to step out in the alley with me? Anytime—just let me know.' Right to the audience! I heard him do that a lot. He wasn't putting on a show. This is what he was really thinking."[75]

It didn't take much to sour Wolf's mood. Saxophonist Willie Young, who played in the band for many years, recalled an incident with a heckler in St. Louis. "One guy hollered out, 'Hey, Wolf—what size shoe you wear?' I said, 'Oh, my God!' I knowed it was going to be a long night." Indeed it was, as Wolf barked at the band for the rest of the gig.[76]

Ida McMahon, wife of bassist Blueblood McMahon, witnessed an encounter Wolf had with another fan. "A lady out in the audience just kept hollerin', 'Hey, Howlin' Wolf! Where did you get those big feet from?' And Wolf would say, 'Lady, leave me alone!' And she would keep on, 'Howlin' Wolf! Where did you get those big feet from?' He would say, 'Lady, leave me alone! I don't want to embarrass you.' So she hollered out again, 'Where'd you get those big feet from?' He said, 'Lady, let me tell you somethin'. If you don't leave me alone, I'm goin' to put a bomb on the end of my penis and I'm goin' to shoot you to the moon faster than the astronauts went!' "[77]

Playing keyboards on the April session was Lee Eggleston. Born in Charleston, Mississippi, in 1919, Eggleston had previously played with the Red Devil Trio and one-armed blues harpist Big John Wrencher. He got his chance to play with Wolf's band when he filled in a few times for an AWOL Henry Gray. Wolf liked what he heard and hired Eggleston. Eggleston saw an altercation between Wolf and S. P. Leary while the band was driving through Mississippi. S.P. wanted Wolf to stop the car so he could relieve himself by the side of the road. Wolf refused and heated words ensued. Wolf ended up slapping S.P. in the face. "Now, I'm gonna sue you," S.P. cried. "You done broke my nose!"[78]

On May 20, 1965, Wolf appeared on the ABC television show *Shindig* with the Rolling Stones, who had had a number 1 hit in Britain with their version of Wolf's "Red Rooster." The Stones told the show's producers they'd only do the show if they could appear with either Wolf or Muddy, their two favorite bluesmen. Wolf got the gig—the first time on American TV for either him or the Stones. The phenomenal house band the Shindogs—Billy Preston, James Burton, Joey Cooper, and Chuck Blackwell—rehearsed with Wolf the day of the show and were raring to play behind one of their favorite bluesmen. As they kicked off Wolf's song, the show's host, Jack Good, stopped them to interview Brian Jones and Mick Jagger. Jones explained that Wolf was one of their favorite singers, and then cut the conversation short by saying, "Now I think it's time for you to shut up and let's bring on the Wolf!" Dressed in a dark suit, Wolf strode majestically onstage, and with the Rolling Stones sitting at his feet performed a scorching version of "How Many More Years." As the first network TV appearance for any Chicago blues star, the Wolf made the most of it—stabbing his massive finger at the camera, shaking his rear end like an elephant suffering a seizure, and blasting blues harp into prime-time TV land.

A surprise visitor backstage at the show's taping was Delta blues legend Son House, rediscovered the year before living in upstate New York and now on a West Coast tour with his young manager, Dick Waterman. They heard about the *Shindig* taping and House said he wanted to see his old friend Wolf again. After getting directions to the TV studio, Waterman and House managed to get inside. Waterman asked House if he'd recognize Wolf after not seeing him for twenty-five years. "Oh yeah, man! I'd know him anywhere. Big, old, skinny guy! Big, old bag of bones!" Waterman said, "Well, there may have been some changes."

"We came around from behind some of the props," Waterman said. "And Wolf was sitting about halfway up alone in a small theater seat and the Stones were off to our left clustered around some of their entourage. So the Stones saw me walking in with this older black man. . . . We got to the front of the stage and Wolf made eye contact with Son and his eyes got big, and Wolf just came straight up like an elephant coming out of a phone booth! He came out of that little theater chair and his eyes got big and Son just watched Wolf coming up, up, up, and out of this chair. Son looked at me and he says, 'Man! He sure got his growth!' "[79]

Wolf and Son were thrilled to see each other and talked about the two sisters they used to date, good times, and long-lost friends. The Stones must've wondered, "Who is this older man that Wolf is so excited to see?" One came up to ask. "Brian Jones was watching me," said Waterman, "and then came up and tapped me and said, 'Excuse me, who is the old man that Wolf thinks is so special? Wolf is in awe of him.' So I said, 'That's Son House.' And he turned to me and said, 'Ah, the one that taught Robert Johnson.' "[80]

The night the show aired, Wolf was in bed at home in Chicago, resting before a gig. Lillie ran into the bedroom and said excitedly, "Wolf, wake up! You fixing to come on now." Wolf turned over and said, "Yeah, I done seen that before," and went back to sleep.[81] Lillie's daughter Barbra was impressed by Wolf's appearance with the Stones, realizing for the first time just how famous her stepfather was.[82]

Having Wolf as a stepfather was a delight for Bettye and Barbra. Wolf doted on them, and they returned his love and devotion. "His kids, man, you know good and well they had a lots to do with him because they loved him so much," S.P. said. "They all, they help him, influenced you know, 'Come on Daddy!' He just like a big, old baby—be fussin' he didn't want to do this or do that, but he go ahead on and do it."[83]

Wolf demanded that Bettye and Barbra always behave like proper young ladies. One can only imagine how intimidating it was for their boyfriends to meet the Wolf at home. If a boyfriend stayed too late, Wolf had a standard ploy. He'd walk into his living room in his underwear and ask in his deepest growl if the boy had brought his pajamas to spend the night. Getting the message, the young man would quickly leave.[84]

Bluesman John Hammond, Jr., son of the legendary talent scout and producer, opened for Wolf at the Ash Grove in Los Angeles in 1965. Hammond was excited and nervous about meeting one of his heroes. "I came off the stage and I'd played a good set, I thought. And I walked into the dressing room, and there was Howlin' Wolf alone, looking right at me. He said, 'You! How in the hell did you ever learn to play like that?' And I felt so intimidated I, I didn't know where my voice was. Finally, I spluttered out, 'Some records, you know?' And he says, 'You know, that's how I learned, too.' He said, 'Give me that guitar!' I handed him my guitar—I had an old Gibson—and he played 'Stone Pony Blues' on it. I was just flabbergasted. My mouth hung open and I said, 'I didn't know you played guitar!' He said, 'Hell yeah, I play guitar! You know who taught me how to play? Charlie Patton. . . . Charlie Patton was an Indian, and he was the baddest motherfucker in the world! If I played a note wrong, he'd whup me upside the head, you know?' I was totally blown away."[85]

Hammond was also blown away by a stunt Wolf did while playing "Stone Pony Blues." "At the end, he flipped the guitar, made three turns, and hit the last three notes!" Hammond said. "It was the slickest thing I've ever seen. I said, 'How come you don't play the guitar?' He said, 'Oh man, I don't like electric guitars. I have my band together and I play the harmonica. I hire a great guitar player.' He had Hubert Sumlin and Hubert was just so good, so different. He was so attached to Wolf; he was Wolf's hands."[86]

Hammond saw Wolf perform several times and was always amazed. "One night he was feeling I don't know what kind of spirit, but he comes up on the stage, he unzips his pants, and pulls the microphone out of his pants! Unbelievable! God help the little girls in the front rows who watched these shows. They must've blanched or whatever. He was a character."[87]

Another young bluesman who heard Wolf at the Ash Grove was Taj Mahal, who at the time fronted a band called the Rising Sons, which included Ry Cooder on guitar. "Wolf was not your pretty guitar player," Taj said. "He was very rudimentary, very direct. I loved his style. Another guy who really liked Wolf's style a lot was Al Wilson from Canned Heat, who used to come over here and jam in my yard and my garage. . . . I liked Wolf's pronunciation. It's very interesting how Eastern European accents and New York City are 'white,' but Wolf used to sing like, 'I been woikin'.' All those cats leaned down on those sounds. Man, I was always thrilled by those guys."[88]

Author Robert Palmer witnessed another outrageous Wolf performance at a Memphis Blues Revue at Ellis Auditorium on August 6, 1965. Sharing the bill with Wolf were blues heavyweights John Lee Hooker, Jimmy Reed, Little Milton, Big Joe Turner, and T-Bone Walker. Palmer brilliantly described Wolf's portion of the show. "The MC announced Wolf, and the curtains opened to reveal his band pumping out a decidedly down-home shuffle. The rest of the bands on the show were playing jump and soul-influenced blues, but this was the hard stuff. Where was Wolf? Suddenly he sprang out onto the stage from the wings. He was a huge hulk of a man, but he advanced across the stage in sudden bursts of speed, his head pivoting from side to side, eyes huge and white, eyeballs rotating wildly. He seemed to be having an epileptic seizure, but no, he suddenly lunged for the microphone, blew a chorus of raw, heavily rhythmic harmonica, and began moaning. He had the hugest voice I had ever heard—it seemed to fill the hall and get right inside your ears, and when he hummed and moaned in falsetto, every hair on your neck crackled with electricity. The thirty-minute set went by like an express train, with Wolf switching from harp to guitar (which he played while rolling on his back and, at one point, doing somersaults) and then leaping up to prowl the lip of the stage. He was The Mighty Wolf, no doubt about it. Finally, an impatient signal from the wings let him know that his portion of the show was over. Defiantly, Wolf counted off a bone-crushing rocker, began singing rhythmically, feigned an exit, and suddenly made a flying leap for the curtain at the side of the stage. Holding the microphone under his beefy right arm and singing into it all the while, he began climbing up the curtain, going higher and higher until he was perched far above the stage, the thick curtain threatening to rip, the audience screaming with delight. Then he loosened his grip and, in a single easy motion, slid right back down the curtain, hit the stage, cut off the tune, and stalked away, to the most ecstatic cheers of the evening. He was then fifty-five years old."[89]

While touring down South, Wolf and Hubert had another fight. Wolf was driving his Pontiac station wagon and Hubert and S.P. were sitting in the seat behind him, whispering about how to beat Wolf up. Finally, Hubert hit Wolf in the back of the head. Wolf stopped the car and all three got out. Wolf had his huge hands up and kept an eye on both men, especially S.P., who was known to carry a knife. While Wolf focused on S.P., Hubert hit Wolf again before Wolf's massive right hand knocked him down. Hubert crawled off to hide in the undergrowth as S.P. took off running. Wolf found Hubert in the weeds and stomped on him with his colossal shoes. Wolf left both men behind and drove off to play his gig. Bluesman Wild Child Butler, who saw Hubert when he managed to get back to Chicago, said, "He was wearing shades and his face was all scratched up."[90] Hubert spent time in the hospital because of his injuries.[91]

Hurt and angered, Hubert left to play with Muddy for the second time, staying away from Wolf for almost six months. Hubert told a writer for *Blues Unlimited* that he would never play for Wolf again.[92] The very next issue reported that Hubert was back with Wolf.[93] Hubert would continue to be Wolf's guitarist for the rest of Wolf's life.

While Hubert was gone, Byther Smith played guitar for Wolf. A man of fiery temperament himself ("I didn't take no small change from nobody!"), Smith was asked to play with Wolf by Hubert, who'd been giving him guitar lessons. Wolf and Smith butted heads one night at Pepper's. "He wanted me to tune his guitar," Smith said. "And I told him and I told the rest of the band that Wolf blowed harp and that's what he was goin' to play as long as I was there. . . . [Wolf then came on-stage and said,] 'Which one of you, blacker than me, tune my guitar? Did you tune my guitar?' And everybody looked at him. And I said, 'Nah, I didn't tune it.' And he said, 'Why didn't you?' I said, 'I'm not gonna tune your guitar tonight, tomorrow night, or any other night, because I play guitar and you blow harp.' . . . Wolf said, 'If you don't shut up, I will take my pistol and beat the hell out of you!' And I just went behind my amplifier and got my gun out and I said, 'Let's get it on!' " Wolf wanted to fire Smith, but it was too late to find another guitar player, so he finished out the night. Fortunately for both men, Smith left the band after a couple more gigs.[94]

Wolf was on the East Coast again in January 1966. He did one gig at Club 47 in Cambridge, Massachusetts, where he played often during the mid-1960s. Peter Wolf (born Peter Blankfield), a Boston R&B deejay who later helped found the J. Geils Band, had an apartment near the club that became an after-hours clubhouse for Muddy, Wolf, and other visiting bluesmen. "You just didn't get that close to Wolf," said the Cambridge Wolf. "He maintained at all times an air of intentional inscrutability that was almost impenetrable. I remember one time at the club, this kid said, 'Isn't it great we've got two Wolfs in the same city?' And even though it wasn't me saying it, Wolf just gave me that icy stare that could go right through you and said, 'As far as I know there's just one Wolf,' glaring at me with a look that I didn't even want to try to comprehend.

"Where Muddy was cool and elegant, with all the glamour of a Hollywood movie star, Wolf sent out a signal that said to all onlookers, 'Look out! Proceed with caution.' Muddy's music was always insinuating that there was something going on behind closed doors, but Wolf's performance was about something else—it was almost like, 'Hey, baby, break down the doors, bust open the windows, you're going deep into the heart of darkness with me tonight.' I remember one time there was a young college girl sitting at the front table with two of her friends, and Wolf just stalked toward her, put his face right up next to hers, dangled the microphone between his legs, and waggled it around not suggestively—altogether explicitly. Then he strutted back and forth across the stage, his eyes rolling back in his head, until suddenly he stopped dead, gave his band members a strange hypnotic stare, waved his hands once in the air, and then from his great height fell with a thud to his knees. I think everyone in the room was tilting as far back in their chairs as they could possibly go—I don't know if I can ever recall a moment quite like it, when an audience was as enchanted as it was petrified. But that was Wolf, on and off the stage."[95]

Performances like this also impressed young East Coast bluesman Geoff Muldaur, who said, "What a character that guy was! He seemed to be a holdover from the nineteenth century, yet urbane—a strange mix in that way, like Muddy. Wolf's personal power went way beyond showmanship. Had he been educated and guided, I do believe he would have given us our finest Othello."[96] Geoff's wife, Maria, the singer, felt Wolf's personal power in a surprising way. "When I went into labor with my daughter, Jenny, I listened to 'Howlin' for my Darling' and that whole album it was on for hours. He was the soundtrack for my labor! Every time he'd sing, 'Oooooooo-ooooooo-oooooo-weee,' I would have a contraction. It was like his visceral, guttural utterances were in sync with the groaning travail of my labor. Geoff was out of town, so I was at a friend's house, and I listened to Howlin' Wolf until it became apparent that I better get to the hospital—and fast!"[97]

In January 1966, Chess released the album *The Real Folk Blues*, a collection of Wolf's most recent singles. The songs were great, but most blues fans already had them, which limited the album's sales.

The February 21, 1966, issue of *Newsweek* profiled Wolf, saying, "He's a giant of a man, a powerful 6-foot 3-inch, 275-pounder, whose short, thick, black hair streaked with white is the only sign that he is 55 years old. When his hands grip a microphone, cup his 'harp' . . . or strong-arm his guitar, the instruments simply disappear from view. When he sings he almost swallows the microphone in his efforts to be heard above the noise of his band—electric guitars, tenor sax and drums, all amplified and played at a frenzied pitch and ear-splitting dynamic level. In his hoarse, rasping voice that sounds like a runaway bucket of nails, he sings 'them mean old blues,' songs about faithless women, loneliness, tomcatting men or nameless trouble 'knockin' on my door.' "

In the article Wolf was quoted as saying, "It's just low-down, gut-bucket blues, the old common music, pleasing to the ear. I just rhyme up a good back-rail sound. This here jingle-jangle stuff ain't no good when you got problems, and a lot of people got problems. The blues ain't never gonna change." Wolf also bemoaned having to keep up with the modern sounds. "I'm on the modern style, all bands are on the modern style now with all the electric stuff," he said. "Not as good as the old guitar. That one with the hole in it, it got a good, sweet sound. But if I walk in a place with it, they'd say, 'Why don't somebody buy that poor boy a guitar?' In this here modern world you got to keep up with modern people."[98]

Sam Lay and Jerome Arnold soon left Wolf's band to play for Paul Butterfield. Lay had no hard feelings toward Wolf. "We was looking at the money part of it," he said. "The money was better. We had a guaranteed four nights a week in one place, didn't have to go nowhere. And the money was, like, 20 bucks a night, man—that was a lot of money then. . . . Working with Wolf we were getting, like, $12.50 a night, and we were working just on the weekends."[99] Taking Lay and Arnold's places were Cassell Burrow and Andrew McMahon, both of whom had been occasional members of the band for years.

On April 11, Wolf cut four more songs for Chess. "New Crawlin' King Snake" was Wolf's hard-charging version of a Delta blues standard. Roaring out his vocal as the band cooked up a musical maelstrom around him, Wolf recorded one of the toughest songs ever. Musical high marks go to Hubert, whose slithery guitar propelled the song into overdrive, and to the riffing saxophones of Eddie Shaw and an unidentified horn man. Wolf used to preface this song in performance with comic remarks such as, "I'm the king of all snakes and you bothered my den. If I bite you, you gonna be snake-bit the rest of your life. You ain't never gonna get well."[100]

"My Mind Is Ramblin' " was an updated version of "Mr. Highway Man." Cruising along like an Oldsmobile running down a lonely stretch of road, "My Mind Is Ramblin' " was another showcase for Hubert's original guitar style. These two songs were released as Chess 1968.

Unreleased at the time were two other songs. "Commit a Crime" was phenomenal: a harsh, hard-rocking, one-chord Delta-style blues that anticipated the angriest sounds of punk, heavy metal, hip-hop, and grunge. It was a simple, savage tale of attempted murder. Wolf may have been thinking of the death of his old friend Robert Johnson, who was poisoned by a woman at the instigation of a jealous husband.[101] When

Wolf sang, "I'm going to leave you woman before I commit a crime," he may also have been thinking of Hubert, who had a very stormy relationship with his wife.[102] Hubert and Evelyn fought so much that Wolf finally refused to let her into the clubs when they played. Hubert said Wolf told him he should leave Evelyn before it led to serious violence.[103]

"Commit a Crime" featured a blistering, repeated lick by Hubert in the key of E, accompanied by bone-crushing drums, punch-press piano, and incandescent sax. Wolf ranted his autobiographical warning in his most scorching voice:

> I'm going to leave you, woman, before I commit a crime. (2×)
> You tried so hard to kill me. Woman it just was not my time.
>
> You put poison in my coffee instead of milk or cream. (2×)
> You 'bout the evilest woman that I ever seen.
>
> You mixed my drink with a can of Red Devil lye. (2×)
> Then you sat down and watched me, hoping that I might die.

"Commit a Crime" remained a hidden gem in Wolf's catalogue and years later became a live showstopper for Stevie Ray Vaughan.

Less successful was "Poor Wind That Never Change," a tame, Dixieland-style remake of Blind Lemon Jefferson's "See That My Grave Is Kept Clean." Wolf's recorded legacy wouldn't have been diminished if it had never been issued. It's hard to believe that this cut and "Commit a Crime" were recorded at the same session. The difference in tone couldn't have been greater.

In July 1966, Wolf played the prestigious Newport Folk Festival. Founded by George Wein in 1959, Newport was a showcase for traditional American music as well as the hottest young folk and blues stars. Wolf's Newport schedule was full as he participated in a blues vocals workshop, played an afternoon set, performed on the main stage at night, and was filmed for two separate documentaries. Waiting his turn to perform at the workshop, Wolf was deeply moved by the gospel music of Reverend Pearly Brown. Wolf performed a couple of numbers on an acoustic guitar, pulling out some of his old Delta repertoire for a rapt audience.

The highlight of the day was Wolf's performance on the main stage. Dick Waterman recalls it vividly thirty years later. "The band is playing and Hubert is leading the band and the band is roaring away and no Wolf is in sight. This is the Newport night concert, which is eighteen thousand people, and they were up in a frenzy. And the band is playing and still no Wolf. And finally from the back left corner of the stage, Wolf enters, wearing work boots, Farmer Brown bib overalls, a long-sleeve work shirt, a white straw hat—a big, big hat. And he has a broom and he's sweeping the stage! The band keeps playing and Wolf keeps sweeping, slowly moving towards the front, and it takes a matter of minutes for him to do this. In Newport in those days, since they put so many acts on, each act had maybe seventeen or eighteen minutes. . . . For somebody to be wasting their stage minutes with these antics—well the Newport people were just totally baffled. Not just baffled, but stunned. Wolf finally comes right up to the front of the stage. He's taken three or four minutes to do this, and the crowd is in a frenzy. They're on their feet, they're roaring, they're just yelling and screaming, and the band has whipped them into a frenzy! And Wolf gets right up to the front of the stage, grabs the microphone, throws down the broom, and right on the chord change sings, 'I'm gonna get up in the mornin'—I believe I'll dust my broom!' He just disintegrated them. Just destroyed them—just destroyed them."[104] Taj Mahal saw Wolf's Newport show and was inspired to wear bib overalls and a big neckerchief for years, including on the cover of his influential 1969 album *Take a Giant Step*.

After his show on the main stage, Wolf and his band rode over to a faux juke joint that Library of Congress folklorist Alan Lomax had set up to film some of the festival's black performers—Wolf, Son House, Bukka White, Pearly Brown, and Skip James. Lomax gave everyone in the room free booze to re-create a juke joint atmosphere. Unfortunately, House, by then a desperate drunk, was in the advanced stage of alcoholism known as "wet brain," where a single drink could overload his damaged liver. Worse, House's manager, Waterman, was not at the filming. With no one to watch his intake, House drank up and started reeling.

When it was his time to perform, Wolf rapped about the blues. "A lot of people's wonderin', 'What is the blues?' I hear lots of people saying, 'The blues, the blues.' But I'm gonna tell you what the blues is:

When you ain't got no money, you got the blues. When you ain't got no money to pay your house rent, you still got the blues. A lot of people's hollerin' about, 'I don't like no blues.' But when you ain't got no money and can't pay your house rent and can't buy you no food, you damn sure got the blues. That's where it's at, let me tell you. That's where it's at. If you ain't got no money, you got the blues, 'cause you're thinkin' evil. That's right. Any time you thinkin' evil, you thinkin' 'bout the blues.

"If you gettin' everything you possess and don't need nothin', you don't have no right to worry about nothin'. But when you ain't got nothing, then you got to worry about somethin'. And that's where the blues come in. And Lord, first thing, say, 'I don't have this. And I don't have that.' And you look over there at these other peoples and they got this and they got that. Then in your heart, you feel like that you ain't nobody. You got the blues."

As Wolf explained the source of the blues, House babbled drunkenly, loud enough to be heard on film. Conscious of the camera, Wolf was incensed, "See, this man got the blues right there," Wolf retorted. "See? That's where the blues come from. Because he done drunk up all of his'n, and he worried." The room erupted in laughter. House continued his drunken ramblings. Priding himself on his self-control, Wolf was aghast to see how low his old mentor had fallen. Finally, he lashed out savagely. "Well, you see, you had a chance with your life, but you ain't done nothin' with it. . . . You don't love but one thing, and that's some whiskey, see, and that's plumb out of it." House gestured at a young woman in the room and said, "No, I love more'n whiskey. Well, I wants her, and she ain't whiskey!"[105] The room broke into nervous laughter. House had the last laugh, but it wasn't one of his or Wolf's finer moments.

Wolf's anger spilled over to his band. Hubert said, "Wolf told us, 'Hey, look at him. Look at this man. The man got drunk. Good musician: old musician. I been knowin' him a long time. Now look at him. Now, don't get me wrong—the man is great. But goddamn, how can he do this?' I said, 'Wolf, the man drink.' 'Oh, you don't understand, son. You don't understand what I'm sayin'.' And he got pissed off then. That's when he got mad with the band. He figured *we* wasn't producing—*we* wasn't playin', you understand? I didn't blame him for it."[106] Wolf was also angry that the band was out of tune. Sax player Sam

Jones, an infrequent player with Wolf's band, readjusted his mouthpiece after the band tuned and then blew off-key, marring the performance.

To compensate for the ragged band sound, Wolf threw himself into the performance with total abandon. He played terrific slide guitar while shaking his massive head and rolling his eyes on "Down in the Bottom." He blew beautifully raw, country-style blues harp for "How Many More Years," and sang an intense version of "Dust My Broom," at one point waving around a twenty-dollar bill while singing that his money was gone. Wolf ended the performance by salaciously licking his harp until House said, "Cut it out, Wolf."

That night back at the house where they were staying on the festival grounds, Wolf lit into his band. "What you think this is?" he roared. "You ain't working on the white man's farm! You ain't going to do me like that!"[107]

Despite the glitches the Newport Festival was a high point in an amazingly successful period for Wolf personally and professionally. At age fifty-six, he was in peak physical and musical form. He was the king of the blues world, lionized at the most prestigious music festivals and cutting records that would anticipate trends in popular music for decades. For now, he was "sittin' on top of the world." But nobody stays on top forever.

12. Change My Way

The charismatic blues singer caressed his microphone suggestively and glared at the crowd. "I am a—a back door man," he growled menacingly. On the dimly lit stage behind him, a pianist from South Chicago pounded out blues rhythms and a guitarist pulled slinky licks from his strings with his bare fingers as a drummer whipped out a narrow groove with rimshots as crisp as a fifty-dollar bill slapped down on a varnished bar. The singer dropped to his knees, unzipped his fly, and moaned, "I am a—I'm a back door man." Slowly pulling the head of a bottle from his pants, he howled, "Well, the men don't know, but the little girls understand." He stood suddenly, popped the bottle top, and sprayed the front of the crowd as a gaggle of young women shrieked in surprise.

Jim Morrison, Ray Manzarek, Robbie Krieger, and John Densmore—the Doors—had a good time with the Howlin' Wolf–Willie Dixon tune "Back Door Man" that night in 1966 at the Whisky A-Go-Go in Los Angeles. The next year, they recorded it on their debut album, which rose to number 2 on the pop charts in 1967. By then, the Yardbirds, Manfred Mann, the Animals, and the Rolling Stones had also recorded versions of songs first done by the Wolf. Within two years, Jimi Hendrix, Cream, the Jeff Beck Group, Electric Flag, and many other bands would follow suit. Bands that didn't cover Wolf's songs often sounded like him anyway. Lowell George of Little Feat was wild about Wolf, and Don Van Vliet—Captain Beefheart—made a career of singing like him. John Fogerty, chief revivalist of Creedence Clearwater Revival, began studying the original Delta bluesmen long after his band had its heyday. He said, "Along the way I did a lot of reading and an awful lot of listening. . . . When I did hear Patton, he sounded like Howlin' Wolf, who was a big influence on me. When I did 'Run Through the Jungle,' I was being Howlin' Wolf, and Howlin' Wolf knew Charlie Patton!"[1] The ultimate tribute came from Led Zeppelin, who used some of the lyrics and the lick from Wolf's "Killing Floor," slowed down and amped up, on "The Lemon Song" on their second album and copyrighted it as their own. Imitation may be the sincerest form of flattery, but carried too far, it'll land you in court. Led Zeppelin paid a large sum in 1972 to settle the infringement with ARC Music, Wolf's publisher.

In the late 1960s, young people were a key market for the bluesmen who made their reputations with Chess in the 1950s. The original audience for their music was shrinking. Even Wolf's stepdaughters ignored his music. Like most children of the 1960s, Bettye and Barbra preferred Martha & the Vandellas, Smokey Robinson, the Jackson Five, the Temptations, and Major Lance to Wolf, Muddy, Sonny Boy, and Little Walter. Blues producer Dick Shurman said, "When I used to go to Howlin' Wolf's house almost too many years ago to admit, his wife and daughter wouldn't let him listen to blues upstairs; he had to go down to the basement. His daughter used to play the Jackson Five and Temptations for me."[2] Until the late 1960s, Bettye and Barbra never went to the blues clubs to hear Wolf. He didn't want them out on the dangerous West and South sides at night.

Wolf knew he had to start appealing to the younger audience. He got along well with most of the young rock 'n' roll musicians he met on the road. Drummer Buddy Miles remembers Wolf trying to recruit him. "He used to say, 'There's that fat drummer, man, that can play that stuff. Man, why don't you come on with me, Buddy Miles? I need some fatback, brother!' It was just an honor because at that time, I was with the Electric Flag."[3]

Wolf also liked the hippies. Nick Gravenites saw Wolf in 1966 at the Family Dog ballroom. "It was just extraordinary, because that was the very height of hippie craziness in San Francisco. People were running around half-naked, mostly naked, people all painted up, some guy running around with a little flag tied to his dick. Crazy! Psychedelic black lights, light shows, and all that stuff, and there's the Wolf.

"That show typified him. He got up there and he saw all these crazy people up there. How do people deal with situations like this? How do people deal with reality? Well, Wolf did a whole lot of crazy shit that night. He would lie down on the stage and play guitar, not doing anything spectacular, but just lying there. He'd get into giving people all kinds of weird looks. He would get into all kinds of weird, strange physical attitudes. You know, it was like one crazy guy and eight hundred crazy people. They were all crazy, but in different ways. This is how the Wolf handled strangeness: He got strange himself. And he could get strange! I saw him just sitting around and lying on the floor and then coming back up and giving looks to the people and making himself look like a monkey or something. That's how he dealt with all this craziness—to get crazy himself! Seemed like a perfect antidote. It was pretty far out, man. I never will forget it. People asked, 'Who's that strange guy up there?' It was sort of like *they* were supposed to be strange, and they're asking, 'Who's that strange guy?' "[4]

After the show, Wolf said to guitarist Sam Andrew of Big Brother & the Holding Company, "Boy, you got more soul than I have on my shoe!" Andrew said, "Now how is a long-haired hippie boy supposed to take that? With a big smile and a lot of laughs."[5]

The next year, singer and pianist Tracy Nelson, who'd heard Wolf many times in Chicago, finally met him at San Francisco's Matrix nightclub. "I was all thrilled and he kind of looked at me and shook my hand and just about broke it and said, 'Get me some joiky!' You know, 'jerky'—the beef sticks. So what are you going to do? I went and got him some beef jerky from the bar."[6]

Chess Records was going through changes in 1967. In April, the brothers moved the company to new headquarters at 320 East 21st Street—seven times as large as the company's old digs. The new building had its own pressing plant and a studio twice as large as the old one. As always, the brothers had big ambitions but knew that hubris could prompt a gurgling corporate spiral down the drain. In her history of Chess Records, Nadine Cohodas wrote, "As the renovation of 320 E. 21st

Street was under way, Leonard and Phil watched the final, sobering collapse of their onetime competitor Vee Jay. . . . But their friends the Ertegun brothers and Jerry Wexler over at Atlantic were demonstrating that a small independent company could become even larger and more successful than Chess. In June of 1967, when the move into the new Chess studio was nearly completed, Atlantic set a record with the number of singles it placed on the Billboard Hot One Hundred—eighteen, including number one, Aretha Franklin singing 'Respect' followed by the Young Rascals and 'Groovin'.' "[7]

In June 1967, Wolf went into the studio to cut something aimed squarely at younger fans. "Pop It to Me" featured Wolf doing a credible job as a soul singer. Cassell Burrow's funk drumming anchored the rest of the band—Hubert, Eddie Shaw, and Bob Anderson on bass—as they riffed away on dance licks. Two other tunes from the same session were traditional Chicago blues shuffles. "I Had a Dream," written by Wolf, was memorable for Hubert's uncanny playing and Wolf's always solid harp. "Dust My Broom" was a raucous, clanging cover of the Robert Johnson–Elmore James blues standard.

Leonard and Phil needed to support their increased overhead—literally, since their new building was eight stories high instead of the two in their old building. They also owned several radio stations, a pressing plant, and had more than two hundred people on the payroll. And they wanted to keep their original blues artists happy by channeling money to them despite the shrinking market for blues. The easiest solution was to get more mileage out of their vast back catalogue. On January 27, 1967, Chess released another repackaged album of Wolf's old hits: *More Real Folk Blues*. The title was a gimmick. Like the *Real Folk Blues* album the year before, it was far from folk blues, with hard-rocking electric blues tunes such as "I'll Be Around," "You're Gonna Wreck My Life," and "Who Will Be Next." It sold modestly but didn't cost Chess much to release.

Leonard's son, Marshall, had big plans for Wolf, Muddy, and the other founding Chess bluesmen. For years, he'd prepared himself to take over the reins of the company. He wanted to excel on both the creative and business ends like his father. Almost single-handedly, he put together the company's international operations, during which he witnessed the potential for blues with young people in Britain, Europe, and, he hoped, the United States, if only the older bluesmen could be properly presented. "I was growing up and became part of that '60s psychedelic revolution, with the Beatles and the Stones changing the whole consciousness of the world," he said. "I really tried to pull some of the blues artists—primarily Muddy and Wolf—into that to get more sales for them, because there was a period where these guys were really hurting. Their original audience died off or converted to Motown and R&B. The blues artists I knew and loved were really struggling to make money. I did whatever I could at that time to try to help them earn more money—to try to move them into this new market because the white blues album market, which was just beginning, wasn't really selling enough to generate real income for them. So I did those kinds of albums and aimed the packaging and the content at a different audience to buy them."[8]

One of Marshall's first projects was producing two "Super Super Blues Band" albums featuring Wolf, Muddy, Bo Diddley, and Little Walter jamming and hamming it up in the studio. These LPs were somewhat of a guilty pleasure for blues fans—musically mediocre, but drop-dead funny. The one with Bo, Muddy, and Wolf was very entertaining. Backed by Hubert on guitar, Buddy Guy on bass, Otis Spann on piano, Clifton James on drums, and singer Cookie Vee, the bluesmen ad-libbed through some of their standards, reveling in their rivalry. After this LP, no one could say they took themselves too seriously. A prime example was "Ooh Baby," on which the three men played the dozens behind singer Vee. Wolf: "You know that brand-new car you bought that girl? I'm drivin' it!" Bo Diddley: "What?" Wolf: "I'm drivin' it now!" Bo: "Well, I heard that Muddy Waters sold it to her!" Muddy: "I sold it to her!" Wolf: "No, you bought it for her!"

While the dissing sounded serious enough on record, Wolf and Muddy were better friends than people thought. At this point in their careers, their competition was partly a put-on: good for business. "Those guys really loved one another, man," said Eddie Shaw, who had played with both. "You know, just maybe they had an incident that happened down through the years that it wasn't feasible that the other one could understand it. But they always respected one another."[9] Onstage, Wolf and Muddy played up their rivalry; offstage, they sometimes drank and dined together. Muddy came over to the Burnetts' house several times for dinner during the late 1960s and early 1970s. By then, both men had mellowed and could commiserate over their common fate as aging bluesmen.

Age wasn't their only problem. The whole country seemed to be coming apart at the seams in 1968. On April 4, Dr. Martin Luther King was assassinated in Memphis, and riots erupted across the country. In Chicago, looting, shooting, and firebombing spread through the West Side, killing nine people. Silvio's was burned to the ground. Wolf and Barbra drove out to survey the damage. When he saw his old club, he wept—the only time Barbra ever saw him cry.[10] "I run a place there, me and a Italian called Silvio," he said. "We run it for about 15, 20 years, and I made a lot of money there. And I was doing good until they killed King, y'know. Then, those people tore up Chicago. . . . They just tore them old houses up, see, and they tore up my shack right with 'em. I lost about, me and that honky lost about, I'd say, about 40,000 dollars each. . . . I fed 'em, I treated 'em nice and I done give 'em whiskey, but you see, they this grudgin'-hearted, you know? A lot of people begrudge you when you're doin' something they can't. They'll do anything to hurt you."[11]

Although not an activist, Wolf supported the civil rights movement by performing at fund-raisers in Chicago. One such show, hosted by the Reverend Jesse Jackson, featured Wolf on a bill with B. B. King, Little Milton, and Marvin Gaye. The day of the show, promoter Pervis Spann asked Wolf to open. Singer Bobby Rush described what happened next. "Wolf went in the back and pulled his shirt off. Had a pair of overalls on! And he came out on the floor with a hammer in one hand and a hacksaw in the other hand, and he came onstage howlin' and draggin'— said, 'I had my fun if I never get well no more.' I'm gonna tell you somethin'—after he did this song, they applauded for 30 minutes! The show was over! Honestly, you never saw anything like it. I mean just nobody could do anything that night."[12]

By May, Wolf was back on the East Coast. Dick Waterman brought his girlfriend, Bonnie Raitt, not yet a professional musician, to hear him at the Scene, a club on the West Side of Manhattan. Waterman and Raitt met Wolf as he came offstage near a bank of strobe lights, which made the sweat pouring down his face look like molten silver. "It was surreal," said Waterman. He introduced Raitt to Wolf, who took her hand and folded it in his massive paw. He looked down at her and purred, "Hello, daaarrrlinnn'!" Waterman said, "She melted! It was one of the great moments of Bonnie's life."[13] Years later, Raitt said, "If I had to pick one person who does everything I loved about the blues, it would be Howlin' Wolf. It would be the size of his voice, or just the size of him. When you're a little pre-teenage girl and you imagine what a naked man in full arousal is like, it's Howlin' Wolf. When I was a kid, I saw a horse in a field with an erection, and I went, 'Holy shit!' That's how I feel when I hear Howlin' Wolf—and when I met him it was the same thing. He was the scariest, most deliciously frightening bit of male testosterone I've ever experienced in my life."[14]

Scary was right, if you were in Wolf's band and refused to follow his rules. He fired everyone in his band at least once—even his bandleader Eddie Shaw, who said, "He'd tell the guys as we get in the station wagon, 'Well, man, you gotta find you another horn player. I done fired this one.' When we'd be leaving Boston, he would fire me. Hubert be drunk so Wolf was driving. I didn't drink. We get about two hundred miles out and I could see his leg starting to shake and he starts wiggling. Hubert dead asleep. Hubert and I did most of the driving. Wolf'd say, 'Man, Hubert drunk and I'm getting tired of driving. Time for some-body else to drive.' I didn't say nothing because he done fired me. I ain't going to drive. 'Hey, man, do you want to drive?' 'Naw, I don't want to drive. Why am I going to drive when you done fired me?' We get on down the road. 'I'm going to wait. I ain't going to fire you till I get home. And we'll talk about it. Right now you ain't fired.' He'd hire me back and I'd drive!"[15]

Some of Wolf's band members came home empty-handed from weeks on the road and told their wives that Wolf didn't pay them. When Andrew McMahon's wife, Ida, complained to Wolf about it, he called a meeting with the band members and invited their wives. Then he recited a litany of crimes and misdemeanors. "Eddie Shaw, you didn't bring your money home because you gambled it up. Hubert Sumlin, you gambled and drank your money up. S. P. Leary, you drank yours up. Andrew McMahon, you know you bought the womens with all your money." McMahon tried to convince his wife that Wolf was lying, but she didn't buy it. "Wolf didn't like that wrongdoing," she said. "I guess he just didn't want his name scandalized that he was not paying his boys when he knew he was."[16]

Wolf was equally blunt with rude audience members. One night on a double bill in Memphis with Muddy Waters, someone in front had the nerve to yell about Wolf's garish yellow tuxedo, "Look at that man in the monkey suit!" Wolf glared and said, "I don't know what you-all talking about. You may think my suit's funny. Yeah—go ahead and laugh. But you here to listen to me tonight—I'm not here to listen to you. And 'cause of that, I got a pile of money big enough to burn up a wet mule!"[17]

Another show in Memphis demonstrated how popular Wolf still was in the South. Appearing at Club Paradise with hometown Stax recording artists Albert King and Johnnie Taylor, Wolf performed for a standing-room-only crowd. "The Paradise seated five thousand people," recalled A. J. Burnett, a dancer unrelated to Wolf, despite her surname. "It was huge! And that place was packed and jammed. It was just elbow-to-elbow trying to get in there. And Johnnie Taylor thought everybody was coming to see him and Albert King did, too. And Howlin' Wolf got up and said, 'Oooohhh! Smokestack Lightnin'!' That was it! Everybody could've went on home. You couldn't hear nary another word! All them people had come out of Mississippi and Arkansas. They all come to see him: Howlin' Wolf."[18]

Wolf played several times a year in the late 1960s at the Club Harlem in Prichard, Alabama, just north of Mobile. Promoter and dee-jay Ruben Hughes, who booked Wolf for the club and had known him in Chicago, never had to worry about him drawing a crowd. "The people was so in love with the Wolf until they just couldn't hardly wait until it was time for him to come back. We'd sell out probably a week or so before the Wolf even got there. That was one of his favorite towns."

Hughes remembered Wolf visiting his radio show in Mobile. "The record 'Killing Floor' was popular and the Wolf came in the door and he said, 'I'm lookin' for a disc jockey named Sugar Daddy.' I said, 'Well, you got him.' He told Hubert, 'Go out to the car and get me a hammer so I can hit Sugar Daddy and put him on the killing floor.' We had a big laugh. . . . We went to the club that night—a double line all around the building. Wolf drew one of the biggest crowds we'd ever seen that night." The last time Wolf played the Club Harlem in the early 1970s, a riot broke out when the club couldn't hold everyone who wanted to get in.[19]

In late June, Wolf drove out to California with Hubert, Eddie Shaw, drummer Cassell Burrow, and bass player B. B. Jones (Alvin Nichols). A review of their show at the Palace in San Diego said, "Burnett, of course gave (or appeared to give) his all in the interests of socking the good old down-home electric Chicago-Mississippi blues right to us, sweat streaming down his craggy face from drenched iron-gray hair, monstrous fist shaking, finger pointing down like an angry black Jehovah/King Kong hybrid deity with a voice that makes Wolfman Jack sound like Tiny Tim."[20]

At the Ash Grove in Los Angeles, Wolf talked about the country's troubles with a journalist. "Somebody has been cashing checks and they've been bouncing back on us. And these people, the poor class of Negroes and the poor class of white people, they're getting tired of it. And sooner or later it's going to bring on a disease on this country, a disease that's going to spring from mid-air and it's going to be bad. It's like a spirit from some dark valley, something that sprung up from the ocean. . . . Like Lucifer is on the earth telling people these obvious things, causing a lot of the people to get irritated. But we can't afford what's going to happen. A lot of innocent people is going to get killed unless they get some kind of satisfaction. . . .

"Too many people have nothing these days but hard work, and when they come to the place where they don't meet their job, they in bad shape. Start 'em to thinking. Start 'em to doing things they wasn't supposed to do, because they got a family and that woman get to crying for bread. That makes a man do things that he's not supposed to do 'cause your wife's sitting there crying and your children's sitting there weeping 'Daddy do this and Daddy do that' and that puts thoughts in your mind.

"You go to the people who have everything and you ask a favor and they go to work and push you off. So you go to work and do things you're not supposed to do. And when you do these things, they going to call the police. And they will shoot at you like you a bird or a rabbit and don't never stop to think that that poor man's got a family. They shoot you like a dog. First they got to stop and think why this man do these problems before you hurt him. 'Cause everybody he does something, he's got a reason.

"The black people fighting in Vietnam now, when they come back they ain't going to settle for these little offers and these back-door hand-outs like they been doing. They ain't going to take it 'cause they realize they been cheated. . . . I don't try to go preaching because we're all wrong and we're all human."[21]

Driving north, Wolf played at the Berkeley Folk Festival with Quicksilver Messenger Service and It's a Beautiful Day. In San Francisco, he played at the Avalon Ballroom, where he befriended another young blues fan, Sandy Guy Schoenfeld. A photography student, Schoenfeld carried a Nikon 35mm camera to the show, got backstage, and encountered the Wolf. "Wolf was intense, focused, happy, bigger than life, actually, and incredibly expressive," he said. "He radiated a unique, powerful charisma and presence, which came through in his music." Wolf asked Schoenfeld if he'd take some new publicity photos for him, and Schoenfeld said he'd be glad to. Later that week, he took his cameras out to where Wolf was staying at the Eddy Street Hotel, in the city's tough Tenderloin district. "There we were, in the sleaziest place I'd ever been in," he said. "There was only one chair, a semi-easy chair with wooden arms that sported a huge, sharp, dangerous coil spring that poked way up from the middle of where the cushion used to be, like a bad joke." Schoenfeld snapped away as Wolf posed with a bottle of whiskey, a box of crackers, and a bag of tobacco while talking about wanting to do product endorsements. They headed out to the hotel parking lot, where Schoenfeld snapped Wolf posing with his guitar, with the rusting buildings, broken windows, barbed wire, empty bottles, and broken glass of the industrial wasteland as a backdrop.

After the shoot, Wolf suggested they get some refreshments. They retired to a seedy local tavern and Wolf ordered them beers. Suddenly, a knot of frightened people began pouring into the bar and moving to the back wall. "I stared at the door, figuring maybe there was a fight going on outside," Schoenfeld said. "Wolf didn't seem to notice, he was so calm and centered." Like a scene out of Dirty Harry, an angry man strode in, took the only empty seat at the bar, next to Schoenfeld, pulled out a pistol, placed it conspicuously on the bar, and announced, "Nobody's moving!" Schoenfeld briefly thought of grabbing the gun, but good sense or cowardice stayed his hand.

Wolf leaned over and whispered, "C'mon, man. Let's get outta here." "Lead the way," said Schoenfeld. They slowly got up and walked out, Schoenfeld expecting any second to feel a bullet in his back. Wolf was so calm that even before they got to the door, he was discussing his photos again. Schoenfeld said, "Can't we wait till we're out of range? I can't think about it now." Wolf said, "Oh yeah, okay," and seemed amused. As they walked back to the hotel, Wolf mentioned that he'd accidentally bumped a man at a corner store the night before when he went to buy liquor. The man pulled out a .38 and pressed it against Wolf's belly. Wolf begged him not to shoot, and the man let him go with a warning.

The next day, Schoenfeld returned with a tape recorder to the hotel, where he recorded a harp lesson with the mighty Wolf while accompanying him by drumming on the room's nightstand. A few weeks later, Schoenfeld sent Wolf two hundred promo shots and one thousand photo-backed business cards showing him with his guitar next to the number thirteen. Wolf wrote him back, enclosed payment and thanked him for his work, adding, "If I ever need a drummer, I will keep you in mind . . . —Your Wolf."[22]

Wolf played another show at the Avalon on July 22 with Quicksilver Messenger Service and Dan Hicks and His Hot Licks. By August 10, he was across the country, up in Toronto for the Mariposa Folk Festival, where he appeared at a workshop with Bukka White, Bill Monroe, and Mike Seeger. "Howlin' Wolf, a veteran urban-blues exponent, delighted an audience of more than 1500 young people with his gutsy, meaningful songs, and his unusual stage antics," wrote a columnist for the *Toronto Globe and Mail*. "The huge, almost evil-looking singer fell to his knees, lay on the floor, and writhed in lyrical agony, much to the delight of those armed with cameras close to the stage."[23]

By mid-August, Wolf was back in the Chicago clubs and taking no guff from his band. One night his piano player passed out drunk onstage. As the rest of the band tried to rouse him, Wolf said, "That's okay: Let him sleep. Long as he's asleep, he's got a job. But when he wakes up, he's a fired motherfucker."[24] Another night, Wolf called Robert "Bilbo" Walker, a guitarist who sat in and played too loud, a "mule-sician."[25]

In November 1968, Wolf went into the studio to do a Cadet Concept album titled simply *Howlin' Wolf*, often referred to as the "electric" Wolf album, like the *Electric Mud* album by Muddy Waters done the

same year. Wolf and Hubert Sumlin plus a troupe of Chess session players redid many of Wolf's classics with "psychedelic" instrumentation.
The result was allegedly "heavy" music, a term of approval then current. Indeed, the album's remakes of "Three Hundred Pounds of Joy"
and "Built for Comfort" sounded like theme songs for a Fat Pride rally.

The biggest problem was the album's lack of dynamics. Blues—
especially Wolf's one-chord, modal blues—is all about the subtle
manipulation of rhythm, tone, and volume to create a mood. But there
was very little subtlety on this album. The arrangements and instrumentation were comically bombastic. The drums were too loud on
almost every cut and sounded as subtle as the switching line at a busy
freight-train yard. Hyperbolic, multitracked guitars screamed distressing
sounds through wah-wahs, fuzz tones, and other distortion devices, all
of which Wolf hated. The final mix sounded like it was done in a
cement truck. The result was a mishmash of sound and fury signifying . . . Well, Wolf said it best in a profile in *Rolling Stone* that drove the
Chess PR team to despair. "Man . . . that stuff's dogshit."[26]

Pete Cosey, a Chess session guitarist who later played with Miles
Davis, remembered how much Wolf hated recording the album. "The
Wolf was outraged at all those electronics. He was angry. He was furious. He hadn't encountered any of those types of electronics and he
didn't consider that the blues. During the sessions he would scowl and
he was mad. Phil Chess came in and tried to console him. That's one of
the pictures I have from that session. The Wolf was looking like his feelings were hurt.

"Wolf dropped a real good lug on me. I had a real long beard, my
shades, a big natural. One day when we were in the sessions, the Wolf
looked at me and he said, 'Why don't you take them wah-wahs and all
that other shit and go throw it off in the lake—on your way to the barber
shop?' He just wiped all my shit out in one stroke!"

Despite the insult, Cosey admired Wolf. "I always considered Howling Wolf the intellectual of the blues," he said. "Very intelligent man: In
observing things, he would always sit down and analyze. He was usually
right on the money. . . . I always had a great respect for Wolf's intuition
and knowledge."[27]

Released in January 1969, the psychedelic *Howlin' Wolf* album was
savaged by the critics. It didn't help that Marshall Chess made light of

Wolf's disgust by prominently placing on its front cover, over a bare white background, big red letters that read, "This is Howlin' Wolf's new album. He doesn't like it. He didn't like his electric guitar at first either." Unlike Muddy's *Electric Mud*, which stayed on the *Billboard* and *Cash Box* charts for months, Wolf's psychedelic album tanked. "I used negativity in the title," said Marshall, "and it was a big lesson: You can't say on the cover that the artist didn't like the album. It didn't really sell that well. But it was just an attempt. They were just experiments."[28]

The best track on the album was the futuristic remake of "Moanin' at Midnight," done with just a couple of subtly distorted guitars plus Wolf's harp and voice. It was eerie and atmospheric, like the acoustic/ electric hybrid tunes done decades later by Otis Taylor, who was heavily influenced by the Wolf. If Wolf's producers had done the rest of *Howlin' Wolf* that way, it might've been a great album.

In fact, they missed their chance to do just that. While Wolf was in the studio for the psychedelic album, producer Charles Stepney recorded him playing a few acoustic blues numbers. The results were spectacular, but went unreleased for decades. Unless someone discovers a trove of acoustic sides by Wolf, this impromptu session provides the best glimpse we'll ever get of what Wolf must've sounded like in a juke joint in the 1930s. Wolf accompanied himself on guitar throughout with a first-position E chord in standard tuning. He played two versions of "Ain't Goin' Down That Dirt Road," combining lyrics from Tommy Johnson's "Big Road Blues," Charlie Patton's "Down the Dirt Road Blues," and Floyd Jones's "Dark Road Blues" (which Wolf taught to Jones in the 1940s). Wolf's first take on the tune is a revelation. His guitar playing is rudimentary and his voice not at his best—he clears his throat noisily several times—but his uncanny musicality shines through. He starts the song at a funereal pace but subtly picks it up from beginning to end while punctuating the lyrics with eerie moans. The song is about much more than a dirt road. As the performance unfolds, the song becomes dark, indeed—a meditation on death. On the second take of "Dirt Road," an up-tempo variation that added lines from Tommy Johnson's "Bye Bye Blues," Wolf started thumping his guitar like a drum—a trick he learned from Patton to keep time in the din of a juke joint. His acoustic version of "Rollin' and Tumblin'," associated with Hambone Willie Newbern and countless others, was equally rock-

ing. The acoustic "I'm the Wolf" cut was a playful, stripped-down version of the song Wolf cut back in February 1952 for RPM Records.
"Woke Up This Morning" mixed stock blues lyrics—"woke up this
morning feeling awful bad"—with a syncopated, danceable rhythm. It's
easy to imagine Wolf scooting his chair around the floor of a juke joint
while thumping away on this.

During this session, producer Charles Stepney recorded a long
interview with Wolf that's been excerpted on several records. "I got a different sound in the blues field from anybody else, you know?" Wolf
said. "See, it's a on-the-beat sound. . . . It's just a good sound, you know,
and today peoples go for the great sound. They done left the music, you
know what I mean? So if you got that sound out there where they can
snatch theyselves and jump around, well, they like that, see?"[29]

Given the exceptional quality of these spur-of-the-moment takes by
Wolf—and with the infallible hindsight of thirty years, during which
the market for acoustic blues has grown enormously—it's hard to
understand why the Chess producers didn't bring Wolf into the studio
to do a full-on acoustic album, as they did with the *Muddy Waters: Folk
Singer* album of 1964. Wolf, after all, played acoustic Delta blues longer
than Muddy did and, unlike Muddy, played with all of the Delta blues
legends: Charlie Patton, Son House, Willie Brown, Robert Johnson,
Sonny Boy II, and others. Chess records producer Gene Barge said,
"You have to understand how record companies work. Traditional blues
wasn't doing that well in the marketplace. Also, Muddy was the star and
Wolf was a star in his own right, and John Lee Hooker and all those
guys. But the new guys like Little Milton and those guys were emerging
as the guys in R&B and blues. They were like a hybrid, a cross between
R&B and the blues, and Little Milton and Johnnie Taylor, these were
the new guys coming on. So the older guys were living basically on their
reputations. . . . At this time, there was still a lot of resistance to these
guys just recording. A lot of record companies would never have
recorded them. . . . Willie [Dixon] was there, but the only thing about
Willie was he was really interested in selling his material. That was his
reason for even producing records. He didn't present himself as a guy to
get the artist out there no matter where the material came from or how
he would do it."[30]

While Wolf was recording his "electric" album, word got out that

Leonard and Phil were considering selling Chess Records to concentrate on their radio stations. In early 1969, they announced the deal: Chess Records would be sold to General Recorded Tapes, a Sunnyvale, California, company that manufactured and sold blank tapes to companies such as Chess. GRT had no experience in the recording business but wanted to acquire a stable of artists. Like all the Chess artists—and Marshall Chess, who didn't know about the deal until it was done— Wolf was stunned. Leonard assured him the company would continue with Phil and Marshall and himself, but Wolf was not happy.

Soon after the deal was consummated, GRT invited Wolf and a few other Chess artists to play at their annual sales convention in New York. "At this time, they had all these diverse artists, all these strange people," said Barge, "and he didn't know any of them. He didn't believe that this was the kind of setting that he would be comfortable in, and to tell you the truth, I didn't either. But we needed him in New York to introduce him to the company. He was the only traditional blues guy we had to go. Muddy had just had an automobile accident. So we got a New York rhythm section and we had a rehearsal. He was still nervous. But the New York rhythm section guys were jazz guys, and they got into it. Wolf had his acoustic guitar and they really made him feel a lot more comfortable. When he did his presentation, he was the only real blues guy there, and he stole the show from all these guys—Funkadelic and Parliament and a whole group of people.

"He was singing for his life. He was just sitting there in the chair, had his acoustic, and just sang the tunes, one of them just straight singing—the blues. All these straight-laced, suit-wearing guys from California were just into the administration of the tape company, and here they have this record company, and they don't know what to do with it. And they meet Wolf. Of course, he was very reserved and quiet and didn't have much to say. He was polite and courteous, and he got back on the plane to go back to Chicago."[31]

Back home, Wolf and his band often played the new North Side club Alice's Revisited. Blues deejay Greg Freerksen saw them there one night in 1969. "The crowd began to dance so I stood up to avoid getting trampled on. When I got up, my face was about two or three feet from the Wolf's face. That's when he broke into 'I Asked Her for Water and She Gave Me Gasoline.' He looked mad when he sang—downright pissed—just like he'd taken a big gulp of gasoline. His eyes were on fire, bulging out of their sockets, his mouth was nothing but a frown, almost a grimace. He opened his huge mouth and sang. His lips were almost wrapped around the microphone and it looked like he was surely going to eat the thing. The Wolf looked mad enough to actually do it."[32]

In May 1969, Wolf headed overseas for another tour of the United Kingdom, arriving at London's Heathrow Airport on Thursday, May 15. The tour agent, Roy Tempest, picked him up and drove him to a rehearsal room off London's Tottenham Court Road to meet the John Dummer Blues Band: Dave Kelly on vocals and slide guitar, John Dummer on drums, Ian "Thump" Thompson on bass, Adrian Pietryga on lead guitar, and sometimes Bob Hall on piano, accompanied by roadie and driver Chris Sladen. They all had idolized Wolf for years. "We were nervous," said Dummer. "Thump and Dave were joking about how to address the man. 'All right, Howlin'?' caused much merriment. (That became our catch phrase: 'I'm the Wolf, but you can call me Howlin'.') Or did he like to be known as Chester? The problem was solved when he loomed in the doorway and beamingly bear-gripped our hands with the greeting, 'Hi! I'm the Wolf.' Then he sat down and blew us through 'Ain't Superstitious,' 'Goin' Down Slow,' 'Smokestack Lightnin',' 'Spoonful,' and the rest."[33] After a one-hour rehearsal, Wolf told them they were playing his kind of music. "I can see by the way you hold your guitars that you're musicians," he said.[34] They were elated—acceptance by their hero. A guitar-effect pedal, though, was banned after it set Wolf off on a five-minute tirade about "that goddamn wah-wah!"

For the next fortnight, the young bluesmen were in for the time of their lives. They drove 275 miles up to Sunderland the next day to play a short evening set. The next night, they backed Wolf at London's Polytechnic School on Regent Street. "The hall was heaving with about a thousand people packed in like sardines," said Kelly. "Wolf connected immediately and grabbed the gig by the scruff of the neck from the instant he boarded the stage. This was the best performance of the tour. He played for nearly two hours. He used every inch of his body to get his songs across, howled at the moon, got on all fours, rolled on his back, rolled his eyes, worked and worked, and the audience knew they'd been worked over by the Tail Dragger. But he didn't wipe out his tracks: Anyone there that night would remember that show for the rest of their lives—or they've got a hole in their soul."[35]

Sunday and Monday, Wolf and the boys played at the Black Prince in Bexley and the Kings Head in Romford on the outskirts of London. "On stage Wolf was incredible," said Dummer. "He never got juiced up to coast through a set. No—every performance he worked, sometimes frighteningly hard, until he got the audience. And it was basically a pub tour and some of those punters didn't honestly merit him giving so much of himself. . . . It was unbelievable. His voice was stronger and more beautiful than you could imagine."[36] Wolf decided he liked the boys enough to travel with them, so he dispensed with his tour agent, who didn't understand the blues anyway. "He traveled with us in our classic rock 'n' roll van," said Kelly, "a six-wheeled Ford Transit with two rows of bench seats, a bulkhead for the amps, a laughably small PA system in back, and a nasty smell."[37] Wolf was a great traveling companion. "He was always good-tempered," said Dummer, "and after gigs especially he was hilarious, roaring out obscure anecdotes and ribald songs, mainly in praise of the miraculous healing properties of 'pussy,' until the atmosphere verged on hysteria."[38] Wolf usually took a spot in the van across two seats in front, crammed in next to the "Squoit," as Wolf pronounced Squirt, his nickname for Sladen. Kelly says, "Wolf would tell him, 'I'm gonna watch you, boy. I'll keep you awake. You start to nod, I'm gonna blow my harp.' We'd be dozing in the back and sure enough loud, wailing harp would disturb our slumber. Wolf thought Chris was getting tired."[39] Sometimes the Squoit would feign fatigue just to hear Wolf's harp. "When Wolf sussed he was being put on," said Dummer, "he laughed like a drain and whapped his massive hand down to apply his dreaded leg-grip on the little Squoit."[40] Wolf told them fascinating stories about musicians he'd played with, bluesmen such as Charlie Patton. "He was only as big as my prick," Wolf said, "but man, what a voice!" He said he loved Jimmy Reed, who, alas, "liked too much juice" and would play "Ain't That Lovin' You Baby" over and over until Wolf had to threaten not to pay him to get him to move on. He did hilarious impressions of Jimmy Reed in his cups. He talked about the civil rights and black power movements and other happenings in the States. He was always on the lookout for a café where he could get a huge plate of ham and eggs "just like back home," though he was invariably disappointed by the results.[41]

The next Saturday, they played just before the weekly ska dance party at the Flamingo Club in London. "The place was heaving with cool, hip young West Indians," said Kelly. "Wolf was definitely up for it. This was the first 'black' venue we'd played. Of course, these hip young dudes were there for the disco. They'd never heard of Howlin' Wolf and couldn't care less about the blues. We came offstage and Wolf laid into us that we'd played badly and let him down, evidenced by the lack of response from the audience. The one show where we played to what he called 'my people,' we had failed. I said, 'Wolf, they're not your people. They're West Indians and they don't know blues music. They've come for the ska later on.' Wolf glared at me, face in my face, and said, 'Don't tell me how to play to coons! I'm a coon myself!' I was shocked at his terminology and a bit scared at having three hundred pounds of heavenly joy turn into three hundred pounds of angry Wolf. I left the dressing room and got on with the load-out. All was fine the next day and the topic wasn't raised again."[42] To pad his own pockets, tour agent Tempest quit booking hotels for Wolf and the band on the road, so Wolf had to return every night to a cheap hotel in London called the White House. Wolf was bored sitting in his room on days off, so Kelly lent him an old Harmony guitar. Wolf accidentally stepped on it and cracked it and was extremely apologetic. "I taped it up on the side of the body where it had split," said Kelly. "It was still playable and I pointed out to him that forever I would be able to show off this guitar and say 'This was played and broken by the great Howlin' Wolf.' He laughed but I don't think he realized that I was serious."[43] Wolf offered to teach Kelly music theory, but only had time to demonstrate his slide guitar part to "The Red Rooster" on the taped-together guitar.

One afternoon they stopped for beer at a pub, and several drunken construction workers, seeing the long-haired "freaks" and a big black man, let the air out of their van's tires. Wolf and the boys were inspecting the damage when one of the louts staggered up. "He came over and slurred, 'Sorry about the tires,' " said Kelly, "and then asked who we were and who was the big guy. We told him he was a blues singer called Howlin' Wolf. He said, 'What? I've met Howlin' Wolf?' THE Howlin'

Wolf?' He staggered away and returned with a couple of his mates and he made them pump up our tires as he sobbed, 'Howlin' Wolf—I've met Howlin' Wolf! We've let down Howlin' fucking Wolf's fucking tires. Oh, no!' "[44] The blues-loving lout succeeded in conveying to his mates just how great Howlin' Wolf was. They all showed up at the gig that night to hear and cheer on Wolf and the boys.

Wolf's performances were frighteningly intense. "About three or four times on the tour something almost mystical happened," Dummer said. "It wasn't my imagination, either, because I'd look across at Thump and afterwards he said he'd felt it too. We remember it happening at the Il Rondo, Leicester. Wolf went down into the audience, mike in hand, and his voice suddenly took on an extra presence, as if some terrifying power had taken over from outside. My immediate reaction behind the drum kit was, 'Christ, what the fuck's happening?' "[45] Kelly remembers the song: Wolf's rendition of "Tell Me What I've Done." "That night, he went out among the students and had them sit on the floor while he pleaded the song on one knee. It seemed he was singing it for his wife, whom he'd phoned that day. He waved his hand back at us onstage, meaning down with the volume, and he met any lick or fill by any of us with a glare. We got quieter and quieter as he gave a master class in blues feeling: less is more. I was shaking at the end of that song, and many girls in the audience had tears in their eyes. I've heard some greats, but I never heard a performance like that before or since."[46]

Wolf wasn't always so pitch perfect. One night they played at the Speakeasy Club in central London. Kelly said, "I don't know if Wolf had too many whiskeys bought for him by the admiring, back-slapping punters, but it was obvious something was wrong at the start of the second set. Wolf decided he was going to play guitar. He turned round to me and said, 'Gimme your guitar, son.' I thought it wasn't a good idea. As I handed it over I said, 'It's in open E tuning.' He growled, 'You don't have to tell me what tuning it's in!' Then he sat down and proceeded to play standard chords on a guitar in open tuning. This did not make for cool music. My colleagues onstage did their best, trying to decide what key to follow in, trying to turn his amp down, trying to hold it together in some way, but it was a lost cause. Predictably, in the music press they reported the debacle as, 'What a shame these visiting artists are given young, inexperienced bands who can't back them properly and ruin their music.' That one hurt."[47]

One Sunday, the Dummer band and Kelly's sister Jo-Ann, a fabulous blues singer, did a benefit at London's Studio 51 for Memphis Minnie, who was ailing in a nursing home in Memphis. Late in the day, Dave and Jo-Ann were onstage with John Mayall, Mick Taylor, Alexis Korner, Paul Kossof, Andy Fraser, and others when the crowd erupted. Wolf had walked in and made his way to the front of the stage. He sang a few numbers to the spellbound crowd before wandering out into the London evening air.[48]

Tour agent Tempest was also promoting a U.K. tour with Freddie King, backed by British blues band Killing Floor. Tempest asked their vocalist and harp player, Bill Thorndycraft, to drive Wolf to his show. "I was told to pick the Wolf up from his Shepherd's Bush hotel at 2:00 p.m.," Thorndycraft said. "When I arrived at the hotel on time, I was shocked to find him waiting in a dingy hallway of a run-down B&B. I expected this great man to be in more luxurious surroundings. He greeted me with little warmth, which was understandable when I discovered that the agent had told him I would pick him up at 10:00 a.m. He'd been sitting in the dark, miserable hallway for four hours without a drink or anything to eat! No wonder he was pissed off when I arrived and felt I was late and responsible for the wait. This obviously did not get our relationship off to a good start. He later mellowed when I got him some food.

"I found Wolf to be both reserved and dignified and a man of few words. However, I remember him sharing with me a few words of wisdom when I asked about his harmonica sound. I was intrigued to know how Wolf managed to get his distinctive sound, so I asked him to share his secret, to which he replied, 'Man, life is like a wheel, and as that wheel goes round you've got to grab a spoke, otherwise you don't go nowhere.' "[49]

Wolf and the Dummer band and Freddie King and Killing Floor played at Manchester Free Trade Hall that night. "The backstage banter and rivalry between Freddie and Wolf was entertaining," said Kelly. "I got the impression that Freddie had at some point been in Wolf's band. It was agreed that he would come out and play with us behind

Wolf on the final encore. Wolf counted in a slow blues and Freddie started with the most beautiful, tasteful, emotional intro. Wolf shouted to him, 'Get it again!' so Freddie started another sequence. About eight bars in Wolf started a fresh sequence on the harp and Freddie immediately dropped in at the top. The performance was good, Wolf and Freddie in friendly but apparent rivalry.

"After the show both artists and bands went for a meal. Freddie proclaimed that he'd buy the drinks if Wolf paid for the food. Freddie thought this arrangement was very amusing. Wolf told me he was aware that he'd been taken a bit, but he went along with the arrangement because he had more money than Freddie. 'Anyway, I'm better looking than him,' Wolf said. 'What kind of figure is that for a man? Look—he's got tits, man. He should wear a brassiere!' Then he leaned over and grabbed my knee while shaking with laughter, which started somewhere in his stomach and built up through his whole body till he had everyone in the vicinity swept up in the joke."[50]

Near the end of the tour, the Squoit invited Wolf to leave his cheap hotel and spend a night at the suburban home of his parents, who were away on vacation. Wolf said, "I didn't know you had a nice house like this. I thought you was a hippie." The next day, Wolf and the five hippies went for Sunday lunch at the Ferry Boat Inn, a genteel, middle-class pub next to the Thames. The Squoit put Wolf at ease by introducing him to the pub's owner, who shook his hand and said, "Good morning, Mr. Wolf. We're very proud to 'ave you in our pub. I 'ope this lot are looking after you well. Would you like a whiskey?"[51]

"Wolf was a gentle giant, but not to be messed with," Kelly said. "He took a paternal interest in his young backing group, was in some ways naive but also sophisticated: complex. I am extremely proud and grateful to have been associated with such a master."[52] Dummer said, "This sounds corny, but it was just as easy to love the man as his music."[53] Wolf returned home on June 3, 1969, after logging more than a thousand miles on the road in the U.K. in less than three weeks.

By July 14, Wolf was in the studio to cut four new tunes, with Lafayette Leake on piano, Hubert on guitar, Calvin Jones on bass, and Cassell Burrow on drums, and three unidentified horn players. One cut from this session is among Wolf's finest: "Hard Luck." Wolf alluded to his hard-luck background in interviews and said his mentor Charlie Patton was "a hard-luck boy like me."[54] Over a stately background of crying horns and Hubert's sensitive, single-string playing, Wolf sang about his childhood, when his mother threw him out and he trudged miles over frozen ground with burlap croker sacks tied around his feet:

> Well, rocks is my pillow. Cold ground is my bed.
> Highway is my home and I'd just rather be dead.
> I'm walkin'. And Lord, I don't have nowhere to go.
> The road I'm travelin' on, oh, the road is mud and cold.

"Mary Sue" was a jazzy mid-tempo blues with phenomenal piano playing by Leake, great horn work, and again, excellent accompaniment by Hubert. The same instruments starred again on "Tired of Crying," with Leake's keyboard trills building an edifice of sound behind Wolf's beleaguered voice and Hubert's eerie guitar lines, punctuated by funky horn lines. "Oh, I'm worried about you, baby, whiles I'm on my job . . . I got to cry over you," sang Wolf, sounding distraught as usual about his woman. "The Big House," driven by horns and piano, was a hard-rocking tune about loneliness: "I'm on my way to the big house. Don't nobody live there but me." Wolf might as well have been singing about the big house of his body.

Wolf got an unexpected call one summer morning in 1969 from photographer Sandy Schoenfeld, who was passing through Chicago on a cross-country jaunt to New York with a friend. Wolf invited them out to his house. The friend, an aspiring blues guitarist, was stunned that they could just drop in to visit the legendary bluesman. Lillie made them a splendid breakfast and Wolf asked them if they had enough money to make it to New York and offered them more, which they declined. They had a long talk about society, politics, and space travel. Then Schoenfeld photographed Wolf and Lillie, Wolf and his dogs, and Barbra and Bettye in their yard. That night, the boys drove out to see Wolf at the Key Largo club and noticed the constant sound of breaking glass in the surrounding neighborhood, which was even grimmer than San Francisco's Tenderloin. A band member mentioned that a robber had recently thrust a pistol through his car window at a red light but backed away when he pulled out an even larger pistol and explained that it fired very lethal dum-dum bullets. Wolf offered to let the boys spend the night at his house, but they had to hit the road. "Despite Wolf's 'tail-dragger' stage persona and beyond his incredible creative talents," Schoenfeld said, "he was clearly a family man: sweet and caring to friends and family alike, and very politically astute and conscious."[55]

At the beginning of August, Wolf and the band headed east to play the first Ann Arbor Blues Festival, one of the first and greatest blues festivals ever convened. Held fourteen days before the famous Woodstock festival and thirteen days after Neil Armstrong walked on the moon, the first Ann Arbor festival focused on big-city, electric blues and included most of the great electric blues players in the world at the time, plus a few acoustic blues players. The organizers were a cabal of blues-loving students at the University of Michigan, led by John Fishel, who during the summer worked at Bob Koester's Jazz Record Mart in Chicago— the starting point for many blues record label owners, musicians, and managers. Fishel and his cronies had talked the university into sponsoring the festival. It all took place on an athletic field owned by the University of Michigan next to the Huron River. Wolf was slated to play just before the Saturday night headliner, Muddy Waters. Preceding them were Sleepy John Estes with Yank Rachell, Luther Allison, Clifton Chenier, and Otis Rush. "The field was outside of town in the county, and the sheriff was very hostile towards doing the show," Fishel said. "So we had a curfew on Saturday night and Wolf was on that performance."[56] The curfew was imposed because of a string of unsolved murders of coeds at the university.

Backstage, Wolf and many other musicians were drinking and eating in a tent, gambling in a trailer, and generally having a great time. Big Mama Thornton approached and said, "Wolf, I'll tell you what: I'll pay you cash money right now if you let me have Hubert." Wolf laughed, pointed at Evelyn Sumlin, and said, "Don't ask me for Hubert. There his wife is. You have to ask her." Thornton laughed and said, "You just don't want to give me Hubert. I could really, really use Hubert." He said, "I could use him too, so I'm keeping him."[57] Wolf told a reporter how much he hated loud music. "I like all music regardless of who plays it," he said. "But some of this music today is too loud. I mean it'll knock your eardrums out. . . . Too loud is nothin' but knockness: just some stuff comin' together and you don't understand what it means. That's what you call real garbage; that's the worst garbage in town. But the peoples just eats it up, just like the rabbit eating the carrot: 'Chomp, chomp chomp—what's up, doc?' " He also talked about race, disenfranchisement, and the recent moonwalk. "You see, I been pushed way back. I could remember when people wouldn't let me up front. And everybody pushed me back, you know, because I was just dirt, and I felt like I was dirt. So I stayed back. . . . I don't care what you say, if somebody behind you got the bread, you can forget about the talk. Sooner or later they gon' push you right up to the front. See what I'm talkin' 'bout? But I can't get my people to understand this. Today this is a new day and if you show some of this stuff called 'in God we trust,' somebody gon' come up to the front and say, 'I am the man.' That's right! There ain't gon' be no hard feelin' and he didn't come for no trouble but he sure gon' let you know that he are the man. . . . We never make it to the moon, they used to say. I say you never know. That's right! You never know what scientists can do. Today we sittin' on the moon—we got a flag up there, y'understand? They said we couldn't do it. Don't never say what we can't do."[58]

Wolf sat with his buddy Big Joe Williams and talked about old times in Mississippi's hill country, where they were born within thirty miles of each other. Muddy Waters joined them. Big Joe left to play tonk, and Wolf and Muddy talked and drank for most of the afternoon, after telling their band members to go about their business. Hubert saw the old rivals together that day. "Wolf's band and Muddy's band, we all got together and we went to playing ball and everything," said Hubert. "And my mind told me, 'Hey, go back there and see how the old man is.' So I come back to the trailer to check on him. Him and Muddy sitting up there huggin' and cryin', man! And then they went to drinking beer together. I told Spann, I said, 'Hey, Spann, come here, man. There's a hole there. Look at these guys, man!' "[59]

But Wolf couldn't resist tweaking Muddy again. He was well lubricated when he hit the stage. The show was running late, and he had an hour to do his act and get offstage so they could get Muddy on. As his band warmed up the crowd of ten thousand, he noticed a three-wheeled motor scooter backstage. He hopped aboard, rode it onstage and posed for the crowd, appearing with his hat turned backward, a set of keys hanging from the belt around his baggy khakis, a beaten-up, short-sleeved shirt flapping—the uniform of a hip-hop idol twenty-five years early. He dragged the motor scooter around the stage and said, "You like it? Get you one!" He dropped it and roamed the front of the stage, drinking from bottles that were offered up by the crowd. As people yelled requests, he kept repeating, "I can only sing 'em one at a time, ladies and gentlemen, one at a time!" Then the band tore into "Killing Floor." "Work, work, work!" Wolf shouted as they vamped furiously on the famous riff.

After the song, he grabbed the microphone and said, apropos of Neil Armstrong's moonwalk, "They say it couldn't be done, but I got my flag on the moon tonight! I got my flag on the moon! I got my flag on the moon!" Then he blew harp and sang like he had just one hour left to live. A reviewer for *Creem* magazine wrote, "He ground out music so heavy it seemed to hang over the stage like a viscous mist."[60] Wolf pulled out all the stops and did all his tricks, playing with the microphone in a phallic way that made Jim Morrison's bust five months before for allegedly exposing himself onstage seem quaint. After Wolf's allotted hour, Fishel and Big Bill Hill, the festival's emcee, beckoned him offstage so they could get Muddy on. Wolf refused to leave. "We were giving him signals, but it became obvious that he was going to do his thing," Fishel said. "We just decided that we'd wing it. . . . It was a classic Wolf performance. It was great!"[61] Late in his set, Wolf and the band heard rumbling—a train approaching on the tracks across the river—and his drummer started playing a train beat. Wolf joined in on harp, imitating a train whistle, interspersed with his patented howl. The train got closer, the band played faster, and Wolf wailed louder till the train passed by just across the river. Then the band tore into "Smokestack Lightnin'." They left the stage after an intense hour-and-a-half performance. The *Creem* reviewer said it all. "If anyone asks you what stage presence is, point to Wolf and tell them to divide by ten!" Muddy had to play a shortened set to beat the curfew, but he remained imperturbable, refusing to let Wolf ruffle his calm.

In October, Chess released *Evil*—a reissue of Wolf's *Moanin' in the Moonlight* album with classic front and back photos by Rae Flerlage. Leonard Chess was having problems with the new GRT team, which was funding some other operations by pulling money out of the company he had built. On October 16, Leonard got into an argument with

GRT's accountant about it. Then he stepped into his car and drove off for a lunchtime appointment. Two blocks away, he slumped over the wheel, dead of a heart attack at the age of fifty-two.[62]

Wolf and the other Chess musicians were shocked. They'd fought with Leonard, but they respected him and many even liked him. "Leonard was a down-home type of guy," said Eddie Shaw. "He could raise hell. He could cuss all day and call you a bunch of motherfuckers and at the end, you'd still love the guy. . . . He was just the head that walked the body. When he died, things got crazy at Chess."[63]

Wolf had butted heads with Leonard many times, and he was bitter about not getting his due, though he claimed he didn't hold a grudge against the Chess family. "They taken advantage of me," he said. "They got thousands, millions of dollars off of me, and I'm still poor and scuffling like a dog trying to live. . . . But now I been to school, and I done woke up and nobody can make no fool of me no more. One time was enough. See, I suffered all through life. But you see, I'm not mad with Chess because he made a fortune off of me. It was just—that was a learning thing, a learning to me that the next man, we gonna have to come right down through the center. So you see, though I was blind one time, oh boy, I done woke up. I can see good."[64]

Throngs of people showed up for Leonard's funeral; the lines extended down the block from the chapel.[65] Wolf arrived late and stayed outside, peering in at the ceremony. "That was a surprise to everybody," said Chess producer Cash McCall. "Wolf showed up at the funeral, so he must've liked the dude."[66]

On May 2, Wolf flew to the U.K. At an old schoolroom in Shepherds Bush, London, Wolf met his backing band on the tour, the Junco Partners: Dave Sproat, bass, Charlie Harcourt, guitar, John Woods, drums, and Bob Sargeant, organ, who were nervous to meet their idol. He put them at ease right away and they rehearsed eighteen songs in an hour and then went out for dinner at a Chinese restaurant in Soho, where the giant bluesman joshed with the tiny waiters. The next night, they played an eight-to-eleven show at the Blues Loft, High Wycombe, just northwest of London, then drove thirteen miles to play a 3:00 a.m. "Midnight Rave" in London's Strand at the Lyceum for Brunel University, where they followed Keith Relf's Renaissance and preceded Deep Purple and Fleetwood Mac. "Wolf rarely announced the song he was about to perform," said Sproat. "We only knew what key the song was in because of the harmonica Wolf selected from the top of Bob's Hammond organ."[67] Peter Green, legendary guitarist for Fleetwood Mac, one of the hottest bands in the U.K. at the time, watched from the wings at the Lyceum. Wolf's voice was so strong that it filled the huge auditorium with just the Juncos' modest PA system.

Two days later, they drove up to Nottingham to play the Britannia Boat Club, where Peter Green and Fleetwood Mac turned up again, having delayed one of their own gigs to hear Wolf. Over the next twenty-one days, Wolf and his backing band crisscrossed the U.K. from Southampton University on the southern coast to Cardiff University in Wales in the southwest all the way up to Aberdeen Music Hall in Scotland. They played sixteen gigs in all, including the Marquee Club in London (where Wolf ran into his diminutive young subterranean friends the Groundhogs), the London School of Economics, the Bull at Richmond, and the University of Lancaster, where they were joined by Freddie King and Wolf's friends from the tour earlier in the year, the band Killing Floor. Wolf upstaged Freddie by crawling onstage on all fours while clutching an empty bottle of bourbon as the Juncos tore into "Killing Floor." Freddie clambered into the lights for a jam at the end of Wolf's set, but Wolf ignored him and sniffed that whoever was running the show shouldn't have let him onstage.

Wolf enjoyed playing with the Junco Partners and introduced them to the audience each night. Their last gig was in Aberdeen. "We had a wonderful reception," Sproat said, "but the gig ran overtime, causing him to miss the night train to London. After the gig we shook his huge hand and sadly waved this greatest bluesman ever goodbye as our manager Joe Robertson chauffeured the living legend off in his tiny, orange Mini Cooper to try to catch up with the long-gone train. Exhausted, we crashed out on a student's floor and contemplated what an experience we had been through. . . . We now realize how knackered he must have been, already forty years our senior."[68] Wolf flew back to the States after putting in more than 3,500 miles on the road in the U.K.

Wolf wasn't feeling well on the flight back to Chicago. He'd been feeling run-down for months, though one would hardly have known it from his schedule so far in 1969: more than ten thousand miles on the road in three countries and two continents. His first gig when he got back was across town at the University of Chicago with his old Delta buddy Johnny Shines. He never made it.

On the way there, he suffered a heart attack. Quick work by Hubert, who was driving Wolf's station wagon, saved his life. "He's sitting over there dressed up and we were on our way to the university," said Hubert. "All of a sudden about halfway, he keeled over and his head hit the dashboard. I said, 'Hey Wolf—you all right?' He wouldn't say nothing, man. I said, 'Oh, Lord have mercy.' I stopped the station wagon, got out and went around on his side, and sweat done popped out on him, and he still wouldn't say nothing, man! I got his head and pulled it back, and I couldn't hear nothing. I couldn't hear his heart. Traffic and everything coming and he just sitting there with his eyes wide. Man, there was a 2 × 4 down by the side of the car. I don't know how it got there. I picked it up and hit the dude in the back one time. 'Hey!' He woke up, man. I didn't know it was a heart attack. Then the cops just passing and I'm trying to stop 'em to get 'em to help, and they just kept on by me. There was a hospital about a half a mile from the university. I got back in the car: 'Hospital: One mile.' I rushed to the hospital, and they taken him first. They had so many people there waiting to get waited on. They hauled Wolf in there and they said, 'Mr. Sumlin, this guy just had a heart attack. It's good you got him here.' "[69] Hubert picked up Lillie and brought her to the hospital.

Wolf's heart attack had probably been brought on by years of undiagnosed high blood pressure, plus other problems not yet evident. Lillie put him in Illinois Central Hospital. On December 1, while Wolf was in the hospital, blues guitarist and singer Magic Sam Maghett died at the age of thirty-two of a heart attack brought on by bad nutrition and stress. Magic Sam had wowed the crowd at the Ann Arbor Blues Festival the day after Wolf played there, and his potential seemed unlimited after two dazzling albums on Chicago's Delmark label; reportedly the Memphis-based Stax label wanted to sign him. Offered a spot on the 1969 American Folk Blues Festival tour of Europe, he'd checked himself out of a hospital to do it. He'd been home for less than a month when he died. Wolf and Hubert were both devastated by the death of the young West Side bluesman. Wolf loved Sam, and Hubert was a like a brother to him. Hubert said Sam wrote his most famous song, "All Your Love," in Hubert's basement.

As if Sam's death weren't bad enough, another great Chicago blues-man, Earl Zebedee Hooker, returned from the same AFBF tour and entered a Chicago sanatorium for end-stage tuberculosis. Zeb kept sneaking out of the TB ward to play gigs, and even played for Wolf at Illinois Central Hospital.[70] Ironically, Jimi Hendrix called Hooker the "master of the wah-wah pedal"—the electronic effect Wolf hated most. But Wolf was impressed by Zeb's slide playing and let him sit in with his band on the rare occasions when Zeb was in Chicago and needed a gig.

After three weeks in the hospital, Wolf said he was feeling well enough to work again. He told Lillie he had to do a date for which he was contracted at the Colonial Tavern in Toronto for two weeks in January. Lillie didn't want him to go; she didn't think he was ready. He was taking his heart medication religiously, but he was still weak.

Wolf went to Toronto anyway, and he not only played his gig at the Colonial but also showed up a mile away on a Sunday night at the Labor Lyceum to perform for an hour and a half to drum up business for his Colonial gig. People lined up for three blocks down the street from the Colonial to see him.

The next day, while shaving, Wolf broke out in a sweat. He told Hubert he was sick. Hubert took him to the hospital, where a doctor said his heart was in bad shape and he'd been taking the wrong medi-cine. Someone called Lillie and she made plans to fly to Toronto. The band went to the club to play without Wolf. Afterward, they stopped by the hospital to see him. He wasn't in his room and no one at the hospi-tal knew where he was, so they went back to the hotel. He wasn't there either, but they figured he'd show up sooner or later.

Sure enough, the next morning, the band's new piano player, Detroit Junior, found Wolf in his room at the hotel. "Why ain't you in the hospital?" he asked. "Well, you see, I had something to do," Wolf said. "I heard them say they couldn't do nothing for me then until the next day." "How'd you get out?" Detroit asked. "Well, I started rolling my eyes and going on and they let me out," Wolf said. Wolf had left the hospital the evening before with no shoes on and wearing just a hospital gown—in Toronto in January. Detroit and Hubert took him back to the hospital.[71]

Lillie arrived at the hospital that evening. Wolf could barely squeeze her hand by then. His test results came back the next day. In addition to heart problems, he had kidney problems. The doctors had to do more tests to find out why. He canceled another tour of England. He wasn't going anywhere.

The new tests showed that Wolf had renovascular hypertension: constriction of the renal arteries, which feed blood to the kidneys. Reduced blood flow to the kidneys leads to excessive release of the powerful hormone renin, which increases blood flow to the kidneys at a heavy price—by increasing blood pressure throughout the body. The condition would probably get worse and could destroy his kidneys or cause a massive stroke or heart attack.[72] Fortunately, the doctor said, an operation to repair the narrowing of the renal arteries could save one or both kidneys and also reduce his blood pressure, which had been high for years. His family attributed his need for occasional "quiet days" to shell-shock from his time in the army. But he never was in combat, so he certainly wasn't shell-shocked. Most likely, on those quiet days, he was suffering from debilitating headaches—a common symptom of high blood pressure.

"I stayed in Canada one whole month, nobody but he and I," said Lillie. "And the doctors and nurses were so nice. I stayed there right with him, eating every meal at the hospital." His doctor explained the surgical procedure to Wolf. It wasn't a dangerous operation, but Wolf would have to wait to get stronger before they could do it. Wolf agreed to the operation.

At the end of the month, Wolf was feeling better. Then he changed his mind about the operation. He told Lillie, "No, I got other jobs to do. My boys walking around." She said, "Wolf, you know those boys can draw unemployment?" He was adamant. He would not have the operation. Lillie and his doctor both cried about his decision, which may have been symptomatic. Renovascular hypertension often causes confusion, an inability to concentrate, hyper-excitability, and hyper-irritability. "He was all wrapped up in that music," Lillie said. "He didn't want to take time out to get that done. He wouldn't have that surgery."[73]

Lillie transferred Wolf to Cook County Hospital in Chicago for another week. After that, she brought him home and didn't tell his friends what had happened. She did put him on a strict diet—reduced fluid intake, no salt, no cigarettes, and no alcohol. He couldn't even eat fruit. One night, she awoke to discover he was not in bed. She found him in the bathroom on his knees, sweating fiercely. She managed to drag him into bed, but he wouldn't let her call an ambulance. He confessed that he'd gone to the kitchen and eaten an apple.[74]

Wolf's doctor ordered him to remain at home for months. While recuperating, he heard that Zeb Hooker had died of TB on April 21 at the age of forty-two. Maybe Zeb's death spurred him, or maybe he was tired of staying at home every night, but Wolf defied his doctor's orders and started playing gigs in the local clubs again.

Chicago blues producer and writer Dick Shurman, who moved from Seattle to Chicago in 1968 to attend school, met Wolf in the late 1960s. "I heard many stories about Wolf, including his physical brutality and his alleged hostility toward whites," Shurman said. "I was awed and slow to approach him, but finally, after I started booking blues shows at the University of Chicago, I gave him a call. He was very friendly and invited me over for dinner, then drove me to his job. Despite what I'd heard, Wolf was more than just polite or courteous to me early in our acquaintance. He seemed to think that I was a young man who could benefit from fatherly advice, which he was quick to volunteer. I'd take a cab to the Burnett home at 88th and Cottage Grove. Often his wife would cook up one of her gourmet meals, then Wolf would drive me over to his job where I'd make a tape. On the way, he loved to give me morality lectures on how to live right, and how other people were living wrong. Some of his malapropisms were amusing, to say the least. In the middle of a lecture about safe driving, someone cut into our lane abruptly. Wolf said, 'See that guy there? He nearly made me have an occlusion!'

"I ended up taping three full evenings of the band in 1969 and 1970. I'm still gratefully amazed at the trust and generosity that resulted in those tapings. At the same time he was telling interviewers about how all the young white blues bands and record companies everywhere were cheating him, he responded to a reassurance from me that I was just making my tapes because I had all of his records and still couldn't get enough of his music by telling me 'That's too bad. I was hoping you'd sell 'em and make yourself some money!' Maybe that's why I never have.

"Pride was another essential element in Wolf's character. He savored his accomplishments and his place in the blues community, for which he worked so hard and gave so much. I remember him . . . giving a little sermon about 'I am the man of the day,' and how he'd triumphed over all the obstacles in his path. . . .

"Possessor of a name that suggested an untamed menace, Wolf spent his last years living in one of the most middle-class settings of any blues artist I knew. When he saw an acquaintance, sometimes he would be warm and friendly; the next time he might look right through the person. The phrase 'brooding majesty' applied strongly. Wolf was also very authoritarian. He once told me, 'My daddy was a plantation fore-man, and he raised me right.' . . . He told me that he made the band learn two new songs every week, so no imitators could keep pace. . . .

"His crowd was mostly older, lower-middle-class blacks, dotted with whites making the pilgrimage to see a living legend. I used to be struck by the sight of the older people with their heads down, actually sleeping through a late or weak set by a man who may have been the most pow-erful blues artist ever in his prime. But just as often, the electricity would return, the eyes would flash, and that iron will would drive the band to play as a unit tailored to the sound of its undisputed leader.

"There are still many Wolf imitators in Chicago. . . . But the act of taking Wolf's name and mannerisms so totally eliminates these people as worthy successors. As Johnny Littlejohn told me Wolf had said once upon being introduced to one of his would-be clones, 'Hell, he ain't no Wolf. He ain't even a little cub!' Chester Burnett didn't choose to live as Little Charlie Patton. He was his own man all the way."[75]

Bob Koester had a brush with one of the Wolf clones at his record store one Saturday. "I went out to the West Side to see a show at some place on a Friday night," he said, "and they announced a guy, 'Now, the star of our show, Little Howling Wolf!' I was going in the store the next day, and some young guy comes in with Willie Dixon. The guy had a single he'd gotten Dixon to produce and he was trying to sell it. I think maybe they thought I'd record him. Dixon says, 'Bob, I want you to meet Little Howlin' Wolf.' It was a totally different guy from who I saw the night before! So I say, 'I saw Little Howling Wolf last night. You're not Little Howling Wolf!' The kid says, 'I'm the *original* Little Howling Wolf—the *real* Little Howling Wolf!' "[76]

By May of 1970, Wolf decided that he'd cut another record. Chess offered him a great deal on one—another trip to England, this time to record with a group of British rock stars. Norman Dayron, a talented young producer at Chess, was instrumental in setting it up. He'd just finished producing Muddy's *Fathers and Sons* album, which also paired a famous bluesman with his young acolytes. Dayron thought the same concept would work with Wolf. "The idea for the session started at Bill Graham's Fillmore West when Mike Bloomfield introduced me to Eric Clapton," Dayron explained. "We were talking backstage and I asked him if he'd like to record with Wolf sometime. Clapton said he'd love to. 'Man, I'd be honored. Anytime!' Then I pitched the idea to Marshall Chess, who liked it. The rock musicians had to sign contracts giving up their rights to the record. Word got out. The way all the other musicians got involved, really, was they requested to be on the record. It was like the event of the year. All the great British players wanted to be in that studio with Howlin' Wolf."[77]

While working toward a humanities professorship at the University of Chicago, Dayron had gotten into the blues through the university's folklore society and by going out to the Chicago blues clubs with Mike Bloomfield, Paul Butterfield, Elvin Bishop, and Nick Gravenites. "I'd heard a lot of stories about Wolf's performances before I ever saw him. I really expected him to do a complete voodoo show. I expected him to eat a live chicken onstage, or at least the head of one. I expected him to walk around on all fours and howl and do all this crazy shit. So when I first saw him, he didn't do all that. He put on a good show—a great show, really—but there was no chicken and no crawling around on all fours, so I was a little disappointed."[78]

Dayron had to fight to make the album—literally. When Wolf found out that Dayron, whom he didn't know, would produce his next album, he wasn't happy. "Wolf was both very defensive and very aggressive," said Dayron. "He'd hold things close to his vest and he would practically never admit anything to you if you asked because he was protecting himself. . . . You had to establish a relationship with him." Dayron talked to Wolf about the upcoming sessions in one of the Chess disc-mastering rooms. "I was alone in that room with him. It was a small room and he had just been told that I was going to be his producer and he wanted no part of it—wanted no part of me. He was mad, like he had gone down in the world if they were giving him this young white boy as

ABOVE: Lucky 13. The photograph on the back of Howlin' Wolf's business cards in the late 1960s *(Photograph © Sandy Guy Schoenfeld at www.howlingwolfphotos.com)*
BELOW: Willie Johnson plays the guitar at home for his son, Tony. *(Photograph © Mick Huggins, courtesy of Cilla Huggins and* Juke Blues *magazine)*

ABOVE: Playing a very
unusual antique harmonica
(Photograph © Sandy Guy Schoen-
feld at www.howlingwolfphotos.com)
RIGHT: Teenage fans Carolyn
Kittle and Linda Schaeffer
photographed with their idol
at Club Rosewood in Mem-
phis, summer 1967 *(Photograph*
© Carolyn Kittle)

ABOVE: Demonstrating the proper technique for playing two harps at once—with nose and mouth *(Photograph © John Phillips)*

RIGHT: Wolf and his size 16 Keds at the Mariposa Folk Festival in 1968 *(Photograph © John Phillips)*

FIRST ANN ARBOR BLUES FESTIVAL, 1969
TOP LEFT: Wolf makes his entrance on a motor scooter *(Photograph © Doug Fulton, courtesy of Doug Fulton)*
TOP RIGHT: The first rap star? Howlin' Wolf! *(Photograph © Charles Sawyer)*
ABOVE: Hubert Sumlin and Howlin' Wolf in action *(Photograph © Charles Sawyer)*
LEFT: Hubert Sumlin at the top of his game *(Photograph © Charles Sawyer)*

ABOVE: Wolf and Muddy hold court at the festival. *(Photograph © Doug Fulton, courtesy of Doug Fulton)*
RIGHT: Wolf pounds on the floor at Hill Auditorium at the University of Michigan in 1971. *(Photograph © Doug Fulton, courtesy of Doug Fulton)*
BELOW: Wolf's baleful stare while singing "Evil" at the Ann Arbor Blues and Jazz Festival in 1972 *(Photograph © Doug Fulton, courtesy of Doug Fulton)*

ABOVE: Recording the *London Howlin' Wolf Sessions*. *Left to right:* Ian Stewart, Eric Clapton, Mick Jagger, Norman Dayron, Howlin' Wolf, Jeff Carp, and Charlie Watts *(Photograph © Jo McDermand, courtesy of the Norman Dayron Archive)*
LEFT: Wolf in his basement lair in 1971 *(Photograph © Peter Amft)*

ABOVE, LEFT TO RIGHT: Koko Taylor, Wolf, Joyce "Cookie" Taylor, and Lillie
Burnett at the Burnett's house *(Photograph © Willie Leiser)*
BELOW, LEFT TO RIGHT: S. P. Leary, Hubert Sumlin, Dorothy Riley, and
Wolf (with a bandage on his wrist from dialysis), backstage at Paul's Mall in
Boston in 1973 *(Photograph © Peter J. Riley)*

ABOVE: Going down slow at Sick's Stadium in Seattle in September 1975.
Left to right: Hubert Sumlin, Wolf, Robert Plunkett, and Eddie Shaw
(Photograph © Diane Voorhees, courtesy of Dave Voorhees)
BELOW, LEFT TO RIGHT: Wolf, Shorty Gilbert, Chico Chism (hidden by
his drums), and Eddie Shaw at the start of Wolf's last big show at the
Chicago Amphitheater in November 1975 *(Photograph © Jim O'Neal)*

a producer. He felt it was an insult and started taking it out on me. It was really interesting. I don't know what happened to me at that moment. Under normal circumstances I might have just folded. I mean, the guy was imposing—he was big. He was threatening! Essentially what he was saying to me was, 'Who the fuck do you think you are, man? I mean, I'm the Howlin' Wolf! You're nobody' And I stood up to him and I don't know why I did it, but he started pushing me around and I put both my hands on his chest and I pushed him back real hard into the disc-cutting lathe. And I said, 'Look, motherfucker, from now on you just call me Mr. Norman!' I just had to deal with him and I think he admired it because he just chuckled and laughed. And when he saw I had the balls to stand up to him, he figured I must be worth something. After that we communicated pretty well." Dayron also worried about Wolf's health. He met with Wolf's doctors to discuss his condition and to make sure he was up for the trip. "He had about fourteen different kinds of pills he had to take: nitro pills, blood-pressure pills, water pills, all these little brown bottles of pills," Dayron said.[79]

The sessions were recorded at Olympic Studios in London. Dayron had done his research, listening to Wolf's records going all the way back to his Memphis days. "I had a song list. I had gone over every song and what I thought every instrument should play on it. And I knew how it should sound and I wanted it arranged a certain way and I was very, very assertive about that."[80] He'd also assembled a great team of backing musicians—besides Clapton and Sumlin, they included nineteen-year-old Chicago harp wizard Jeffrey Carp, plus the Rolling Stones' rhythm section, Charlie Watts and Bill Wyman, along with the Stones' unacknowledged sixth member, pianist Ian Stewart.

When the Chicago entourage showed up on Saturday, May 2, to record, they found that Watts and Wyman were unavailable due to a scheduling foul-up. Studio time was expensive, so Dayron put out the word that he needed a rhythm section pronto, and Beatle Ringo Starr and his friend, bass player Klaus Voorman, showed up with several other players. They cut sturdy new versions of "I Ain't Superstitious," "Goin' Down Slow," and "I Want to Have a Word with You," a slowed-down variant of "Love Me Darlin'." But Ringo was a rock 'n' roll drummer who wasn't used to playing blues shuffles. He played solidly on "I Ain't Superstitious" and the other tracks, but he was put off by Wolf's gruff manner, and he knew that Watts and Wyman would be the rhythm section the next day, so there was no point in his coming back.

Eric Clapton had wanted to meet Hubert for years. "One reason I did that session," he said, "was that for a long time I'd really wanted to meet his guitarist, Hubert Sumlin, because he did some things that really freaked me out when I was picking up the guitar—that stuff on 'Goin' Down Slow,' just the weirdest playing."[81] Despite his reputation, Clapton was quite modest about his playing and was, surprisingly, intimidated by meeting two of his blues idols. "Eric Clapton walked in the first day and Hubert was tuning up his guitar in the corner of the room," Dayron said. "Eric turned around and looked like he was going to leave immediately. . . . He looked at me and said, 'What do you need me for? I mean, you got Hubert in there. You don't need me!' I told him Hubert was going to play rhythm. He said, 'What? How could you ever have Hubert play rhythm? He's my idol! He's a great lead guitar player. He plays the perfect style for Howlin' Wolf!' " Once Clapton realized he was there just to play guitar, he relaxed. Dayron later got some criticism that it should have been more of a Clapton album, but that was never the concept for the sessions. Dayron also had to talk Wolf into telling Clapton that he needed him, which wasn't easy to do. "I don't think Eric really thought Wolf needed anybody," Dayron said.[82]

"Initially there was a lot of attitude going on, where people's egos are on display, Wolf's among them," he said. "The only thing that could ever humble Mick Jagger would have been Howlin' Wolf. And he did come in humbled." Jagger asked to play tambourine on a track where Dayron wanted to make the rhythm section sound like Sam Lay. At one point, Dayron said, "Mick turned around and said, 'Well, who does his royal majesty think he is?' He was used to being the Queen of England, and here I was acting like that."[83]

Dayron also had some problems with the session's engineer. "Glyn Johns was a real prima donna. I was very rough on him because he didn't work fast enough and the standard I had was Chess Records and he wasn't getting that sound. He was getting a clean, white, ball-less, wimpy sound, and it wasn't what I wanted, so I really bricked him. He thought I was a real asshole." Dayron, only twenty-six years old, was brash in dealing with Johns. "I was too abrupt with him," he said, "but I was used to Ron Malo's engineering. I was young and arrogant. In terms of the overall management of the session, though, I think the results speak for themselves."[84]

Watts, Wyman, and Stewart showed up on the second day of the sessions, and the assembled musicians cut three tracks: "Rockin' Daddy," "Poor Boy," and "Wang Dang Doodle." They cut three more the next day: "Sittin' on Top of the World," "Do the Do," and "Highway 49."

That night, the whole project almost came to a messy end. "I couldn't find Wolf," Dayron said. "I asked, 'Where's Howlin' Wolf? He's disappeared!' And so I go back into the studio building and it's about 2:30 in the morning. I go through all the rooms, searching. It's empty—deserted. It's like a grave. And so finally I send all the cabs back to the hotel and I have one cab hang on in the hopes I could find him. I start to panic, and I don't know what to do. I'm trying to be responsible for him because before I took him to London, he'd just recovered from a heart attack.

"Finally I go into one of the men's bathrooms and I see that one of the stalls at the far end is closed. I go back there, and sure enough, he's in there. I'm knocking on the door, 'Come on, Wolf, we're all ready to go.' No answer. So I actually stick my head under the stall and crawl in there. And he's got his pants down and he's slumped over like he's passed out. I move back and I kick the door down—just smash it with my foot. I go in and he's unconscious and he's turning gray, just a light gray, and he's cold and he's slumped over. I must say, the first thought in my mind was, 'I'm going to go down in history as the guy who killed Howlin' Wolf.' Another image that sticks in my mind was the size of Wolf's shoes with his pants down around them."[85]

Wolf was still breathing and Dayron got a couple of guys to help pick him up. Wolf slowly came around as they called an ambulance. But he wouldn't get in the ambulance, insisting that he just had indigestion. He wouldn't even let them put an oxygen mask on him. Despite their entreaties, Wolf got in a cab and went back to the hotel.

"He had a lot of dignity and it was like, you don't fuck with Howlin' Wolf's dignity or you get your ass handed to you," Dayron said. A few days before, Dayron had gone to Wolf's hotel room to have a talk with him. The first thing he noticed was an empty bottle of whiskey. Dayron told him he shouldn't be drinking. They argued about it, and Dayron had to take away his room service. He also examined Wolf's pill bottles and saw that he hadn't been taking his pills. "I think because there was nobody else in the room but him and me, he could finally just face up to the truth. And he got sheepish and sort of hung his huge head and said, 'Alright, alright, alright, Mr. Norman. I won't do that.' I had to get him to stop saying 'Mr. Norman.' It was like a Mr. Charlie thing and I think he used it to put me down. I finally said, 'You better just call me Norman, motherfucker!' " Then I asked him how he'd feel if I called him 'nigger.' It put a big smile on his face because he got the point."

"Wolf was extremely complicated. One part of him was voodoo. One part of him was the devil. Another part of him was a very decent and generous man. One part of him was a homebody. He loved his home and his family and his quiet. One part of him was a street guy. And one part of him was a performer who at one time in his life would probably have done things onstage that no other bluesman would have ever done. One part of him was connected to show business, so he knew how to exploit his unique properties. That's why he took the name Howlin' Wolf. . . . He had his own rationality. You had to learn what that was if you wanted to argue with him. Conventional wisdom was of little interest to him. . . . I think at that point in his life, too, he had many, many concerns in his life other than building relationships with musicians. He was certainly not going to do that."[86]

The next day, the band was working on "The Red Rooster" when Clapton did something very insightful. Dayron said, "He handed the guitar over to Wolf and said, 'Man, you've gotta show us how to do this. Could you play the basic lick so that we can learn the song?' And Wolf looked at him like he was crazy. He was like, 'Are you kidding me?' And [Clapton] said, 'No, man. We want to get the right feel for it.' And Wolf said, 'Oh. Okay.' And he took up a guitar, which was his own. If I remember correctly, it was an old Sears Silvertone guitar, and he started playing slide, bottleneck, actually. . . . The ice was broken, because they had extended themselves to him. Eric did. By sort of submitting to Wolf, it broke the ice and he got nicer. At that point, the space opened up. There was room for them to create something. And from that point, things just got better and better."[87] That day, they tore through "The Red Rooster" and five other tunes: "Worried About My Baby," "Commit a Crime," "Built for Comfort," "Who's Been Talking?," and "Killing Floor."

Wolf was happy about the album, despite his grumbling in the studio. Asked about it by a reporter for *Melody Maker*, he said, "The sessions over here so far have been really wonderful."[88] Asked by a reporter for *Rolling Stone* about his sidemen, he said, "Well, that boy [Clapton] on gi-tar over there, he's outasite."[89] On the last day of the session, the British "boys" presented Wolf with an appropriate gift—a fishing rod. Wolf was touched and said he couldn't wait to try it out back home. The gift was Clapton's idea; like Wolf, he was an avid fisherman.

Dayron brought the tapes back to Chicago, where he had carte blanche from Chess to improve whatever he wanted. One big problem: No one had noticed that Hubert's amp was shorting out during the recording sessions, so several of his guitar tracks were mostly unusable. Dayron brought some Chicago musicians into the studio, overdubbing a few guitar parts by Paul Asbell and BeBop Sam, and adding piano bits by Lafayette Leake, John Simon, Erwin Helfer, and Joel Smirnoff, bass by Phil Upchurch, and horns by Joe Miller, Jordan Sandke, and Dennis Lansing. Then he had Stevie Winwood sweeten many of the tracks with keyboards.

Dayron's meticulous work paid off. It was a fine album, and many of the new versions of Wolf's tunes were at least as good as the originals. Clapton's playing, in particular, was sensational, and the other musicians all played well. Released in May 1971, *The London Howlin' Wolf Sessions* was Wolf's only album to appear on the Billboard 200. It spent fifteen weeks on the chart and peaked at number nineteen. For a blues album, it was a major hit. "The snobs and the blues-nerds who wrote for the magazines at the time generally resisted liking the album," said Dayron. "I think it was reverse racism. But when I sent a copy of the record to B. B. King, he called me up and said, 'That's a good record, son. You ought to be proud of it.' "[90]

After he returned from England, Wolf did a short tour of the South and came back surprisingly refreshed. By August, he was in Michigan for the second Ann Arbor Blues Festival, where, as the opening-night headliner, *his* set was cut short by the curfew. His monologue during "Hard Luck" illustrated the real-life source of his blues. "Some of you been mistreated and some of you have been drove from your door and some of you been treated like a dog. I know it, 'cause I been treated that way myself. Some of you, your folks is growing old. They didn't care about you. 'I have so much of worry. Sometime I could cry. But I'm going back to my mama's grave, fall on her tombstone and die.' "[91] A reporter discussed Wolf's unhappiness with Chess Records. "Wolf does not like what is happening to him at Chess. Five years ago, he talked bitterly of Willie Dixon's influence on his recording. The sad thing is Wolf would undoubtedly produce better records if he was doing what he wanted."[92]

Wolf had good reason to fuss. Chess Records was about to foist another misguided concept album on him, *Message to the Young*, full of transparent appeals to the youth market. The message of the title tune seemed to be, "If we say the right buzzwords, you will buy this vinyl." It was a tie-dyed, hippie-headed plea for peace, love, and understanding, man. Tongue firmly embedded in cheek, Wolf sang lines like, "You girls—you want to wear your dresses short? Go on and wear your dresses short. I'll appreciate it if don't nobody else will. Awooo!" On "If I Were a Bird," he sang, "We need more love!" He may have been thinking, "We need less fuzz-tone guitar!" "Turn Me On" holds a sort of grim fascination, with rock licks laying down a base for lyrics such as, "You give me a heart attack, baby, and my love is comin' down on me."

Even on this album, the nadir of Wolf's recording career, there were a few decent cuts. "She's Looking Good" and "Just As Long" were credible funk and soul songs. But *Message to the Young* died on the record store shelves. It has never been re-released.

Cash McCall produced the album when Willie Dixon dropped out at the last minute. Dixon offered McCall sympathy and advice: "Just ignore the jive and keep on going." Days before the first session, McCall delivered song tapes and lyric sheets to Wolf. The morning of the first session, Wolf went to Studio B and watched as the band ran through the first song. He didn't utter a sound. The band started again. He still wouldn't sing. He hadn't learned the songs, so McCall rescheduled for the next week. A week later, Wolf hadn't learned the songs yet, so in a familiar routine, he wore earphones and sang the lyrics as McCall recited them to him. "That's how we did the whole album," McCall said. "Wolf was a different dude, but he was a cool dude in a lot of ways. You had to find a way to communicate with him. If you didn't do that, you were just in trouble. . . . He didn't let nobody take him down too many roads he didn't want to travel. He was much more comfortable

dealing with straight-ahead blues. I always did love and respect him—
even after working with him!"[93]

After playing in Chicago for a few more months, Wolf went to the
East Coast for some gigs, including the first Washington Blues Festival,
billed as "the first blues festival produced by blacks" and held at the pre-
dominantly black Howard University in the heart of Washington,
D.C.'s, northwest ghetto. It nevertheless attracted a largely white crowd
with electric bluesmen B. B. King, Muddy Waters, Buddy Guy and
Junior Wells, Luther Allison, and acoustic blues players such as John
Jackson, Fred McDowell, and Elizabeth Cotton. Wolf did his old tricks
for a new audience. At times, crawling on his hands and knees, he
looked like he was delivering a lecture about yoga.

On March 17, Wolf and Lillie had a guest at their home: Gene
Goodman, brother of jazz giant Benny Goodman and co-founder of
ARC Music, Wolf's publishing company. Goodman knew that GRT
was trying to sign Wolf to a publishing contract. He asked Wolf to renew
his publishing contract with ARC. The new contract was complicated.
Wolf and Lillie looked it over and signed it, and Goodman produced a
bottle of whiskey and offered Wolf a drink.[94] The contract and whiskey
would come back to haunt all of them.

On the morning of May 2, a year to the day after his first London
session with the cream of the British rock stars, Wolf suffered yet
another heart attack. While he was hospitalized in Chicago, his band
went to Detroit to fulfill a commitment for a two-week gig at the Chess-
mate Coffee House, a venue they had played for years. In Detroit Wolf
often visited his and Lillie's friend Margaret Malkentine, who loved
Wolf's stories and would cook his favorite Sunday dinner: roast beef
with yams, and mashed potatoes with gravy, topped off by Seagram's
Seven Crown whiskey. One evening Wolf and Hubert heard Margaret's
neighbor, guitarist Wilson Lindsey, rehearsing with his rock band. Not
long after, Wolf asked Lindsey to fill in for an ailing Hubert for a few
weeks at a gig in Chicago. Lindsey later worked for twenty years in various jobs in the music business, often at Creed Taylor's CTI label, where
he met some of the world's finest jazz musicians. He never forgot his
weeks playing with the Wolf. "I can't think of very many people at all
that had his magnetism," he said. "That's the God's honest truth. He
had so much depth as a human being. He was a powerful man. He

didn't talk a hell of a lot. Onstage, for instance, if I would play some-thing he liked, he would flash me this approving look that I can't even begin to describe. It would just fill you up with joy and you really wanted to do your best. It was just a look, but it was powerful. And when you did something that wasn't so hot, that look was flashed at you, too!

"A guy that reminded me a lot of Wolf, from the viewpoint of a deep knowledge of people and a grasp of what he was doing, was Dizzy Gilles-pie. . . . They weren't egocentric. All of Dizzy's focus seemed to be to consolidate everything for his family and his wife, and that was the same way with Wolf. Wolf and Dizzy had a lot in common in that they had seen so much in their years. I would wager that those guys at one time in their lives probably pushed it so close to the edge that they had to back off and say, 'Well, I can't go that way any more. I'm going to have to get it together . . . pursue the music and not fall over into the abyss.' "[95]

Wolf was facing another abyss in 1971. His kidneys were shot. Soon after his heart attack in May, he had to start getting hemodialysis treat-ments once a week in a Chicago hospital. Lillie said, "A lot of days, he would be sitting on the machine and he would look and say, 'Baby, I wished that I had listened to you and the doctor.' I'd say, 'It's too late now, you know?' "[96]

The giant who'd wowed audiences everywhere with his stamina was finding it difficult to perform. He was just sixty-one, but his health was failing. His doctor wanted him to stop performing altogether.[97] His doc-tor didn't understand the Wolf.

13. Goin' Down Slow

The Pontiac station wagon barreled up Highway 61 at dawn, pulling a small, two-wheeled trailer emblazoned with "The Original Howling Wolf and His Orchestra." The Wolf and his orchestra had gotten a late start on the road after playing in Baton Rouge. The sky was lightening as Wolf instructed Hubert to turn toward downtown Natchez, near the mighty Mississippi. At the Highway 84 sign, Wolf said, "Turn right," and they drove west on St. Catherine Street. The rest of the band was snoozing and Hubert was tired and lost in thought as Wolf mumbled something. "What's that, Pa Shot?" Hubert asked. "I'm too late, Hubert," said the Wolf.

"What you mean?" Hubert asked. The old man told Hubert to pull over next to a pile of burnt wood covered with kudzu. "That's where all them people died, Hubert. That's what I was singing about in "The Natchez Burnin'." Wolf and Hubert stared at the charred remains of the Rhythm Club, where 203 people were trapped in an inferno in 1940. "It took me forty years to get myself together, you know," Wolf said. "I should've been on top now. Times is changing. I can feel it, man. I was born forty years too soon, and I'm going to miss it." "Well, hey, you still a young man. How old are you anyway, man?" "Be fifty-nine this year," Wolf said, and they both laughed. Wolf had been telling Hubert he was fifty-eight for years. Leaving town, they passed a fork in the road at D'Evereaux Drive where, a century before, human beings were yoked together like cattle and sold to the highest bidder. Then the bluesmen headed out on Highway 61.

The show went well that night at the VFW Hall out on Highway 49 south of Clarksdale. Wolf, as usual, rose to the occasion, despite his continuing fatigue. Afterward, they crossed a small bridge over the Sunflower River and slept at the Riverside Hotel, where classic blues singer Bessie Smith bled to death after a car accident in 1936, directly above the room where Ike Turner wrote and rehearsed the first rock 'n' roll record, "Rocket 88," in 1952. The next morning, Wolf chatted with Mrs. Hill, the hotel's owner, whom he'd known for decades. Then he and the band went to breakfast.

At the café, a policeman approached Wolf and said he'd seen him at the VFW show—and knew someone who knew his mother. Wolf was stunned. He hadn't seen Gertrude Burnett in years. The cop told him to go down to the Big Six barbershop on Issaquena Avenue and talk to barber and bluesman Wade Walton. At the barbershop, Wolf announced, "I'm the Wolf," and Walton said, "Yeah, I know." "Do you know where my mama is?" Walton said he'd just seen her—said she lived nearby above Mr. Lee's restaurant, where she'd recently been robbed of most of her meager worldly possessions. "If you wait a few minutes, she'll probably be by here," Walton said. Wolf sat in a barber chair and, uncharacteristically, fidgeted. After Walton finished cutting a man's hair, he took Wolf and Hubert out the back door to Issaquena, where they waited. "There your mama is—right there," Walton said, pointing at a short, stout woman, walking toward them, dressed in black. Wolf ran to her and yelled, "Mama!" He lifted her into the air, set her back on the ground, kissed her on both cheeks, and hugged her. He was crying. He reached into his pocket, and while hugging her balled something up and slipped it into a pocket on her smock.

Mother and son talked for fifteen minutes. Then she felt something in her smock. "Turn me loose!" she said, pushing him away. She fished it out of her smock, looked at it, spat on it, and threw it down and stomped on it. "I told you I don't want your dirty old money!" she yelled. "You play them dirty blues!" She started to walk away, then turned and screamed, "Dirty!" Wolf sobbed as she walked away. Hubert ran up to comfort him and noticed something in the dirt. "Lord, have mercy!" he said as he picked up and brushed off a five-hundred-dollar bill. He'd never seen one before. Wolf sent Eddie Shaw to beg his mother to come back, but she refused. She wouldn't have anything to do with his devil's music.

"Wolf cried all the way to Memphis," Hubert said. "When we got to Memphis, we managed to get him quieted down. He said, 'Hubert, you see what I'm talking about?' I say, 'Wolf, that's sure your mama?' He say, 'Yeah. I love her, but she put me out on account of I wouldn't work for 15 cents a day, 'cause I was sittin' around trying to play this guitar. Told me, 'Don't come back. I don't want you back here.' "[1]

Wolf's life was full of woe in 1971. Hard work was his solace. In October, he played at Hunter College in New York City, where his band backed John Lee Hooker, with solo bluesman Larry Johnson opening. Wolf's show impressed Hunter College student Kim Field, now a leading authority on harmonica, who'd never heard him in person. "He was unbelievable!" Field said. "He was striding back and forth across the stage, howling, and he'd do the howl and he'd get down on his hands and knees and pound his fists on the stage floor while he was howling into the microphone. . . . I'd never seen a guy throw so much energy into a song. It was just incredible. I'd always liked Wolf's records, but I was a real Muddy Waters guy. I liked the Wolf but it seemed like they must've done something to his voice on the board or something in the studio. So when I saw him and heard that voice coming out of a human being and not some weird creature or some device, it was really astounding. He was real intimidating. Big finish on the song and he just collapsed into a chair. Eddie Shaw whisked the chair under him and he did the rest of the set kind of hunched over. It was like he put everything he had into that one song. But it was really an experience to catch the guy operating on that level, even for just five minutes. So then I began to listen to Wolf a lot more and began to be more in awe of the guy."

Field, who was taking harp lessons from Muddy's young harp man Paul Oscher, tried to ask Wolf a technical question at a gig later that year. "Paul had just shown me the tongue-blocking technique, which is really the hallmark of the Chicago sound, and this just exploded in my brain. I had tongue-block fever. I was twenty.

"They had a break and the band hit the bar, but the Wolf just stayed sitting on his stool, in the spotlight, staring at his big feet, sort of lost. He was very much one of those in-your-own-world kind of guys. I think the Wolf had this 'invisible shield' aura about him. He was not a guy that you would walk up to and slap on the back and say, 'Hi, how you doing?'

"I have to ask him if he tongue-blocks when he plays harmonica. I have to know this. So with great trepidation, I make my way up to the front of the stage. And what do I call the guy? 'Mr. Wolf?' 'Mr. Burnett?' That seemed bizarre. 'Chester?' Too familiar in some way. So finally I say, 'Excuse me, Wolf, I hate to bother you, but I'm a harp player from New York. I'm taking lessons from Paul Oscher. You're playing some fantastic harp tonight. I really love your sound. I'd really like to know if you tongue-block when you play the harp.' But I was completely incoherent. And he just started staring at my feet, and slowly, very slowly as I'm stammering out this incomprehensible stuff, was working his way up past my knees and finally locked eyes with me just as I came to a halt. Then there was this ten seconds of total silence. And I was just about to turn and bolt, and he looks at me and says, 'The Wolf don't tell nobody his tricks. If you find out, the Wolf don't mind. But the Wolf don't tell you about 'em.' So I said, 'Okay, that's fine, man! Fantastic! Take it easy! See you later!' And then I turned and bolted."[2]

By November, Wolf and his band were playing to packed houses in Columbus and Ann Arbor, where a crowd at Hill Auditorium gave him two encores and would have kept him onstage all night if they could. In late November, Wolf was back in Toronto at the Colonial, where he'd had the heart attack the year before. He was taking his lunch at the bar downstairs when a chubby child named Colin Linden sneaked in from the restaurant upstairs. Linden was learning to play guitar and loved Wolf's music. He'd begged his mother to take him to the show three hours early so he could meet his idol. "I went right up to him and said, 'Mr. Wolf, you're my hero. I'm only eleven years old, but would you come upstairs and talk with me?' In spite of the fact that he didn't know me from anybody and he was a sixty-year-old man at the time, he came upstairs and we spent the afternoon talking. It was great!

"I asked him what he thought of all these musicians like Eric Clapton and Mick Jagger and Steve Winwood and Charlie Watts, all these guys who played on the *London Sessions*. He said they treated him like a king. He said they treated him so nice, and he thought they were all real sweet. And he was a sweet, gentle, soft-spoken person to me. I've heard from other people that he was real tough, but to me he was really warmhearted and fantastic.

"I remember certain things that he said to me the very first time I met him. He said, 'You know, I'm not going to be around forever, so it's important that young people keep on playing and keep on learning the blues. I'm not going to be around to keep making music.' For me as an eleven-year-old, that was like someone giving me a mission. It was not something I'd heard someone else say before, and I took it very much to heart." Wolf also offered performance advice. "He said, 'Whenever you're playing for other people, no matter who they are, if they're rich or poor—they could be white or black or Puerto Rican or Mexican or whatever—you have to play the same, whether there's three thousand people out there or thirty. You have to do your best even if there's just a few people there.' " Linden was astonished by Wolf's dedication. "He was as committed an artist as I've ever heard of in my life. You know what he had to go through just to make music, and I don't think he shucked it. . . . He was such an incredible life force. Even when he was an older man and sick, there was just so much life pouring through him, completely without filter. . . . I loved him."[3] Wolf also turned Linden on to musicians such as Charlie Patton. "He said, 'If you want to learn how to play, listen to the people who taught me.' "[4]

Linden had his picture taken with Wolf that day and kept it in his wallet for decades until it started to disintegrate. He still carries the matchbook on which Wolf wrote his address. He saw Wolf whenever he played Toronto after that. "He would tell me about the times when he was growing up, how much he wanted to be a man and how hard he tried to be a good person," said Linden. "The Wolf spent most of his time on the road, but he would never complain to anybody. He could sing away his blues and troubles. He was tired, he would say. I once asked him if the road was getting him down. He just replied, 'I wouldn't do it if I didn't love it.' I remember shortly after his sixty-third birthday, my family and I brought him a home-baked birthday cake that read, 'Happy Birthday to the World's Greatest Blues Singer.' When we gave it to him, he cried. No one had ever done that before."[5] Today Linden is a leading blues guitarist, producer, and songwriter.

In early December, Wolf headed south with Andrew McMahon to

go hunting and fishing and to pick up one butchered calf, which he bought every year from a friend in West Point. McMahon had had some trouble fishing with Wolf the year before in Wisconsin when he caught and kept seventy undersized fish. A game warden collared him and hauled him off to jail. Wolf bailed him out to the tune of $90 and said, "From now on, you better read that book you got up there when you got your license to fish, 'cause you ain't got no suit now. I'm gonna get my money from you, 'cause I got to pay you off."[6]

On January 26, 1972, Wolf cut a live album on Chicago's North Side: *Live and Cookin' at Alice's Revisited.* Produced by Ralph Bass, the band included Wolf's regulars—Hubert, Eddie, and Sunnyland Slim—plus L. V. Williams on guitar, Dave Myers, formerly of Little Walter's band, on bass, and Fred Below on drums. It's the only official live LP by the Wolf. Hubert did his best dive-bomb finger-slides, Sunnyland and Eddie added tasteful flourishes, and Below, one of the greatest blues drummers ever, kicked the band along nicely. Wolf sang mainstays such as "Call Me the Wolf," "Don't Laugh at Me," "Sittin' on Top of the World," "Just Passing By," and "Mr. Airplane Man," along with the old Tampa Red tune "Mean Mistreater."

A few days after recording it, Wolf flew to California for some gigs, including one in Oakland that inspired drummer Pat Ford, who was playing in a blues band with his brothers Robben and Mark. Pat and his wife, Sharon, picked Wolf and the band up at the airport. "We're down in the luggage area, and it's the first time I've met Wolf, and I'm not only in awe of this guy, but I'm also sort of intimidated by him. . . . It was winter and he had on a big, long overcoat and a hat on his head, and he was just a big man. So I'm trying to round all these guys up and . . . I say, 'Does anybody know where Hubert is?' Hubert's standing over by the doors going out of the luggage area. He's opening up the door for all these ladies and all these old guys, and they all think he's a bellhop! They think it's his job! So I say, 'Come on, Hubert, we gotta go.'

"We get to the Paramount, and we can hear the sound barreling out of this big theater house. It's Alice Cooper doing their sound check. Wolf was supposed to open for them. This is a pretty bizarre match of acts, but somebody in Oakland thought this was a great idea. So when we go through these big sliding doors to get in with the gear, the sound is just so loud it's overpowering. They had this curtain backdrop that you could kind of see through and the band was on the other side of it. But we could see through the curtain this giant guillotine onstage that was one of their props, and it absolutely freaked the band out.

"Wolf just looked at me and said in his gravelly voice, 'What's that there for?' And I told him it was just a prop, and he thought it was just the most bizarre thing. He said, 'I just don't understand. I just don't understand.' There was a grand piano backstage and a piano bench in front of it, and he sits on this piano bench. He looks at Sharon and he slides over and he pats the bench, so she sits down next to him. The two of them just sit there and exchange pleasantries as best as they can over the volume of Alice Cooper's band.

"All of a sudden Sharon comes over and grabs my arm and says, 'Patrick, I think something's wrong with Wolf.' And I go over and he's sort of bent over and he's massaging his chest. And he says, 'My pills.' I grab Hubert and he comes over with the pills, and Wolf is having this minor heart attack right there onstage—triggered by this guillotine. It just freaked him out. He's sitting there and Sharon's sitting next to him and Hubert's rubbing his chest and he's giving him these little pills and finally Alice Cooper's band finishes.

"Wolf bounces back by the time the gear's all set up. He comes on and they do a couple of songs, and I'm actually quite impressed at how strong the band sounds. I take them to their rooms to rest up.

"Then I bring 'em back for the concert. As they get ready to go on, the funniest thing happens. Sunnyland starts to walk onstage, and then he turns around and comes back off. He reaches into his pocket and pulls out a fifth and says to me, 'My Daddy said, "Never drink while you're performing." ' He sets it down by the side of the stage near the curtain and he slips it into the folds so nobody will see it.

"So he goes on and the band does a tune or two upfront and then they bring on the Wolf. He's in this gray sharkskin suit with a pin tie and he's looking really good, and I'm not kidding you, he comes on and he starts singing his heart out. He starts literally doing the Wolf thing on a level that surprised me, because I was expecting a lot less out of him. Besides my wife and I, there were probably two other people in the whole place who even knew who he was. And within two songs, you hear people going, 'Alice Cooper! Alice Cooper!' They just start chanting over the top of the band. And Wolf steps up to the front of the stage and he's digging down really deep. He stayed on and he gave it a hundred percent. He did his whole set. As soon as a song was over, they went right into the next one. And the band really, really cooked.

"I've never been so impressed. It taught me a serious lesson about being a professional in this business. You know, if Wolf could perform in that situation—he had every right to just walk off. I mean, this was a day when most people would never, ever have gone through the whole ball game, and he did it all.

"Of course there were no encores, and at the end of the show, he came off the stage and he walked up to me and I looked at him and I just said, 'I'm really sorry, Wolf.' And he looked at me and said, 'I'll never come to California again.' And he didn't! He said, 'I been treated disrespectfully. These people do not care about me.' All Sunnyland said was, 'Let's go to Kentucky! Let's go to the Colonel!' So I drove them all to the Colonel and they got Kentucky Fried Chicken. The next day I took 'em to the airport and they were gone.

"So on my wall, one of my favorite mementos is me with Howlin' Wolf and his band. It's a great joy to me every time I look at it. He showed me the greatness that this bluesman had. He wasn't a clown. He was the real deal—and very, very serious about his business."[7]

Later in February, Wolf was back in Toronto during a blizzard to play the University of Waterloo. Billed as the closer, Wolf showed up at the auditorium long before Freddie King and Big Mama Thornton, who arrived well past show time. Wolf went on first and played a long set highlighted by his usual antics—down on all fours, leering at the girls, and howling.[8] At the end of April, Wolf opened in Milwaukee for rock organist Lee Michaels and rock band Jo Jo Gunne. A reviewer wrote, "He gave a worthy performance, but there was an aura of sadness. It's a shame . . . that he must be relegated to being a lead-in act for two rock groups."[9]

Though he opened for rock groups if the money was right, Wolf kept playing for his own crowd at tough West Side clubs such as Big Duke's Flamingo Lounge. "He wasn't goin' to turn his people down to go play a job for the white people," said S. P. Leary "just because they give him a few more dollars and he done already signed a contract here. He's goin' to fill his contract. He wouldn't break no contract wherever. . . . He believed in doin' what was right and givin' you services rendered for the price that you paid to see him."[10] *Living Blues* magazine cofounder Jim O'Neal said, "I always respected Wolf for continuing to play in those black clubs on the South and West sides when he didn't really have to and when he wasn't making anywhere near the money he could have made if he would have accepted some offers from some of the rock stars or promoters."[11]

On June 8, Wolf was slated to receive an honorary doctorate from Chicago's Columbia College along with former Boston Celtics star Bill Russell, *New York Times* reporter Neil Sheehan, *New Yorker* film critic Pauline Kael, health activist Dr. Quentin Young, and former FCC chairman Newton Minnow. Wolf was too sick to attend, so Lillie went in his place. Wolf was proud to get a Ph.D. By then he'd been taking classes at Wendell Phillips High School for six years, plus weekly guitar lessons from Reggie Boyd for more than a decade.

Wolf appeared at the new Ann Arbor Blues and Jazz Festival in September 1972. John Sinclair and Peter Andrews, two Ann Arbor music personalities, revived and expanded the festival to include jazz in 1972 when the University of Michigan canceled funding after the money-losing 1970 event. Sinclair had previously managed the rock band the MC5 and had an international reputation as a troublemaking political polemicist and poet. (A Michigan judge called him a "menace to society.") Sinclair was thrilled to book Howlin' Wolf, whom he listened to on the radio while growing up in a small Michigan town. "There was no one in the vicinity that I knew of even remotely with a name like Howlin' Wolf, so that was pretty fascinating to a kid. Then he sang a song about how he asked this woman for water and she gave him gasoline. The concept just twisted my mind. I couldn't imagine anyone who could be so rough." During the 1969 and 1970 festivals, Sinclair had been in jail on a controversial marijuana rap commemorated in a song by Beatle John Lennon, who played at a local benefit concert that prompted the Michigan Supreme Court to overturn Sinclair's conviction. Sinclair knew all about Wolf's set-stretching antics at the 1969 show. "I heard about this and I had my laughs," Sinclair said. "I realized that if I was going to do a festival, I was going to have Howlin' Wolf and Muddy Waters as long as they were alive. But I booked them for separate nights."[12]

Sinclair's staff got grim news a week before the festival: the great

Howlin' Wolf was dead. The news leaked to the *Detroit Free Press* and the wire services, and local blues fans were devastated.

Reports of Wolf's death were greatly exaggerated. The story was the handiwork of Johnny "Bee" Badanjek, legendary rock 'n' roll drummer for Mitch Ryder and the Detroit Wheels and world-class practical prankster. Johnny Bee had called the festival office as "Wolf's widow" but thought they knew it was a joke. He was mortified to find out otherwise and confessed to Sinclair, who quickly revealed the hoax. Even so, Sinclair had to get a signed statement from Lillie Burnett attesting that her husband was alive and well enough to play. While dead, Wolf vacationed in West Point. "My wife got hundreds of calls, including some from behind the Iron Curtain," he said.[13]

On Friday, September 8, before his Ann Arbor appearance, Wolf was passing a bottle with some of his hippie friends backstage. A staffer walking by said they were breaking festival rules. Wolf was incensed. "These boys are my friends!" he said. "If the Wolf can't be with his friends, drink a little gin, an' talk a little blues, then the Wolf don't howl tonight!' "[14]

Onstage in front of fifteen thousand people, Wolf sat violently in his chair, blew harp, goggled his eyes like a gland case, and growled and howled his otherworldly songs. A reporter for the *Ann Arbor News* called it "one of the best performances he has ever given in this area: controlled, powerful, and yet full of the old irascible Wolf. It was a classic."[15] To many listeners, Wolf sounded more futuristic than Sun Ra and his Arkestra, who followed him onstage.

Sinclair also booked Wolf into the Rainbow Room in the Shelby Hotel in Detroit in 1973 and 1974. "He was supposed to sit in a chair and take it easy—doctor's orders," Sinclair said. "He couldn't do it! Couldn't do it: He was rolling on the floor and on his back! Now I'm sixty years old, so it doesn't seem so far-fetched, because I might do that tonight, you know? But thirty years ago, the idea of a guy in his sixties giving an exuberant, high-energy performance was not only thrilling, but also a tremendous inspiration. In our world, where all the people of sixty were old white people who were just really lame and didn't have anything to offer that you could think of, to see a guy in his sixties give an exuberant, dynamic performance like that was just an incredible experience to see."[16]

In late November, Wolf was back at the Colonial in Toronto, where he saw his young friend Colin Linden, who'd spent the previous year learning to emulate his idol. Toronto blues fan Dave Richardson also heard Wolf there. Richardson remembers Wolf's take-charge stage persona. "Maybe part of that was being a big man, but he just was in charge. It wasn't like he was attempting to be. He just was. He was in charge of the band; he was in charge of everybody in that room. The Wolf is in your town. You just don't go wrong with the Wolf around!

"He had Big Walter Horton with him. . . . Usually the Wolf didn't play a lot of harp live. He tended to sing and then he played a little bit, but when I saw him, he didn't play a lot of harp. It struck me strange that he brought Big Walter along."[17] Wolf's doctor had forbidden him to play harp in live performances because it put stress on his kidneys. Wolf would play harp anyway sometimes and told a friend simply, "It's my job."[18] On another Toronto trip, Wolf brought Cary Bell, a very skilled, jazzy harp player. But Bell wouldn't play simple harp lines like the Wolf, so Wolf fired him at the end of the week.

One morning in Toronto, Wolf left the hotel, was gone all day, and hadn't returned by show time. His band went to the club without him and started playing. Two songs into the first set, Wolf showed up with a big smile on his face. Eddie Shaw said, "Wolf, we gonna fine *you* now for being late!" Wolf said, "That's okay. Go ahead and fine me. I'll pay anything you want!" Wolf had been invited to dinner and couldn't tell his band; barbecue was strictly forbidden on his diet.[19]

On New Year's morning, 1973, Wolf was heading home from a gig, driving Congress Boulevard, a main Chicago thoroughfare. What happened next is unclear. Some say Wolf came within a hair of uttering his last howl, others that he was in a minor car accident. In an interview five months later, he said, "There was about 200 cars all going about 60 miles an hour in the same direction, and this one in front of me had to stop. So my car came to a sudden stop and I continued forward through the windshield. They told me later I wound up in a field beside the road, but I don't know for sure. The next thing I remember was when I woke up in the hospital. That finished my kidneys. Now I have to go in every two or three days to have my blood purified."[20]

Hubert Sumlin said he heard a different story from Wolf. "He said, 'Hubert, I just put on the brakes. This motherfucker, this big, black son-of-a-bitch: I don't know where he come from. I got out and boxed that motherfucker. Knocked him down.' . . . No, he didn't go through the windshield. . . . They carried Wolf to the hospital, but he didn't want to go. He said there wasn't nothing wrong then, but he went on anyway. . . . I believe Wolf's kidneys were already stirred up."[21] Eddie Shaw said Wolf had the accident because he passed out at the wheel. "Well, he hit the windshield, but he was already passed out." Shaw said Wolf's kidney problems preceded the accident. "Wolf went on a dialysis machine in 1971. . . . I don't think it was the accident that was the cause of it all. He had high blood pressure and everything."[22] Wolf's step-daughter Barbra also said the accident was minor. "The kidney problems started on a New Year's morning on the way from work. And he was hit from behind—not a serious accident, it seems, but I understand that certain things can sometimes trigger a failed kidney, and it started out like that."[23]

The car accident may have aggravated Wolf's kidney problems, but didn't cause them. He was on dialysis before the accident. His kidneys got worse after the accident, so Wolf thought the accident destroyed them—though they probably would have gotten worse anyway. Soon after the accident, Wolf had to increase the frequency of his dialysis treatments to three times a week. He'd been paying $150 a treatment at St. Joseph's Hospital in Chicago. When his doctor found out Wolf was a veteran, he pointed out that he could get free dialysis at the Edward Hines, Jr., VA Hospital on Chicago's West Side.

Wolf was reluctant to go to the Hines VA hospital. The first time Lillie left him there overnight, she cried all the way home. She went back the next day and found him surrounded by patients, laughing. Wolf was in the VA hospital for a month. The doctors finally told him he could take a dialysis machine home on a trial basis. Lillie took intensive training to learn how to operate the machine, and when she took Wolf home, she started doing Wolf's dialysis three times a week in the seclusion of Wolf's private lair, their basement. The dialysis machine looked like a washing machine and performed a similar task—washing impurities from Wolf's blood. Lillie had to stick a large needle into Wolf's arm, attach it to a catheter, and run his blood through the machine for four to six hours at a time. When the treatment was over, Lillie would remove the needle and bind Wolf's inner elbow with a gauze bandage. Some fans, seeing the bandage he wore onstage after treatments, thought he was a drug addict.

Wolf would emerge from dialysis nearly as good as new—for one day. On the second day, he'd be visibly flagging, and on the third, he'd be tottering like an old man. Sheer willpower kept him going at times. "The doctor would tell me, 'This man got the strongest constitution of any man I ever saw!' " Lillie said. More than ever, Wolf leaned on her for advice and support. "He wouldn't let nothing go on unless they got in contact with me—day or night," she said. "He would have to call me. 'Call my wife. Call my wife.' He had some rough days. . . . I told him that the day and hour he needed me, I would be there."[24] Wolf was stoic about his fate. Evelyn Sumlin said, "He never complained about it too much. He wasn't a complaining person."

Home hemodialysis can be messy, with blood leaking out around the catheter and the patient groggy. Evelyn Sumlin remembers a disturbing visit to Wolf's basement when she saw him lying in a puddle of blood. "I couldn't stand blood. . . . I see the blood come up and it scared me. I run upstairs and tell Lillie that he was bleeding. And she just come down there and she take and turn the tubes so that there wasn't no more blood would come in. And she took it out and she changed it and she say, 'Evelyn, nothing's wrong. I just have to change the tube.' But he would sleep. If he had to ride a long ways [to a gig], she would put him on at six o'clock in the morning and go six hours. Then when he come off, he would lie around maybe an hour, an hour and a half, and he was ready to go."[25]

Eddie Shaw, Wolf's road manager, had to schedule all of Wolf's shows around towns where he could get dialysis from a VA hospital. By the end of May 1973, he was ready to hit the road again. His first gig back was at Joe's Place in Cambridge, Massachusetts, owned by Joe Spadafora and Dick Waterman. Opening acts there included the fiery young Bonnie Raitt, an unknown Bruce Springsteen, and a solo, acoustic George Thorogood.

Bluesman Paul Rishell, then in his early twenties, opened for Wolf at Joe's Place for a week and like so many other budding bluesmen was amazed by the old man's power, dedication, and generosity. "Looking at him, it was almost like a little kid looking at a Christmas tree, and your eyes keep going up and keep going up and at the top is the star—and there would be his face looking down at you with this beautiful skin and this big, huge head, an enormous head.

"He was just a big, scary guy, but there was a gentleness there. He was a real gentleman—that's how I would describe him. His manners were always courtly when women were around. And he was the eye of the whole thing and people would crowd around him because he had this charisma about him. . . . He'd get up and start playing and the room would just sort of bend into a groove, like he'd taken the room and bent it and everyone was sliding into the middle.

"He was just so dedicated. I was so impressed that they would drive into town from Chicago. . . . They'd be driving for eight, nine, ten hours at a time. . . . When you're on dialysis and in your sixties—and he was a sick man—he knew it, everybody knew it. It was like, 'Man, I'm going to die on this fucking stage. There's no way I'm going to stop.'

"He was almost theatrically courtly in his manners towards women. He was sitting in back of Joe's Place one night. He'd had dialysis that day or the day before. These women came in who were nurses. They probably worked at the hospital where he had the dialysis. I was the only person in the room with him. He was just sitting there chewing on ice cubes, glaring at the wall. These women came in and he was like, 'Oh, I can't stand up. I'm sorry. So nice to see you ladies.' And he was very wonderful and friendly to these women, asking them questions—how they got over here; were they with someone who could take care of them, because it might be kind of a rough joint? He paid a lot of attention to them. Finally he said, 'You better go now because I have to get ready for my show. You get yourself a nice seat out front and we'll come and see you.' They were giggling and laughing. They were in their forties or fifties. They leave. He turns right to me and says, 'A woman that big *got* to wash.' He could be two guys at once—really earthy.

"Of all the blues guys I ever met, Wolf and Son House both lived up to my ideal of what they would be like. They were so unique and so dynamic and in their own way so brilliant. . . . I had so much respect for both of those guys because they were so dedicated to what they were doing. They didn't for one minute question the importance of what they were doing. It was made all the more important because of their belief in it. I learned that from them—that if you're going to play music for a living, you have to believe in yourself 200 percent. You have to believe that what you're doing is the right thing and that there's no other thing for you to do, and till the day you die, you don't ever stop playing. It's your religion. It becomes who you are and what you are and what you do."[26]

Wolf also did a week at Max's in New York City. *The Village Voice* said, "He took his seat, picked up his mike, and began belting out the blues with an energy that would make Rod Stewart shrivel. About halfway through the set, Wolf produced a harp and started feeding beautiful, intense harp runs to the crowd through his mike. . . . Howlin' Wolf seemed to be enjoying the attention of the young white crowd he'd drawn and talked with them a bit, leaned out into them during his hotter numbers, and gesturing and posturing far more than one would expect a man his age to."[27]

Other East Coast shows followed in June, including one at the Village Gate that Kim Field heard. "He used to do 'Goin' Down Slow' a lot in those days," Field said, "and he'd act the whole thing out. He was an incredibly gifted actor. . . . There's a harp player named Danny Russo, a really great harp player. He used to wear these dark glasses. I remember Wolf doing 'Goin' Down Slow' and I turned to Danny and saw tears just streaming down under these dark glasses. Wolf would take on this sorrowful visage and his whole body would sag, and he'd lean on one knee and dangle the microphone in front of his face. It was like you were sitting there in his living room and he was telling you his trials and tribulations.

"He knew how much power he had. He was the most incredible physical specimen of a human that I've ever seen—by a long shot. Nobody even came close to the Wolf. His head was massive, his hands were like big hams. He was six foot four, but he looked twice that. He was so massive in his bulk and his chest. You try to imagine guys like that at thirty or thirty-five, it would've been just unbelievable."

Field glimpsed another side of Wolf that sweltering summer night. "It was really hot, and it was hot inside the club after the show. This friend of mine went to the men's room and I went out to the street and leaned up against a brick wall there in front of the club and was trying to get a little air. And the Wolf comes out and does the same thing—stands up against the brick wall. We were the only two people out on the street, really. He leans up against the wall about six feet away from me. So we're both kind of leaning up against the wall, and this woman who'd been in the club came out by herself and started walking down the sidewalk. She's about six feet tall and weighs about 120 pounds and she had really long legs and she had a miniskirt on. And this is the glitter era, so she had these six-inch platform shoes, so it was quite a visual. She was walking down the sidewalk and we're both watching her. Then the Wolf turns to me and says, 'You know, pretty soon they won't wear no clothes at all—just a little thing in front like the Apache Indians. Ha ha ha ha ha!' I just lost it and had to hang on to the wall."[28]

By August, Wolf and his band were back home to record what would be his last studio album, *The Back Door Wolf.* Produced by Ralph Bass and engineered by Malcolm Chisholm, it featured Wolf's core band—Hubert Sumlin, Eddie Shaw, Detroit Junior, S. P. Leary, and Andrew McMahon—plus Willie Harris on guitar and James Green on bass on a few cuts. Some of Wolf's most passionate singing can be heard on this album—remarkable, considering the shape he was in— along with some of Hubert's finest playing. Chisholm said, "It was Hubert's demo for his next job and he played just incredibly well."[29] The rest of the band was outstanding. Coming after the mediocre *Howlin' Wolf* and *Message to the Young* albums, *The Back Door Wolf* is a neglected gem. Wolf returned to his roots and did the elemental blues album he'd wanted to make for years.

The first cut, "Moving," was a fast twelve-bar shuffle with lively, subtle guitar and vehement singing that really was moving. Chisholm said, "Wolf was a world-class musical talent. . . . He was a singer, not a vocalist. You remembered the words when Wolf sang them."[30] Alas, Wolf didn't always remember those words. On "Moving," Wolf did the same old trick: Shaw repeated lyrics to him seconds before he sang them. Surprisingly, "Moving" was credited to Wolf as composer.

"Coon on the Moon," written by Shaw, was, despite the mordant title, a song about black pride. Wolf was fascinated by space flight, and he asked Shaw to come up with a song on the subject. Wolf also wanted to record something that reflected the progress of black Americans in the 1960s. Shaw combined both themes in one song that worked quite well—and that anticipated the verbal shock techniques of rap and hip-hop by at least a decade. "I wrote that tune when all the astronauts was heading to the moon and all this Sputnik and stuff," Shaw said. "We had to do an album, so this was one of the tunes I wrote about how things are changing now from picking cotton to driving trucks and being educated, and soon we even going to have a black man on the moon. We had this old saying in those days; Wolf would call black guys 'coons,' you know? 'Hey, man, look at that coon over there.' So I just wrote us a song: 'Soon there's going to be a coon on the moon.' It turned out okay. There was a lot of laughter in it."[31]

Like rappers who freely use the word "nigger," Shaw and Wolf claimed the racial slur as their own to drain it of its power. The song's details sketched Wolf's life. He sang it in a tone so caustic it should've been sold as paint remover:

> We used to pick the cotton till we got too old.
> (Tell me, who was the first man to go to the North Pole?)
> Things have changed. Yes, we on the move now. . . .
> You gonna wake up one morning and it'll be a coon sitting
>   on the moon.

"Trying to Forget You" was a hypnotic one-chord romp in the style of "Smokestack Lightnin' " and so many other Wolf tunes—melodically repetitive but tonally and rhythmically lush, with fluid bass, precise drumming, right-on-the-dot guitar and piano, and churning harp. Shaw's lyrics were all about the pain of infidelity, real or imagined. Jealousy never sounded so incensed.

Another keeper was "Stop Using Me," credited to Wolf and driven by Detroit Junior's prancing piano, including a spectacular intro run down the keys, plus Sumlin's and Harris's clipped guitars, McMahon's and Leary's loping bass and sizzling drums, and Wolf's throbbing harp. Wolf, again fed lines seconds before he sang them, flubbed a few words. Nonetheless, he delivered the droll lyrics with dainty grace.

An interesting though dated topical song, "Watergate Blues," also written by Shaw, was about Frank Wills, the $80-a-week security guard who one night in 1972 noticed adhesive tape covering the lock on a door at the Watergate office complex, leading to the arrest of five burglars and the scandal that destroyed Richard Nixon's presidency. Had Wills, a low-paid black man, not found the tape, Nixon would have served out his second term as president. "Leave Here Walking," written by Shaw, was a fine, fast twelve-bar shuffle distinguished by Hubert's liquid guitar licks and Wolf's shredded voice and harp.

A few songs were less successful. "Speak Now Woman," a slow blues written by St. Louis Jimmy Oden, didn't quite take off, partly due to Detroit Junior's use of electric harpsichord—an attempt by Bass to update Wolf's instrumentation that sounded out of place on a blues song. The same tinkling keys marred the title song, "The Back Door Wolf," a slow blues credited to Shaw and Bass and starring Shaw's lascivious sax, punctuated by Wolf's wordless moans. "You Turn Slick on Me," written by Detroit Junior, was a nondescript slow blues on which Wolf several times broke the twelve-bar structure as the band did its best to follow him. It's memorable mainly for Hubert's talkative lead guitar.

"Can't Stay Here," the album's last song, was credited to McMahon, apparently to push publishing royalties his way. It's a reworking of Charlie Patton's "Down the Dirt Road Blues." Wolf's last studio cut harked back to his first and greatest mentor:

> *Feel like choppin', chips flying everywhere. (2×)*
> *No, I can't make a dollar—no, and I can't stay here.*

Paul Rishell said, "Wolf was an artist who was trying to do a lot of different things at the same time. He was trying to establish a kind of music and make it modern and also to support where it came from. He wasn't ashamed of the old music. He loved that old music, and he was trying to uphold that tradition, too. . . . He looked as far back as he did forward."[32]

Harp player Danny Russo, another young bluesman Wolf befriended, remembers how thrilled Wolf was with a special gift he gave him in 1973. "I wanted to convince him I was legitimate. I told him about the double Charlie Patton album on Yazoo and I went out and bought it for him. And when he saw that, he was going nuts. He loved it! I told him, 'They got the words in there.' He went, 'Yeah, man, I'd like to do some of them numbers.' He was always nice to me. We were twenty or twenty-one years old and we were actually afraid to go near him, and he used to tell Hubert, 'Why don't you send the boys up to my room?' And Hubert would say, 'Why don't you go up and see him?' One time I knocked on the door and he came to the door and he was in his shorts and undershirt and he was brushing his teeth and he said, 'Come on in, have a seat.' He was very friendly. He had an F-hole guitar on the bed and he was watching the Bowery Boys and he was laughing!"[33]

By August 1973, Wolf was finished with recording. *The Back Door Wolf* was released to very favorable reviews. *Blues Unlimited* said, "Long live Howlin' Wolf. This album is absolutely fantastic. . . . Welcome home, Wolf—it's great to have you back."[34]

Driving to gigs was torturous for the Wolf by then, so he started flying to gigs whenever he could. One Sunday in late August, for example, he drove down to St. Louis with the band, did a gig that night, and then had them drop him at the airport. As he left the band, he said, "You guys get in that bus and you take that motherfucker to Denver, and when I get there, if anybody been arguin' and fightin', I'm gonna whup everybody's ass in the bus. I mean carry that fucker to Denver and don't put a scratch on it! I don't want *no* arguin' and fightin'. Detroit, I don't wanna hear nothing about you been arguin' and fightin' or I'm gonna whup your ass when I get there."[35] Sermon delivered, he took a late flight back to Chicago, where Lillie did his dialysis the next day. On Tuesday, he flew to Denver and Eddie picked him up at the airport and took him to their hotel to rest up for their show at a Denver club, Ebbet's Field. That night, Eddie and the band launched into six instrumentals and cover tunes, including songs as unlikely as "I Can't Stop Loving You," "How Blue Can You Get," and "What'd I Say?" Wolf finally came out and sang "The Red Rooster," and then did a long, dramatic version of "Goin' Down Slow," followed by "Killing Floor," and ending with "Shake for Me." He gave it his all in half an hour onstage, and then introduced his "baby brother" J.D., who lived in Denver.

"Goin' Down Slow" highlighted almost every show in his last years. Everyone close to him knew it was highly charged for him. "We would often talk about that," said Evelyn Sumlin. "When he would sing that song, he would sort of get a little stressed out, you know? He would get like he was sad. . . . We all thought it was dedicated to his mother."[36]

Wolf often refused to stop after just three or four songs, and then he and Shaw would argue about it. If Wolf got too excited, Shaw would grab the microphone and announce the end of his set, and Wolf would hang his head in shame. "Even when he was sick," Shaw said, "Wolf would always give a hundred percent. In his mind, he could do it all the time. He was that type of man. He just had so strong a belief in music and what he was doing that he wouldn't even let his health be no object to hold him back."[37] As Peter Guralnick pointed out in his remarkable portrait of Wolf in the book *Lost Highway*, "It was a little like James Brown with his cape, but this was real life, a continuing and weird drama of affirmation."[38]

One of Wolf's constant companions in the summer of 1973 was Eddie Shaw's teenaged son, Vaan. "I can remember my exact first impression of him," Vaan said. "He was a nice man, but people definitely irritated him. He did the *Back Door Wolf* sessions and he wanted a glass of water. People handed him beer, people handed him wine, people handed him everything. And finally he got so mad that he cursed everybody out and he said, 'All I wanted was some water!' And I remember that I thought that was so stupid because I didn't know why these people were catering to him the way they were, 'cause they were overboard—constant overkill. It was like they were finally appreciating him, but he didn't really need it."

Wolf often baby-sat Vaan, who said he was an excellent baby-sitter. "All you had to do was listen to his lectures and stuff like that. Actually a lot of the stuff that he said makes sense now. It didn't make sense then, but he got talking about changes in the world and stuff like that. 'Underwear talk,' I think he called it: what you say when you're around your wife with nobody else to pay attention—how you can change the world. I wouldn't talk back, so basically I was his ears. He knew I was a good listener and he'd talk and talk and talk and talk.

"I didn't know him as a musician, just as an older gentleman figure that would tell you when to sleep, when to eat, when to go to bed, how much to eat or watch, stuff like that. I got dropped off there because my father would be out playing cards with Freddie King, something like that, and Wolf didn't mind keeping me.

"He was not a people person at all, 'cause people would either irritate him or exploit him. I think he knew a little bit of both. . . . Most times when Wolf went into the studio, he would get exploited, and he knew he was getting exploited."[39]

In the fall of 1973, Wolf had a visit from his son, Floyd, who'd recently moved to Connecticut. They hit the Chicago clubs and Floyd said, "Everywhere we goes, man, peoples know him. . . . They buy him liquor. He didn't buy it; they was givin' it to him." Floyd and his father drank until 2:00 a.m. The next day Wolf showed him around Chicago. "We passed a bank. He said, 'Son, see that bank there?' I said, 'Yeah, Dad.' 'I got money there and I live on the interest.' So we turned a corner and went on down about two or three blocks and it was another big, old, tall bank. 'See that bank there, son?' I said, 'Yes.' 'I got money there, too, and I live on the interest. And I tell you what, didn't no Lord put ne'er a damn penny in there!' And when he said that, looked like somethin' started burnin' me in the bottom of my feet comin' up my legs and tellin' me to get away from him. Get away from him! So when I got back to the house . . . I went in there and got all my bags. Said, 'Take me to the bus station.' He wanted to know why I was leavin' so early, but I couldn't—I just couldn't tell him."[40]

By late 1973, Wolf was increasingly despondent about being exploited by the music industry. He saw the younger musicians, most of them white, making millions with his kind of music while he was still doing club gigs despite ill health. His band was driving to gigs in a Pontiac station wagon instead of a limousine. He was out of sync with the times—certainly not what the star-making machinery was looking for. "They need the images of their weekly gods—the boy coming of age every month and blah blah blah," Vaan said. "Wolf did not fit the nice scenario. He did not look how he was supposed to look. He was bigger than he was supposed to look. He didn't sound the way he was supposed to sound. He was like a prepackaged, total anti-hero. You would not go into your son's room and see a picture of Wolf on the wall. If you did, you'd drop dead! You'd go, 'Why is this black farmer-looking guy up on your wall, Johnny?' "[41]

In October of 1973, Wolf played at Barbra's marriage. It was one of the few times she and her sister ever heard him with his band in person. Wolf doted on his stepdaughters. Long before, they learned to go to him if Lillie turned them down when they wanted something. Wolf would tell them, "Don't worry about that. That stingy woman!" Then he'd give them whatever they wanted.[42]

By December, Wolf was on the East Coast for another round of gigs: a night at Avery Fisher Hall in New York City, six nights at Grendel's Lair in Philadelphia, a week at Paul's Mall in Boston, and other venues. At Paul's Mall two nights before New Year's, two blues fans,

David Little and Peter Riley, came to hear the Wolf. Riley brought his mother, Dorothy "Ma" Riley, who was curious about the blues and close to Wolf's age, and had lived for years down South. Wolf enjoyed talking to her; she seemed to draw him out. A beautiful young woman approached and asked Wolf to sign an album; David and Peter certainly noticed her. As she left, Dorothy leaned over and said, "Wolf, she's attractive!" "Aw, she don't show me nothin'!" Wolf said, and they all laughed.[43]

Then he agreed to do an interview. "Now, you take me when I started out with it," he said, "I'd sit up and play all night long for a fish sandwich. I didn't know no better. Have a packed house, and people be makin' a lot of money off of us, give us a fish sandwich and a drink of whiskey, and I thought, 'That was it!' I didn't want nothin' else." They asked if he was bitter about playing for so little in his early days. "No, no! No, I don't think—y'know, don't never do that. Once you get drownded, you just got drownded, y'know what I mean? Just don't worry about that. Look forward to something else, y'know what I mean? So I didn't feel bad about it. I go back 'round through that country now. A lot of them old peoples are dead out, but their little undergrowths done growed up. We sit down and laugh about it."

What about white people playing the blues? "A lot of poor white folks come out of the South playing good music, y'know what I mean? You see, the peoples that come up the hard way—that come up suf-ferin'—they can play that music, and they can sing them songs, them old songs. . . . We got some white players play good music that come out of the South. Now you take these white kids in the North, y'know, they don't know what it means. They're just playing. They just want to be out there under the blue lights. . . . Now you take the white peoples way back, they used to play that long-haired music. You'd get tired and brood over it over the night. But they'd done had a plenty, them rich folk, and they haven't had no ups and downs back there like the poor white man. The poor white man come out of Arkansas, Mississippi, and Alabama . . . them guys could play some music. . . . They come along on that same track that I fall on."

He turned morose when asked if he'd been home for the holidays. He hadn't. As he did too often, he'd taken this gig out of a sense of duty. "I started to turn it down, but you see, the company had booked it. If he'd've called me, I'd've turned him down. I didn't want to come here anyway. I want to stay home with my family on Christmas."[44] Wolf apologized for his mood and they thanked him profusely for his time. Little and Riley saw Wolf every time he played in the area from then on, and always brought "Ma" Riley with them to break the ice.

Like many of the Chess blues stars, Wolf wondered why, with all the rock stars covering his songs, he wasn't getting more money. The changed circumstances of the rock era had everything to do with his discontent. In the 1950s, Chess artists were paid two cents a record, the industry standard.[45] By the 1970s, those rates looked paltry when rock artists were getting a percentage of a record's selling price. The Chess brothers bailed out their many profligate artists time and again with loans, all records of which were destroyed when GRT took over the company and Leonard died. But Wolf was not one of their profligate artists. He always paid his own way and never came down to the Chess building to beg for advances. He was incensed that he wasn't getting his share when he saw the rock stars doing his music and getting rich and the Chess brothers making millions by selling the company he helped make famous.

Wolf discussed the matter with Lillie and Eddie Shaw. They agreed that he'd been exploited, and he decided to sue ARC Music and Chess. The law firm of Abeles, Clark & Osterberg filed a suit for $1,250,000 on his behalf in United States District Court in the Southern District of New York on May 6, 1974.[46] The suit described Wolf as "a renowned black performer and composer of rhythm and blues music. . . . He lacks the personal knowledge, experience and sophistication necessary to fully appreciate and comprehend the nature, character and significance of certain legal rights in intellectual property and contracts." The suit leveled broad charges against Gene Goodman, ARC Music, and the Chess brothers, alleging that among other acts:

- Goodman and the Chess brothers had entered into a "plan and scheme to defraud" Wolf of his composition rights.
- On March 17, 1971, with full knowledge of Wolf's ill health and of the efforts of General Recorded Tapes to sign an agreement with him, Goodman traveled to Wolf's home and convinced him to sign an agreement with ARC Music. To cloud Wolf's judgment

during their discussions, Goodman showed him a check for $2,000, offered him a bottle of whiskey, and invited him to drink from it.

- The March 1971 agreement contained a clause whereby Wolf signed away his rights to everything he'd written and recorded before March 1971 as a retroactive "employee-for-hire" of ARC Music.

- Goodman failed to reveal to Wolf that ARC Music was about to settle a copyright infringement suit for more than $80,000 for just one of his compositions; also, that his early copyrights would soon be up for renewal and that he could sell them for a great deal of money, but if he died after signing the new agreement, Lillie could not renew his copyrights.

The royalty issue was complicated. Wolf had certainly received songwriting royalties from ARC. Documents filed by his own lawyers show that from December 1966 to June 1974, ARC sent him $105,673 accompanied by royalty statements—$45,123 of it in one sum in December 1972, after ARC settled with Led Zeppelin over "The Lemon Song." During the same period, he received other checks from ARC totaling $12,908. The essence of Wolf's suit was whether those amounts were fair, and whether he and Lillie could renew and control his copyrights.

In a formal answer filed with the court, Goodman's lawyers denied Wolf's charges. Among other defenses, they claimed that the purpose of the "employee-for-hire" language in the March 1971 agreement "was to assure defendant ARC MUSIC CORP that it would have renewal rights even if the plaintiff did not survive the renewal term. . . . Said defendant's desire to acquire this right was fully disclosed and discussed with plaintiff and his wife, both of whom, with full understanding that the renewal rights had potential value, acquiesced to the defendant's request."[47]

The cliché is that the Chess brothers had exploited an oppressed group of artists. Indeed, it would be hard to find Americans more oppressed in the twentieth century than black people from the Deep South. But the Chess brothers—two Jewish immigrants whose family fled Poland before the Holocaust—had their own firsthand knowledge of the worst kind of oppression.

When they started their company, they were hoping just to create the hits of the day, without much thought for tomorrow. It's hard to believe they foresaw that song publishing rights and their fabulous catalogue would be worth a fortune even twenty years down the road, let alone fifty. The Chess brothers seem lucky rather than unscrupulous: the fortunate recipients of the equity that their own drive for quality helped create. By suing them, their artists were merely stating the obvious: They thought they should share in the good fortune. It was like working for decades in a gold mine that regularly yielded small amounts of pay dirt after a lot of heavy lifting, sifting, and washing. Suddenly, with the rock stars of the 1960s, they'd struck a vein of solid gold. Everybody working the mine wanted some. As Leonard might have put it, they'd hit the MOTHER lode!

News of Wolf's suit ran in *Variety* on May 15, 1974, and walloped the close-knit Chicago blues community like a bomb. Within two years, Willie Dixon and Muddy Waters brought similar suits against Goodman, ARC, Phil Chess, and the estate of Leonard Chess.

Wolf wouldn't enjoy the fruits of his suit. Lillie settled with ARC and the Chess brothers for an undisclosed sum after his death, and ARC retained the publishing rights to his songs.

Wolf kept traveling and working throughout the spring, summer, and fall of 1974. In April, he played the Easter Blues Festival in Cocoa Beach, Florida, where a reviewer wrote, "The band reached new heights on 'Killing Floor' as Hubert Sumlin destroyed the audience with his hot picking. In all, the Wolf played an hour and a half and undoubtedly made many converts to the blues here."[48] In June, he was in Atlanta for a three-night stint at Richard's, where a reviewer wrote, "He's suffered a couple of heart attacks in the past few years and he's had to go easy, rest a bit, but good lord, this old man can sing!"[49] In July, they were at the International Blues Festival in Summerville, Kentucky, where a reviewer wrote, "His set, which included 'Goin' Down Slow' and 'Sittin' on Top of the World,' was short but very enjoyable. Wolf sang with more initial strength and power than I heard from him two years ago at Ann Arbor, but towards the end of the set, he began to sound short-winded and looked to be gasping for breath."[50] Wolf also played in 1974 at the University of Vermont, where Peter Guralnick and Johnny Shines were startled to find him hiding in a backstage broom closet: the grownup version of returning to the dark sanctuary under his great-uncle's house.[51]

In October 1974, Wolf's son, Floyd, telephoned. Elven Frazier was dead. Floyd was broke and had two young sons to support. Would his father give him money enough to bury his mother? Wolf turned him down. "He told me, 'I ain't got no money,' and hung up the phone in my face!" Floyd claimed. "That did it. From that day on, I didn't talk to him no more. I didn't call him or nothin'."[52]

Wolf did a lot of shuffling of band members in 1973 and 1974. Bob Anderson took over on bass from Andrew McMahon in 1973, then "Shorty" Gilbert took over for Anderson in 1974. Called "Shorty" because his legs were stunted by polio, Gilbert sat in on bass one night in 1973 while Anderson went to "get something to eat." (Anderson actually went to visit a girlfriend.) After all the stories he'd heard about the Wolf, Shorty was petrified when the old man yelled, "Get the bass, little thing!" He played well, and Wolf asked him for his phone number and said he wished he'd had him in his band years before. He joined Wolf's band in May of 1974. "It made me feel better than anything I ever felt in my life playing with Wolf," he said. Wolf always paid well and the band worked steadily, often playing gigs without Wolf when he was sick.[53]

S. P. Leary became ill in 1974, so Robert Plunkett took over the drum chair—reluctantly at first. "I was afraid of Wolf because I had heard all these rumors that he beat up on his guys," he said. Wolf's looks also gave him pause. "A great big black man with nice curly hair and blue eyes. I thought, 'Blue eyes? A white man got blue eyes! Something wrong with this motherfucker! No, I'm not playing with the man!'" Wolf wooed Plunkett for five years to join his band, sending someone every year to implore the drummer. "Hubert'd come say, 'Wolf wants you to work with him.' 'I ain't gonna work with him.' 'Why not, man?' "'Cause I'm scared of him! He beat you all up! I ain't gonna let him beat me up! I like his music. Let's keep it like that, 'cause I don't want nobody hittin' me.'" Then Wolf secretly paid for Plunkett's breakfast every Sunday at a restaurant where they both ate. He finally asked a waitress for the name of his breakfast benefactor. "The Howlin' Wolf always pays," she said. He asked her to thank him.

In 1974, Wolf sent Eddie Shaw to request Plunkett's drum favors for the fifth time. "I say, 'Hey Eddie, I told somebody to tell Wolf four years in a row I am not going to work with him.' 'Why not?' 'I'm afraid of him and I don't want to kill him.' 'Oh man, Wolf's a nice guy.' 'Well, from what I heard, he ain't nice.' 'Well, I tell you what, the man wants you to work with him.' 'Well, you tell him for the fifth time I ain't gonna work with him.' 'Look, Robert, I tell you what. I'm the bandleader. If you work with us, Wolf won't give you no order. He won't have nothing to do with you. I'll be your boss. Can you handle that?' 'Yeah. Are you sure he ain't gonna have nothing to do with me?' 'He ain't gonna have nothing to do with you.' And he didn't! He didn't tell me to do nothing. I said, 'Okay. If you can do it like that, I'll work with him.'"

Plunkett discovered that Wolf was a generous, businesslike band leader. "I wished I had played with Wolf the first time he sent for me. One of the nicest persons I ever worked for! I thought he was a mean guy, but it wasn't that. It was the guys. It wasn't the Wolf. He was trying to keep regulations on the level and they was drunks. . . . He'd have to fine 'em. He'd jump on 'em and knock 'em around.

"I had to go home, down South again, and when I quit the band, I didn't want to tell Wolf I was leaving the band. I told Eddie, 'Tell Wolf that this'll be my last week. I'm going back home.' 'No, you go tell him.' 'No man, I ain't gonna tell him.' 'Why can't you tell him?' 'I don't wanna tell him. You tell him.' 'No, man, you gotta tell him.' But finally Eddie says, 'Okay, I'll tell him for you.' So Eddie went and told Wolf, 'Robert got to leave the band because he got to go home and join his family.' Wolf said, 'Tell Plunkett to come over here. I want to talk to him.' I said, 'Oh shit, he mad.' He was over in the corner and I went over there. He looked over at me and said, 'Have a seat.' I said to myself, 'Damn.' I sit down. 'What you drinking?' 'I drink Scotch.' 'Bring him a half a pint.' Wolf don't buy no drinks! I know he mad now. So I sit down and he says, 'I really hate that you gotta leave the band. You're a nice person and I like the way you carry yourself. You don't get drunk and stuff. You don't be late. I hate to lose you.' I said, 'Well, my family down there — I have to go back.' He said, 'I understand. But I had to ask you to work for me for a long time. I almost had to beg you to work with me. So tell me the truth: How do you really feel about me?' I looked at him and laughed and said, 'I had you all wrong, old man. You're one of the nicest persons I ever worked with in my life.'

"That sticks to right now. If I had known Wolf was nice as he was, I'd have begged to work with him. That's right! I'd have got on my knees!"[54]

Plunkett left in 1975 and Kansas City Red filled his drum chair, but Wolf didn't like Red's sense of rhythm. He replaced him with Chico Chism, who had worked with Wolf before. "You do what he ask you to do and you had no problems," Chico said. "Play his music like it's supposed to be played, and conduct yourself accordingly. Wolf treated me nice. I had played with a lot of people, but I just taken to Wolf for some reason. . . . He was just like a daddy. It was really neat being with Wolf like that. The man was not at all like people said he was. If you screwed up, he wouldn't get all like they said: hitting people physically and all that stuff. He didn't do that; not to me. You would have to really do something drastic, you know? Like him and Hubert and Junior—they was there before me—they'd have little rows, but not when I was there."[55]

Drummer Casey Jones also played with Wolf during the 1970s. Wolf called him "Longhair" because he had a long, processed hairdo. "I liked the hell out of him," Jones said. "When I did a riff Wolf didn't like, he'd say, 'That was a little too much there, Longhair. You got to make it easy.' " Jones saw Wolf and Hubert argue constantly. "Wolf would knock fire from you!" he said. "Yeah, man! His eyes would turn different colors, man. He was mad then! I seen it! Scary!"[56] Jones quit to start his own band, but remained friendly with the Wolf.

Vaan Shaw noticed the unusual dynamic between Wolf and Hubert. "I tell you, man, everything a Gypsy is supposed to be, Hubert Sumlin is. A Gypsy don't care about money! If Hubert got money, it's fine. If he don't, it's fine. Hubert attracts women. He attracts women like flies. He got the kindest heart. . . . If Hubert looked out the window and there was a guy on the street, he's grab him and ask him, 'Did you have a meal?' Playing cards, he'd cheat you. Hubert was the Gypsy.

"Hubert was the heart, and that's the way Wolf planned it. Don't think that Wolf just went and said 'I'm going to get this guy off the street.' He picked Hubert for a specific reason. Hubert had enough love in his heart—he had enough fire. He was the opposite of Wolf—he wasn't Wolf at all. Where Wolf was disciplined, Hubert was a maverick. He could care less. Where Wolf was structured, Hubert was sponta- neous. They were totally opposite. Wolf knew exactly what he was doing when he picked Hubert. He couldn't have planned it better. Hubert was Wolf's counterpart. Wolf did all the planning, and Hubert was the heart and soul. That's the bottom line.

"To see them both together was a trip. It was like watching a father and a son: from one extreme to the other. In a half hour they could kiss and say 'I love you' to each other verbally and touch and hug, and in next half hour be knocking around fighting. It was like a car with a stuck accelerator going from 0 to 60: Oh, boy, here we go! Wolf would say, 'Hubert, time to get the band. Hubert, you gotta be back at a certain time. Are you listening to me, Hubert? Are you listening?' 'I'm listening, old man, I'm listening. I love you. I'm listening.' 'You got that watch I bought you?' 'Yeah, old man, I got it. I love you, Wolf.' 'Okay, I love you, too. You look okay. Your hair combed? Okay.' Hubert'd go outside and suddenly Hubert ain't here—he'd be down at a bar somewhere. Come back late, sweating: 'I'm sorry. I'm sorry.' 'Hubert, now you didn't do right. You know you were supposed to be back at seven.' 'I'm sorry! Sorry!' Then they'd fight and make up again.

"But when they were on, I never saw two people more in sync. It was the best sight you'd ever wanna see because it was really special. Hubert just took the shit to a whole other level. The truth is, to this day, Wolf was the only one that could get Hubert there. When Hubert played with Wolf, it was to make Wolf proud of him. And that meant more than money or people yelling or his own ego. It was like Wolf could wink at him and say, 'You did right, boy!' It was like that pat on the head that he wanted more than anything, and it worked. And they were magic!"[57]

Wolf worried about Hubert constantly. Many nights, he'd come home from gigs and cry about Hubert. "What's going to happen to Hubert when I'm gone, Lillie?" he'd sob.[58]

Wolf himself worried his friends. They thought the old man was getting senile. "He let me use one of his harps and he thought I didn't give it back to him, but I did," said Billy Boy. "He kept saying, 'He didn't give me my harp back!' "[59]

Wolf also worried what would happen to his band if he couldn't work. Eddie Shaw had a solution. He was thinking about buying a club at 1815 West Roosevelt Road on Chicago's West Side. Lillie offered to lend him some money, and he also won some money at the racetrack in Boston when they played at Joe's Place. Driving back to Chicago, Shaw told Wolf he was thinking about buying a club. Wolf said, "Hey, man, I'm ready to come off the road. If you open a club, I'll come in there and play with you and make it the biggest club in Chicago." Shaw said, "Hey, I ain't going to be able to pay you for a whole week at a time." Wolf said, "I ain't worried about the money."[60]

Shaw opened his new club in June 1975, renaming it Eddie Shaw's 1815 Club. During the grand opening weekend, more than thirty blues musicians played, including Wolf imitators James "Tail Dragger" Jones, William "Highway Man" Holland, and Lee "Little Wolf" Solomon. Shaw booked Wolf there on Fridays, Saturdays, and Sundays, with Jimmy Dawkins, Tail Dragger, and Casey Jones on other nights. B. B. King dropped by the club a few weeks after it opened to see his old friend Wolf.

Wolf helped Shaw make ends meet. "Wolf was always in my corner. He'd say, 'Eddie, how much you make tonight?' I'd say, 'I made $1,100.' 'Paid the band?' 'Yeah.' 'You got enough money to buy your whiskey with?' 'Yeah.' 'Give me $200 and go ahead.' He would do stuff like that for me."[61]

Harp player, producer, and Phoenix club owner Bob Corritore, who grew up in Chicago, first heard Wolf at the 1815 Club in 1974. It was his first trip to a real blues club. He was eighteen years old, had a fake ID, and nervously noticed people chugging pints on the street corner and as much broken glass as gravel in the club's parking lot. Walking in, he saw Wolf playing cards by the bandstand. Then Wolf started playing blues, and Corritore was bowled over. "It was flawless how Hubert and the Wolf used to work together," he said. "Hubert was always so inventive and so magical with his guitar. . . . He was a guitar master, and he owned those songs." Corritore loved Wolf's harp sound. "He just had a hard-hitting, beautiful tonal thing that he did, kind of a Sonny Boy sound but rawer and with more vibrato. Wolf always played great harmonica." He returned to the club for months. "He'd throw in these things I had never heard before that probably he could have made great records of. They seemed to be fully developed songs."[62]

Drummer Twist Turner, who moved to Chicago from Seattle in 1974, also heard Wolf at the 1815. "The first time I saw him was the best, 'cause I walked into this smoke-filled bar and Wolf was crawling on the floor and had his finger out pointing, and he was doing a bunch of stuff. He was crawling up to women and he was prowling." Turner couldn't help but notice Wolf's health problems. "I seen him grab his chest and start holding it like it was hurting and then pop some—I'm assuming it was nitroglycerine pills—in his mouth and just sit there for a while and then keep on singing. . . . I was really scared that he was going to die while I was watching." Turner heard Willie Johnson sit in with Wolf one night at the club. "That was the first time I heard him and it cracked me up because he sounded just like Hubert, only better. When I heard that I said, 'So, that's where Hubert got it!' "[63]

In March of 1975, Wolf and Lillie traveled to the Grammy Awards in Los Angeles. Wolf had been nominated twice in the same category—Best Traditional or Ethnic Album—for *The Back Door Wolf* and *London Revisited*, a package of alternate tracks from his and Muddy's London sessions. Other nominees were Bukka White, Willie Dixon, and Doc and Merle Watson. Wolf fell asleep at the ceremony and Lillie had to wake him for the awards in his category. She needn't have bothered. Doc and Merle Watson won.

One day, Wolf and Lillie showed up unexpectedly at the old Chess studios. Wolf had a gripe about something on *The Back Door Wolf* and blamed it on Ralph Bass, who cussed Wolf out and told him to get out of his office. Wolf stormed out but Lillie briefly stayed behind, and Bass apologized to her for his language.

Wolf had other worries in 1975. Even with dialysis three times a week, he was constantly tired. He was staying home as much as possible, spending a lot of time fishing with his young buddy Vaan, who liked to listen to him talk about life and music. "Even as a kid, I'd say, 'Listen up, Vaan. He's about to say something. Retain it in your brain.' . . . When we would go fishing or something, he'd start talking. And he'd talk to the fish or talk to the air and I'd be there. He'd say everything from aggressive talk to 'This is a fucked-up world' to 'I'm going to make it after all.'

"Or he'd talk about his mother. They didn't get along because of music: 'cause of just music, nothing else. She literally had nothing to do with the devil's music. It was the weirdest thing in the world. They took it to a level that you wouldn't believe, like it was not the career she wanted for him at all.

"When I caught Wolf in a moment like that, he'd go, 'Yeah I missed a lot. Ain't no love like your mother's love.' He'd say stuff like that, and you knew where it was coming from. 'Ain't no love like your mother's love. Damn, let me tell you that, young boy.' I always remember that. 'Ain't no love. Ain't no love. I missed a lot.' And then he'd go off.

"He also said, 'You think the blues is gone down for the count? It'll all change. Blues is going to be played in people's homes. Even to this day, I wouldn't be allowed to come in their houses—but my music is going to be in their houses. My music is going to be in their culture.' I remember him saying it to me and me going, 'Whoa, this is heavy words.' I remember thinking over and over, 'This is not ego talk.' . . . He said, 'Watch and see. This stuff going to sell big. Everything going to change. There's going to be a blues McDonald's.'

"I've had a lot of people say, 'Yeah, I would've liked to have met Wolf.' And I keep telling them, 'You wouldn't have liked him.' He was a person you would not like but you would understand. He treated you with the right amount of respect. But by the same token, he would also say what's wrong. He was not a person to say, 'Hey, nice tie!'

"He was honest to the point where I think sometimes it was his downfall. It's like, if you said, 'Good morning,' he'd probably say, 'The day just started. I don't know.' Or 'How are you?' 'I'm the same way I was. Am I supposed to change?' It was not an average answer, and it was continual to where it would get on your nerves. And times were bad and he didn't say times were good. It was 'Damn, my arm cut off and I'm bleeding: I'm supposed to go with a smile? To hell with that!' It was too much reality. He was bitter about a lot of things. Shit, he was bitter about his life. And I'll tell you, he was bitter because he didn't get his dues and I think he knew it.

"It's like he was in the wrong body, the wrong everything, and he adapted to it. But he could create. That was his whole thing—he could create. Out of him being what he was, he could create.

"Out of all the elements, that's the hardest element of all. Everybody can steal another's idea, manufacture it, clone it, or whatever. But it's hard to just create. It's the hardest thing of all. You gotta remember, these guys didn't have blueprints. . . . The thing that makes Wolf so magical is that you see a person create a whole genre of music through just their mind, and you ain't supposed to do it. You're supposed to have a sheet of paper, a desk, a quiet room, you're supposed to think and concentrate. And here's a guy using just his ego, creating lyrics in a room full of smoke, alcohol, four-letter words, and intimidating individuals—and yet he still creates. And that's the magic."[64]

Wolf was often at the 1815 Club during 1975. Jim O'Neal, blues producer and co-founder of *Living Blues* magazine, said, "I can remember a lot of times he'd be sitting at the bar by himself and everybody knew that he was the center of everything—that old man sitting at the bar leaning over and not doing anything, not talking to anybody. . . . Wolf had a lot of respect on the scene there and considering that Muddy wasn't performing on the local club scene any more I think pretty much everyone acknowledged that Wolf was the king of the scene there, even though he wasn't making the most money maybe, or even drawing the biggest crowds. . . . He had a certain position in the hierarchy of blues that few people are ever going to obtain and I sensed that people knew that already back then."[65]

In July, the Rolling Stones came to Chicago and invited Wolf and Lillie to be special guests at one of their shows. Wolf said, "Well, I don't think I want to hear that noise." Bill Wyman made arrangements to send a limousine to pick them up for the show. Wolf wasn't interested; he liked the Stones personally but really preferred to spend the evening resting at home. Then reporter Bob Greene from the *Chicago Sun-Times* called for an interview. Wolf said tongue-in-cheek that he couldn't afford tickets to the Stones' show, and Greene took him seriously and wrote an article that made him sound like a pauper disowned by princes. Wolf and Lillie were deluged with calls offering free tickets to the show. Lillie had to call Greene to explain that Wolf's comment was a joke and she and Wolf decided to go to the show after all. That night, the Stones' limousine picked Wolf and Lillie up and took them to the Continental Hotel, where the Stones had an entire floor. Wolf hugged "his boys," as he still called them, talked about old times, and they all retired to dinner. Then Wolf and Lillie went to the show, sitting next to Wyman's son, and were touched that Mick introduced them as the light crew turned a spotlight on them. Afterward, said Lillie, "You would've thought Wolf was one of the Rolling Stones. . . . Them kids was screaming and hollering and we were trying to get into the limo." A young woman ran up, unbuttoned her blouse, and asked Wolf to sign her bra. Wolf had Lillie sign it for him as he laughed nervously.

The next night, the Stones were going to have dinner at Wolf's house. Lillie prepared a big soul food dinner, but no one showed up until well after dinnertime, so Wolf went to the 1815 Club. Finally, Wyman and his son and Ron Wood showed up. Wyman apologized for their tardiness and the absence of the others. Lillie called Wolf, who came home from the club to spend the evening with them listening to records, passing a guitar, and having a good time. Wolf's "boys" left the next morning, "as drunk as they wanted to be," said Lillie.[66]

In late September 1975, Wolf and his band headed out west for a show at Sick's Stadium in south Seattle, less than forty miles from Camp Murray, where Wolf had had his problems during World War II. Sick's was where a young Jimi Hendrix watched Elvis in 1957; it was also the site of Jimi's last Seattle concert in 1970. It was a mile downhill from where Wolf would get dialysis at a VA hospital—now the corporate headquarters of Amazon.com, the Web retailer.

Wolf was very sick that day. He got his dialysis and then headed outside into the gloomy Seattle air to catch his ride down the hill. His driver didn't show up on time, so he started walking down toward the stadium. His driver finally picked him up several blocks away.

Wolf was headlining, with Ace of Straits and Shuffles (harp player Kim Wilson's band), Albert Collins, and John Lee Hooker preceding him. When Wolf's band started playing, it was 7:00 p.m. and getting cold, dark, and drizzly—normal weather for Seattle in September. The show was sparsely attended—no more than two thousand people.

Seattle guitarist John Stephan went to the show to hear Hubert. "I couldn't believe my eyes that I was actually seeing this guy that I'd been listening to all this time. And I thought, 'God, he sounds just like himself!' He had this real cheesy Rickenbacker, but he sounded just the same. . . . Then Howlin' Wolf walked out and he picked up a microphone, a Shure 57, and plugged in. I was about fifteen feet from him. There was a piano bench right in front of the stage. He sat down on this old wooden piano bench and I could tell right away that he was ill. I thought he had the flu or something. He was coughing. He sat down and he had his legs apart and he had the microphone laid over one leg so it was just hanging down. He had his head down and he was just rocking back and forth. And he'd kind of look around and scan the audience. People were just mesmerized. He was just looking at all the people and the band was just going. He had on a black suit and a white shirt and no tie. And he had really cool nylon or silk socks, dark with a really cool pattern on them. He opened up his suit and pulled out a really crumpled-up paper bag, a sandwich bag. He held it and rocked back and forth as he looked the audience over. He opened up this bag and started pulling out harmonicas. He'd look at 'em up close and check the key and set 'em on the piano bench to the left of him— probably four or five harps. He laid 'em out in order. He picked up the mike and grabbed a harp and just started making that sound that just came out from the depths—just the most soulful sound. He played harp for quite a while and then stood up and sang. He only did about five songs: 'How Many More Years,' 'Wang Dang Doodle,' and some others. 'How Many More Years' was Wolf's last song. When he sang 'I'm going to fall on my knees, I'm going to raise up my right hand,' he kind of bent down a little bit and he raised his hand up. He couldn't even quite raise his hand all the way.

"I remember how bad I felt because I knew how sick he was. He left the stage and didn't come back for an encore. I remember how stupid the audience was. They wanted him to do another one and a few people were booing. I turned around and yelled at them to shut up, because I knew he was sick. I just didn't know how sick he was. . . . It was raining when he finished.

"I damn near cried because I felt so bad that people were booing him. I felt guilty for going. Being a performer myself, I've played sick and I know what it feels like. It was just hippies. They were drunk and stoned and they didn't give a shit. They just wanted to hear more Howlin' Wolf. They paid their $3 and they expected to hear more. But he did his best. He sat down just for the first couple of songs, but he played harp for a long time sitting down, and he sat there for a long time before he played. He was kind of stalling. He had enough work ethic and love for what he was doing to know he had to deliver, but I could tell he really didn't want to be there."[67]

After the show, the band went back to their hotel and everyone prepared to head to the airport but Robert Plunkett, back for one gig, and Detroit Junior. "Wolf came down and brought me my money," said Plunkett. "See, they went back the same day, and me and Detroit Junior stayed over until Monday. Wolf gave me my money and gave me a fifth of Scotch and his door key. I said, 'Wait a minute.' I'm staring at my pay and the Scotch and this door key, and I said, 'What the fuck's this for?' 'They got these fine-looking girls here,' Wolf said. 'You ought to find you one, take her up and get her one time in my bed.' And I did! I did, and I told her, 'This is for Wolf!' "[68]

By November, Wolf was noticeably weaker. He'd lost sixty pounds during the previous four years, and he looked gaunt and drawn. Chicago deejay Pervis Spann had booked him for a big package show at the Chicago Amphitheater on Friday, November 7, and a follow-on show the next night in Memphis. Spann called Lillie several times to find out if Wolf would make either show. Wolf was determined to do both, but Lillie doubted he could do either.

She finally agreed to let him do the show in Chicago, which had a dream lineup: Luther Allison, Little Mack Simmons, Wolf, O. V. Wright, Albert King, Little Milton, Bobby Bland, and B. B. King. "Wolf determined he was going to go," Lillie said.[69] Lillie helped Wolf dress, drove him down to the Amphitheater, and parked close to the artists' entrance. It was cold outside and it took a long while for Wolf and Lillie to walk in. Backstage, he talked to his band—Eddie, Hubert, Chico, and Shorty. "I want you to make me sound good tonight," he said. "I don't know how long I'm going to be down here." He joked around and seemed in good spirits. Chico said, "Wolf, when I go out, I want to go out on my feet with my drumsticks and my drum key in my hand." "Me, too, Chico. Me, too."[70] Other bluesmen came by to talk with the Wolf, and seeing him alert and joshing with his band, quickly spread the word: The old man's going to get down tonight. Word filtered backstage that the show was sold out. People were being turned away at the box office.

Spann begged Lillie to let Wolf do the show in Memphis the next night, but she said Wolf was in no shape to travel. "Wolf looked like he wanted to make a liar out of me!" she said.[71]

At 9:30, after Little Mack Simmons finished his set, Wolf got ready to perform. Eddie Shaw set up a chair for him and the band launched into an instrumental. Wolf walked up to the side of the stage and was preparing to head into the spotlights when he seemed to have a sudden attack of pain or panic. He turned and started offstage, then froze in place. "It looked like he thought, 'This is my last time,' " said Lillie. Wolf slowly spun around and headed out into the lights as Lillie took her seat in the front row.[72]

The crowd roared. Wolf surveyed them sadly as the band started into "Built for Comfort." Wolf sang it sitting down, concentrating on every syllable. The band hit "Highway 49," and before it was half over, Wolf rose unsteadily to his feet and started stalking the stage, bravely doing his old antics. Many in the crowd clapped wildly. The band launched into "Shake It for Me" and Wolf stayed on his feet, shaking and waggling his hips and moving from one side of the huge stage to the other. After twenty minutes, Wolf was tiring, but Eddie let him have another song. As the band tore into "Killing Floor," Wolf crawled across the stage, then got to his feet and ran in place while singing over and over, "God knows, I should-a been gone." The crowd rose like a flame and cheered. They gave him a standing ovation. Dripping with sweat, he waved and blew kisses. Then Eddie helped him off.

Backstage, Wolf called Shorty and Chico over. "Little short dick," he said to Shorty, "I wished I had you and this little motherfucker here back in the '50s. We'd have made so much money this amphitheater couldn't hold it all. Y'all make me sound better than I ever sounded in my life."[73]

Then he sat, exhausted. Soon he was gasping. Someone called the paramedics while local deejay E. Rodney Jones went to the front row to get Lillie. She asked, "Has he had a heart attack?" Jones said, "I think so." They rushed into the dressing room. "I knew he hadn't," said Lillie, "but he was like—you know, he worked too hard. So everybody was around there. They even called the paramedics before they called me, and I'm sitting right by the stage. And I go in and I said, 'Let me get to him, because I know what to do for Wolf.' And the medic comes running in and he says, 'Let me get to him. I can—' I said, 'No, you can't work with him like I can. I know exactly what to do.' I knew he was tired, so I loosened his belt and I gave him his medication. And everybody was standing around. They said, 'Let him go to the hospital.' Wolf said, 'I don't want to go to the hospital, baby.' I said, 'You won't have to go.' So

the paramedic says, 'Let us take him. Let us take him.' Everybody saying, 'We don't have another Wolf.' I said, 'No, he'll be all right.' And so
finally he rolled over, and says, 'And B. B.' I says, 'No, we gonna get
ready and go home.' He says, 'Just listen at B.!' He *never* discussed other
musicians. It was a funny thing. So he said, 'Listen to that old B.! You
may pay the boys. I think I want to listen to B. tonight.' I say, 'You?' He
said, 'Yeah! . . . I'm gonna stay here and listen to B.' I said, 'Okay.' So I
did. Wolf sat there all night until the show was over. And that was so
unusual because you never heard him discuss musicians and what he
thought about them. He never did. Because sometimes I'd be waiting,
you know, and he never, he never—he *never* did. And I was surprised for
him to even say he wanted to stay and listen to B. B. King that night.
And I said, 'Well, okay.' So we did and we were about one of the last
ones to leave because E. Rodney and all of them, you know, they took
him to the car. I was doing the driving, of course. And they wanted to
know if I wanted any of them to go home with me to help me with him.
But he was in walking condition and everything."[74]

The Wolf went home and slept soundly. Saturday night, he went to
the 1815 Club for his regular gig. Vaan Shaw saw him there. "I remember the last thing he said to me in his life," Vaan said. "I was sitting there
at the 1815 and a bass player friend of mine came up and I said, 'It's
Howlin' Wolf.' And he said, 'Who?' And I said, 'Nothing. You wouldn't
understand.' I walked up to Wolf and I said, 'Why are you here? Why
are you in this shitty little club?' I remember what was playing: something by KC and the Sunshine Band. Wolf looked at me and said,
'Don't worry. When I'm dead, I'll get all the greatness I was supposed to
get when I was alive. But I have to die first.' I said to him, 'I really don't
want to hear that shit! I really don't want to hear about you having to
die.' And he said, 'You'll understand years from now.' "[75]

On November 17, Wolf entered a hospital complaining of fatigue.
The doctors couldn't figure out what was wrong with him, and he
stayed in the hospital for weeks. One day, Lillie went to the old Chess
building to see Ralph Bass. Wolf wanted to know if Bass was still mad at
him. Bass had forgiven him. Wolf was relieved when Lillie told him.

On December 17, Hound Dog Taylor died, and Wolf was deeply
distressed. He loved Hound Dog. Ironically, he himself seemed to be
better, and his doctors released him. The next day, Hubert got a call

from Lillie. Wolf was back in the hospital. "I get to the hospital," said Hubert, "and he's sitting there eating chicken and laughing and telling jokes! . . . And he got to talking, sitting around with the patients in the hospital, other veterans, and he brought up Hound Dog and said, 'Hey, man, I'm gonna be seeing Hound Dog soon, you know? Yeah! I'm gonna be seeing Hound Dog!' I thought, 'Hey, what shit is he talking about? Hound Dog's dead!' "[76] Hubert left the next day for Paris to work on an album.

Wolf's condition soon deteriorated again. His eyesight was going, and his wits. Something was terribly wrong, and the hospital he was at was at a loss to figure out what it was, so Lillie transferred him to Hines VA hospital. The doctors there ran every test at their disposal.

Wolf told Lillie, "Call my mama and tell her I said if I ever needed her, I need her now." Lillie called Gertrude to deliver the message. Gertrude laid the phone down and walked away. A man came on the line and Lillie begged him to get her back on the line. He said, "She won't come back." Lillie said, "You tell her that Wolf said if she agrees, I'll bring her up here." Gertrude refused to come to her son's side. When Lillie went back to the hospital, Wolf asked, "Did you get my mother?" "Yeah," "What did she say?" "She didn't say anything." "That's okay, Lillie." Wolf didn't ask about his mother again.[77]

On Wednesday, January 7, the doctors delivered devastating news. Wolf had a brain tumor—probably a large one. They told him he would need an operation within days and, because of his weakened heart, there was some chance he wouldn't survive it.

Hubert got a call on Thursday in Paris. "People at the hospital said, 'Your daddy want to talk to you. He got something to say.' I said, 'Well, I'll be there quick as I can.' I got the next plane, man—Air France to Chicago."[78]

On Thursday, January 8, 1976, Wolf's doctors operated to relieve pressure on his brain. His heart gave out during the operation. The doctors put him on a heart pump and respirator, but his mind and spirit were already gone.

Arriving back in Chicago, Hubert went straight to the hospital. "They had his eyes taped up when I got there," he said. "He was dead then. . . . He's dead—cold as ice. He's dead.' "[79]

After consulting with Wolf's family, the doctors removed the machines and his body ground to a halt at 3:00 p.m. on January 10. The cause of death was listed as "metastatic brain carcinoma."[80]

Floyd Burnett was in a hospital in Connecticut when his father died, and Lillie couldn't contact him. When he got home, he thought he heard a voice in his kitchen asking him for water. "I said, 'That's my daddy's voice! Wait a minute! Somethin' ain't right.' " He called Lillie and asked, "My daddy is dead, ain't he?" She said, "How do you know?" He said, "He just called me from the grave to bring him some water. And from the Bible speaking, that's hell-bound."[81]

Radio station WVON played Wolf's music all day Sunday after he died. Monday night, Eddie Shaw held a jam session in Wolf's honor at the 1815 Club. Bluesmen famous and obscure showed up to sing out their sorrows: Hubert Sumlin, Chico Chism, Lucille Spann (Otis's widow), "Earring George" Mayweather, "Jewtown Eddie" Burks, and Wolf imitators Tail Dragger, the Highway Man, and Little Wolf. Bob Corritore hugged Hubert, who looked lost. "His head was just down and droopy," said Corritore. "I told him I was sorry and he mumbled some words. He was really, really depressed."[82]

Wolf's family held the memorial service on Friday, January 16, at A. R. Leak Funeral Chapel on South Cottage Grove Avenue. It was a bitterly cold day—so cold that Dick Waterman shivered in the back seat of a limousine with a blanket around him all the way from the airport to the funeral home. Between 7:00 a.m. and 6:00 p.m., more than ten thousand people showed up to view Wolf's body. For a few hours, the city had to close South Cottage Grove Avenue. "They had the body in a room that hold five hundred people," Tail Dragger said. "It was full. They had another room hold five hundred . . . and that was full. The hallway was full. The funeral home was full. People standing all out the door!"[83] The funeral home set up TV cameras and monitors for people who couldn't get into the main grieving room to see Wolf's body. Wolf's music played over the funeral home's intercom—much of it from the psychedelic album that he hated.

It felt like a funeral for a prince or president. Eddie Shaw, Hubert Sumlin, and other friends of the Wolf stood in front of his open casket all day in respect. "I can remember Eddie Shaw and Little Milton standing there kind of straight up, like warriors standing over their fallen king," said Jim O'Neal.[84] The funeral program listed Hubert Sumlin and Floyd Lee Burnett as Wolf's sons.

Notably absent was Muddy Waters, who was on the road. Muddy called Lillie and also sent a telegram to offer his condolences. His flower arrangement was one of the biggest at the funeral. He later visited Lillie to offer his condolences in person. "He did more than a lot of them," she said.[85]

At the funeral service, Willie Dixon spoke for ten minutes about the life, sorrows, and joys of the Wolf. Then the Reverend Henry Hardy delivered a rousing eulogy, using lyrics from Wolf's songs and ending with an exhortation: "You ain't dead, Wolf. Howl on, Wolf! Howl on!"[86] Tough bluesmen like Sam Lay wept openly.

The wake started at 8:00 p.m. "That was the damndest funeral I ever seen," said S. P. Leary. "He wanted everybody to feel good at his funeral, 'cause he had every kind of whiskey you could name on both sides of the hall. He didn't want nobody crying. He wanted them to rejoice!"[87] Rejoice they did: hundreds of Wolf's band members, family members, friends, and fans.

Late the next morning, Ralph Bass, Sam Lay, S. P. Leary, Andrew McMahon, Sunnyland Slim, Eddie Taylor, Detroit Junior, and Willie Young carried the Wolf across icy ground at Oak Ridge Cemetery on Chicago's West Side. The graveside gathering was intimate, as Wolf would've wanted. His friends shared a few stories and then were lost in their thoughts about the great bluesman . . . took a hard life and turned it into songs that could break your heart . . . sure could make you laugh, too . . . a great friend, man . . . didn't jive you, even when you wanted him to . . . had a soft spot for folks in pain, 'cause he'd been there himself . . . adored his wife and daughters . . . yes, sir: a good, good man, no matter what his mama thought. At noon, they eased the Wolf down into the frozen ground.

That evening, a full moon rose over Chicago. At the Brookfield Zoo, three miles from Wolf's grave, the captive wolves howled long into the night.[88]

Epilogue: Tail Dragger

In the end, a lesser artist struggling through those last dismal gigs might have fretted that his fame would fade as fast as a name written in water. In the mid-1970s, Wolf's kind of music seemed to be dying under the onslaught of soul, hard rock, heavy metal, disco, and the beginnings of punk and rap. But the Wolf simply would not quit. No matter what, he put on his game face every night, stepped onstage, and did his job like a man — "singing for the peoples," as he called it.

Just as Wolf predicted, he's had a hell of an afterlife. He has become his admirers: not just his family, but the millions of blues lovers who still listen to his music, and the countless others who unknowingly feel his pulse in all of popular music. They include thousands of musicians worldwide, from his Chicago protégés and the American and British bluesmen of the sixties and seventies, now venerable blues elders, to the blues, hip-hop, grunge, and punk-blues singers of the eighties, nineties, and beyond, now the mainstream of popular music. More than a quarter of a century after Wolf's death, "the sound he was giving off," as Johnny Shines called it, and his brand of theatrical, over-the-top showmanship, is pervasive in popular music. His image lends a certain hip cachet to hit movies and advertisements, and his colossal spirit mesmerizes millions who see him in TV documentaries. In 1975, he was play-

320

ing tiny taverns on Chicago's seedy West Side. Today he's considered one of the giants of American music.

Wolf left his last wife in good shape financially. After an out-of-court settlement with Arc Music over back royalties in 1977, Lillie Burnett and her daughters moved to an upscale suburb south of Chicago, and she became one of the most active widows of any blues star. In 1997, she joined Willie Dixon's widow, Marie, and daughter, Shirli, in founding the Blues Heaven Foundation, an educational resource for musicians and fans in the old Chess Records building at 2120 South Michigan Ave. Lillie was present when the city of Chicago erected a life-sized statue of Wolf in a city park in 1978, when Wolf was elected to the Blues Foundation Hall of Fame in 1980, and when he was inducted into the Rock and Roll Hall of Fame in 1991. She helped unveil a United States postage stamp bearing his likeness in 1994 and a life-sized statue of Wolf in West Point in 2000. On May 11, 2001, she passed away from congestive heart failure, ending one of the great love stories in American music. She's buried next to the Wolf at Oakridge Cemetery on Chicago's far West Side. Her daughters live in the same suburb where their mother spent her last decades.

Wolf's son, Floyd, died in March 2000. His stepsister Rosie died in 1996, and his stepbrother, J.D., died in 1987. J.D.'s son, Chester Burnett—Wolf's namesake—played football for the Minnesota Vikings and other NFL teams in the 1990s. Wolf's stepsister Sadie lives in Gary, Indiana, and his stepsister Lucy lives near Memphis. His half sister, Dorothy, died in September 2001. Wolf's nieces and nephews—Dorothy's daughters Ivory Upshaw, Charlie Mae Clay, Elizabeth Clay, and Doris Brown, all living in or near Gary, and sons David, Isaac, and Carl Clay, scattered across the country—are thriving.

After Wolf died, his band soldiered on as Eddie Shaw & the Wolf Gang. Lillie funded their first album in 1977, and they've released nine more albums. Eddie lost the 1815 Club in the late 1970s. He still blows sax and harp and sings up to two hundred nights a year with the Wolf Gang, which includes guitarist Vaan Shaw, bass player Shorty Gilbert, and drummer Tim Taylor (son of blues guitarist Eddie Taylor). Eddie's son Vaan has also released three fine albums.

Hubert Sumlin took Wolf's death hard. "I quit for three or four months when Wolf died," he said. "The people used to walk up and tell me, 'Hubert—you dead.' . . . I had to leave Chicago to go to Texas to work."[1] During his two-year sojourn in the Lone Star State, Sumlin played at Antone's Blues Club in Austin and gave tips on the fine points of blues guitar to two genuine blues brothers, Jimmie and Stevie Ray Vaughan. His influence is evident in Jimmie's powerful yet subtle bare-fingered style and in his late brother's kamikaze glissandos and go-for-broke-on-every-solo approach. In the 1980s and 1990s, Hubert toured with Albert King, Otis Rush, Pinetop Perkins, and many other artists, and released seven albums under his own name. In 1982, he married Willie "Bea" Reed, Sunnyland Slim's cousin, and moved with her in 1991 to a small, farm-style house they bought in a Milwaukee suburb. Bea died in 1999 and Hubert lost a lung to cancer in 2002, but he has recovered and continues to tour in the United States, Europe, and Japan. His latest album, *About Them Shoes*, due out in 2004, features the playing of friends such as Eric Clapton, James Cotton, Levon Helm, Bob Margolin, Paul Oscher, and Keith Richards.

The saga of Jody Williams is one of the great comeback stories in blues history. He became disillusioned with the music business after his guitar licks turned up as the basis for other people's hits. Disgusted by the rip-offs, he stuck his guitar under his bed in the late 1960s, vowing never to touch it again, and went to school in electronics. He spent the next thirty years raising a family and working as a technician at Xerox. He kept his creative juices flowing by building elegant dioramas filled with scenes from African-American history. Then one night in 1997, he went to hear his old friend Robert Lockwood, who urged him to start playing again. Williams did his first gig in thirty years at a club in Chicago on June 10, 2000—Wolf's ninetieth birthday. In the audience was his twenty-nine-year-old daughter, Yolanda, who had never heard her father play. Offers for gigs started coming in from all over the world. His chops came back; his creativity never left. In September 2001, he went into the studio in Chicago with producer Dick Shurman and a host of admiring musicians to craft *Return of a Legend*, a CD that sounded like a classic 1950s Chess album recorded on modern equipment. It won a Handy Blues Award in 2003 for Comeback Album of the Year.

It's debatable whether a producer like Sam Phillips, who relied on great ears and instincts instead of a marketing budget and focus groups, would be a driving force in today's record business. Phillips died in

Memphis in 2003. Phil Chess is living in Tucson, Arizona. Phil's nephew Marshall and son Kevin run a record company called Czyz, their family name in Polish. Chess producer Ralph Bass died of a heart attack aboard an airplane in March 1997. Chess producer Norman Dayron is producing albums for the Fuel 2000 label.

Hardcore blues fans often lament the "death of the blues," as if the genre died with Wolf, Muddy, Little Walter, and Sonny Boy. The list of Wolf's one-time band members, musical associates, and close musical friends who have passed away is certainly long enough to give anyone the blues. But the blues genre sounds relatively healthy in 2004. Many one-time band members and musical associates of the Wolf are still living and most continue playing: Abb Locke, Abu Talib, Aron Burton, Big Joe Duskin, Billy Davenport, Bobby Rush, Bo Diddley, Billy Boy Arnold, Buddy Guy, Byther Smith, Calvin Jones, Casey Jones, Chico Chism, Clifton James, Detroit Junior, Eddie C. Campbell, Etta James, Francis Clay, Gene Barge, James Cotton, Koko Taylor, Lester Davenport, Little Arthur Duncan, Little Hudson Showers, Little Smokey Smothers, Lucky Lopez, Mary Lane, Nick Charles, Pete Cosey, Phil Upchurch, Robert Plunkett, Robert Bilbo Walker, Sam Lay, Wild Child Butler, and Willie Kent. The indestructible veterans Robert Lockwood, Honeyboy Edwards, and Homesick James are still playing. Others, such as Hosea Kennard, last seen working as a short-order cook in Chicago in the 1990s, have simply vanished from the music world or, like Matt Murphy, who has suffered a stroke, are ailing.

Wolf's band members haven't forgotten him. Sam Lay, Hubert Sumlin, Eddie Shaw, Henry Gray, James Cotton, and Calvin Jones plus a cadre of guest artists including Taj Mahal, Colin Linden, Kenny Neal, Debbie Davies, Cub Koda, Lucky Peterson, Ronnie Hawkins, Lucinda Williams, Colin James, Christine Ohlman, and Tim Taylor helped create the album A Tribute to Howlin' Wolf, which earned a Grammy nomination in 1998.

Bonnie Raitt, Taj Mahal, John Hammond, Joe Louis Walker, Marcia Ball, Robert Cray, Deborah Davies, Keb' Mo', Maria Muldaur, Otis Taylor, Rory Block, and many other middle-aged blues performers continue to thrill blues lovers. Dynamic younger performers such as Alvin "Youngblood" Hart, Corey Harris, Eric Bibb, Guy Davis, Deborah Coleman, and Michael Burks are still moving the blues forward. And a

whole crop of younger bluesmen and blueswomen is waiting in the
wings: Chris Thomas King, Ana Popovic, Derek Trucks, Susan
Tedeschi, Jonny Lang, the North Mississippi All-Stars, and Sean
Costello are just the tip of the iceberg. Many British blues performers
whom Wolf inspired are keeping the smokestack burning: Chris Barber,
Ian McLagen, Long John Baldry, Sam Mitchell, the Groundhogs, the
Junco Partners, the T-Bones, Killing Floor, Dave Kelly, John Dummer,
Peter Green, Eric Clapton, the Rolling Stones, Jeff Beck, Jimmie Page,
and others.

Wolf imitators continue to channel the spirit of the man. James
"Tail Dragger" Jones and Lee "Little Wolf" Soloman still do gigs on
occasion in Chicago. Jesse "Little Howlin' Wolf" Sanders gigs around
Memphis; his wife, Diane, is the daughter of Wolf's stepsister Lucy.

Seattle's grunge groups got into the Wolf groove in the 1990s. Kurt
Cobain captured the Wolf's outsized spirit as much as anyone ever has
with his shredded vocals. No coincidence: Cobain tried to form a Creedence Clearwater Revival cover band, doing songs influenced by Wolf.
In the hit movie *Singles*, about Seattle's grunge scene, a Howlin' Wolf
poster was prominently placed in the practice room of the mythical
band Citizen Dick, played by real-life rockers Pearl Jam. Soundgarden
recorded a frenzied version of "Smokestack Lightnin'."

In 1994 hip-hop guitarist Skip McDonald, aka Little Axe, sampled
Wolf's voice from a 1968 interview and cut it with guitar licks and
sounds to create "The Wolf That House Built," a dub-blues masterpiece. Since the 1990s, Wolf's songs have been covered by artists as varied as Lucinda Williams, Megadeth, PJ Harvey, Iggy Pop (who once
took drum lessons from Sam Lay), Bill Frisell, and others.

Older bluesmen influenced by Wolf such as R. L. Burnside, James
"T-Model" Ford, Magic Slim, and Willie King have released some of
the most impressive blues albums of the last decade. Burnside, who
hails from Holly Springs, Mississippi, not far from Wolf's birthplace,
unexpectedly became a cult favorite of young music lovers in the late
1990s. He rocks the house with the kind of one-chord, slide-and-drone
blues that Wolf pioneered. T-Model Ford, Burnside's label-mate on Fat
Possum, plays north Mississippi hill country blues in the style of the
Wolf at his most primitive, and often does Wolf's songs in concert.
Magic Slim and the Teardrops from Chicago are among the best pro-

ponents of the intense, electric blues style of the Wolf. Slim often breaks
into a feral, Wolf-like voice as he prowls the boards. "It took me twenty
years to get that voice," Slim says.[2] He and his Teardrops won a Handy
Award in 2003 for Blues Band of the Year. Willie King and the Libera-
tors are best known for their powerful songs about social injustice, many
done in the hypnotic style of the Wolf. King pays explicit homage to
Wolf in almost every show.

An encouraging recent trend in popular music has been the birth of
the punk-blues movement. Appalled by what passes for music on today's
programmed radio and inspired by bluesmen like Wolf, Hound Dog
Taylor, and the Fat Possum crew and by blues-inspired punk-rockers
like the Gun Club, bands like the John Spencer Blues Explosion, the
Immortal Lee County Killers, and the White Stripes have taken a neo-
primitive, take-no-prisoners approach to music. A two-woman punk-
blues band from Boston, Mr. Airplane Man, even named themselves for
a Wolf song.

Wolf often pops up in unexpected places. Clothier the Gap used his
image in an ad for khakis in the 1990s. He showed up as a character in
the 1994 film *Foreign Student*, about a French exchange student who
falls in love with a black woman in the American South in 1955.

The Wolf continues to amaze viewers of documentaries such as
Martin Scorsese's *The Blues*, a six-part series shown on PBS in 2003—
proclaimed the Year of the Blues by the United States Senate—full of
club footage shot in the 1960s by Sam Lay. Wolf's backstage performance at the 1966 Newport Folk Festival was released on video in
"Devil Got My Woman" in 1996. His amazing TV studio performances
on the American Folk Blues Festival tour were released on DVD in
2003. And he was the subject of a superb full-length documentary on
DVD in 2003, *The Howlin' Wolf Story—The Secret History of Rock &
Roll*, directed by respected filmmaker Don McGlynn and produced by
Joe Lauro of Historic Films, Inc.

The Wolf has stalked away in the end, but he didn't wipe out his
tracks. He had a very rocky furrow to plow in life, out of which he created music of incomparable beauty. In it, you hear all the joys and sorrows of a hard life fully lived. His art speaks to people across oceans and
ages. It whispers about morality while moaning of mortality. It's the
blues.

Notes

1 • POOR BOY

1. Robert E. Jakoubek, *Jack Johnson* (New York: Chelsea House, 1990), pp. 81–85.
2. Ruth White Williams, *On the Map 145 Years: The History of West Point, Mississippi, 1846–1991* (West Point, MS, 1996), p. 206.
3. Ibid., p. 210.
4. Ibid., p. 203. There is no birth certificate for Chester; Mississippi did not register births until 1912.
5. Ibid., p. 92. White Station was named for Frank S. White, a state legislator who lured the railroad to West Point in 1882. He was also instrumental in naming Clay County for Kentucky Democrat Henry Clay.
6. Ibid., pp. 66–68.
7. Letter, Organization of 59 Black Men In White Station, Mississippi, to the President of the United States, May 26, 1890, transcribed by Elijah W. Halford, Private Secretary of the President, quoted by War Department, Office Commissary General of Subsistence, Washington, D.C., June 3, 1890, National Archives.
8. Neil R. McMillen, *Dark Journey: Black Mississippians in the Age of Jim Crow* (Champaign: University of Illinois Press, 1989), p. 192.
9. James W. Silver, *Mississippi: The Closed Society* (New York: Harcourt, Brace & World, 1966), p. 19.
10. Death certificate for Gertrude Burnett.
11. Howlin' Wolf interview by David Little, Peter Riley, and Dorothy Riley in Boston, 30 December 1973.
12. Ibid.
13. Marriage certificate, Monroe County Courthouse Docket no. 26 (1909–1911), p. 125.

14. Pete Welding, "An Interview with Bluesman Howlin' Wolf," *Downbeat*, December 14, 1967, p. 22.
15. Ibid.
16. Howlin' Wolf interview, *Howlin' Wolf: The Chess Box*, Chess MCA CHD3-9332, 1991.
17. Frank "Bluesboy" Brown, "Howlin' Wolf: Primeval Passion Electrified," *WKCR Program Guide*, April 1987, p. 3.
18. Annie Eggerson interview with Mark Hoffman; Annie Eggerson interview with James Segrest in White Station, Mississippi, 31 August 1996.
19. Pat Quinn interview with Mark Hoffman by telephone, 25 October 2003; Mike Leadbitter, "Mike's Blues," *Blues Unlimited* (September 1969), p. 17.
20. Leadbitter, *Nothing but the Blues* (London: Hanover Books, 1971), p. 45.
21. Hubert Sumlin interview with Mark Hoffman in Milwaukee, 6 June 2001.
22. Lillie Burnett interview with Ralph Metcalf, Jr., in Chicago, 15 February 1991, from *Speaking of the Blues* series, Chicago Public Library.
23. Evelyn Sumlin interview with Mark Hoffman in Chicago, 29 May 2002.
24. The 1920 census record for Gertrude Burnett shows her living with Jim Price, age forty-seven. The occupation for both is listed as "cook."
25. Annie Malkentine interview with Mark Hoffman by telephone, 20 April 2003. Annie's mother, Margaret, was a good friend of Wolf's and used to let him stay at her house in Detroit.
26. Hubert Sumlin interview with Don McGlynn and Joe Lauro in New Orleans, 1 May 2002, for film *The Howlin' Wolf Story*.
27. 1920 United States Census Records for Clay County, Mississippi. Lucy Wiseman interview with Mark Hoffman by telephone, 30 March 2003; Gertrude Burns interview with Mark Hoffman in White Station, Mississippi, 7 October 1996; William Hardy, Jr., interview with James Segrest in White Station, Mississippi, 31 August 1996. According to Wiseman and Hardy, Will Young raised another child named Rebecca, also Chester's aunt. Gaddis Burnett died as a young man from ptomaine poisoning. Wiseman married Jessie Swift and moved to St. Louis with her husband.
28. Annie Eggerson interview with Mark Hoffman in White Station, Mississippi, 6 October 1996.
29. Leroy Swift interview with Mark Hoffman in White Station, Mississippi, 9 October 1996.
30. Silla Swift interview with Mark Hoffman in White Station, Mississippi, 9 October 1996. Silla married twice and survived both husbands. Her last husband was Louis Henderson.
31. Hardy, Wiseman, and Eggerson interviews. Will Young had two daughters, Susie and Flora, and a son, Nelius, with Mary A. "Miss Monk" Walker, unmarried daughter of Wess Walker, who lived in White Station.
32. McMillen, *Dark Journey*, p. 128.
33. Ibid., p. 130.
34. Lillie Burnett interview with James Segrest in Chicago, 15 July 1991.
35. Silla Swift interview.

36. Annie Eggerson interview with Hoffman.
37. Wiseman interview.
38. Eggerson interview with Hoffman.
39. Deacon R. L. Larry interview with James Segrest in White Station, Mississippi, 31 August 1996.
40. Wiseman interview.
41. Deacon R. L. Larry interview with Mark Hoffman in White Station, Mississippi, 6 October 1996.
42. Wiseman interview. Wiseman finally got her GED after she retired. "I was determined that my children get an education, and I thank the Lord for that," she said. Her daughter is now the respected mayor of Centreville, Illinois.
43. Annie Eggerson interview with Hoffman.
44. Silla Swift interview.
45. Ibid.
46. Leroy Swift interview.
47. Ibid.
48. Ibid.
49. Ibid.
50. Ada Swift interview with Mark Hoffman in Chicago, 4 June 2001.
51. Leroy Swift interview.
52. Ibid.
53. Silla Swift interview.
54. Eggerson interview with Hoffman.
55. Leroy Swift interview.
56. Larry interview with Segrest. Larry himself learned to play blues harmonica, but now plays only religious music.
57. Lillie Burnett interview with Segrest.
58. Hardy interview and Eggerson interview with Hoffman.
59. Howlin' Wolf interview with Sandy Guy Schoenfeld in San Francisco, July 1968. © 1968 Sandy Guy Schoenfeld. Used with permission.
60. McMillen, p. 133.
61. Ibid.
62. Leroy Swift interview.
63. Ibid.
64. Silla Swift interview.
65. Lillie Burnett interview with Metcalf.
66. Lillie Burnett interview with Segrest.
67. Ibid.
68. Vaan Shaw interview with Mark Hoffman by telephone, 7 March 1998.

2 • DOWN IN THE BOTTOM

1. Stephen Calt and Gayle Wardlow, *King of the Delta Blues: The Life and Music of Charlie Patton* (New Jersey: Rock Chapel Press, 1988), p. 48.

2. William Faulkner, *The Mansion* (New York: Random House, 1959), p. 48.

3. Nicholas Lemann, *The Promised Land: The Great Black Migration and How It Changed America* (New York: Vintage, 1991), pp. 9–10.

4. David L. Cohn, *Where I Was Born and Raised* (Boston: Houghton Mifflin, 1948), pp. 22–23.

5. Joel Slotnikoff, "Gayle Dean Wardlow: The Blues World Interview" (October 1996).

6. Ibid.

7. Schoenfeld interview.

8. Jannie Taylor interview with James Segrest in Drew, Mississippi, 27 May 1991.

9. Peter Guralnick, *Feel Like Going Home: Portraits in Blues and Rock 'n' Roll* (New York: Harper & Row, 1989), p. 153.

10. Taylor interview.

11. Dorothy Spencer Scott interview with James Segrest in Cleveland, Mississippi, 24 June 1997.

12. Dorothy Spencer Scott interview with James Segrest in Cleveland, Mississippi, 29 June 1997.

13. Sadie Davis Jones interview with James Segrest in Gary, Indiana, 10 July 1991. The authors made several attempts to interview Wolf's sister Dorothy Burnett (Clay) for this book, but she declined to talk about her brother.

14. Taylor interview and Dorothy Spencer Scot interview, 24 June 1997.

15. Dorothy Spencer Scott interview, 24 June 1997. Blues scholar David Evans in his research of the blues tradition around Drew, Mississippi, heard of a bluesman named John Dee, who called himself Howlin' Wolf, but Evans did not discover that John Dee and Chester Burnett were one and the same person. See David Evans, *Big Road Blues: Tradition and Creativity in the Folk Blues* (New York: Da Capo Press, 1987), p. 194.

16. Dorothy Spencer Scott interview, 24 June 1997, and Morrow interview.

17. Ibid.

18. James Hart Morrow interview with James Segrest in Webb, Mississippi, 27 May 1991.

19. Taylor interview.

20. Morrow interview.

21. Dorothy Spencer Scott interview, 24 June 1997.

22. Welding, "Interview," p. 21.

23. For more on Handy's role in popularizing the blues see W. C. Handy, *Father of the Blues* (New York: Collier, 1970).

24. Patton's first name is sometimes spelled "Charley," but we spell it "Charlie" throughout.

25. Ruffin Scott interview with James Segrest at Dockery Plantation, Mississippi, 27 May 1991. Ruffin Scott married Dorothy Mae Spencer. When both knew Wolf in the late 1920s, they were not yet married and knew him under very different circumstances.

26. Osborn Holloway interview with James Segrest in Cleveland, Mississippi, 30 May 1997.

27. For more on Charlie Patton see Calt and Wardlow's *King of the Delta Blues*, and Robert Sacré, editor, *The Voice of the Delta* (Liège, Belgium: Presses Universitaires de Liège, 1987).

28. Little, Riley, and Riley interview.

29. Chris Morris, liner notes for *Howlin' Wolf: The Chess Box*.

30. *Newsweek* (February 21, 1966), p. 91.

31. Hubert Sumlin interview with Mark Hoffman in Milwaukee, Wisconsin, 8 June 2001.

32. Welding, "Interview," p. 20.

33. Guralnick, *Feel Like Going Home*, p. 153.

34. Ibid.

35. Welding, "Interview," p. 21.

36. Ibid.

37. Hammond interview with Mark Hoffman in Seattle, 8 June 1997.

38. Sacré, *Voice of the Delta*, p. 151.

39. Tom Cannon interview with James Segrest in Cleveland, Mississippi, 24 May 1991.

40. Wolf would later tip the scales at 275 pounds.

41. Estimates of the Wolf's shoe size vary from 13 to 17. His feet were also unusually wide, and he often slit the sides of his shoes to give his bunions room to breathe. "I haven't seen anyone with shoes on look like John D's," Dorothy Spencer Scott said on 24 June 1997.

42. Taylor interview.

43. Leadbitter, *Nothing but the Blues*, p. 45, and Welding, "Interview," p. 20.

44. Guralnick, *Feel Like Going Home*, p. 153.

45. "Howlin Wolf," *Ann Arbor Argus*, p. 30.

46. Samuel Charters, *The Bluesmakers* (New York: Da Capo, 1991), p. 53.

47. Paul Rishell interview with Mark Hoffman by telephone, 16 September 1997.

48. Welding, "Interview," p. 21. Charlie Patton died on April 28, 1934.

49. Leadbitter, *Nothing but the Blues*, p. 45.

50. Welding, "Interview," p. 21.

51. Evans, *Big Road Blues*, p. 178.

52. Ibid.

53. Ray Flerlage and Mike Bloomfield, "Interview with Howlin' Wolf," *Rhythm & Blues* (February 1965), p. 18.

54. There were a number of musicians around Drew named Nathan. Besides Taylor and Scott, Dick Bankston's real first name was Nathan.

55. Taylor interview.

56. Welding, "Interview," p. 21.

57. Jacques Demêtre and Marcel Chauvard, "Son Utilisation des 'Field-Hollers' a valu a Chester Burnett le Surnom de Howlin' Wolf," *Jazz Hot* (December 1961), pp. 28–29. English translation, translator unknown. Courtesy of Mark Jickling.

58. Dorothy Spencer Scott interview, 24 June 1997.

59. Little, Riley, and Riley interview.

60. Honeyboy Edwards interview with James Segrest in Chicago, 28 July 1991.

61. Welding, "Interview," p. 21.

62. Demêtre and Chauvard, "Son Utilisation," page unknown.

63. Barry Gifford, "Couldn't Do No Yodeling, So I Turned to Howlin'," *Rolling Stone* (August 24, 1968), p. 6.

64. Honeyboy Edwards interview.

65. David "Honeyboy" Edwards as told to Janis Martinson and Michael Robert Frank, *The World Don't Owe Me Nothing: The Life and Times of Delta Bluesman Honeyboy Edwards* (Chicago: Chicago Review Press, 1997), p. 95.

66. Welding, "Interview," p. 22.

67. Taylor interview. Mrs. Taylor did not know the name Chester Burnett and only knew him as John D. Burnett or Howlin' Wolf. She was emphatic that he was using the name Howlin' Wolf by 1928 when she met him and his family.

68. Clyde Stats interview with Mark Hoffman by telephone, 15 October 2003.

69. Dick Shurman notes, *Howlin' Wolf: The Chess Box*.

70. Ruffin Scott interview.

71. Dock Burnett interview with the American Red Cross, 29 September 1943.

72. Notes to CD "Mahlathini: The Lion of Soweto" (Virgin Records Ltd., 1987). Mahlathini, like Wolf, was suspected of witchcraft and inspired a legion of imitators.

73. Paul Pena interview with Mark Hoffman by telephone, 8 August 1999.

74. Dorothy Spencer Scott interview, 24 June 1997.

75. Welding, "Interview," p. 21.

76. Vernon Gibbs, "Howlin' Wolf Bemoans the Blues," *Crawdaddy* (December 5, 1971), p. 47.

77. Dorothy Spencer Scott interview, 24 June 1997.

78. Ibid. Spencer Scott didn't like Wolf's music. "He just couldn't sing to suit me," she said. She didn't like Charlie Patton's music, either.

79. Ruffin Scott interview, and Evans, *Big Road Blues*, p. 194.

80. Robert Palmer, *Deep Blues* (New York: Penguin, 1981), p. 61.

81. Paul Trynka, *Portrait of the Blues* (New York: Da Capo, 1996), p. 43.

82. Dorothy Spencer Scott interviews, 24 and 29 June 1997.

83. Dorothy Spencer Scott interview, 24 June 1997.

84. Welding, "Interview," p. 21.

85. Calt and Wardlow, *King of the Delta Blues*, p. 68.

86. Ibid.

87. Conversation with Mark Hoffman, 8 October 1996.

88. Mike Leadbitter and Mike Rowe, "Sunnyland Slim," *Blues Unlimited* 105 (December 1973/January 1974), p. 30.

89. Guralnick, *Feel Like Going Home*, p. 154.

90. Welding, "Interview," p. 22.

91. Edwards, *World Don't Owe Me Nothing*, pp. 95–96.

92. Honeyboy Edwards interview.

93. Edwards, *World Don't Owe Me Nothing*, p. 96.

94. Johnny Shines interview with James Segrest in Montgomery, Alabama, 30 October 1991.

95. John Earl, "A Lifetime in the Blues: Johnny Shines," *Blues World* 46/49 (1973), p. 10.

96. Guralnick, *Feel Like Going Home*, p. 100.

97. Earl, "Lifetime in the Blues," p. 10.

98. Pete Welding, "Ramblin' Johnny Shines," *Living Blues* 22 (July/August 1975), p. 23.

99. Shines interview.

100. Welding, "Ramblin' Johnny Shines," p. 24.

101. Earl, "Lifetime in the Blues," p. 10.

102. Welding, "Ramblin' Johnny Shines," p. 24.

103. Shines interview.

104. Demêtre and Chauvard, page unknown.

105. Alex Cramer, "Johnny Shines," *Coda*, Vol. 11, No. 12 (October 1974), p. 11.

106. Welding, "Ramblin' Johnny Shines," p. 29.

107. Rosie Davis Griffin interview with James Segrest in Gary, Indiana, 10 July 1991.

108. Ibid.

109. Ibid.

110. Ibid.

111. Ibid.

112. Sadie Davis Jones interview with James Segrest in Gary, Indiana, 10 June 1991.

113. Lucy Davis Marshall interview with James Segrest in Wynne, Arkansas, 6 June 1991.

114. Dorothy Burnett Clay interview with Elizabeth Clay in Gary, Indiana, May 2001. Dorothy taped her reminiscences for her daughter four months before she died of cancer. "They treated her so bad, you know, like Cinderella the stepsister," said Elizabeth. "According to my mom, they weren't even very nice to Wolf, because Wolf had a different mother."

115. Rosie Davis Griffin and Sadie Davis Jones interviews.

116. Taylor interview.

117. Ibid.

118. Ida McMahon interview with James Segrest by telephone, 28 March 2000.

119. Taylor interview.

120. Rosie Davis Griffin interview.

121. Sadie Davis Jones interview.

122. Gibbs, "Howlin' Wolf Bemoans the Blues," p. 47.

123. Shines interview.

124. Ibid.

125. Sunnyland Slim interview with Jim O'Neal, 28 September 1981, Blues Archive, University of Mississippi.

126. Eddie Shaw interview with James Segrest in Chicago, 27 June 1991.

127. Zora Young interview with James Segrest by telephone, 17 July 1998.

128. John Anthony Brisbin, "Detroit Junior: You Got to Put Somethin' in It," *Living Blues* 129 (September/October 1996), p. 38. Despite what Detroit Junior said, Wolf would not have been incarcerated in Parchman for a murder committed in Arkansas. After extensive searching, we have found no documents to verify this incident, but we believe that Wolf did kill someone in the 1930s, either in Arkansas or Mississippi. The records clerk at Parchman penitentiary told us that no records exist there of inmates incarcerated before 1940.

129. Honeyboy Edwards interview.
130. Hubert Sumlin interview with Mark Hoffman in Seattle, 8 May 2003.
131. Lyrics from "Can't Stay Here" (adapted from "Down the Dirt Road Blues" by Charlie Patton) from Howlin' Wolf's album *The Back Door Wolf* (1973).

3 • SADDLE MY PONY

1. Demêtre and Chauvard, page unknown.
2. Rosie Davis Griffin interview, and interview with Floyd Jones in Justin O'Brien, "The Dark Road of Floyd Jones," *Living Blues* 58 (Winter 1983), p. 7.
3. Myrtle Gordon interview with James Segrest in Earle, Arkansas, 5 June 1991.
4. Rosie Davis Griffin interview.
5. Ibid.
6. Lucy Davis Marshall interview with James Segrest in Wayne, Arkansas, 6 June 1991.
7. Rosie Davis Griffin interview.
8. Lucy Davis Marshall interview.
9. Ruby Sims interview with James Segrest in Hughes, Arkansas, 6 June 1991.
10. Gordon interview. The Harrises, a black family, owned a three-hundred-acre farm and hired their own sharecroppers. Despite being much better off, they were good friends with the Burnetts.
11. Sadie Davis Jones interview.
12. Rosie Davis Griffin interview.
13. Gordon interview.
14. Lucy Davis Marshall interview.
15. "Howlin' Wolf," *Ann Arbor Argus*, p. 31.
16. O'Brien, "Dark Road of Floyd Jones," p. 7, and Mike Rowe, "Floyd Jones," *Blues Unlimited* 137–38 (Spring 1980), p. 15.
17. Rowe, "Floyd Jones," p. 16.
18. Ibid.
19. O'Brien, "Dark Road of Floyd Jones," p. 8.
20. Ibid.
21. Chris Robinson, "Lazy Bill Called Me Homesick (I Wasn't Though)," *Blues Unlimited* 84 (September 1971), p. 6.
22. O'Brien, "Dark Road of Floyd Jones," p. 9.
23. Shines interview.
24. "Howlin' Wolf," *Ann Arbor Argus*, p. 31.
25. Welding, "Ramblin' Johnny Shines," p. 27.
26. Brisbin, "Detroit Junior," p. 38.
27. Lee Eggleston interview with James Segrest in Chicago, 1 July 1991. "Sweet Melvina" was "49 Highway Blues" by Big Joe Williams, released in 1935.
28. Reverend Johnny Williams interview with James Segrest by telephone, 23 February 1998.
29. Minnie McKenzie interview with James Segrest in Shelby, Mississippi, 2 June 1991.
30. Edwards, *World Don't Owe Me Nothing*, p. 113.

31. Bob Eagle, "Luther Huff," *Living Blues* 22 (July/August 1975), p. 33, and Cannon interview.
32. Burns interview.
33. Annie Eggerson interview with James Segrest.
34. Larry interview with Mark Hoffman. The song "My Baby Not at Home" was John Lee "Sonny Boy" Williamson's "Blue Bird Blues," recorded in 1937. Wolf later recorded the song both in its original version and modified as "Mr. Airplane Man."
35. Larry interview with James Segrest.
36. Annie Eggerson interview with Mark Hoffman.
37. Welding, "Interview," p. 21.
38. Demêtre and Chauvard, "Son Utilisation," page unknown.
39. Amy van Singel and Jim O'Neal, "Living Blues Interview: Howling Wolf," *Living Blues* 1 (Spring 1970), p. 14, and Guralnick, *Feel Like Going Home*, p. 154.
40. Sonny Payne interview with Mark Hoffman by telephone, 15 March 2003. Payne's story could explain why Wolf described the mystery sibling as his sister, half-sister, or stepsister; she was actually his sister-in-law. Sonny Boy researcher Bill Donoghue has what looks like a wedding photo of Sonny Boy with an unidentified woman. Wolf's half-sister Dorthy never mentioned Sonny Boy when she told her life story to her daughter shortly before she died. By all accounts, Wolf's mother had only one child.
41. Guralnick, *Feel Like Going Home*, p. 154.
42. Gordon interview. Julius Rosenwald, the president of Sears, Roebuck, founded Rosenwald schools across the South for the educational improvement of blacks.
43. Rosie Lee Whitehead interview with James Segrest in Earle, Arkansas, 5 June 1991.
44. Hubert Sumlin, "My Years with Wolf," *Living Blues* 88 (September/October 1989), p. 13.
45. All quotations from Welding, *Feel Like Going Home*, pp. 21–22.
46. For a good account of Robert Johnson's life see Peter Guralnick, *Searching for Robert Johnson* (New York: Dutton, 1989).
47. Mike Rowe and Mike Leadbitter, "I Was the Baby Boy," *Blues Unlimited* 96 (November 1972), p. 5.
48. Ibid., p. 4.
49. David Evans, "Peck Curtis: Interview," *Blues Unlimited* 69 (January 1970), p. 11.
50. Mark Hoffman interview with Robert Lockwood, Jr., in Cleveland, Ohio, 20 April 2002.
51. Ibid.
52. Pete Welding, "Gambler's Blues: Shakey Jake," *Living Blues* 10 (Autumn 1972), p. 11.
53. Rick Milne, "Shakey Jake," *Blues Unlimited* 42 (March/April 1967), p. 10.
54. Welding, "Interview," p. 22.
55. Guralnick, *Feel Like Going Home*, p. 50.
56. Bob Groom, "An Interview with Son House," *Blues World* 18 (January 1968), p. 7. Mike Leadbitter's *Nothing but the Blues*, p. 45, says that Wolf married Brown's sister in the 1930s. We found no record of this marriage in the Mississippi and

Arkansas vital records archives or in the reminiscences of anyone in Wolf's family, so we think the story of this marriage is inaccurate.

57. Guralnick, *Feel Like Going Home*, p. 60.

58. Welding, "Interview," p. 23.

59. Tommy Bankhead interview with James Segrest by telephone, 20 February 1998.

60. Bill Greensmith, "Still in the Woods," *Blues Unlimited* 145 (Winter 1983–1984), p. 9.

61. In another interview, Johnson identified this first meeting as being at Dooley Square, a store in Tunica, Mississippi. Jimmy Dawkins, Dick Shurman, Keith Tillman, and Mike Leadbitter, "Willie Johnson: Boppin' the Blues," *Blues Unlimited* 93 (July 1972), p. 4.

62. John Anthony Brisbin, "Willie Johnson," *Living Blues* 124 (November/December 1995), p. 43.

63. Ibid., p. 44.

64. John Anthony Brisbin, "Jimmy Rogers: I'm Havin' Fun Right Today," *Living Blues* (September/October 1997), p. 18.

65. Magnolia Frazier interview with James Segrest in Cleveland, Mississippi, 22 June 1997.

66. Holloway interview.

67. Magnolia Frazier interview.

68. Ibid.

69. Emma Towner Williams interview with James Segrest in Pace, Mississippi, 18 May 1998.

70. Laura Towner interview with James Segrest in Pace, Mississippi, 18 May 1998.

71. Willie Richard, Sr., interview with James Segrest in Pace, Mississippi, 8 October 1997.

72. Emma Towner Williams interview.

73. Holloway interview.

74. Emma Towner Williams interview.

75. Ibid.

76. Laura Towner interview.

77. Richard interview.

78. Magnolia Frazier conversation with James Segrest in Cleveland, Mississippi, 5 August 2001.

79. Magnolia Frazier interview.

80. Emma Towner Williams interview.

81. Richard interview.

82. Mike Rowe, "They Know I'm Not Playing Anything but the Blues: James DeShay," *Blues Unlimited* 143 (Autumn/Winter 1982), p. 33.

83. Magnolia Frazier interview.

84. Ibid.

85. Gibbs, p. 47.

86. Richard interview.

87. Floyd Frazier interview with James Segrest by telephone, 27 October 1997.

4 • HOW MANY MORE YEARS

1. Military service record for Chester A. Burnett, United States Army.
2. Jessie "Little Howlin' Wolf" Sanders interview with James Segrest in Memphis, Tennessee, 17 May 1997.
3. Mr. Charlie was a term used derisively by Southern blacks for their white bossman.
4. It's tempting to think this was Texas bluesman Babe Turner, better known as Black Ace, but Turner didn't enter the army until 1943, according to Sheldon Harris, *Blues Who's Who: A Biographical Dictionary of Blues Singers* (New York: Da Capo, 1981), p. 518.
5. Archie Edwards interview with Mark Hoffman by telephone, 1996. A talented musician who lived in Washington, D.C., Edwards never achieved the success or fame that Wolf felt he deserved.
6. Stuart Tucker, "If You Had Two Guitars You Had a Big Band: Buddy Folks," *Living Blues* 85 (March/April 1989), p. 30.
7. Wilson County Marriage License and Marriage Bond and Record, 22 February 1941, for marriage of James Freeman and Lillie Crudup. Crudup was not related to bluesman Arthur "Big Boy" Crudup, whose family came from Mississippi.
8. American Red Cross interview with Dock Burnett, 29 September 1943.
9. We found no marriage certificate for Chester Burnett and Lillie Crudup in the records of Davidson, Wilson, or Shelby counties in Tennessee, in Pierce or King counties in Washington state, or anywhere in Arkansas or Mississippi.
10. Rowe, "Floyd Jones," p. 16.
11. Fort Lawton was the site of a controversial so-called race riot between black soldiers and Italian POWs on August 14, 1944, a year after Wolf was there. At the ensuing trial of forty-three black soldiers—the largest American military courts-martial of World War II—twenty-eight soldiers were convicted of crimes ranging from rioting to manslaughter. Many received astonishingly long sentences: up to twenty-five years. All were released by 1949, under suspicious circumstances that the army still refuses to explain. The army's prosecutor was Leon Jaworski, later famous as the special prosecutor in the Watergate case. Jack Hamann, *The Broken Column* (Chapel Hill, NC: Algonquin Books of Chapel Hill, 2004).
12. Rosie Davis Griffin interview.
13. Sadie Davis Jones interview.
14. Monroe Burnett interview with James Segrest in Webb, Mississippi, 27 May 1991.
15. Progress notes, Chester Burnett's military medical records.
16. His military medical records state that he was treated in 1926 for both syphilis and gonorrhea. It's hard to tell from the terse records how the army doctors determined this, especially since the records also state that he refused a spinal tap to test for syphilis. It's quite likely that he simply didn't trust their diagnosis.
17. Dock Burnett interview with American Red Cross.
18. Johnny Littlejohn interview with James Segrest in Chicago, Illinois, 4 July 1991.
19. Wolf received the American Campaign Medal for service in the American Theatre of Operations, plus the World War II Victory Medal, both of which were given to

anyone who served in the military within the continental United States for one year between 1941 and 1946. He never received the Asiatic-Pacific Campaign Medal or the Eastern Campaign Medal, given for service of any kind in a foreign war zone or for actual combat duty during the war.

20. Jones interview.

21. Howlin' Wolf interview with Peter Guralnick at Cook County Hospital, Chicago, 1970.

22. Detroit Junior interview with James Segrest in Chicago, 29 July 1991.

23. Application for Social Security Account Number for Chester Arthur Burnett, 29 November 1943. In his application, he listed his birth date as June 10, 1909. Wolf always said in interviews that he was born in 1910, the birth year shown on his military service record and his death certificate. Wolf made an amusing mistake on the Social Security Number application when he marked "Female" for "Sex of Applicant," apparently thinking they were asking him about his preference in partners.

24. Griffin interview.

25. Susan Stroud interview with Mark Hoffman by telephone, 14 August 2003.

26. *In Their Own Voices: An Account of the Presence of African Americans in Wilson County; The Lebanon Democrat* (Lebanon, TN, 1999), p. 257.

27. Rowe, "Floyd Jones," p. 16, and O'Brien, "Dark Road of Floyd Jones," p. 11.

28. Pat Dawson, "Man, We Was Jumpin' Like Crazy," *Blues & Rhythm* (August 1990), p. 11.

29. Welding, "Interview with Howlin' Wolf," p. 22. Wolf was in his mid-thirties by this time!

30. Israel "Wink" Clark interview with James Segrest in Tunica, Mississippi, 30 May 1991.

31. Will Jones interview with James Segrest in Robinsonville, Mississippi, 29 May 1991.

32. Lonnie Bailey interview with James Segrest in Lake Cormorant, Mississippi, 29 May 1991.

33. Clark interview.

34. Interview with Ida McMahon, whose husband, Andrew, later played bass with Wolf.

35. Clark interview.

36. Nathaniel Richardson, Jr., interview with James Segrest in Robinsonville, Mississippi, 29 May 1991.

37. Clark interview. Fiddlin' Joe Martin was born in Edwards, Mississippi, in 1904.

38. David Evans, "The Fiddlin' Joe Martin Story," *Blues World* (July 1968), p. 4.

39. David Evans, "The Woodrow Adams Story," *Blues Unlimited* (July 1968), p. 7.

40. Fred Hay, "Fiddlin' Joe Martin: Obituary," *Living Blues* (March/April 1976), p. 10.

41. Dan Curry interview with James Segrest in Prichard, Mississippi, 19 August 1997.

42. Aron Burton interview with James Segrest by telephone, 18 September 1998.

43. Maxwell Street Jimmy Davis interview with James Segrest in Clarksdale, Mississippi, 7 August 1994.

44. Monroe Burnett interview.

45. Monroe Burnett interview, and Jim O'Neal, "Living Blues Interview: Houston Stackhouse," *Living Blues* (Summer 1974), p. 33.

46. Clark interview.

47. Walter J. Brown interview with James Segrest in Robinsonville, Mississippi, 29 May 1991.

48. Clark interview.

49. Curry interview.

50. Hubert Sumlin interview with Jim O'Neal, 23 September 1981, Blues Archive, University of Mississippi.

51. Howlin' Wolf interview with David Booth, quoted in *Howlin' Wolf: Memphis Days—The Definitive Edition, Vol. 1*, Bear Family CD 15460; and Demêtre and Chauvard, "Son Utilisation," page unknown.

52. Clark interview.

53. Curry interview.

54. Ibid.

55. Monroe Burnett interview.

56. Clark interview.

57. Marriage license registered in De Soto County, Mississippi, on 8 May 1947. Wolf and Katie Mae gave as their address Cordova, Tennessee, a rural community known for its fireworks factory (a converted army munitions facility) and its easy access to Memphis, twenty miles west. It's quite likely that Wolf and Katie Mae did not reside in Cordova for long. Two of the town's leading citizens, both living there in 1947, did not remember them. Dr. Howard Pinkston and Margaret Schwam interviews with Mark Hoffman by telephone, 21 October 2003.

58. Magnolia Frazier interview.

59. Peter Guralnick, *Lost Highway: Journeys and Arrivals of American Musicians* (New York: Harper and Row, 1989), p. 283.

60. Corrinia Wallace, "Corrinia Wallace Remembers Willie Johnson and Howlin' Wolf," *Living Blues* (November/December 1995), p. 46.

61. Curry interview.

62. Magnolia Frazier interview.

63. Willie Walker interview with James Segrest in Renova, Mississippi, 22 June 1997.

64. Floyd Frazier interview.

65. Floyd Frazier interview with James Segrest by telephone, 27 October 1997. Floyd Frazier was not familiar with the legend of Robert Johnson and did not take pride in relating this story.

66. David Little interview with Mark Hoffman, 10 November 2003.

67. Little, Riley, and Riley interview.

68. Lillie Burnett interview with Metcalf.

5 • HOUSE ROCKIN' BOOGIE

1. Compiled by Workers of the Writer's Program of the Works Progress Administration in the State of Arkansas, *Arkansas: A Guide to the State* (New York: Hastings House, 1941), p. 222.

2. Demêtre and Chauvard, "Son Utilisation," page unknown.

3. Charles Radcliffe, "Sweet Home Chicago: The Blues 1945–65, Part Two," *Friends* (21 August 1970), p. 16.
4. Welding, "Interview," pp. 22–23.
5. Demêtre and Chauvard, "Son Utilisation," page unknown.
6. Palmer, *Deep Blues*, pp. 231–32.
7. Dick Shurman notes, *Howlin' Wolf: The Chess Box*.
8. Volume dials even in West Memphis didn't go up to 11 before the sonic breakthrough in 1984 pioneered by English guitarist/hotrod enthusiast Nigel Tufnel of Squatney, East London.
9. Rubin quoted in Brisbin, "Willie Johnson," p. 41.
10. Charlie Gillett, *The Sound of the City: The Rise of Rock and Roll*, revised edition (London: Souvenir Press, 1983), p. 137.
11. Quoted in Willie Johnson Artist File, Blues Archive, University of Mississippi.
12. Joe Roesch and Michael "Red Dog" Downes, "The Invisible Legend: Matt 'Guitar' Murphy," *Blues Connection* (October 1997), p. 6.
13. Robert Neff and Anthony Connor, *Blues* (Boston: David R. Godine, 1975), p. 37.
14. Calvin Newborn interview with Jim O'Neal, 3 June 1978, Blues Archive, University of Mississippi.
15. Oliver Sain interview with James Segrest by telephone, 9 December 1997.
16. Listen to Hare's guitar playing on James Cotton's "Cotton Crop Blues" for a prime example of his power.
17. Kevin Hahn, "Pat Hare: A Blues Guitarist," *Juke Blues* (Summer 1991), p. 8.
18. Colin Escott with Martin Hawkins, *Good Rockin' Tonight: Sun Records and the Birth of Rock 'n' Roll* (New York: St. Martin's, 1991), p. 53.
19. Abu Talib interview with James Segrest by telephone, 22 March 1999.
20. Bill Greensmith, "Carl Tate AKA Bob Starr," *Blues Unlimited* (May/June 1976), p. 7.
21. Neff and Connor, *Blues*, p. 37.
22. Roesch and Downes, "Invisible Legend," p. 7.
23. Talib interview.
24. Trynka, *Portrait of the Blues*, p. 45.
25. Helen Doob Lazar, "Living Blues Interview: James Cotton," *Living Blues Magazine* (1987), p. 24.
26. Trynka, *Portrait of the Blues*, p. 45.
27. Ernestine Mitchell interview with James Segrest in Memphis, Tennessee, 15 May 1997.
28. Tot Randolph interview with James Segrest in Memphis, Tennessee, 13 June 1997.
29. Big Amos Patton interview with James Segrest, Clarksdale, Mississippi, to Memphis, Tennessee, 3 August 1994.
30. *Crittenden County Times*, West Memphis, 21 February 1947, p. 7.
31. Welding, "Interview," p. 23.
32. Roesch and Downes, "Invisible Legend," p. 6.
33. Mike Leadbitter, " 'Somethin' to Tell You': Dr. Ross," *Blues Unlimited* (December 1972), p. 6.
34. Stuart was the brother-in-law of rockabilly musician Charlie Feathers. Peter Gural-

nick, *Lost Highway: Journeys and Arrivals of American Musicians* (New York: Harper & Row, 1989), p. 110.

35. Ronnie Smith interview with Mark Hoffman by telephone, 5 June 1998.

36. Brisbin, "Willie Johnson," p. 45.

37. Edwards, *World Don't Owe Me Nothing*, p. 167.

38. Paul Burlison interview with Mark Hoffman in Seattle, Washington, 20 February 1998.

39. Ibid.

40. Ronnie Hawkins interview with Mark Hoffman by telephone, 8 May 2001.

41. Mitchell interview.

42. Roscoe Gordon interview with James Segrest by telephone, 26 April 2001.

43. Palmer, *Deep Blues*, p. 153.

44. Honeyboy Edwards interview.

45. Peter Hatch, "This Is the Blues," *Coda* (May/June 1971), p. 14.

46. Hugh Merrill, *The Blues Route* (New York: William Morrow, 1990), pp. 63–64.

47. John Anthony Brisbin, "Easy Baby: We Seen Some Good Days," *Living Blues* (March/April 1999), p. 60.

48. John Anthony Brisbin, "Brewer Phillips, Part 2: The Early Years," *Living Blues* (January/February 1995), p. 42.

49. Tommy Williams interview with James Segrest in Memphis, Tennessee, 17 May 1997.

50. Sonny Blake interview with James Segrest in West Memphis, Arkansas, 15 August 1997.

51. Gordon interview.

52. Mitchell interview.

53. Tommy Williams interview.

54. B. B. King interview with Mark Hoffman by telephone, 21 August 1998.

55. Blake interview.

56. Patton interview.

57. Ibid.

58. Roesch and Downes, "Invisible Legend," p. 6.

59. Floyd Murphy interview with James Segrest by telephone, 5 March 1999.

60. Little Mack Simmons interview with James Segrest by telephone, 12 April 1999.

61. Bill Greensmith, "East St. Louis Blues: Little Cooper and the Drifters," *Blues & Rhythm* (April 1995), p. 5.

62. Mary Lane interview with James Segrest by telephone, 13 April 1998.

63. Frank Frost interview with James Segrest in Helena, Arkansas, 31 May 1991.

64. Norman Darwen, "We Play Classier Places Where They Don't Throw Bottles," *Blues & Rhythm* (January 1990), p. 4.

65. Sumlin, "My Years with Wolf," pp. 12–13.

66. Blake interview.

67. Bankhead interview.

68. Bill Greensmith and Cilla Huggins, "Still Hanging Right On in There: Dirty Jim Tells All, Part 1," *Blues Unlimited* (Spring 1981), p. 9.

69. Honeyboy Edwards interview.

70. Sain interview.
71. Bankhead interview.
72. Willie Kent interview with James Segrest by telephone, 22 September 1997.
73. Walker interview.
74. Brett J. Bonner, "Smokey Wilson: Corn Shuckin' Blues," *Living Blues* (November/December 1996), p. 20.
75. Arthur Williams interview with James Segrest by telephone, 1 September 1999.
76. Tommy Williams interview.
77. Patton interview.
78. Sain interview.
79. Ernest Gatewood interview with James Segrest by telephone, 22 January 1999.
80. Bankhead interview.
81. Patton interview.
82. Lane interview.
83. Blake interview.
84. Gordon interview.
85. Randolph interview.
86. Sain interview.
87. Murphy interview.
88. Wallace, "Remembers," p. 46.
89. Blake interview.
90. Brian Baumgartner, "Eddie Snow and Floyd Murphy: Partnership in the Blues," *Juke Blues* (Autumn 1998), p. 17.
91. Sain interview.
92. Edwards, *World Don't Owe Me Nothing*, p. 168.
93. Sumlin interview with O'Neal.
94. Hahn, "Pat Hare," p. 8.
95. Ibid., p. 10.
96. Sain interview.
97. Randolph interview.
98. Roesch and Downes, "Invisible Legend," pp. 6–7.
99. Randolph interview.
100. Blake interview.
101. Sain interview.
102. Robert Williams interview with Don McGlynn and Joe Lauro for the film *The Howlin' Wolf Story*, 5 May 2002.
103. Randolph interview.
104. Ibid.
105. Sain interview.
106. Abb Locke interview with James Segrest in Chicago, Illinois, 25 July 1991.
107. Williams interview.
108. Willie Mitchell interview with James Segrest by telephone, 15 April 1999.
109. Arthur Williams interview. Unable to do field work, Barber Parker hauled laborers around in an old school bus from which he sold cold cuts and sodas. He died in the late 1960s.

110. Roesch and Downes, "Invisible Legend," p. 7.
111. Jones interview.
112. Griffin interview.
113. Rosie Griffin interview with James Segrest by telephone, 4 April 1997.
114. Marshall interview. There is no marker over Dock Burnett's grave. Wolf's niece Abbie Mitchell Harris, who died in a motorcycle accident, is buried in the same graveyard in a marked grave.
115. Floyd Frazier interview.
116. Floyd's grandmother died in 1951 of a heart attack and his grandfather died a week later in a mysterious house fire the same day he attended his wife's funeral. Magnolia Frazier conversation.
117. Eddie Shaw, *The Blues and Me*, unpublished autobiography.
118. Floyd Frazier interview.
119. Roesch and Downes, "Invisible Legend," p. 8. Little Junior Parker died of a brain tumor in 1971.
120. Sumlin interview with O'Neal.

6 • I'M THE WOLF

1. Palmer, *Deep Blues*, p. 233.
2. Escott and Hawkins, *Good Rockin' Tonight*, pp. 18–19.
3. Guralnick, *Lost Highway*, pp. 329–30.
4. Sam Phillips interview with James Segrest in Memphis, Tennessee, 14 October 1997.
5. Ibid.
6. Liner notes to *Sun Records: The Blues Years, 1950–1958*.
7. Phillips interview.
8. Brisbin, "Willie Johnson," p. 47.
9. Phillips interview.
10. Dawkins et al., "Willie Johnson," p. 4.
11. Brisbin, "Willie Johnson," p. 45.
12. Ibid.
13. Welding, "Interview," p. 21.
14. Nadine Cohodas, *Spinning Blues into Gold: The Chess Brothers and the Legendary Chess Records* (New York: St. Martin's, 2000), p. 64.
15. List of *Cash Box* chart hits for Howlin' Wolf compiled by blues researcher Mark Jickling.
16. Galen Gart, *First Pressings: The History of Rhythm & Blues, Volume 1: 1951* (Milford, NH: Big Nickel Publications, 1991), p. 89.
17. Ibid., p. 90.
18. Joe Bihari interview with James Segrest by telephone, 6 April 1999.
19. Ike Turner interview with James Segrest by telephone, 6 April 1999.
20. Brisbin, "Willie Johnson," p. 45.
21. Turner interview.

22. Kerry Kudlacek and Dave Sax, "The Ike Turner Blues Story," *Blues Unlimited* (November 1968), p. 5.
23. Turner interview.
24. Bihari interview.
25. Kudlacek and Sax, "Ike Turner Blues Story," p. 5.
26. Greensmith, "Still in the Woods," p. 10.
27. Bihari interview.
28. *Billboard*, October 6, 1951, p. 33.
29. Gart, *First Pressings, Volume 1*, p. 125.
30. Bihari interview.
31. Gordon interview.
32. Gart, *First Pressings, Volume 1*, p. 119.
33. Phillips interview.
34. Bill Wyman and Richard Havers, *Bill Wyman's Blues Odyssey: A Journey to Music's Heart and Soul* (New York: DK Publishing, 2001), p. 296.
35. Phillips interview.
36. Welding, "Interview," p. 23.
37. Phillips interview.
38. Jerry Portnoy interview with Mark Hoffman by telephone, 17 January 2003.
39. Kim Field interview with Mark Hoffman in Redmond, Washington, 10 April 2000.
40. Shurman liner notes, *Howlin' Wolf: The Chess Box*.
41. Escott and Hawkins, *Good Rockin' Tonight*, p. 16.
42. Phillips interview.
43. Mitchell interview.
44. Arthur Williams interview.
45. Galen Gart, *First Pressings: The History of Rhythm & Blues, Volume 2: 1952* (Milford, NH: Big Nickel Publications, 1992), p. 17.
46. Ibid., p. 20.
47. Gordon interview.
48. Bihari interview.
49. Gart, *First Pressings, Volume 2*, pp. 21 and 24.
50. Phillips interview.
51. Gart, *First Pressings, Volume 2*, p. 85.
52. Ibid., p. 86.
53. Patton interview.
54. See Mike Leadbitter and Neil Slaven, *Blues Records, 1943–1970: A Selective Discography, Volume 1: A–K* (London: Record Information Services, 1987), p. 628, and Dave Sax, "Howlin' Wolf—The Memphis Recordings," in liner notes for *Howlin' Wolf: Memphis Days—The Definitive Edition, Vol. 2*, Bear Family CD15500.
55. Hubert Sumlin has claimed that this song was recorded in Chicago with him and Jody Williams on guitar, but the guitar sounds distinctly like Willie Johnson. Sumlin, "My Years with Wolf," p. 14.
56. Escott and Hawkins, *Good Rockin' Tonight*, p. 32.
57. Shurman liner notes, *Howlin' Wolf: The Chess Box*.

58. Greil Marcus, *Mystery Train: Images of America in Rock 'n' Roll Music* (New York: Dutton, 1990), pp. 42–43.
59. Welding, "Interview," p. 23.
60. Howlin' Wolf interview with David Booth, quoted in *Howlin' Wolf: Memphis Days*, Bear Family CD 15460.
61. Sumlin interview with O'Neal.
62. Floyd Frazier interview.
63. Peter Guralnick, *The Listener's Guide to the Blues* (New York: Quarto, 1982), p. 80.
64. Phillips interview.
65. Wyman and Havers, *Bill Wyman's Blues Odyssey*, p. 297.

7 • SMOKESTACK LIGHTNIN'

1. Lemann, *The Promised Land*, p. 6.
2. Mike Rowe, *Chicago Blues: The City and the Music* (New York: Da Capo, 1981), p. 35.
3. Ibid., pp. 32–35.
4. Cohodas, *Spinning Blues into Gold*, pp. 5–56.
5. Robert Gordon, *Can't Be Satisfied: The Life and Times of Muddy Waters* (Boston: Little, Brown, 2002), p. 4.
6. Wolf interview with Booth, Bear Family CD 15460. Willie Dixon claimed to have picked Wolf up at the bus station when Wolf first came to Chicago, but his memory was faulty in this instance. Both Wolf and Muddy, who rarely agreed on anything, said that Wolf drove to Chicago. Bob Corritore, Bill Ferris, and Jim O'Neal, "Willie Dixon, Part II," *Living Blues* (September/October 1988), p. 21.
7. Jim and Amy O'Neal, "Muddy Waters," *Living Blues* (March/April 1983), p. 39.
8. Howlin' Wolf interviewed by Ralph Bass, from the documentary *Wolf* by Len Sauer, 1971.
9. Jim and Amy O'Neal, "Muddy Waters," p. 39.
10. Ibid.
11. Sumlin, "My Years with Wolf," p. 13.
12. Welding, "Interview," p. 23.
13. Demêtre and Chauvard, "Son Utilisation," page unknown.
14. Sumlin, "My Years with Wolf," pp. 10–11.
15. Hubert Sumlin interview with Mark Hoffman in Seattle, 8 May 2003. Hubert's mother eventually came around about her son's music. "I got my mama to come out where I was playing before she passed," he said. "About seven months before she died, I taken her to Antone's [a famous blues club in Austin, Texas]. I went and got her and, shit, she loved it! She said, 'You know what? I been thinking about this all these years. God gave you what you had. God gave you this. I think you turned out to be one of the best in the world. Son, I didn't know.' I said, 'Well, thank you!' That was a ease off my mind. All them years, man, she didn't believe in me and she didn't like what I was doing."

16. Dan Forte, "Chicago Blues Legend Hubert Sumlin: Howlin' Wolf's Sideman," *Guitar Player* (April 1980), p. 58.

17. Trynka, *Portrait of the Blues*, pp. 46–47.

18. Ibid., pp. 89–90.

19. Jody Williams interview with Mark Hoffman by telephone, 22 June 1997.

20. Welding, "Interview," p. 23.

21. Steve Cushing, "Behind the Beat of Blues," *Living Blues* (March/April 1991), p. 18.

22. Ibid.

23. Jody Williams interview.

24. Sain interview.

25. Born in 1931, Hubert was actually in his early twenties. It was probably Jody Williams, just eighteen then, who had to get his union card.

26. Rowe, "Floyd Jones," p. 18.

27. American Federation of Musicians Local 208 files, courtesy Harold Washington Library, Chicago.

28. Sumlin, "My Years with Wolf," p. 14.

29. Sumlin interview with O'Neal.

30. HPI Blues Chat with Hubert Sumlin, 5 April 1998, Blueschat.com.

31. Jody Williams interview.

32. Lacy Gibson interview with James Segrest by telephone, 29 January 1999.

33. Dusty Brown interview with James Segrest by telephone, 5 May 1999.

34. Billy Boy Arnold interview with James Segrest by telephone, 11 February 1999.

35. Jody Williams interview.

36. Edwards, *World Don't Owe Me Nothing*, p. 168.

37. Dave Myers interview with James Segrest by telephone, 24 September 1997.

38. Arnold interview.

39. Reverend Hudson Showers interview with James Segrest by telephone, 12 November 1997.

40. James Rooney, *Bossmen: Bill Monroe and Muddy Waters* (New York: Dial, 1971), p. 130.

41. Paul Oliver, *Blues off the Record: Thirty Years of Blues Commentary* (New York: Da Capo, 1988), p. 265.

42. Sumlin, "My Years with Wolf," p. 14.

43. Hubert Sumlin interview with Mai Cramer, January 1996, Realblues.com.

44. Sumlin, "My Years with Wolf," p. 14.

45. Jody Williams interview.

46. Hubert Sumlin interview with Hoffman, 8 May 2003.

47. Little Arthur Duncan interview with James Segrest by telephone, 6 November 1998.

48. Arnold interview.

49. John Anthony Brisbin, "The Lost American Bluesmen," *Living Blues* (July/August 1997), p. 30.

50. Gibson interview.

51. Jody Williams interview.

52. John Anthony Brisbin, "Robert Plunkett: I Think I Had a Little Magic," *Living Blues* (March/April 1994), p. 43.

53. Mike Rowe and Bill Greensmith, " 'I Was Really Dedicated': An Interview with Billy Boy Arnold, Part 3: 'Whatever I Did It Was Me and I'm Proud of It,' " *Blues Unlimited* (January/February 1978), p. 22.

54. Cushing, "Behind the Beat of the Blues," p. 18.

55. *Cash Box*, May 22, 1954, p. 30.

56. Sam Myers interview with James Segrest by telephone, 9 June 1999.

57. Gibbs, p. 47.

58. Cohodas, *Spinning Blues into Gold*, p. 93.

59. Jickling list of *Cash Box* hits.

60. Patton interview.

61. Norman Darwen, "Wolf Taught Me How to Work," *Blues & Rhythm* (February 1992), p. 5.

62. Sumlin, "My Years with Wolf," p. 14.

63. Jody Williams interview.

64. Jickling list of *Cash Box* hits.

65. *Billboard*, September 4, 1954, p. 32.

66. T. E. Mattox, "Blues in Black and White," *Blues Access* (Summer 1993), p. 12.

67. Galen Gart, *First Pressings: The History of Rhythm & Blues, Volume 4: 1954* (Milford, NH: Big Nickel Publications, 1990), p. 108.

68. Hubert Sumlin interview with Hoffman, 8 May 2003.

69. Jody Williams interview.

70. Jickling list of *Cash Box* hits.

71. *Chicago Defender*, February 19, 1955.

72. Rowe and Greensmith, "Billy Boy Arnold," p. 21.

73. Arnold interview.

74. Jody Williams interview. Williams is one of the few musicians who had money problems with Wolf. Almost all the dozens of musicians we've interviewed for this book said that as long as you did your job onstage, Wolf never shortchanged you. When Williams quit, it probably taught Wolf a valuable lesson.

75. Brisbin, "Willie Johnson," p. 47.

76. Jim and Amy O'Neal, "Muddy Waters," p. 39.

77. Jimmie Lee Robinson interview with James Segrest by telephone, 19 November 1997.

78. Brisbin, "Willie Johnson," p. 48.

79. American Federation of Musicians Local 208 files.

80. Hubert Sumlin interview with Hoffman, 8 May 2003.

81. Galen Gart, *First Pressings: The History of Rhythm & Blues, Volume 5: 1955* (Milford, NH: Big Nickel Publications, 1990), p. 123.

82. Sain interview.

83. Hubert Sumlin interview with Hoffman, 8 May 2003.

84. Sain interview.

85. Cohodas, *Spinning Blues into Gold*, p. 121.

86. Wolf interview, *Howlin' Wolf: Chess Box*.

87. Philip Larkin, *All What Jazz: A Record Diary 1961–68* (London: Faber and Faber, 1970), pp. 145–6.

88. *Billboard*, February 18, 1956, p. 62.

89. *Cash Box*, February 25, 1956, p. 36.

90. Jickling list of *Cash Box* hits.

91. Mark Humphrey liner notes, *Howlin' Wolf: His Best*, Chess CD9375.

92. Mighty Joe Young interview with James Segrest by telephone, 24 April 1998.

93. Wallace, "Remembers," p. 46.

94. Brisbin, "Willie Johnson," p. 48.

95. Randle interview.

96. Brown interview.

97. Jim and Amy O'Neal, "Muddy Waters," p. 39.

98. Arnold interview.

99. Mighty Joe Young interview.

8 • I BETTER GO NOW

1. Sumlin, "My Years with Wolf," p. 15.

2. Forte, "Hubert Sumlin," p. 60.

3. Sumlin interview with McGlynn and Lauro.

4. Sumlin, "My Years with Wolf," p. 15.

5. Jim and Amy O'Neal, "Muddy Waters," p. 39.

6. Sain interview.

7. Randle interview.

8. Darwen, "Wolf Taught Me," p. 5.

9. Ibid.

10. Monroe Burnett interview.

11. Mike McCracken, "Interview: Little Whit," *The Alabama Blues Society Newsletter* (August 1994), p. 9.

12. Cushing, "Beat," p. 23.

13. Dorothy Spencer Scott interview.

14. Sain interview.

15. Ad in Howlin' Wolf File, Blues Archive, University of Mississippi.

16. *Chicago Defender*, April 14, 1956.

17. *Chicago Defender*, July 7, 1956.

18. Rowe and Greensmith, "Billy Boy Arnold," p. 25.

19. *Chicago Defender*, September 8, 1956.

20. *Chicago Defender*, December 22, 1956.

21. *Billboard*, September 1, 1956, p. 50.

22. Peter Lee and David Nelson, "From Shoutin' the Blues to Preachin' the Word: Bishop Arnold Dwight 'Gatemouth' Moore," *Living Blues* (May/June 1989), pp. 11–12.

23. Steve Wisner, "Chicago Blues, Yesterday and Today: 'Smokey' Smothers: Big Otis and Little Abe," *Living Blues* (March/April 1978), p. 19.

24. Galen Gart, *First Pressings: The History of Rhythm & Blues, Volume 6: 1956* (Milford, NH: Big Nickel Publications, 1991), p. 118.

25. Jickling list of *Cash Box* hits.

26. *Cash Box*, February 23, 1957.

27. Galen Gart, *First Pressings: The History of Rhythm & Blues, Volume 7: 1957* (Milford, NH: Big Nickel Publications, 1991), p. 21.

28. Jickling list of *Cash Box* hits.

29. Bobby Rush interview with James Segrest in Clarksdale, Mississippi, 3 May 1997.

30. Cilla Huggins, "Luther: The Chicago Years," *Juke Blues* (Spring 1999), p. 16.

31. Rowe and Greensmith, "Billy Boy Arnold," pp. 24–25.

32. Arnold interview.

33. Norman Darwen, "The Phillip Walker Story: From Port Arthur to Los Angeles," *Blues & Rhythm* (April 1994), p. 12.

34. *Cash Box*, August 17, 1957.

35. *Howlin' Wolf: The Complete Records, 1951–1969* (Charly Records, 1993).

36. Jickling list of *Cash Box* hits.

37. Cohodas, *Spinning Blues into Gold*, pp. 136–39.

38. Yannick Bruynoghe, "In Chicago with Big Bill and Friends: *Chicago Scrapbook* Excerpts," *Living Blues* (Winter 1982/1983), p. 7.

39. Malcolm Chisholm interview with James Segrest in Chicago, Illinois, 25 July 1991.

40. Stan Lewis interview with James Segrest by telephone, 8 April 1999.

41. Alex Cramer, "Jimmy Rogers," *Coda* (June/July 1974), p. 7.

42. Phil Chess interview with Mark Hoffman by telephone, 27 September 1998.

43. Chisholm interview.

44. Discographies disagree as to whether Abb Locke or Billy Duncan played on this session. More than likely, it was Locke, who had joined the band before this session.

45. Locke interview with Segrest.

46. Abb Locke interview with Jim O'Neal, 3 December 1981, Blues Archive, University of Mississippi.

47. Locke interview with Segrest.

48. Jeff Hannusch, "Henry Gray: Lucky, Lucky Man," *Living Blues* (July/August 2001), p. 23.

49. Brisbin, "Willie Johnson," p. 48.

50. Locke interview with Segrest.

51. Hannusch, "Henry Gray," p. 23.

52. Locke interview with O'Neal.

53. S. P. Leary interview with James Segrest in Chicago, 24 June 1991.

54. Milne, "Shakey Jake," p. 10.

55. S. P. Leary interview with James Segrest in Chicago, 24 June 1991.

56. Ibid.

57. Jickling list of *Cash Box* hits.

58. *Cash Box*, May 9, 1959.

9 • HOWLIN' FOR MY DARLING

1. Hubert Sumlin interview with Hoffman.
2. Lillie Burnett interview with Segrest.
3. Lillie Burnett interview with Ralph Metcalf, Jr., "Speaking of the Blues" series, Blues Archive, Chicago Public Library, 15 February 1991.
4. Lillie Burnett interview with Segrest.
5. Lillie Burnett interview with Metcalf.
6. Hubert Sumlin interview with Hoffman.
7. Ibid.
8. Lillie Burnett interview with Segrest.
9. Hubert Sumlin interview with Hoffman.
10. Evelyn Sumlin interview with Mark Hoffman in Chicago, Illinois, 29 and 30 May 2002.
11. Mick Vernon, "Hubert Sumlin: Guitar Class No. 1," *R&B Monthly* (December 1964), p. 5.
12. John Anthony Brisbin, "Little Smokey Smothers: They Smell My Onions," *Living Blues* (November/December 1993), p. 26.
13. Little Smokey Smothers interview with Mark Hoffman by telephone, 6 October 1997.
14. Brisbin, "Little Smokey Smothers," p. 26.
15. Gordon, *Can't Be Satisfied*, p. 175.
16. Smothers interview.
17. Brisbin, p. 26.
18. Smothers interview.
19. Brisbin, p. 27.
20. Smothers interview.
21. Lee "Shot" Williams interview with James Segrest by telephone, 4 September 1997.
22. John Anthony Brisbin, "Lester Davenport: It's All About Havin' a Good Time," *Living Blues* (January/February 1993), p. 23.
23. Lester "Mad Dog" Davenport interview with James Segrest in Chicago, Illinois, 21 July 1991.
24. Hubert Sumlin interview with Hoffman in Seattle, 8 May 2003.
25. Ibid.
26. *Howlin' Wolf: Complete Records* (Charly Records).
27. Brisbin, "Little Smokey Smothers," p. 26.
28. Paul Ackerman's liner notes, *Moanin' in the Moonlight*, Chess LP 1434.
29. Jacques Demêtre and Marcel Chauvard (translated from the French by Ian McLean), "Land of the Blues—Chicago," *Jazz Journal* (August 1960), p. 17.
30. Demêtre and Chauvard, "Son Utilisation," page unknown.
31. Demêtre and Chauvard, "Land of the Blues," pp. 18–19.
32. Demêtre and Chauvard, "Son Utilisation," page unknown.
33. Locke interview with Segrest.
34. Jimmie Lee Robinson interview.
35. Sacré et al., *Voice of the Delta*, p. 281.

36. Bill Dahl, "Abu Talib: The Real Thing at Last," *Living Blues* (March/April 1999), p. 53.
37. Lockwood interview with Hoffman.
38. Talib interview.
39. Ralph Bass interview with James Segrest in Chicago, Illinois, 23 July 1991.
40. Shurman notes, *Howlin' Wolf: The Chess Box.*
41. Talib interview.
42. "The Session Men," *Blues Unlimited* (August 1966), p. 10.
43. Talib interview.
44. Lawrence Cohn, *Nothing but the Blues: The Music and the Musicians* (New York: Abbeville Press, 1993), p. 373.
45. Willie Dixon with Don Snowden, *I Am the Blues: The Willie Dixon Story* (New York: Da Capo, 1989), p. 149.
46. Rowe, *Chicago Blues*, p. 172.
47. Dixon and Snowden, *I Am the Blues*, p. 147.
48. Ibid., p. 88.
49. *Billboard*, 23 January 1961, p. 42.
50. Dixon and Snowden, *I Am the Blues*, p. 147.
51. Guralnick, *Feel Like Going Home*, p. 162.

10 • THREE HUNDRED POUNDS OF JOY

1. Sam Lay interview with James Segrest in Chicago, Illinois, 11 July 1991.
2. "Folsom Prison Blues" by Johnny Cash with W. S. "Fluke" Holland on drums.
3. Sam Lay interview with Mark Hoffman in Chicago, Illinois, 10 June 1999.
4. Michael Richardson, "Chicago Shuffle Master: Drummer Sam Lay Steps Out Front with His New Six-String Instrument," *Big City Blues* (October/November 2002), p. 14.
5. For more on Little Walter's life and music, including his tragic decline, read Tony Glover, Scott Dirks, and Ward Gaines, *Blues with a Feeling: The Little Walter Story* (New York: Routledge, 2002).
6. Lay interview with Segrest.
7. Bass interview.
8. Arnold interview.
9. Lillie Burnett interview with Segrest.
10. Evelyn Sumlin interview.
11. Lay interview with Segrest.
12. Kell, "Double Shuffle," p. 31.
13. Lay interview with Segrest.
14. Eddie Shaw, *The Blues and Me*, chapter 3: "Muddy Waters," and chapter 4: "Howling Wolf."
15. Bob Rusch, "Eddie Shaw: Interview," *Cadence* (March 1984), p. 13.
16. Eddie Shaw interview with Mark Hoffman in Seattle, Washington, 7 March 1998.
17. Trynka, *Portrait of the Blues*, p. 96.
18. Evelyn Sumlin interview.

19. Francis Clay interview with Mark Hoffman by telephone, 20 September 1999.
20. Bass interview.
21. Larry interview with Hoffman.
22. Darwen, "Wolf Taught Me," p. 5.
23. Mark Hoffman and James Segrest, "Hubert at Home: Sumlin's Friends Keep Him Young," *Blues Access* (Fall 2001), p. 44.
24. Hubert Sumlin interview with Mark Hoffman by telephone, 8 July 2001.
25. Ibid.
26. Hoffman and Segrest, "Hubert at Home," p. 44.
27. Ibid.
28. Sumlin, "My Years with Wolf," p. 15.
29. Forte, "Chicago Blues Legend," p. 60.
30. Ibid.
31. Shurman liner notes, *Howlin' Wolf: The Chess Box*.
32. Huggins, "Luther," p. 16.
33. Hubert Sumlin interview with Jim Fricke, Experience Music Project, Seattle, Washington, 10 February 2001.
34. Sadie Davis Jones interview with Segrest.
35. Evelyn Sumlin interview.
36. Lay interview with Segrest.
37. Showers interview.
38. Evelyn Sumlin interview.
39. Lay interview with Segrest.
40. Ernest Withers interview with Mark Hoffman in Seattle, Washington, 12 July 2002.
41. David Hervey interview with James Segrest by telephone, 4 September 2000.
42. When Wolf first came to Chicago, he had been handled by the Moe Gale Agency. Gale was the owner of the famous Savoy Ballroom in Harlem.
43. Hervey interview.
44. Perry Payton interview with James Segrest in Greenville, Mississippi, 11 June 1997.
45. Bill Morris interview with James Segrest by telephone, 1 September 2000.
46. Lay interview with Segrest.
47. Morris interview.
48. Hervey interview.
49. Lay interview with Segrest.
50. Hervey interview.
51. Lay interview with Segrest.
52. Other albums usually cited by critics in this regard include *The Best of Muddy Waters*, Magic Sam's *West Side Soul*, *Best of Little Walter*, and Junior Wells's *Hoodoo Man Blues*.
53. Lay interview with Segrest.
54. John S. Wilson, "Amplifying System Drowns Out Music at Capital Festival," *New York Times*, June 2, 1962.
55. Dick Lillard, *Blues-L*, 25 September 1997.
56. Clay interview.
57. Nick Charles interview with Mark Hoffman in Seattle, Washington, 22 July 1999.

58. Lay interview with Segrest.
59. Keith Tillman, "Bringing It to Jerome," *Blues Unlimited* (June 1969), p. 12.
60. Arnold interview.
61. Evelyn Sumlin interview.
62. Lillie Burnett interview with Segrest.
63. Eddie Shaw interview with Segrest.
64. Hannusch, "Henry Gray," p. 24.
65. Reuben Hughes interview with James Segrest in Greenwood, Mississippi, 15 August 1998.
66. Lay interview with Segrest.
67. This album was re-released on Chess as *Blues from "Big Bill's" Copa Cabana*.
68. Dixon and Snowden, *I Am the Blues*, p. 149.
69. Billy Boy Arnold interview with McGlynn and Lauro, May 2002, for film *The Howlin' Wolf Story*.

11 • SITTIN' ON TOP OF THE WORLD

1. Johnny Littlejohn interview with James Segrest in Chicago, Illinois, 4 July 1991. When Johnny was not available, Wolf would hire talented guitarist Eddie Taylor, best known for his seminal guitar work on Jimmy Reed's records for Vee-Jay in the 1950s.
2. Bob Rusch, "John Littlejohn: Interview Oral History," *Cadence* (February 1979), p. 6.
3. Littlejohn interview with Segrest.
4. Neff and Connor, *Blues*, p. 37.
5. Lay interview with Segrest.
6. Johnny Littlejohn interview with Jim O'Neal, 23 August 1981, Blues Archive, University of Mississippi.
7. Littlejohn interview with Segrest.
8. Evelyn Sumlin interview.
9. Littlejohn interview with Segrest.
10. Lillie Burnett interview with Segrest.
11. Marriage certificate for Chester Burnett and Lillie Jones, Office of County Clerk, Cook County, Illinois.
12. Lillie Burnett interview with Segrest.
13. Evelyn Sumlin interview.
14. Arnold interview.
15. Bass interview.
16. Evelyn Sumlin interview.
17. Lillie Burnett interview with Segrest.
18. Ibid.
19. Lillie Burnett interview with Metcalf.
20. B. Kimberly Taylor, "Remembering Howlin' Wolf: An Interview with Howlin' Wolf's Widow: Lillie Burnett," *Blues Revue* (April/May 1996), pp. 37–38.
21. Duncan interview.

22. Barbra Jones Marks conversation with James Segrest in West Point, Mississippi, 29 August 1997.
23. Koko Taylor interview with Mark Hoffman by telephone, 13 February 1998.
24. Robert "Huckleberry Hound" Wright interview with Mark Hoffman in Chicago, Illinois, 2 June 1999.
25. Frank Scott, "My Stay in Chicago," *Blues Unlimited* (January 1965), pp. 7–8.
26. Mark Humphrey liner notes for *Howlin' Wolf: His Best*, MCA/Chess 9375.
27. Dixon and Snowden, *I Am the Blues*, p. 198.
28. Sumlin, "My Years with Wolf," p. 16.
29. Ibid., p. 17.
30. Bob Koester interview with Mark Hoffman by telephone, 1 June 1997.
31. Hubert Sumlin interview with Don McGlynn and Joe Lauro in New Orleans, Louisiana, 1 May 2002.
32. Chris Strachwitz interview with Mark Hoffman by telephone, 24 November 1997.
33. Dixon and Snowden, *I Am the Blues*, pp. 139–40.
34. Strachwitz interview.
35. Sugar Pie DeSanto interview with James Segrest by telephone, 26 February 1999.
36. Strachwitz interview.
37. Koester interview.
38. Sumlin, "My Years with Wolf," p. 17.
39. Strachwitz interview.
40. DeSanto interview.
41. Koester interview.
42. Lillie Burnett interview with Metcalf.
43. Dixon and Snowden, *I Am the Blues*, pp. 136–37.
44. Long John Baldry interview with Mark Hoffman by telephone, 1 June 2003.
45. Neil Slaven, "Howlin' Wolf," *R&B Monthly* (August 1964), p. 3.
46. Neil Slaven, "The American Folk Blues Festival," *R&B Monthly* (December 1964), p. 8.
47. Alan Stevens, "R&B? No, I'm a Folk Singer—Howlin' Wolf," *Melody Maker* (November 7, 1964), p. 12.
48. Charles Keil, *Urban Blues* (Chicago: University of Chicago Press, 1966), p. 37.
49. Simon A. Napier, "The Third 'American Folk-Blues Festival'—1964," *Blues Unlimited* (November/December 1964), p. 4.
50. Dixon and Snowden, *I Am the Blues*, p. 135.
51. Tony McPhee interview with Mark Hoffman by telephone, 25 January 2003.
52. Stevens, "R&B?," p. 12.
53. John J. Broven, "Howlin' Wolf at the Marquee," *Blues Unlimited* (January 1965), p. 8.
54. Chris Barber interview with Mark Hoffman by telephone, 30 January 2003.
55. Baldry interview.
56. Winston Weatherall telephone interview with Mark Hoffman, 30 August 2003.
57. Andy McKechnie e-mail to Mark Hoffman, 14 September 2003.
58. Weatherall interview.
59. McKechnie e-mail.

60. Stuart Parkes interview with Mark Hoffman by telephone, 31 August 2003.

61. Ibid.

62. Weatherall interview.

63. Dave Hatfield interview with Mark Hoffman by telephone, 15 January 2003.

64. Ian McLagan interview with Mark Hoffman by telephone, 13 January 2003.

65. T. E. Mattox, "Blues with an Attitude: Memphis Charlie Was Born to Blow," *Blues Access* (Summer 1990), p. 7.

66. Charlie Musselwhite interview with Mark Hoffman at Everett Blues Festival, Everett, Washington, 2 August 1997.

67. Jan Mark Wolkin and Bill Keenom, *Michael Bloomfield: If You Love These Blues* (San Francisco: Miller Freeman, 2000), p. 24.

68. Elvin Bishop telephone interview with Mark Hoffman, 28 July 2003.

69. Norman Dayron interview with James Segrest by telephone, 25 April 1999.

70. Barry Goldberg telephone interview with Mark Hoffman, 14 August 2003.

71. Tracy Nelson interview with Mark Hoffman at Chicago Blues Festival, 30 May 2003.

72. Mattox, "Blues with an Attitude," p. 8.

73. Nick Gravenites interview with Mark Hoffman by telephone, 14 December 1999.

74. Billy Davenport interview with Mark Hoffman by telephone, 2 November 1997.

75. Musselwhite interview.

76. Willie Young interview with James Segrest by telephone, 31 October 1997.

77. McMahon interview.

78. Lee Eggleston interview with James Segrest in Chicago, Illinois, 1 July 1991.

79. Dick Waterman interview with James Segrest in Oxford, Mississippi, 15 August 1996.

80. Bill Wyman, *Rolling with the Stones* (London: DK Publishing, 2002), p. 186.

81. Lillie Burnett interview with Segrest.

82. Barbara Marks conversation with James Segrest in Chicago, Illinois, 4 July 1991.

83. Leary interview.

84. Conversation with Barbra Marks.

85. John Hammond, Jr., interview with Mark Hoffman in Seattle, Washington, 17 August 1997.

86. Jas Obrecht, "John Hammond," *Guitar Player* (July 1991), p. 116.

87. Hammond interview.

88. Taj Mahal telephone interview with Mark Hoffman, 2 November 1997.

89. Palmer, *Deep Blues*, pp. 232–33.

90. Wild Child Butler interview with James Segrest by telephone, 20 October 1999.

91. Byther Smith interview with James Segrest by telephone, 15 September 1997.

92. Rick Milne, "The Muddy Waters Band: On-the-Spot from Washington, D.C., October 1965," *Blues Unlimited* (January 1966), p. 4.

93. Bob Koester, "Chicago Blues Scene," *Blues Unlimited* (February 1966), p. 3.

94. Smith interview.

95. *Martin Scorsese Presents the Blues* (New York: Amistad, An Imprint of Harper-Collins Publishers, 2003), p. 192.

96. Geoff Muldaur e-mail to Mark Hoffman, 4 January 2003.

97. Maria Muldaur telephone interview with Mark Hoffman, 10 November 2003.
98. "Mean Old Blues," *Newsweek* (February 21, 1966), p. 91.
99. Wolkin and Keenom, "Michael Bloomfield," p. 86.
100. Chicago club performance recorded by Dick Shurman in the late 1960s.
101. Poisoned drinks have a venerable history in the blues world. The same year Robert Johnson was poisoned, his stepson, Robert Lockwood, got involved with a young woman he met at a juke joint. When he told her he was leaving her, she put Lysol in his whiskey. "I drank that whole half a pint of whiskey down and it wouldn't stay on my stomach," he said. "Throwed it back up." Days later, he was still sick. He went to see a root doctor who gave him a compound to drink that made him feel better. The root doctor also said something that Lockwood simply didn't believe. Years later, Lockwood was playing in a club when a stout, middle-aged woman came in and introduced herself. That night she begged him to come home with her. When they were in bed, she asked, "You ever seen me before? If I tell you who I am, would you be mad?" Lockwood said, "No, what the fuck am I gonna be mad about?" She said, "I tried to poison you once." It was just as the root doctor had prophesied. "He told me when I found her, I wasn't going to know who she was," Lockwood said. Needless to say, the rekindled romance was over, but Lockwood learned a valuable lesson. "I found out a long time ago, women is hard losers," he said. "They're the hardest losers that there is." (Lockwood interview with Hoffman.)
102. Evelyn claimed that she, not Wolf, knocked Hubert's teeth out. "We were coming from work one morning and whenever Hubert wanted to go someplace else outside of coming home, he had a way of trying to do it. He kept complaining, complaining. . . . We got back to the house, and Hubert had his way of getting even with me when I wasn't looking. And he grabbed me in my chest and broke the buttons off of my blouse. That was one thing that I didn't like—you would never see me half-dressed. And it was early in the morning and people were coming out and going to church or going to their jobs, and he had caught me and he was pulling me and all the buttons had fell off my blouse, and you could see my bra, and I got upset. I had me a little .22, and I hit him. . . . That was the only way I could get him to turn me loose, because he was, like, dragging me by my blouse and all my clothes was off from the top, and I wasn't going to let him keep dragging me" (Evelyn Sumlin interview).
103. Hubert Sumlin interview with Mark Hoffman in Milwaukee, Wisconsin, 23–24 May 2003.
104. Waterman interview.
105. *Devil Got My Woman: Blues at Newport, 1966* (Vestapol Productions, 1996).
106. Hubert Sumlin interview with Mark Hoffman in Seattle, Washington, 8 May 2003.
107. Sumlin interview with Hoffman.

12 • CHANGE MY WAY

1. Harold Stienblatt with Chris Gill, "John Fogerty: New Moon Rising," *Guitar World* (July 1997).
2. Dick Shurman posting to Blues-L Internet list server, used with permission.

3. Buddy Miles interview with Mark Hoffman by telephone, 6 June 2003.
4. Gravenites interview.
5. Sam Andrew, "Recollections of Janis" (*The Writings of Sam Andrew*, www.bbhc.com), used with permission.
6. Tracy Nelson interview with Mark Hoffman in Chicago, Illinois, 30 May 2003.
7. Cohodas, *Spinning Blues into Gold*, p. 270.
8. Marshall Chess interview with Mark Hoffman by telephone, 15 January 1998.
9. Eddie Shaw interview with Segrest.
10. Barbra Jones Marks conversation with James Segrest during Burnett family's Fourth of July picnic, 1991.
11. Little, Riley, and Riley interview.
12. Rush interview.
13. Waterman interview.
14. Interview by Alan Paul with Bonnie Raitt in *Guitar World* magazine.
15. Shaw interview with Segrest.
16. McMahon interview.
17. Pinetop Perkins interview with Mark Hoffman by telephone, 29 April 1998.
18. A. J. Burnett interview with James Segrest in Memphis, Tennessee, 5 May 1997.
19. Ruben Hughes interview with James Segrest in Greenwood, Mississippi, 15 August 1998.
20. *Teaspoon and Door*, 2 August 1968, p. 8.
21. *Open City*, 5–11 July 1968, p. 3.
22. Sandy Guy Schoenfeld, letter and memoir from www.howlingwolfphotos.com, used with permission.
23. *Toronto Globe and Mail*, 12 August 1968, p. 14.
24. Ernest Gatewood interview with James Segrest by telephone, 22 January 1999.
25. Robert Walker interview with James Segrest by telephone, 7 September 1999.
26. *Rolling Stone*, 15 February 1969, p. 8.
27. Robert Gordon interview with Pete Cosey in 1997, courtesy of Robert Gordon.
28. Marshall Chess interview.
29. *Howlin' Wolf: The Chess Box*.
30. Gene Barge interview with Mark Hoffman in Chicago, Illinois, 9 June 2001.
31. Ibid.
32. Story courtesy of Greg Freerksen, host of *Blues Edition* at WDCB Public Radio, College of DuPage.
33. John Dummer, *Melody Maker*, 24 January 1976, p. 49.
34. Memoir by Dave Kelly, used with permission.
35. Ibid.
36. *Melody Maker*, p. 49.
37. Kelly memoir.
38. *Melody Maker*, p. 49.
39. Kelly memoir.
40. *Melody Maker*, p. 49.
41. Kelly memoir.
42. Ibid.

43. Ibid.
44. Ibid.
45. *Melody Maker*, p. 49.
46. Kelly memoir.
47. Ibid.
48. Ibid.
49. Bill Thorndycraft, from the Killing Floor Web site, www.killingfloor.com, used with permission.
50. Kelly memoir.
51. Ibid.
52. Ibid.
53. *Melody Maker*, p. 49.
54. Little, Riley, and Riley interview.
55. Schoenfeld memoir.
56. John Fishel interview with Mark Hoffman by telephone, 17 January 1998.
57. Evelyn Sumlin interview.
58. "The Real Blues," *Ann Arbor Argus* (Vol. 1, No. 10, 1969), p. 21.
59. Hubert Sumlin interview with Don McGlynn and Joe Lauro.
60. *Creem*, Vol. 2, No. 4, 1969, p. 5.
61. Fishel interview.
62. Cohodas, *Spinning Blues into Gold*, p. 299.
63. Eddie Shaw interview with Segrest.
64. Howlin' Wolf interview with Dan McClosky in Ann Arbor, Michigan, 7 August 1970.
65. Cohodas, *Spinning Blues into Gold*, p. 300.
66. Cash McCall interview with James Segrest by telephone, 4 March 1999.
67. Dave Sproat, "Howlin Wolf British Tour '69: A Legend Remembered," www.juncopartners.com, used with permission.
68. Ibid.
69. Hubert Sumlin interview with McGlynn and Lauro.
70. Sebastian Danchin, *Earl Hooker: Blues Master* (Jackson: University Press of Mississippi, 2001), p. 243.
71. Detroit Junior interview.
72. Dr. Robert Fortner (nephrologist) interview with Mark Hoffman by telephone, 5 September 2003.
73. Lillie Burnett interview with Metcalf.
74. Lillie Burnett interview with Segrest.
75. Dick Shurman, "Memories of Howlin' Wolf," *The Voice of the Delta*, pp. 274–78.
76. Bob Koester interview with Mark Hoffman, 6 November 2003.
77. Dayron interview.
78. Ibid.
79. Ibid.
80. Ibid.
81. *Guitar Player* magazine, August 1976.
82. Dayron interview.

83. Ibid.

84. Ibid.

85. Ibid.

86. Ibid.

87. Bill Dahl, liner notes from *The London Howlin' Wolf Sessions, Deluxe Edition*, p. 12.

88. "Wolf Gathers His Flock in London," *Melody Maker* (16 May 1970), p. 3.

89. Chris Holdenfield, "Wolf Has Got This Weird Time," *Rolling Stone* (11 June 1970), p. 30.

90. Dayron interview.

91. Howlin' Wolf interview with McClosky.

92. Charles Radcliffe, "Sweet Home Chicago: The Blues 1945–65, Part Two," *Friends* (21 August 1970), p. 16.

93. McCall interview.

94. Court record filed with the National Archives: 1974 Civil 1959.

95. Wilson Lindsey interview with Mark Hoffman by telephone, 13 November 2003.

96. Lillie Burnett interview with Metcalf.

97. Evelyn Sumlin interview with McGlynn and Lauro.

13 • GOIN' DOWN SLOW

1. Hubert Sumlin interview with Hoffman in Seattle, Washington, 23 May 2003.

2. Field interview.

3. Colin Linden interview with Mark Hoffman by telephone, 8 January 1998.

4. From Colin Linden's Web site, www.colinlinden.com, used with permission.

5. *Blues Magazine*, vol. 2, No. 1, February 1976.

6. Leary interview.

7. Pat Ford interview with Mark Hoffman by telephone, 12 March 2003.

8. Posting from Robert Crocker to the Blues-L Internet list server.

9. *Bugle-American*, 3–10 May 1972, p. 40.

10. Leary interview.

11. Jim O'Neal interview with James Segrest by telephone, 2 December 1999.

12. John Sinclair interview with Mark Hoffman in New Orleans, 2 May 2003.

13. *Ann Arbor News*, 9 September 1972.

14. Posting from Steve Hoffman to the Blues-L Internet list server.

15. *Ann Arbor News*, 9 September 1972.

16. Sinclair interview.

17. Dave Richardson interview with Mark Hoffman by telephone, 11 February 2003.

18. Danny Russo interview with Mark Hoffman by telephone, 9 August 2003.

19. Detroit Junior interview.

20. *The Real Paper*, 30 May 1973, p. 18.

21. Hubert Sumlin interview with Hoffman.

22. Eddie Shaw interview with Hoffman.

23. Bettye Kelly and Barbra Jones Marks interview with Don McGlynn and Joe Lauro in film *The Howlin' Wolf Story*.

24. Burnett interview with Metcalf.
25. Evelyn Sumlin interview.
26. Paul Rishell interview with Mark Hoffman, 16 September 1997.
27. *Village Voice,* 7 June 1973, p. 68.
28. Field interview.
29. Chisholm interview.
30. Ibid.
31. Eddie Shaw interview with Hoffman.
32. Rishell interview.
33. Danny Russo interview with Mark Hoffman, 9 August 2003.
34. *Blues Unlimited,* February/March 1974, p. 106.
35. Eddie Shaw interview with Segrest.
36. Evelyn Sumlin interview.
37. Eddie Shaw interview with Segrest.
38. Guralnick, *Lost Highway,* p. 287.
39. Vaan Shaw interview.
40. Floyd Frazier interview.
41. Vaan Shaw interview.
42. Lillie Burnett interview with Metcalf.
43. David Little interview with Mark Hoffman, 11 November 2003.
44. Little, Riley, and Riley interview.
45. Cohodas, *Spinning Blues into Gold,* p. 308.
46. Court record filed with the National Archives: 1974 Civil 1959.
47. Ibid.
48. *Living Blues* 17 (Summer 1974), p. 41.
49. *Great Speckled Bird,* 10 June 1974, p. 9.
50. *Living Blues* 18 (Autumn 1974), p. 30.
51. Guralnick, *Lost Highway,* p. 287.
52. Floyd Frazier interview.
53. Shorty Gilbert interview with James Segrest in Chicago, Illinois, 18 July 1991.
54. Robert Plunkett interview with Mark Hoffman in Chicago, Illinois, 4 June 1999.
55. Chico Chism interview with Mark Hoffman by telephone, 2 October 1997.
56. Casey Jones interview with James Segrest in Chicago, Illinois, 27 July 1991.
57. Vaan Shaw interview.
58. Lillie Burnett interview with Segrest.
59. Billy Boy Arnold interview.
60. Eddie Shaw interview with Segrest.
61. Ibid.
62. Bob Corritore interview with James Segrest by telephone, 15 September 1999.
63. Twist Turner interview with James Segrest by telephone, 15 October 1998.
64. Vaan Shaw interview.
65. O'Neal interview.
66. Lillie Burnett interview with Segrest.
67. John Stephan interview with Mark Hoffman in Seattle, Washington, 15 January 2003.

68. Plunkett interview.

69. Lillie Burnett interview with Segrest.

70. Chism interview.

71. Lillie Burnett interview with Metcalf.

72. Lillie Burnett interview with Segrest.

73. Gilbert interview.

74. Burnett interview with Metcalf.

75. Vaan Shaw interview.

76. Hubert Sumlin interview with Hoffman.

77. Lillie Burnett interview with Segrest.

78. Hubert Sumlin interview with Hoffman.

79. Ibid.

80. State of Illinois Medical Certificate of Death for Chester A. Burnett.

81. Floyd Frazier interview.

82. Corritore interview.

83. James "Tail Dragger" Jones interview with James Segrest by telephone, 24 June 1998.

84. O'Neal interview.

85. Lillie Burnett interview with Segrest.

86. Showers interview.

87. Leary interview.

88. Brookfield Zoo librarian interview with Mark Hoffman by telephone, 30 July 2003.

EPILOGUE: TAIL DRAGGER

1. Hubert Sumlin interview with Hoffman in Milwaukee, 6 June 2001.

2. Magic Slim interview with Hoffman in Seattle, 31 August 2003.

Discography

HOWLIN' WOLF ON COMPACT DISC

"Good evening everybody, the Wolf is comin' into town," sang the Howlin' Wolf in the raucous "House Rockin' Boogie" in 1951. While you can no longer see the Wolf in your town, sadly, you can still hear his unforgettable voice on CD. But which Wolf CDs should you buy? As fans of the Mighty Wolf, we say buy them all! But for those who just want to add a Wolf CD or two to their music collection, here's a brief survey to help you choose.

WEST MEMPHIS AND MEMPHIS RECORDINGS

Wolf's unique sound was fully in evidence from his first recording session for Sam Phillips. Nobody before or since has sung the blues quite like the Wolf. Supported by the molten guitar of Willie Johnson and the crudely powerful drumming of Willie Steele, Wolf growled, moaned, howled, and blew harp through one dynamic recording after another. This is music for scaring the living and waking the dead.

   Memphis Days: Definitive Edition, Vol. 1 (Bear Family 15460) collects twenty-one of Wolf's rare early sides from the studio of Sam Phillips. They fully live up to his statement upon first hearing the Wolf: "This is for me. This is where the soul of man never dies." From deep, slow blues to rollicking boogies, these cuts are rough and raw in all the best ways. They're not for the faint of heart. They're musical Viagra—the hard stuff. Bonus: This CD includes Wolf's previously unreleased audition recordings for Phillips.

   Memphis Days: Definitive Edition, Vol. 2 (Bear Family 15500) collects the rest of Wolf's Memphis recordings for Sam Phillips, including previously unreleased alternate takes of Wolf classics "How Many More Years?" and "Baby Ride With Me." Along with Vol. 1, this is the lupine beast in his prime, at his primitive best.

Cadillac Daddy: Memphis Recordings, 1952 (Rounder 28) covers the same ground as the above CDs in an abbreviated, twelve-song version. Your best choice would be the two Bear Family CDs, but if you cannot find or afford them, this is a solid second choice.

Howlin' Wolf Rides Again (Ace 333) collects eighteen sides (including alternate takes) that Wolf recorded for the Bihari brothers' RPM label. Recorded on portable equipment in makeshift studios in West Memphis, these songs are every bit as good as what Wolf was recording for Sam Phillips in Memphis at the time. Wolf's voice and harp work were in their prime and his band was hotter and more alarming than a five-dollar pistol.

CHICAGO RECORDINGS

Wolf put together a new band when he moved to Chicago to record for Chess Records, but his sound remained essentially unchanged. He would be the Wolf wherever he recorded. But studios and equipment were better in Chicago, and Wolf took advantage of them to create one Chicago blues classic after another.

Howlin' Wolf/Moanin' in the Moonlight (MCA/Chess 5908) combines Wolf's classic first two Chess albums (including the legendary "rocking chair" album) on one disc—a terrific bargain. It's loaded with signature songs such as "Smokestack Lightnin'," "Evil," "Spoonful," "Howlin' for My Darling," and "Goin' Down Slow," to name just a few. A stellar cast of musicians ably assisted Wolf, with Jody Williams and Willie Johnson outstanding on guitar on the early tracks and Hubert Sumlin's genius on full display on the later ones. These are the songs that made Wolf's legend and influenced a generation of blues and rock musicians. It's absolutely the best the blues has to offer and the best single CD with which to start any Wolf collection.

The Real Folk Blues/More Real Folk Blues (MCA/Chess 112820) is another terrific twofer, combining Wolf's third and fourth Chess albums on one disc. Again this CD features fabulous singing from Wolf and dynamic band work. Among its twenty-four cuts are such Wolf classics as "Killing Floor," "Sittin' on Top of the World," "Tail Dragger," and "I'll Be Around." While not as essential as the previous disc, these are all marvelous songs.

The London Howlin' Wolf Sessions [Deluxe Edition] (MCA/Chess 112985) has stood the test of time very well. Wolf sounded remarkably strong, considering his ill health during recording, and Eric Clapton, Bill Wyman, Charlie Watts, and the rest provided solid, restrained, and at times dazzling accompaniment. While not the best place to start a Wolf collection, it's a good bet for a later purchase. You can buy the original album on a single CD, but for diehard fans, there's a new, two-disc "deluxe edition" that includes alternate takes and mixes, revealing studio chatter, and astute liner notes by Bill Dahl.

Live And Cookin' at Alice's Revisited (MCA/Chess 9339) was Wolf's late-career live album for Chess. Recorded at a popular North Side club, this is a potent showcase for Wolf's ability to rock the house even in the twilight of his career. The CD has two cuts not on the original vinyl album: "The Big House" and "Mr. Airplane Man." Unless someone can come up with a live album recorded at Silvio's, this is the definitive live Wolf.

The Back Door Wolf (MCA/Chess 9358) was Wolf's last album of new material and a fitting finale to a brilliant career. Wolf was in fine voice, despite his infirmities, and Hubert's guitar playing was among his best. Many of the songs had a topical flavor, like the acerbic "Coon on the Moon," or reach back to Wolf's early Delta influences in tunes such as "Can't Stay Here." A hidden gem, this album is ripe for rediscovery by Wolf fans.

Change My Way (MCA/Chess 93001) is a fine compilation of Wolf singles that was first released in 1975. Songs such as "Hidden Charms," "I Ain't Superstitious," and "Do the Do" feature Hubert at his brilliant best.

COMPILATION CDS

The Chess Box (MCA/Chess 9332) is the Wolf fan's dream collection. A three-CD box set beautifully packaged with comprehensive musical and biographical notes by Wolf experts Chris Morris and Dick Shurman, plus superb photos from the best sources, it provides the best overview available of Wolf's entire recording career for Chess. It features all of Wolf's greatest hits and includes several snippets of Wolf talking about his life and music. It also includes two unusual acoustic cuts that Wolf recorded while fooling around in the studio in 1968. This is the definitive collection for anyone who wants a total Wolf fix.

Ain't Gonna Be Your Dog (MCA/Chess 9349) is an excellent two-disc, forty-two-track collection of rare or previously unreleased Wolf recordings, plus first-rate liner notes by Dick Shurman. With some artists, a collection like this might be mostly filler. Don't fear; there are many great cuts here. Bonus: It includes four more astonishing Howlin' Wolf acoustic tracks.

His Best (MCA/Chess 9375) is a twenty-song Wolf collection released during Chess's fiftieth anniversary celebration. The packaging is terrific, with good liner notes by Mark Humphrey. The music, it goes without saying, is superb. It's a good CD for someone who has never heard the Wolf or for a devoted fan who wants a single CD of his hits.

His Best, Vol. 2 (MCA/Chess 12026) is a follow-up to the previous CD—a twenty-track selection of Wolf's other hits. Not as essential as the previous CD, it's still solid.

The Best of Howlin' Wolf (MCA/Chess 35802) is MCA's recent repackaging of Wolf hits in their Twentieth Century Masters Series. Song selection is brief, though, including just twelve tracks. A better value in a single CD is **Howlin' Wolf/Moanin' in the Moonlight** (MCA/Chess 5908) or **His Best** (MCA/Chess 9375), mentioned above.

Sessionography

This list includes every known recording session by Howlin' Wolf. With the exception of one official live album and part of another, it does not include his live recordings, many of which are of questionable provenance, nor does it include alternate takes from the same session. Singles are noted in parentheses.

EARLY 1951: MEMPHIS RECORDING SERVICE, MEMPHIS
Howlin' Wolf's audition session, produced by Sam Phillips and sent to the Bihari brothers in Los Angeles. Howlin' Wolf, vocal, harmonica; Albert Williams, piano; Willie Johnson, guitar; Willie Steele, drums

"Baby Ride with Me"; a.k.a. "Ridin' in the Moonlight"

MAY 14, 1951: MEMPHIS RECORDING SERVICE, MEMPHIS
Howlin' Wolf, vocal, harmonica; Albert Williams, piano; Willie Johnson, guitar; Willie Steele, drums

"Baby Ride with Me"; a.k.a. "Ridin' in the Moonlight"
"How Many More Years"

JULY 1951: MEMPHIS RECORDING SERVICE, MEMPHIS
Produced by Sam Phillips, this session yielded two sides that he sent to the Chess brothers in Chicago, resulting in Wolf's first record: Chess 1479, issued on August 15, 1951. Howlin' Wolf, vocal, harmonica; Albert Williams or Ike Turner, piano ("How Many More Years"); Willie Johnson, guitar; Willie Steele, drums

"How Many More Years" (rerecorded; Chess 1479)
"Moanin' at Midnight" (Chess 1479)

Joe Bihari flew in from Los Angeles to record Wolf's first session for RPM. With the help of his teenaged talent scout Ike Turner, Bihari cut four tunes on a Magnecord or Ampex portable recorder, including one that Chess had just released: "Moanin' at Midnight," which RPM released as "Morning at Midnight." Howlin' Wolf, vocal, harmonica; Ike Turner, piano; Willie Johnson and Tommy Bankhead, guitars; Willie Steele, drums

> "Baby Ride with Me"; a.k.a. "Ridin' in the Moonlight" (rerecorded; RPM 333)
> "Dog Me Around"
> "Morning at Midnight" (RPM 333)
> "Keep What You Got"

Joe Bihari produced Wolf's second session for RPM at a private home and not at the YMCA, as some discographers believe. Howlin' Wolf, vocal, harmonica; Ike Turner, piano; Willie Johnson, guitar; Willie Steele, drums

> "Passing by Blues" (RPM 340)
> "Crying at Daybreak" (RPM 340)
> "My Baby Stole Off"
> "I Want Your Picture"

Another session for Chess, produced by Sam Phillips. Howlin' Wolf, vocal, harmonica; L. C. Hubert, piano; Willie Johnson, guitar; Willie Steele, drums; bass and sax unknown

> "Howlin' Wolf Boogie" (Chess 1497)
> "California Blues #1"
> "California Boogie"
> "Look-a-Here Baby"
> "The Wolf Is at Your Door"; a.k.a. "Howlin' for My Baby" (Chess 1497)
> "Smile at Me"
> "Worried All the Time" (Chess 1515)

Howlin' Wolf, vocal, harmonica; L. C. Hubert, piano; Willie Johnson, guitar; Willie Steele, drums; bass and saxes unknown

> "Mr. Highway Man"; a.k.a. "Cadillac Daddy" (Chess 1510)
> "My Troubles and Me"
> "Getting Old and Grey" (Chess 1510)
> "My Baby Walked Off"
> "Chocolate Drop"

FEBRUARY 12, 1952: PRIVATE HOME, WEST MEMPHIS, ARKANSAS

Last session for Joe Bihari's RPM Records. Howlin' Wolf, vocal, harmonica; Ike Turner, piano; Willie Johnson, guitar; Willie Steele, drums; bass unknown

"House Rockin' Boogie"
"Brown Skin Woman"
"Worried About My Baby"
"Driving This Highway"
"The Sun Is Rising"
"My Friends"
"I'm the Wolf"

APRIL 17, 1952: MEMPHIS RECORDING SERVICE, MEMPHIS

Howlin' Wolf, vocal, harmonica, guitar; James Cotton, harmonica; L. C. Hubert or William " 'Struction" Johnson, piano; Willie Johnson, guitar; Willie Steele, drums; bass unknown. Cotton's undeveloped harp style is evident on "Saddle My Pony." He and Wolf probably both played harp on "Dorothy Mae." Wolf played harp on "Sweet Woman" and "Decoration Day."

"Everybody's in the Mood"; a.k.a. "All in the Mood"
"Color and Kind"
"Bluebird"
"Saddle My Pony" (Chess 1515)
"Dorothy Mae"
"Sweet Woman"; a.k.a. "I've Got a Woman"
"(Well) That's All Right"
"Decoration Day"

OCTOBER 7, 1952: MEMPHIS RECORDING SERVICE, MEMPHIS

Howlin' Wolf, vocal, harmonica; James Cotton, harmonica; L. C. Hubert, piano; Walter "Tang" Smith, trombone; Charles Taylor, tenor sax; Willie Steele, drums; bass unknown

"Oh Red" (Chess 1528)
"My Last Affair" (Chess 1528)
"Come Back Home"
"Drinkin' C.V. Wine Blues"

MASTERED BY CHESS RECORDS ON SEPTEMBER 24, 1953, BUT RECORDED EARLIER AT MEMPHIS RECORDING SERVICE, MEMPHIS

Howlin' Wolf, vocal, harmonica; Willie Johnson, guitar; others unknown

"I've Got a Woman"
"Just My Kind"

"Work for Your Money"
"I'm Not Joking"
"Mama Died and Left Me"

MASTERED BY CHESS RECORDS ON OCTOBER 28, 1953,
BUT RECORDED EARLIER AT MEMPHIS RECORDING SERVICE,
MEMPHIS
Wolf's last session in Memphis. Howlin' Wolf, vocal, harmonica; Willie Johnson,
guitar; others unknown

"Highway My Friend"
"Hold Your Money"
"Streamline Woman"
"California Blues #2"
"Stay Here Till My Baby Comes Back"
"Crazy About You Baby"
"All Night Boogie" (Chess 1557)
"I Love My Baby" (Chess 1557)

MARCH 1954: CHESS STUDIOS, CHICAGO
Wolf's first session in Chicago. Howlin' Wolf, vocal, harmonica; Otis Spann, piano;
Lee Cooper, Hubert Sumlin, guitars; Willie Dixon, bass; Earl Phillips or Fred
Below, drums

"No Place to Go" (Chess 1566)
"You Gonna Wreck My Life" (Chess 1744)
"Neighbors"
"I'm the Wolf"
"Rockin' Daddy" (Chess 1566)

MAY 25, 1954: CHESS STUDIOS, CHICAGO
Howlin' Wolf, vocal, harmonica; Otis Spann, piano; Jody Williams, Hubert Sumlin, guitars; Willie Dixon, bass; Earl Phillips, drums

"Baby How Long" (Chess 1575)
"Evil" (Chess 1575)

OCTOBER 1954 CHESS STUDIOS, CHICAGO
Howlin' Wolf, vocal, harmonica; Otis Spann, piano; Jody Williams, Hubert Sumlin, guitars; Willie Dixon, bass; Earl Phillips, drums

"I'll Be Around" (Chess 1584)
"Forty Four" (Chess 1584)

MARCH 1955: CHESS STUDIOS, CHICAGO
Howlin' Wolf, vocal, harmonica; Henry Gray, piano; Jody Williams, Hubert Sumlin, guitars; Willie Dixon, bass; Earl Phillips, drums

"Who Will Be Next" (Chess 1593)
"I Have a Little Girl" (Chess 1593)
"Come to Me Baby" (Chess 1607)
"Don't Mess with My Baby" (Chess 1607)

JANUARY 1956: CHESS STUDIOS, CHICAGO
Howlin' Wolf, vocal, harmonica; Hosea Lee Kennard, piano; Hubert Sumlin, Willie Johnson, guitars; Willie Dixon, bass; Earl Phillips, drums

"Smokestack Lightnin' " (Chess 1618)
"You Can't Be Beat" (Chess 1618)

JULY 19, 1956: CHESS STUDIOS, CHICAGO
Howlin' Wolf, vocal, harmonica; Hosea Lee Kennard, piano; Hubert Sumlin or Willie Johnson and Otis Smothers, guitars; Willie Dixon, bass; Earl Phillips, drums

"I Asked for Water" (Chess 1632)
"So Glad" (Chess 1632)
"Break of Day"
"The Natchez Burnin' " (Chess 1744)

DECEMBER 1956: CHESS STUDIOS, CHICAGO
Howlin' Wolf, vocal, harmonica; Adolph "Billy" Duncan, tenor sax; Hosea Lee Kennard, piano; Willie Johnson, Otis Smothers, guitars; Alfred Elkins, bass; Earl Phillips, drums

"Going Back Home" (Chess 1648)
"Bluebird"
"My Life" (Chess 1648)
"You Ought to Know"

JUNE 24, 1957: CHESS STUDIOS, CHICAGO
Howlin' Wolf, vocal, harmonica; Adolph "Billy" Duncan, tenor sax; Hosea Lee Kennard, piano; Otis Smothers, Willie Johnson (last session with Wolf), guitars; Alfred Elkins, bass; Earl Phillips, drums

"Who's Been Talking?" (Chess 1750)
"Tell Me" (Chess 1750)
"Somebody in My Home" (Chess 1668)
"Nature" (Chess 1668)

DECEMBER 1957: CHESS STUDIOS, CHICAGO
Howlin' Wolf, vocal, harmonica; Hosea Lee Kennard, piano; Hubert Sumlin, Jody Williams, guitars; Alfred Elkins, bass; Earl Phillips, drums

"Walk to Camp Hall"
"Poor Boy" (Chess 1679)

"My Baby Told Me"
"Sittin' on Top of the World" (Chess 1679)

MARCH 1958: CHESS STUDIOS, CHICAGO
Howlin' Wolf, vocal, harmonica; Abb Locke, tenor sax; Hosea Lee Kennard, piano; Hubert Sumlin, guitar; probably Willie Dixon, bass; S. P. Leary, drums

"I Didn't Know"
"Howlin' Blues"; a.k.a. "I'm Going Away" (Chess 1726)
"I Better Go Now" (Chess 1726)

APRIL 3, 1958: CHESS STUDIOS, CHICAGO
Howlin' Wolf, vocal, harmonica; Adolph "Billy" Duncan, tenor sax; Hosea Lee Kennard, piano; Hubert Sumlin, Jody Williams, guitars; Abb Locke, tenor sax; Alfred Elkins, bass; Earl Phillips, drums

"I Didn't Know" (rerecorded, Chess 1695)
"Moaning for My Baby" (Chess 1695)
"Midnight Blues"

SEPTEMBER 1958: CHESS STUDIOS, CHICAGO
Howlin' Wolf, vocal, harmonica; Hosea Lee Kennard, piano; L. D. McGhee, Hubert Sumlin, guitars; S. P. Leary, drums

"I'm Leavin' You" (Chess 1712)
"You Can't Put Me Out"
"Change My Way" (Chess 1712)
"Getting Late"

JULY 1959: CHESS STUDIOS, CHICAGO
Howlin' Wolf, vocal, harmonica; Abb Locke, tenor sax; Hosea Lee Kennard, piano; Hubert Sumlin, Abe Smothers, Freddie King ("I've Been Abused" only, according to Hubert Sumlin) guitars; S. P. Leary, drums

"I've Been Abused" (Chess 1735)
"Howlin' for My Darling " (Chess 1762)
"My People's Gone"
"Mr. Airplane Man" (Chess 1735)
"Wolf in the Mood"

JUNE 1960: CHESS STUDIOS, CHICAGO
Howlin' Wolf, vocal; Otis Spann, piano; Freddie Robinson (Abu Talib), Hubert Sumlin, guitars; Willie Dixon, bass; Fred Below, drums. (Some experts claim it was Freddy King, not Freddie Robinson, on guitar, but both Hubert Sumlin and Robinson insist it was Robinson.)

"Wang Dang Doodle" (Chess 1777)
"Back Door Man" (Chess 1777)
"Spoonful" (Chess 1762)

MAY 1961: CHESS STUDIOS, CHICAGO
Howlin' Wolf, vocal; Johnny Jones, piano; Jimmy Rogers, Hubert Sumlin, guitars;
Willie Dixon, bass; Sam Lay, drums

"Down in the Bottom" (Chess 1793)
"Little Baby" (Chess 1793)

JUNE 1961: CHESS STUDIOS, CHICAGO
Howlin' Wolf, vocal; Johnny Jones, piano; Hubert Sumlin, guitar; Willie Dixon,
bass; Sam Lay, drums

"Shake for Me" (Chess 1804)
"The Red Rooster" (Chess 1804)

DECEMBER 1961: CHESS STUDIOS, CHICAGO
Howlin' Wolf, vocal, guitar; Henry Gray, piano; Hubert Sumlin, guitar; Jimmy
Rogers, Willie Dixon, bass; Sam Lay, drums

"You'll Be Mine" (Chess 1813)
"Just Like I Treat You" (Chess 1823)
"I Ain't Superstitious" (Chess 1823)
"Goin' Down Slow" (Chess 1813)

SEPTEMBER 27–28, 1962: CHESS STUDIOS, CHICAGO
Howlin' Wolf, vocal; J. T. Brown, tenor sax; other sax unknown; Johnny Jones,
piano; Hubert Sumlin, guitar; Jerome Arnold, bass; Junior Blackmon, drums

"Mama's Baby" (Chess 1844)
"Do the Do" (Chess 1844)
"Tail Dragger" (Chess 1890)
"Long Green Stuff"

JULY 26, 1963: COPA CABANA CLUB, CHICAGO
Blues from "Big Bill's" Copa Cabana album. Howlin' Wolf, vocal; J. T. Brown,
tenor sax; Donald Hankins, baritone sax; Lafayette Leake, piano; Hubert Sumlin,
Buddy Guy, guitars; Jerome Arnold, bass; Sam Lay, drums

"Sugar Mama"
"May I Have a Talk With You"

AUGUST 14 1963: CHESS STUDIOS, CHICAGO
Howlin' Wolf, vocal; J. T. Brown, tenor sax; Donald Hankins, baritone sax; Lafayette Leake, piano; Hubert Sumlin, Buddy Guy, guitars; Jerome Arnold, bass; Sam Lay, drums

"Hidden Charms" (Chess 1890)
"Three Hundred Pounds of Joy" (Chess 1870)
"Joy to My Soul"
"Built for Comfort" (Chess 1870)

AUGUST 1964: CHESS STUDIOS, CHICAGO
Howlin' Wolf, vocal, harmonica; Arnold Rogers, tenor sax; Donald Hankins, baritone sax; Lafayette Leake, piano; Hubert Sumlin, Buddy Guy, guitars; Andrew McMahon, electric bass; Willie Dixon, acoustic bass; Sam Lay, drums

"Love Me Darlin' " (Chess 1911)
"Killing Floor" (Chess 1923)
"My Country Sugar Mama" (Chess 1911)
"Louise" (Chess 1923)

APRIL 15, 1965: CHESS STUDIOS, CHICAGO
Howlin' Wolf, vocal; Eddie Shaw, tenor sax; Lee Eggleston, piano; Hubert Sumlin, Buddy Guy, guitars; Billy Davenport, drums; bass unknown

"I Walked from Dallas" (Chess 1945)
"Tell Me What I've Done" (Chess 1928)
"Don't Laugh at Me" (Chess 1945)
"Ooh Baby" (Chess 1928)

APRIL 11, 1966: CHESS STUDIOS, CHICAGO
Howlin' Wolf, vocal; Eddie Shaw, tenor sax; unknown baritone sax and clarinet; Henry Gray, piano; Hubert Sumlin and unknown, guitars; Cassell Burrow, drums; bass unknown

"Poor Wind That Never Change"
"New Crawlin' King Snake" (Chess 1968)
"My Mind Is Ramblin' " (Chess 1968)
"Commit a Crime"

JUNE 1967: CHESS STUDIOS, CHICAGO
Howlin' Wolf, vocal, harmonica; Eddie Shaw, tenor sax; unknown piano and organ; Hubert Sumlin, guitar; Cassell Burrow, drums; Bob Anderson, bass

"Pop It to Me" (Chess 2009)
"I Had a Dream" (Chess 2009)
"Dust My Broom"

SEPTEMBER 1967: CHESS STUDIOS, CHICAGO
Super Super Blues Band album. Howlin' Wolf, vocal, harmonica; Muddy Waters and Bo Diddley, vocals, guitars; Cookie Vee, vocal, tambourine; Otis Spann, piano; Hubert Sumlin, guitar; Clifton James, drums; Buddy Guy, bass

> "Long Distance Call"
> "Ooh Baby" and "Wrecking My Love Life"
> "Sweet Little Angel"
> "Spoonful"
> "Diddley Daddy"
> "The Red Rooster"
> "Goin' Down Slow"

NOVEMBER 1968: CHESS STUDIOS, CHICAGO
Howlin' Wolf album. Howlin' Wolf, vocal, harmonica; Gene Barge, sax; Donald Myrick, flute; Hubert Sumlin, Pete Cosey, Roland Faulkner, Phil Upchurch, guitars; Louis Satterfield, bass; Morris Jennings, drums

> "Spoonful"
> "Tail Dragger"
> "Smokestack Lightnin' "
> "Moanin' at Midnight"
> "Built for Comfort"
> "The Red Rooster"
> "Evil"
> "Down in the Bottom"
> "Three Hundred Pounds of Joy"
> "Back Door Man"

NOVEMBER 1968: CHESS STUDIOS, CHICAGO
Acoustic session: Howlin' Wolf, vocal, guitar

> "I'm the Wolf"
> "Rollin' and Tumblin' "
> Howlin' Wolf interview
> "I Ain't Gonna Be Your Dog No More"
> "Woke Up This Morning"
> "Ain't Going Down That Dirt Road"

JULY 14, 1969: CHESS STUDIOS, CHICAGO
Howlin' Wolf, vocal; Lafayette Leake, piano; Hubert Sumlin, guitar; Calvin Jones, bass; Cassell Burrows, drums; unknown trumpet, tenor sax, and baritone sax

> "Mary Sue" (Chess 2081)
> "Hard Luck" (Chess 2081)

"The Big House"
"Tired of Crying"

MAY 2–7, 1970: OLYMPIC STUDIOS, LONDON
The London Sessions album. Howlin' Wolf, vocal, guitar, harmonica; Joe Miller, Jordan Sandke, Dennis Lansing, horns; Jeff Carp, harmonica; Ian Stewart, John Simon, Lafayette Leake, Erwin Helfer, Joel Smirnoff, and Steve Winwood, keyboards; Eric Clapton, Hubert Sumlin, Paul Asbell, and BeBop Sam, guitars; Bill Wyman, Klaus Voorman, Phil Upchurch, bass; Ringo Starr, Charlie Watts, Mick Jagger, drums, percussion
   "I Want to Have a Word with You"
   "Goin' Down Slow"
   "I Ain't Superstitious"
   "Rockin' Daddy"
   "Poor Boy"
   "Wang Dang Doodle"
   "Sittin' on Top of the World"
   "Do the Do"
   "Highway 49"
   "Commit a Crime"
   "Worried About My Baby"
   "Built for Comfort"
   "Who's Been Talking?"
   "The Red Rooster"
   "Killing Floor"

OCTOBER 1971: CHESS STUDIOS, CHICAGO
Message to the Young album. Howlin' Wolf, vocal; John Jeremiah, organ; Sonny Thompson, piano; John Stocklin, Bryce Robinson, guitars; Bob Crowder, bass; Tyrone Smith, drums; unknown backing vocals and brass instruments

   "If I Were a Bird"
   "Message"
   "I Smell a Rat"
   "Miss Jones"
   "Message to the Young"
   "She's Looking Good"
   "Just As Long"
   "Romance Without Finance"
   "Turn Me On"

JANUARY 26, 1972: "ALICE'S REVISITED" CLUB, CHICAGO
Live and Cookin' at Alice's Revisited album. Howlin' Wolf, vocal, harmonica; Eddie Shaw, tenor sax; Sunnyland Slim, piano; Hubert Sumlin, unknown, guitars; Dave Myers, bass; Fred Below, drums

"When I Laid Down I Was Troubled"
"I Don't Know"
"Mean Mistreater"
"I Had a Dream"
"Call Me the Wolf"
"Don't Laugh at Me"
"Just Passing By"
"Sittin' on Top of the World"
"The Big House"
"Mr. Airplane Man"

AUGUST 14 AND 17, 1973: CHESS STUDIOS, CHICAGO
The Back Door Wolf album. Howlin' Wolf, vocal, harmonica; Detroit Junior, piano and harpsichord; Hubert Sumlin, unknown, guitars; Andrew McMahon, bass; S. P. Leary, drums

"Moving"
"Coon on the Moon"
"Speak Now Woman"
"Trying to Forget You"
"Stop Using Me"
"Leave Here Walking"
"The Back Door Wolf"
"You Turn Slick on Me"
"Watergate Blues"
"Can't Stay Here"

Bibliography

BOOKS

Calt, Stephen, and Gayle Wardlow. *King of the Delta Blues: The Life and Music of Charlie Patton.* Newton, N.J.: Rock Chapel Press, 1988.

Charters, Samuel. *The Bluesmakers.* New York: Da Capo Press, 1991.

Cohn, David L. *Where I Was Born and Raised.* Boston: Houghton Mifflin, 1948.

Cohn, Lawrence. *Nothing but the Blues: The Music and the Musicians.* New York: Abbeville Press, 1993.

Cohodas, Nadine. *Spinning Blues into Gold: The Chess Brothers and the Legendary Chess Records.* New York: St. Martin's Press, 2000.

Danchin, Sebastian. *Earl Hooker: Blues Master.* Jackson: University Press of Mississippi, 2001.

Dixon, Willie, with Don Snowden. *I Am the Blues: The Willie Dixon Story.* New York: Da Capo Press, 1989.

Edwards, David "Honeyboy," with Janis Martinson and Michael Robert Frank. *The World Don't Owe Me Nothing: The Life and Times of Delta Bluesman Honeyboy Edwards.* Chicago: Chicago Review Press, 1997.

Escott, Colin, with Martin Hawkins. *Good Rockin' Tonight: Sun Records and the Birth of Rock 'n' Roll.* New York: St. Martin's Press, 1991.

Evans, David. *Big Road Blues: Tradition and Creativity in the Folk Blues.* New York: Da Capo Press, 1987.

Faulkner, William. *The Mansion.* New York: Random House, 1959.

Field, Kim. *Harmonicas, Harps and Heavy Breathers.* New York: Simon & Schuster, 1993.

Gart, Galen, ed. *First Pressings: The History of Rhythm & Blues: Volume 1: 1951.* Milford, N.H.: Big Nickel Publications, 1991.

———, ed. *First Pressings: The History of Rhythm & Blues: Volume 2: 1952*. Milford, N.H.: Big Nickel Publications, 1992.

———, ed. *First Pressings: The History of Rhythm & Blues: Volume 3: 1953*. Milford, N.H.: Big Nickel Publications, 1989.

———, ed. *First Pressings: The History of Rhythm & Blues: Volume 4: 1954*. Milford, N.H.: Big Nickel Publications, 1990.

———, ed. *First Pressings: The History of Rhythm & Blues: Volume 5: 1955*. Milford, N.H.: Big Nickel Publications, 1990.

———, ed. *First Pressings: The History of Rhythm & Blues: Volume 6: 1956*. Milford, N.H.: Big Nickel Publications, 1991.

———, ed. *First Pressings: The History of Rhythm & Blues: Volume 7: 1957*. Milford, N.H.: Big Nickel Publications, n.d.

Gillett, Charlie. *The Sound of the City: The Rise of Rock and Roll*. Rev. ed. London: Souvenir Press, 1983.

Glover, Tony, Scott Dirks, and Ward Gaines. *Blues with a Feeling: The Little Walter Story*. New York: Routledge Books, 2002.

Gordon, Robert. *Can't Be Satisfied: The Life and Times of Muddy Waters*. New York: Little, Brown & Company, 2002.

Guralnick, Peter. *Feel Like Going Home: Portraits in Blues and Rock 'n' Roll*. New York: Harper & Row, 1989.

———. *Lost Highway: Journeys & Arrivals of American Musicians*. New York: Harper & Row, 1989.

———. *Searching for Robert Johnson*. New York: E. P. Dutton, 1989.

———. *The Listener's Guide to the Blues*. New York: Quarto Books, 1982.

Guralnick, Peter, and Robert Santelli, Holly George-Warren, and Christopher John Farley, eds. *Martin Scorsese Presents the Blues*. New York: HarperCollins, 2003.

Hamann, Jack. *The Broken Column*. Chapel Hill, N.C.: Algonquin Books of Chapel Hill, 2004.

Handy, W. C. *Father of the Blues*. New York: Collier, 1970.

Harris, Sheldon. *Blues Who's Who: A Biographical Dictionary of Blues Singers*. New York: Da Capo Press, 1981.

Jakoubek, Robert E. *Jack Johnson*. New York: Chelsea House, 1990.

Keil, Charles. *Urban Blues*. Chicago: The University of Chicago Press, 1966.

Leadbitter, Mike, and Neil Slaven. *Blues Records, 1943–1970: A Selective Discography, Volume 1: A–K*. London: Record Information Services, 1987.

Leadbitter, Mike, ed. *Nothing but the Blues*. London: Hanover Books, 1971.

Lemann, Nicholas. *The Promised Land: The Great Black Migration and How It Changed America*. New York: Alfred A. Knopf, 1991; Vintage Books, 1992.

McMillen, Neil R. *Dark Journey: Black Mississippians in the Age of Jim Crow*. Champaign: University of Illinois Press, 1989.

Marcus, Greil. *Mystery Train: Images of America in Rock 'n' Roll Music*. New York: Dutton, 1990.

Merrill, Hugh. *The Blues Route*. New York: William Morrow, 1990.

Neff, Robert, and Anthony Connor, eds. *The Blues: In Images and Interviews*. Boston: Cooper Square Publishers, 1999.

Oliver, Paul. *Blues Off the Record: Thirty Years of Blues Commentary.* New York: Da Capo Press, 1988.

Palmer, Robert. *Deep Blues.* New York: Viking Penguin, 1981.

Rooney, James. *Bossmen: Bill Monroe & Muddy Waters.* New York: Dial Press, 1971.

Rowe, Mike. *Chicago Blues: The City & the Music.* New York: Da Capo Press, 1981.

Sacré, Robert, ed. *The Voice of the Delta: Charley Patton and the Mississippi Blues Traditions.* Liège, Belgium: Presses Universitaires Liège, 1987.

Silver, James W. *Mississippi: The Closed Society.* New York: Harcourt, Brace & World, 1966.

Trynka, Paul. *Portrait of the Blues.* New York: Da Capo Press, 1996.

Williams, Ruth White. *On the Map 145 Years: The History of West Point, Mississippi, 1846–1991.* West Point, Miss., 1996.

Wilson County Black History Committee. *In Their Own Voices: An Account of the Presence of African Americans in Wilson County.* Lebanon, Tenn.: The Lebanon Democrat, 1999.

Wolkin, Jan Mark, and Bill Keenom. *Michael Bloomfield: If You Love These Blues.* San Francisco: Miller Freeman Books, 2000.

Workers of the Writer's Program of the Works Progress Administration in the State of Arkansas. *Arkansas: A Guide to the State.* New York: Hastings House, 1941.

Wyman, Bill. *Rolling with the Stones.* London: DK Publishing, 2002.

Wyman, Bill, and Richard Havers. *Bill Wyman's Blues Odyssey: A Journey to Music's Heart & Soul.* New York: DK Publishing, 2001.

PERIODICALS

"Ann Arbor Blues Festival." *Creem* 2, no. 4 (1969).

"Caught in the Act." *Melody Maker,* November 15, 1969.

"Electric Wolf: 'Man, It's Dogshit.' " *Rolling Stone,* February 15, 1969.

"Howlin' Wolf." *Anne Arbor Argus,* September 17, 1969.

"Mean Old Blues." *Newsweek,* February 21, 1966.

"The Session Men." *Blues Unlimited,* August 1966.

Barnes, Harper. "Honey Don't You Hear Me Howling." *The Real Paper* (May 30, 1973).

Baumgartner, Brian. "Eddie Snow & Floyd Murphy: Partnership in the Blues." *Juke Blues* (Autumn 1998).

Billboard, September 4, 1954.

Billboard, February 18, 1956.

Billboard, September 1, 1956.

Billboard, January 23, 1961.

Bonner, Brett J. "Chicago Sax: Eddie Shaw." *Living Blues,* November/December 1995.

———. "Smokey Wilson: Corn Shuckin' Blues." *Living Blues,* November/December 1996.

Brisbin, John Anthony. "Brewer Phillips, Part 2: The Early Years." *Living Blues*, January/February 1995.

——. "Corrinia Wallace Remembers Willie Johnson and Howlin' Wolf." *Living Blues*, November/December 1995.

——. "Detroit Junior: You Got to Put Somethin' in It." *Living Blues*, September/October 1996.

——. "Easy Baby: We Seen Some Good Days." *Living Blues*, March/April 1999.

——. "Jimmy Rogers: I'm Havin' Fun Right Today." *Living Blues*, September/October 1997.

——. "Lester Davenport: It's All About Havin' a Good Time." *Living Blues*, January/February 1993.

——. "Little Smokey Smothers: They Smell My Onions." *Living Blues*, November/December 1993.

——. "Robert Plunkett: I Think I Had a Little Magic." *Living Blues*, March/April 1994.

——. "The Lost American Bluesmen." *Living Blues*, July/August 1997.

——. "Willie Johnson." *Living Blues* 124 (November/December 1995).

Broven, John J. "Howlin' Wolf at the Marquee." *Blues Unlimited*, January 1965.

Brown, Frank. "Howlin' Wolf: Primeval Passion Electrified." *WKCR Program Guide*, April 1987.

Bruynoghe, Yannick. "In Chicago with Big Bill & Friends: *Chicago Scrapbook* Excerpts." *Living Blues*, Winter 1982/1983.

Bryan, John. "The Blues Is the Truth." *Open City*, July 5–11, 1968.

Cash Box, May 22, 1954.

Cash Box, February 25, 1956.

Cash Box, February 23, 1957.

Cash Box, August 17, 1957.

Cash Box, May 9, 1959.

Chicago Defender, February 19, 1955.

Chicago Defender, April 14, 1956.

Chicago Defender, July 7, 1956.

Chicago Defender, September 8, 1956.

Chicago Defender, December 22, 1956.

Corritore, Bob, Bill Ferris, and Jim O'Neal. "Willie Dixon, Part II." *Living Blues*, September/October 1988.

Cramer, Alex. "Jimmy Rogers." *Coda*, June/July 1974.

——. "Johnny Shines." *Coda* 11, no. 12 (October 1974).

Crittenden County Times (West Memphis), February 21, 1947.

Cushing, Steve. "Behind the Beat of Blues." *Living Blues*, March/April 1991.

Dahl, Bill. "Abu Talib: The Real Thing at Last." *Living Blues*, March/April 1999.

Darlington, Sandy. "The Groove and the Rut." *San Francisco Express Times*, July 10, 1968.

Darwen, Norman. "The Phillip Walker Story: From Port Arthur to Los Angeles." *Blues & Rhythm*, April 1994.

——. "We play classier places where they don't throw bottles." *Blues & Rhythm*, January 1990.

——. "Wolf Taught Me How to Work." *Blues & Rhythm*, February 1992.

Dawkins, Jimmy, Dick Shurman, Keith Tillman, and Mike Leadbitter. "Willie Johnson: Boppin' the Blues." *Blues Unlimited* 93 (July 1972).

Dawson, Pat. "Man, we was jumpin' like crazy." *Blues & Rhythm*, August 1990.

Demêtre, Jacques, and Marcel Chauvard. Translated from the French by Ian McLean. "Land of the Blues—Chicago." *Jazz Journal*, August 1960.

——. "Son Utilisation des 'Field-Hollers' a valu a Chester Burnett le Surnom de Howlin' Wolf." *Jazz Hot*, December 1961.

Dummer, John. "None of That Goddamn Wah Wah." *Melody Maker*, May 31, 1969.

——. "On the Road with the Howlin' Wolf." *Melody Maker*, January 24, 1976.

Eagle, Bob. "Luther Huff." *Living Blues* 22 (July–August 1975).

Earl, John. "A Lifetime in the Blues: Johnny Shines." *Blues World* 46/49 (1973).

Evans, David. "Peck Curtis: Interview." *Blues Unlimited*, January 1970.

——. "The Fiddlin' Joe Martin Story." *Blues World*, July 1968.

——. "The Woodrow Adams Story." *Blues Unlimited*, July 1968.

Flerlage, Rae, and Mike Bloomfield. "Interview with Howlin' Wolf." *Rhythm & Blues*, February 1965.

Forte, Dan. "Chicago Blues Legend Hubert Sumlin: Howlin' Wolf's Sideman." *Guitar Player*, April 1980.

Fulton, Doug. "City's First Jazz, Blues Festival." *Ann Arbor News*, September 9, 1972.

Gibbs, Vernon. "Howlin' Wolf Bemoans the Blues." *Crawdaddy*, December 5, 1971.

Gifford, Barry. "Couldn't Do No Yodeling, so I Turned to Howlin'." *Rolling Stone*, August 24, 1968.

Gilbert, Jeremy. "Wolf Gathers His Flock in London." *Melody Maker*, May 16, 1970.

Greene, Bob. "Howlin's for the Stones, but Wolf's not in pack." *Chicago Sun-Times*, July 23, 1975.

Greensmith, Bill, and Cilla Huggins. "Still Hanging Right On in There: Dirty Jim Tells All, Part 1." *Blues Unlimited*, Spring 1981.

Greensmith, Bill. "Carl Tate, a.k.a. Bob Starr." *Blues Unlimited*, May/June 1976.

——. "East St. Louis Blues: Little Cooper and the Drifters." *Blues & Rhythm*, April 1995.

——. "Still in the Woods." *Blues Unlimited* 145 (Winter 1983/1984).

Gronda, Steve. "Easter Blues in Cocoa Beach." *Living Blues*, Summer 1974, p. 41.

Groom, Bob. "An Interview with Son House." *Blues World*, January 1968.

Guitar Player magazine, August 1976.

Hahn, Kevin. "Pat Hare: A Blues Guitarist." *Juke Blues*, Summer 1991.

Hannusch, Jeff. "Henry Gray: Lucky, Lucky Man." *Living Blues*, July/August 2001.

Hatch, Peter. "This Is the Blues." *Coda*, May/June 1971.

Hay, Fred. "Fiddlin' Joe Martin: Obituary." *Living Blues*, March/April 1976.

Hoffman, Mark, and James Segrest. "Hubert at Home: Sumlin's Friends Keep Him Young." *Blues Access*, Fall 2001.

Holdenfield, Chris. "Wolf Has Got This Weird Time." *Rolling Stone*, June 11, 1970.

Huggins, Cilla. "Luther: The Chicago Years." *Juke Blues*, Spring 1999.

Joyce, Mike. "James Cotton: Interview." *Cadence*, January 1980.

Koda, Cub. "Howlin' Wolf: The Wolf Is at the Door." *Goldmine*, April 16, 1993.

Koester, Bob. "Chicago Blues Scene." *Blues Unlimited*, February 1966.

Koppel, David. "Trouble Can't Keep a Big Good Wolf Down." *Chicago Daily News*, June 14–15, 1975.

Kudlacek, Kerry, and Dave Sax. "The Ike Turner Blues Story." *Blues Unlimited*, November 1968.

Lazar, Helen Doob. "Living Blues Interview: James Cotton." *Living Blues Magazine*, 1987.

Leadbitter, Mike. "Mike's Blues." *Blues Unlimited*, September 1969.

———. "Somethin' to Tell You: Dr. Ross." *Blues Unlimited*, December 1972.

Leadbitter, Mike, and Mike Rowe. "Sunnyland Slim." *Blues Unlimited* 105 (December 1973/January 1974).

Lee, Peter, and David Nelson. "From Shoutin' the Blues to Preachin' the Word: Bishop Arnold Dwight 'Gatemouth' Moore." *Living Blues*, May/June 1989.

Linden, Colin. "In Memoriam: Howlin' Wolf, 1910–1976." *Blues Magazine*, February 1976.

McCracken, Mike. "Interview: Little Whit." *The Alabama Blues Society Newsletter*, August 1994.

Manoff, Mark. "Howlin' Wolf Feels What He Sings." *Philadelphia Evening Bulletin*, December 5, 1973.

Mattox, T. E. "Blues in Black and White." *Blues Access*, Summer 1993.

———. "Blues with an Attitude: Memphis Charlie was Born to Blow." *Blues Access*, Summer 1990.

Miller, Francis, Jr. "Payin' Some Dues: Blues at Ann Arbor." *Great Speckled Bird*, August 18, 1969.

Milne, Rick. "Shakey Jake." *Blues Unlimited* 42 (March/April 1967).

———. "The Muddy Waters Band: On-the-Spot from Washington, D.C., October 1965." *Blues Unlimited*, January 1966.

Napier, Simon A. "The Third 'American Folk-Blues Festival'—1964." *Blues Unlimited*, November/December 1964.

Nusser, Richard. "Ann Arbor Blues & Jazz Festival." *Crawdaddy*, December 1972.

Obrecht, Jas. "John Hammond." *Guitar Player*, July 1991.

O'Brien, Justin. "The Dark Road of Floyd Jones." *Living Blues*, Winter 1983.

O'Neal, Jim. "Living Blues Interview: Houston Stackhouse." *Living Blues*, Summer 1974.

O'Neal, Jim, and Amy O'Neal. "Muddy Waters." *Living Blues*, March/April 1983.

Paul, Alan. "Bonnie Raitt: The Hour of Music That Rocks My World." *Guitar World*, February 1999.

Radcliffe, Charles. "Sweet Home Chicago: The Blues 1945–65, Part Two." *Friends*, August 21, 1970.

Richardson, Michael. "Chicago Shuffle Master: Drummer Sam Lay Steps Out Front with His New Six-string Instrument." *Big City Blues*, October–November 2002.

Robinson, Chris. "Lazy Bill Called Me Homesick (I Wasn't Though)." *Blues Unlimited*, September 1971.

Roesch, Joe, and Michael "Red Dog" Downes. "The Invisible Legend: Matt 'Guitar' Murphy." *Blues Connection*, October 1997.

Rowe, Mike. "Floyd Jones." *Blues Unlimited* 137–38 (Spring 1980).

———. "They Know I'm Not Playing Anything but the Blues: James DeShay." *Blues Unlimited* 143 (Autumn/Winter 1982).

Rowe, Mike, and Bill Greensmith. " 'I Was Really Dedicated': An Interview with Billy Boy Arnold, Part 3: 'Whatever I did it was me and I'm proud of it.' " *Blues Unlimited*, January/February 1978.

Rowe, Mike, and Mike Leadbitter. "I Was the Baby Boy." *Blues Unlimited* 96 (November 1972).

Ruble, Alonzo. *Teaspoon and Door*, August 2, 1968.

Rusch, Bob. "Eddie Shaw: Interview." *Cadence*, March 1984.

———. "John Littlejohn: Interview Oral History." *Cadence*, February 1979.

Salsberg, Larry. "What's New." *Toronto Daily Sun*, January 30, 1970.

Schaefer, Tom. "The Mere Presence of Wolf." *The Bugle-American*, May 3–10, 1972.

Scott, Frank. "My Stay in Chicago." *Blues Unlimited*, January 1965.

Shurman, Dick. "Chicago." *Living Blues*, November/December 1975.

Slaven, Neil. "Howlin' Wolf." *R&B Monthly*, August 1964.

———. "The American Folk Blues Festival." *R&B Monthly*, December 1964.

Slotnikoff, Joel. "Gayle Dean Wardlow Interview." *Blues World*, October 1996.

Smith, Bill. "Howlin' Wolf, Freddie King, Big Mama Thornton." *Coda*, April 1972.

Stevens, Alan. "R&B? No, I'm a Folk Singer—Howlin' Wolf." *Melody Maker*, November 7, 1964.

Stienblatt, Harold, with Chris Gill. "John Fogerty: New Moon Rising." *Guitar World*, July 1997.

Sumlin, Hubert, and Jim Kent. "My Years with Wolf." *Living Blues*, September/October 1989.

Taylor, B. Kimberly. "Remembering Howlin' Wolf: An Interview with Howlin' Wolf's Widow: Lillie Burnett." *Blues Revue*, April/May 1996.

Tillman, Keith. "Bringing it to Jerome." *Blues Unlimited* (June 1969).

Tracy, Steve. "Review: The Back Door Wolf." *Blues Unlimited*, February/March 1974.

Tucker, Stuart. "If You Had Two Guitars You Had a Big Band: Buddy Folks." *Living Blues*, March/April 1989.

Van Singel, Amy, and Jim O'Neal. "Living Blues Interview: Howling Wolf." *Living Blues*, Spring 1970.

Vernon, Mick. "Hubert Sumlin: Guitar Class No. 1." *R&B Monthly* (December 1964).

Ware, Burnham. "International Blues Festival, Somerville, Kentucky." *Living Blues*, Autumn 1974.

Welding, Pete. "An Interview with Bluesman Howlin' Wolf." *Downbeat*, December 14, 1967.

——. "Gambler's Blues: Shakey Jake." *Living Blues*, Autumn 1972.

——. "Ramblin' Johnny Shines." *Living Blues*, July/August 1975.

West, Hollie I. "A Blues Festival for Black People." *Rolling Stone*, December 2, 1970.

Wilson, John S. "Amplifying System Drowns out Music at Capital Festival." *New York Times* (June 2, 1962).

Wise, Steve. "Howlin' Wolf." *Great Speckled Bird*, June 10, 1974.

Wisner, Steve. "Chicago Blues, Yesterday & Today: 'Smokey' Smothers: Big Otis & Little Abe." *Living Blues*, March/April 1978.

Wright, Robin. "Are You Comin' Along with Me?" *Ann Arbor News*, August 8, 1970.

Wuelfing, Howard. "Riffs: Wolf at Max's." *Village Voice*, June 7, 1973.

Yorke, Ritchie. "Mariposa Festival Swings to the Finish." *The Toronto Globe and Mail*, August 12, 1968.

DOCUMENTS

American Red Cross interview with Dock Burnett, September 29, 1943.

Application for Social Security Account Number for Chester Arthur Burnett, November 29, 1943.

Certificate of death, Chester A. Burnett. Hines, Cook County, Illinois, January 10, 1976.

Certificate of death, Gertrude Burnett. Marks, Quitman County, Mississippi, June 24, 1986.

Certificate of marriage, Chester Burnett and Katie Mae Johnson. Office of County Clerk, De Soto County, Mississippi, May 8, 1947.

Certificate of marriage, Chester Burnett and Lillie Jones. Office of County Clerk, Cook County, Illinois, March 14, 1964.

Certificate of marriage, Lee Burnett and Gertrude Jones. Monroe County Courthouse Docket #26 (1909–1911).

Court record filed with the National Archives: 1974 Civil 1959.

Letter, Organization of 59 Black Men In White Station, Mississippi, to the President of the United States, May 26, 1890, transcribed by Elijah W. Halford, Private Secretary of the President, quoted by War Department, Office Commissary General of Subsistence, Washington, D.C., June 3, 1890 (United States National Archives).

United States Census Records, 1870–1930.

United States Military Records, Chester Arthur Burnett.

FILMS AND DVDS

The American Folk Blues Festival: Volume 2, 1962–1966. Produced by David Peck and Janie Hendrix. Reelin' in the Years Productions and Experience Hendrix, 2003. DVD.

Devil Got My Woman: Blues at Newport 1966. Vestapol Productions, 1996. Video-cassette.

The Howlin' Wolf Story — The Secret History of Rock & Roll. Produced by Joe Lauro, directed by Don McGlynn. BMG/Arista, 2003. DVD.

Hubert Sumlin: Living the Blues. Produced and directed by Jim Kent and Sumner Burgwyn/Juke Joint Films, 1986. Videocassette.

LINER NOTES

Ackerman, Paul. Liner notes. *Howlin Wolf/Moanin' in the Moonlight.* MCA Records, 1986.

Booth, Stanley. Liner notes. *Howlin' Wolf: Memphis Days — The Definitive Edition, vol. 1.* Bear Family Records, 1989.

Dahl, Bill. Liner notes. *The London Howlin' Wolf Sessions, Deluxe Edition.* MCA Records, 2003.

Escott, Colin, and Hank Davis, Bez Turner, Martin Hawkins, and Rob Bowman. Liner notes. *Sun Records: The Blues Years, 1950–1958.* Charly Records, 1996.

Humphrey, Mark. Liner notes. *Howlin' Wolf: His Best (Chess 50th Anniversary Collection).* MCA Records, 1997.

McRae, Donald. Liner notes. *Mahlathini: The Lion of Soweto.* Virgin Records, 1987.

Morris, Chris, and Dick Shurman. Liner notes. *Howlin' Wolf: The Chess Box.* MCA Records, 1991.

Sax, Dave, Colin Escott, and Jim Dickinson. Liner notes and discography. *Howlin' Wolf: Memphis Days — The Definitive Edition, vol. 2.* Bear Family Records, 1990.

OTHER INTERVIEWS

Howlin' Wolf interview with Paul Williams and Peter Guralnick in 1966 at Club 47 in Cambridge, Massachusetts, for *Crawdaddy.*

Howlin' Wolf interview with Sandy Guy Schoenfeld in June 1968 in San Francisco.

Howlin' Wolf interview with Charles Stepney in November 1968 at Chess Studios. From *Howlin' Wolf: The Chess Box.*

Howlin' Wolf interview with Dan McClosky on August 7, 1970, at the Ann Arbor Blues Festival in Ann Arbor, Michigan.

Howlin' Wolf interview with David Little, Peter Riley, and Dorothy Riley on December 30, 1973, at Paul's Mall in Boston.

Howlin' Wolf interview with Eric Benjamin on March 7, 1974, for *The Valley Advocate.*

Calvin Newborn interview with Jim O'Neal on June 3, 1978. From the Blues Archive, University of Mississippi.

Johnny Littlejohn interview with Jim O'Neal on August 23, 1981. From the Blues Archive, University of Mississippi.

Hubert Sumlin interview with Jim O'Neal on September 23, 1981. From the Blues Archive, University of Mississippi.

Sunnyland Slim interview with Jim O'Neal on September 28, 1981. From the Blues Archive, University of Mississippi.

Abb Locke interview with Jim O'Neal on December 3, 1981. From the Blues Archive, University of Mississippi.

Hubert Sumlin interview with Mai Cramer in January 1996 at the House of Blues in Boston.

Pete Cosey interview with Robert Gordon in 1997. Courtesy of Robert Gordon.

Hubert Sumlin interview on April 5, 1998. From Howell Productions, Inc. (HPI) *Blues Chat.*

Hubert Sumlin interview with Jim Fricke on February 10, 2001, at the Experience Music Project, Seattle.

ARCHIVES, MANUSCRIPTS, AND PRIVATE PAPERS

American Federation of Musicians Local 208 files. Courtesy of Harold Washington Library, Chicago.

Andrew, Sam. "Recollections of Janis." From the Big Brother & the Holding Company site, www.bbhc.com.

Freerksen, Greg. Posting to the Blues-L Internet list server, March 3, 1997.

Griggs, Baby Dave. "Full Moon Over Chicago: The Passing of Howlin' Wolf," an unpublished memoir.

Hoffman, Steve. Posting to the Blues-L Internet list server, March 13, 1997.

Kelly, Dave. "Howlin' Wolf Remembered." A memoir.

Lillard, Dick. Posting to the Blues-L Internet list server, September 25, 1997.

List of *Cash Box* chart hits for Howlin' Wolf. Compiled by blues researcher Mark Jickling.

Schoenfeld, Sandy Guy. "The Howling Wolf Photos Story." From www.howling-wolfphotos.com.

Shaw, Eddie. "The Blues and Me." A memoir.

Shurman, Dick. Posting to the Blues-L Internet list server, June 19, 1995.

Sproat, Dave. "Howlin' Wolf British Tour '69: A Legend Remembered." From the Junco Partners site, www.juncopartners.com.

Thorndycraft, Bill. "Howlin' Wolf." From the Killing Floor site, www.killingfloor.com.

Index

385

A NOTE ABOUT THE AUTHORS

James Segrest has an M.A. in history from Auburn University. He has written liner notes for such CDs as the Grammy-nominated *A Tribute to Howlin' Wolf* for the Telarc label and has also written for *Blues Access* magazine. He speaks about Howlin' Wolf at blues festivals throughout the country. He lives in Notasulga, Alabama, and works as a teacher in Tallassee, Alabama.

Mark Hoffman has a bachelor's degree in English literature from the University of Washington and has written about music for such nationally circulated magazines as *Blues Access, Living Blues,* and *Blue Suede News,* and for regional publications such as *Blues to Do Monthly, Pacific Northwest* magazine, the *Bellevue Journal-American,* the *Seattle Weekly,* and *Eastsideweek.* He was the chief consultant on the prize-winning film *The Howlin' Wolf Story—the Secret History of Rock & Roll.* He lives on Bainbridge Island, near Seattle.